OUR CATHOLIC HERITAGE IN TEXAS

IN SEVEN VOLUMES

1519-1936

PREPARED UNDER THE AUSPICES OF
THE KNIGHTS OF COLUMBUS OF TEXAS

PAUL J. FOIK, C. S. C., PH. D., *Editor*
Chairman
TEXAS KNIGHTS OF COLUMBUS HISTORICAL COMMISSION
St. Edward's University
Austin

From the murals of John Bednar, C. S. C., at
St. Edward's University, Austin, Texas

THE VENERABLE PADRE FRAY ANTONIO MARGIL DE JESÚS, O. F. I., PIONEER MISSIONARY,
FOUNDER OF MISSIONS, AND PATRON OF TEXAS

OUR CATHOLIC HERITAGE IN TEXAS
1519-1936

PREPARED UNDER THE AUSPICES OF
THE KNIGHTS OF COLUMBUS OF TEXAS
PAUL J. FOIK, C. S. C., PH. D., *Editor*

THE MISSION ERA:

THE WINNING OF TEXAS
1693-1731

by

CARLOS E. CASTAÑEDA, PH. D.

VOLUME II

AUSTIN
VON BOECKMANN-JONES COMPANY, *Publishers*
1936

NIHIL OBSTAT

JOSEPH MAGUIRE, C. S. C.
President, St. Edward's University
Austin, Texas
Censor Deputatus

IMPRIMATUR

✠ ARTHUR J. DROSSAERTS, D. D., LL. D.
Archbishop of San Antonio

✠ CHRISTOPHER E. BYRNE, D. D., LL. D.
Bishop of Galveston

✠ JOSEPH P. LYNCH, D. D., LL. D.
Bishop of Dallas

✠ EMMANUEL B. LEDVINA, D. D., LL. D.
Bishop of Corpus Christi

✠ ANTHONY J. SCHULER, S. J., D. D., LL. D.
Bishop of El Paso

✠ ROBERT E. LUCEY, D. D., LL. D.
Bishop of Amarillo

TEXAS KNIGHTS OF COLUMBUS HISTORICAL COMMISSION

Honorary Chairman of the Commission

THE MOST REV. ARCHBISHOP ARTHUR J. DROSSAERTS, D. D., LL. D.

Executive Committee

REV. PAUL J. FOIK, C. S. C., PH. D., Chairman
REV. JOEPH G. O'DONOHOE, LL. D., Secretary
REV. JOHN S. MURPHY, LL. D.
HON. JOSEPH I. DRISCOLL, LL. D., K. S. G., Past State Deputy
HON. WILLIAM P. GALLIGAN, State Deputy
RIGHT REV. MONSIGNOR PETER GUILDAY, PH. D., LL. D.

Diocesan Historians

RIGHT REV. MONSIGNOR M. S. GARRIGA, Archdiocese of San Antonio
REV. JOHN S. MURPHY, LL. D., Diocese of Galveston
REV. JOSEPH G. O'DONOHOE, LL. D., Diocese of Dallas
REV. DANIEL A. LANING, Diocese of Corpus Christi
REV. CONSTANT M. KLEIN, O. M. C., Diocese of El Paso
REV. ARNOLD A. BOEDING, Diocese of Amarillo

Historiographer

CARLOS EDUARDO CASTAÑEDA, PH. D.

PREFACE

The period of Texas history covered in this volume is one about which there is little definite information. In fact the years from 1694 to 1714 have been generally referred to as silent years in the history of the State. But a careful search of the numerous manuscript sources gathered by the University of Texas and the Texas Knights of Columbus Historical Commission in the last twenty years has made it possible for the writer to reveal for the first time many details and facts little known or ignored entirely heretofore. It is the purpose of this volume to present a connected narrative of life in Texas during the period covered, of the motivating forces that resulted in the permanent occupation of the State, of the conflicting interests of individuals and of nations, and of the sterling nature of the pioneering *Padres* and Spanish officials who laid the foundations of civilization in the wilds of Texas. The history here presented is much more than that of the missions in Texas. It is rather as complete a narrative of events as the author has been able to weave together from all the sources at his command.

Heretofore the only connected narratives available were Bancroft's *History of the North Mexican States and Texas* and Bolton's *Texas in the Middle Eighteenth Century*. Recently, with the publication of *Pichardo's Treatise on the Limits of Louisiana and Texas* by Dr. Charles W. Hackett, an invaluable general work of reference for Spanish Texas was brought within the reach of students. More recently the author published the long sought *History of Texas* of Fray Juan Agustín Morfi. But the treatment in these various works is unsatisfactory because of their documentary character. In the present volume a more systematic, continuous, and complete account of the permanent occupation of Texas is given for the first time, the detailed development of mission life is revealed and the authentic record of the establishment of the first civil settlement in Texas is made available. The early exploration of the Big Bend country, which has generally been neglected by historians of the State, forms a part of our narrative. It goes without saying, that here is to be found the fullest account of the establishment of the missions in Texas, and of the heretofore untold labors and sacrifices of the saintly *Padres,* who worked patiently for the salvation of souls and even faced death for their faith.

The author wishes to acknowledge his indebtedness to the Texas

Knights of Columbus who, through their Historical Commission, have made possible the writing of the present volume. He is further indebted to the Rev. Dr. Paul J. Foik, C. S. C., of St. Edward's University, Austin, Chairman of the Commission, for constant advice and encouragement; to Dr. Eugene C. Barker for helpful criticism; to Dr. Charles W. Hackett for useful suggestions and friendly advice, and to Miss Maurin T. Wilson, Mr. E. W. Winkler, and Miss Winnie Allen, of the University of Texas Library, for their tireless coöperation in checking materials and sources. To the many other unnamed friends who have given kind assistance and encouragement, the author makes known his appreciation.

C. E. Castañeda,
Latin-American Librarian
University of Texas

CONTENTS

Chapter I

French Settlement of Louisiana and Spain's Renewed Interest in

ILLUSTRATIONS AND MAP

THE WINNING OF TEXAS

CHAPTER I

French Settlement of Louisiana and Spain's Renewed Interest in Texas, 1693-1714

Loss of interest in Texas. With the danger of foreign aggression apparently past, the ardor displayed by colonial officials in driving the French from Texas cooled considerably, and growing indifference soon caused the temporary abandonment, in 1693, of the project to occupy the province. Repeated expeditions and investigations during the preceding eight years had disclosed that the French had lost interest in the establishment of a settlement in that region; that the Gulf coast, particularly that portion lying west of the Mississippi River, offered no inducement for colonization; and that the maintenance of a garrison or settlement was impracticable because of the great expense involved and the grave dangers and almost insurmountable obstacles encountered in transporting the necessary supplies.[1] The distance to the projected establishment was too great from the frontier outposts of New Spain.

Up to the time of the abandonment it should be noted that it had been the colonial officials who had taken the initiative in the occupation of Texas, impelled by a sense of duty to the king and to God. Their firm belief that the king's domain was threatened by foreigners, and that the establishment of missions in this remote field would bring thousands of Indians to ultimate salvation through conversion, was the driving force of the first heroic effort to establish a permanent settlement. The home government had given little encouragement at any time to the enterprise and had limited itself to the approval of such measures as had already been put into execution. Spain was too deeply involved in European politics, and the rapidly declining Charles II had neither the vision to realize the importance of the movement, nor the means to carry it through.

But when the immediate danger of French aggression seemed past, interest in Texas might have persisted, had it not been that the endeavors of the tireless Franciscan missionaries to Christianize the natives met

---

[1]Testimonio de auttos sobre las prouincias Dadas Por el Emo. Señor Conde de Galve Virrey de esta nueua España pra. los socorros y Permanencia de los Religiosos Misioneros en la Proua. de los Tejas hasta su retirada y razones Porque se executo. pp. 71-75, *Archivo General de Indias, Audiencia de Guadalajara,* 67-4-11 (Dunn Transcripts, University of Texas). Reference to these transcripts will be hereafter referred to as *Dunn Transcripts.*

with scant success. Everything seemed to conspire against them. A flood destroyed one of the newly founded missions;[2] sickness decimated the little troop of Spaniards left to guard the priests and gave an opportunity to the designing medicine men to lay the blame for the numerous deaths on the waters of baptism; one of the faithful missionaries died; and lastly, the crops planted with untold hardships and under the most trying circumstances by the dauntless sons of Saint Francis proved a complete failure.[3]

Disheartening as all these material misfortunes were, what in reality hurt the missionaries most was the intractable nature of the Indians, their indifference, their obstinate refusal to attend services. Father Massanet, who may rightly be called the father of Texas missions, reluctantly had to come to the conclusion that the natives had deceived him. "More than a year of misery and disappointment had sufficed to break even his iron resolution."[4]

The discouraging report written by this enthusiastic and holy man towards the close of 1693, after his sad experiences, effectively put an end to further endeavors for the time being, coming as it did, at a time when interest in Texas had begun to wane considerably among the officials of the viceregal government. Texas was to be relegated to oblivion and the natives were to be left without the paternal care of the missionaries for twenty years after this attempt to bring them into the fold of the Church.

It is significant, however, that the order for the abandonment was couched in terms which clearly indicated that the measure was temporary. The missionaries were instructed to return to their respective colleges of Querétaro and Zacatecas "until a more fitting occasion arose for the continuance of the work."[5]

If Father Massanet's faith in the ultimate success of the enterprise had been shaken, that of others, like Father Hidalgo, was to remain undimmed

---

[2]The second mission, Santísimo Nombre de María was founded by the missionaries who accompanied De León, after his departure, in 1689. It was situated on the bank of the Neches River and was in charge of Fr. Jesús María Casañas. This was the mission that was destroyed by a flood shortly after the departure of Terán in 1692. W. E. Dunn, *Spanish and French Rivalry in the Gulf Coast Region of the United States,* 134-141.

[3]Massanet to the Viceroy, June 14, 1693, in *Testimonio sobre las Providencias Dadas,* 61-68 (Dunn Transcripts).

[4]Dunn, *op. cit.,* 140-141.

[5]Respuesta del Fiscal, March 11, 1694, in *Prosiguen los Autos de la Retirada de los Religiosos Misioneros y Soldados . . .,* 13-15. (Dunn Transcripts).

and to burn steadily through the years like a flaming beacon upon the outposts of New Spain. From the missions in Coahuila this remarkable missionary was to watch constantly for an opportunity to return to his beloved Tejas Indians who one day were to come in search of him, even though it should be in company with the traditional and inveterate enemies of Spain, the French.

Effect on Spain of French Settlements. The time came sooner, perhaps, than the officials anticipated, for French interest in Texas had not died but had merely been temporarily diverted. France, like Spain, was absorbed in the devastating wars that marked the closing years of the reign of the ambitious Louis XIV. But before the close of the century French vessels searched again for the mouth of the Mississippi and Frenchmen succeeded at last in establishing the settlement which the unfortunate La Salle had tried to found.

"So close are the events of the history of Louisiana connected with those of Texas that it is not possible to narrate with clearness what took place in the second without giving at least a brief summary of the first."[6] With these words the ablest Franciscan historian of the eighteenth century, Father Fray Juan Agustín Morfi, points out why it is necessary to digress in treating of the history of Texas during the first years of the century. It was the successful establishment of the French on the Mississippi that unmistakably led to the reoccupation of Texas by Spain as a defense movement, and this step led to the renewal of missionary activity in this vast field.

The conclusion of the Treaty of Ryswick enabled Louis XIV to turn his attention once more to his colonial possessions in America. The growing weakness of Spain, the rapidly failing health of the idiotic Charles II, and the keen rivalry of England and France made it imperative for the French king to take immediate steps to secure the lion's share of the colonial empire of Spain. Serious consideration was given again to the establishment of a colony at the mouth of the Mississippi as attempted by La Salle thirteen years before. Several months' preparations for a new enterprise under royal patronage resulted in the organization of an expedition under the direction of Iberville, a Canadian nobleman.[7] Four

---

[6]Castañeda, C. E., *Morfi's History of Texas,* 1673-1779.

[7]Pierre Le Moyne d'Iberville had distinguished himself in Hudson Bay against the English. He was the third son of Charles Le Moyne, who migrated to Canada in his early youth and became Sieur de Longueil in 1676. Pierre was born in Mon-

vessels were fitted out at Rochefort and the expedition at last set out from Brest on October 24, 1698. Its first destination was Santo Domingo, where it was to be joined by a powerful frigate under the command of the Marquis of Chasteaumorant, ordered there in advance to guard the fleet against the English. From here the five vessels had instructions to proceed to the mouth of the Mississippi to establish a colony.[8]

Fully aware of the impotence of Spain, these preparations had been carried on publicly, and no attempt was made to conceal either the destination or the purpose of the expedition. A Spanish subject living in La Rochelle was the first to write, on March 14, 1698, to one of the Spanish ministers concerning the matter. In his report he declared that the French were going to establish a settlement somewhere on the Gulf coast, presumably Pensacola Bay, and that families would be sent from Martinique, Santo Domingo, and Guadalupe for the purpose.[9] This information was immediately forwarded by special messenger, together with the translation of a pamphlet recently published in France, giving the details of the organization of a trading company for the purpose of colonizing Louisiana under the patronage of Louis XIV. With unusual promptness the report reached the king who, on April 1, transmitted the documents to the Council of the Indies.

Occupation of Pensacola Bay. The news of the designs of the French aroused the Council to action, and the whole machinery of the government, both in Spain and in America, was at once set in motion to forestall the impending crisis. On April 7, the Council ordered a summary to be drawn up of all the information available on the subject; on the 12th, the matter was discussed by a special *Junta de Guerra;* and on the19th, a royal *cédula* was issued in the name of the king. This order reviewed the whole course of events from the attempted settlement by La Salle to the new preparations now being made to renew the efforts to establish a colony on the Gulf coast, and ended by commanding the immediate occupation

---

treal, July 16, 1661. He died July 9, 1706. A. Fortier, *History of Louisiana,* I, 32-33.

[8]The sources for the Iberville expedition are printed in Pierre Margry, *Découvertes et Etablissements des Français,* Volume IV. Good secondary accounts are found in Fortier, *History of Louisiana;* Ogg, *The Opening of the Mississippi,* 171-182; Dunn, *op. cit.*

[9]Diego de Peredo to Enrique Enriquez de Guzmán, *A. G. I., Aud. de Guadalajara,* 61-6-21 (Dunn Transcripts).

of the Bay of Santa María de Galve, the point suspected of being the objective of the French expedition.[10]

The royal *cédula* reached Mexico on July 14, 1698. The effect was immediate. After hurried consultations, active preparations for an expedition to carry out the order just received were begun immediately in Veracruz. Four months of feverish activity saw Andrés Arriola,[11] the newly appointed governor and commander-in-chief of the expedition, ready to set out. On October 15, the little fleet sailed from Veracruz in search of Pensacola Bay. Arriola was given two sets of instructions, one to be followed in case the French were found in possession of the bay, the other in case the place was found unoccupied.[12]

Unfavorable weather detained the expedition on the high seas for more than a month and it was not until November 21 that the coast of Florida was reached. Imagine the surprise of Arriola when he found the bay already occupied. A cautious reconnaissance revealed, however, that the occupants were Spaniards. Four days before, on November 17, Captain Juan Jordán had taken possession of the port and all the surrounding country in the name of the king of Spain. Jordán had come directly from Spain to Havana in the fleet of Zavala, with special instructions to proceed to Pensacola without delay. Agreeable to his orders he had, with the coöperation of the officials in Havana, fitted two vessels, and taking fifty men—his orders asked for one hundred—he had set out from Havana for Florida on November 6, to carry out his instructions.[13] Spain had won in the race for Pensacola Bay.

It was not until January 26, 1699, that early in the morning five cannon shots announced to the bewildered Spanish garrison the presence of a small foreign fleet just outside the harbor. Arriola and his men, unable to perceive clearly the movements of the new arrivals, and suspecting hos-

---

[10]Real Cédula, April 19, 1698, in *Testimonio de Autos ejecutados en Virtud de Rl. Cédula de su Mgd. . . . A. G. I., Aud. de México,* 61-6-22 (Dunn Transcripts).

[11]Andrés de Arriola was a typical Spanish adventurer. Up to 1691 when he became sergeant major of the Presidio of Veracruz, he had seen service in three different fleets. In 1694, he was made general of a relief expedition to the Philippines. By a fortunate coincidence he made the trip from Acapulco to Cavite in less than four months, making the round trip in less than eleven months, the best record in those days for trans-Pacific navigation. This put him in line for promotion and secured for him the appointment as governor. Dunn, *op. cit.,* 176-177.

[12]Instrucción dada al Mre. de Campo D. Andrés de Arriola, in *Testimonio de Autos ejecutados en Virtud de Rl. Cédula* . . . (Dunn Transcripts).

[13]Jordán to the Viceroy, December 6, 1698, in *Testimonio de Autos ejectuados, A. G. I., Aud. de México,* 61-6-22 (Dunn Transcripts).

tility, immediately replied unceremoniously by firing three shots charged with ball. A boat was forthwith sent to reconnoiter the strangers, which found the fleet to consist of five vessels—three large frigates and two small ketches. When the sun dispelled the fog a little later, the flag of France was clearly seen floating in the breeze. The Spanish colors were promptly raised over the unfinished fort and the garrison put under arms in expectation of an attack. The day passed without any hostile movement. On the following day M. Escalette was sent by the commander of the French squadron, the Marquis of Chasteaumorant, to get permission of the Spanish commander to land and replenish their water and wood supply. M. Chasteaumorant declared he had come at the order of the king of France to drive out certain Canadian adventurers who were suspected of taking refuge in this region.

The request was courteously but firmly refused and the French were instructed by Arriola to look for another place along the coast where they could get the desired water and wood. On the 29th, the French tried to sound the entrance to the harbor but were curtly ordered away. On January 30, the little squadron put out to sea and was lost in the horizon, after having registered a formal protest with the Spanish commander against the inhospitable manner in which it had been received.

It is to be noted that during the four days which the little fleet was anchored before Pensacola, Iberville and the colonists—for the expedition was no other—had been kept well in the background. The two ketches in which the settlers were quartered remained a safe distance away and no indication of the real purpose of the expedition was given to the Spaniards.[14]

The French, it seems, had not expected to find Pensacola occupied by the Spaniards. Iberville had made careful inquiry, while in Santo Domingo, as to the location of the Mississippi and the presence of the English in the region, but had obtained no definite information about either. Fearful of repeating La Salle's mistake, he had decided to sail directly from Santo Domingo to Florida with the intention of following the coast westward from there until the Mississippi River was reached. Little did he think he would find the Spaniards already there.

---

[14]The Spanish sources for this incident are all included in the *Testimonio de Autos ejecutados*, A. G. I., *Audiencia de México*, 61-6-22, already referred to, (Dunn Transcripts), which consists of 343 typewritten pages. The French sources have been published in Margry, *Découvertes et Etablissements de Français*, IV. A good account is found in Dunn, *Spanish and French Rivalry in the Gulf Coast Region*, 146-191.

French settle Louisiana. Upon leaving Pensacola on January 30, the French expedition made its way to Mobile Bay, where it spent a few days before proceeding along the coast to present day Ship Island. From here the exploration of the coast was continued in canoes until the mouth of the Mississippi was finally discovered on March 2.

In order to avoid any risk of passing by the river, Iberville hit upon the idea of using two long canoes to explore the coast more minutely. Fifty men and a missionary, the experienced Father Anastasius Douay, who had been with La Salle fourteen years before, accompanied Iberville. With almost no difficulty he came upon the goal of his search. "We perceived a pass between two banks which appeared like islands. We saw that the water had changed; tasted and found it fresh . . . As we advanced we saw the passes of the river, three in number . . . On the third a *Te Deum* was sung in gratitude for having found the river."[15] In April a temporary fort was built at Biloxi and Iberville, having accomplished the main purpose of his expedition, prepared to return home at once to make further plans for the development of the new colony. Out of regard for his powerful protector he named the fort Maurepas.[16]

But let us return to the Spaniards at Pensacola. It seems strange they did not take more active measures to prevent the French from landing on the coast. As a matter of fact, it was a full year before they even discovered the existence of the French settlement at the mouth of the Mississippi, and fourteen years before definite steps were taken to prevent their efforts to penetrate into Texas. To understand this paradox, let us see what effect the visit of the French had upon Arriola, and why the viceregal government, after displaying such activity in occupying this harbor, did nothing to oust the French from the coast region.

No sooner had the French squadron departed than Arriola called a council of war. The Spanish garrison had not been deceived by the visitors. It was plain that they intended to found a settlement somewhere on the Gulf coast. Arriola now submitted three questions to the assembled officers. First, was it advisable to send a boat to observe the movements of the French? Second, should Arriola remain at Pensacola or embark for Mexico without loss of time to secure the necessary naval force and supplies to prevent the French from carrying out their designs? Third, were there any suggestions for defence? The council of war was unanimous on the inadvisability of sending a boat to watch the movements of the French

---

[15]French, *Historical Collections of Louisiana and Florida,* II, 52-57.

[16]French, *Historical Collections of Louisiana and Florida,* II, 110-113.

fleet. The boat would be easily captured and precious time would be lost. With but one dissenting vote it was agreed that Arriola should leave immediately for Mexico. Accordingly on February 2, he embarked for Veracruz, leaving Francisco Martínez,[17] an experienced officer, in charge of the fort.

Upon his arrival in Veracruz, Arriola found Spanish officials deeply concerned over what at that time was considered the most serious aggression of Spain's colonial empire. From Caracas and from Havana conclusive evidence of a contemplated Scotch settlement on the Isthmus of Darien had been sent to the viceroy with an urgent appeal for immediate help to ward off this grave menace to the interests of the king. The disquieting news of the French on the Gulf coast now brought by Arriola only added to the already tense situation.

Special councils were ordered to meet both in Veracruz and in Mexico City to discuss the situation and decide on a course of action. The majority of the officials was inclined to consider the danger from the French as more imminent and of more serious consequences to New Spain than the remote peril of Darien. But the viceroy, with a broader view of things, would not be convinced, and steadfastly refused to allow any action to be taken with regard to the French until the threat of a Scotch settlement at Darien was past. He firmly believed that the French, upon finding Pensacola previously occupied, had returned home. In spite of all the efforts of Arriola, action was deferred for almost a year.[18]

In the meantime the French settlers gained a secure foothold. Iberville returned to the settlement at Biloxi on January 8, 1700. During his absence an English corvette carrying twelve guns, had entered the Mississippi but Bienville had succeeded in forcing it to leave. This news, however, and the fact that English traders from Carolina were among the Chickasaws, made Iberville take immediate steps to establish a fort on the banks of the river. He placed four guns there and gave the command to Bienville and M. de Saint Denis, "a Canadian of noble birth,"

---

[17]Francisco Martínez had accompanied De León's expedition to Texas in 1689 and had also been in Texas with Terán in 1691. When it was decided to occupy Pensacola, he was made sergeant major and second in command of the expedition under Arriola. Dunn, *op. cit.*, 108, 132, 133, 137, 179.

[18]*El Virrey de Na. España Da quenta á V M. con Autos de las providencias que aplico pa. que los nauios del gl. Don Man. de Zavala pasasen al exterminio de escozeces* . . . July 14, 1699. 16 pp. (Dunn Transcripts).

declared Morfi, "whom we shall shortly see playing an important role in the history of Texas."[19]

Perhaps, because Spain and France were nominally at peace, it is curious to note how the French in Louisiana resorted to a clever ruse to deceive the Spaniards during the first year of their establishment. After Arriola left for Veracruz, Martínez sent a scouting party to Mobile Bay to ascertain if the French were still there. The men reported that signs of their short stay were visible, but that no ships had been seen. The fears entertained as to the designs of the French now rapidly subsided, but persistent rumors of the presence of Englishmen in the vicinity of Pensacola greatly alarmed the half-starved and sick-ridden Spanish garrison.

Fear of the English.   Early in February, 1699, a dispatch from Governor Laureano de Torres y Ayala reached the distressed troops at Pensacola, warning them of the designs of the English. The letter went on to state that Francisco Romo de Uriza had been sent to the colony of St. George (Carolina) in the summer of 1698. While there he learned that the English were contemplating the occupation of the Gulf coast in the neighborhood of the Mississippi River and the Bay of Espíritu Santo.[20] The news greatly alarmed Martínez, and the garrison was almost thrown into a panic by further details of the English designs sent by Governor Torres soon after. The governor declared that in January an English vessel was wrecked near St. Augustine and some of the survivors were given shelter at the presidio there. Later, Torres had sent back the Englishmen escorted by a group of Spanish soldiers to the colony of St. George for the purpose of finding out more about the intended occupation of the Gulf coast. The report was brought back that five vessels ready for sail had been observed in the English fort and that a settlement at Apalache was being planned.[21]

The suspicions of Martínez and the famished soldiers left at Pensacola seemed at last confirmed when on May 2 two English sailors arrived at the presidio in a small boat and claimed they had been shipwrecked while on their way from Jamaica to New England. Cross-examination of the men revealed that they knew of no English colony to the west. Nevertheless, Martínez decided to send them to Mexico for further questioning. On May 4, a small vessel which had brought some needed supplies from

---

[19]Castañeda, *Morfi's History of Texas.*

[20]Martínez to the Governor of Havana, February 21, 1699, in *A. G. I., Audiencia de México,* 61-6-22 (Dunn Transcripts).

[21]Torres to the King, September 16, 1699, *A. G. I., Audiencia de México,* 61-6-22 (Dunn Transcripts).

Havana, set sail for Veracruz, carrying the disabled men and the two English sailors with a detailed report of the fears entertained concerning the activities of that nation.[22]

But neither the viceroy nor the viceregal officials gave much credence to the tales of an English settlement. Curious enough, the *fiscal,* Baltasar de Tobar, without any concrete evidence, arrived at the correct conclusion and affirmed that the supposed English vessels were in reality French.[23] But his urgent recommendation that steps be taken to drive them out of the Gulf region went unheeded. It was the continued and persistent rumors of the presence of Englishmen, as reported by the Indians, which at last resulted in the issuance of orders to Arriola, when he was about to return to Pensacola at the close of 1699, to undertake the expulsion of the intruders.

After setting things in order, Arriola finally succeeded in organizing an expedition to go in search of the supposed English colony. With one hundred of his best men, he set out with four vessels on March 4, 1700, to find it west of Pensacola. Both Martínez and Franck accompanied Arriola. The expedition made its way first to Mobile Bay. A few miles west a party of Indians was sent ashore to reconnoiter. They soon returned to report that a short distance away was a fort garrisoned by about two hundred men and that it was further protected by a fleet of several vessels. Before the excitement of this discovery died down, there came in sight a small boat flying the English flag. It was immediately overtaken, and, to the surprise and bewilderment of the Spaniards, it was found to contain ten Frenchmen instead of Englishmen.[24] The men declared that they were on their way to Biloxi, where the French had a fort which they had built in April the year before, immediately after the departure of M. Chasteau-morant; that another fort had been established twenty-five leagues up the river; and that about four hundred leagues still further up there was a third French fort. The English mystery was thus cleared up and Arriola was now faced with the accomplished fact of the French occupation of the Mississippi.

He released the prisoners and sent them on to the French fort with a

[22]Martínez to the Viceroy, May 4, 1699, *A. G. I., Audiencia de México,* 61-6-22 (Dunn Transcripts).

[23]Respuesta fiscal, June 5, 1699, in *Testimonio del Segundo Quaderno de Autos . . . sobre. la Poblazón y fortificazión de la Bahía de Santa Ma. Galve. A. G. I., Audiencia de México,* 61-6-22 (Dunn Transcripts).

[24]Franck to the King, June 4, 1700, *A. G. I., Audiencia de México,* 61-6-22 (Dunn Transcripts).

strong protest against the invasion of Spanish territory in time of peace. He sent word that he would follow shortly and pay the fort a personal visit. When on March 23 the Spanish expedition reached Biloxi, they were politely entertained and feasted by the French. But the courtesy of the invaders, who regaled the Spaniards with such delicacies as fresh bread, milk, eggs, wine, and even brandy, did not make Arriola forget his duty. He again protested in the strongest terms against the French settlement of Spanish territory and demanded the evacuation of the settlers. The commander of Biloxi politely replied he had taken possession of the land by order of his king to keep the English out; that he could do nothing without orders from France.

To attack the fort was out of the question. Arriola remained at Biloxi four days and started on his return trip on March 27. But misfortune haunted the Spaniards. Three days later a terrific hurricane destroyed all but one vessel. Most of the men swam ashore and drifted into the French fort where they were given gracious hospitality until new vessels could come from Pensacola to take them home.[25] The reports of Arriola and his officers convinced the Spanish officials in New Spain that to attempt to oust the French was futile with the resources at hand. It was necessary to await the pleasure of the king before any further steps were taken. Thus the French gained a permanent foothold on the Gulf coast, which, like a thorn, rankled constantly the sensitive honor of Spain's officials and resulted ultimately in the formal occupation of Texas.

Death of Charles II. The imbecile Charles II was rapidly reaching the end of his inglorious reign. Spain and its immense colonial empire seemed crushed under an evil genius that paralyzed all action. The impotence of the viceregal officials in coping with foreign aggression on the Gulf coast was but a faint reflection of the incapacity of the ruler and his equally worthless advisers. France had violated the sovereignty of Spain in America with impunity and firmly established herself at the mouth of the Mississippi, laying the foundation for the permanent occupation of the vast territory of Louisiana. At last, death stepped in to end the feeble existence of Charles II, who died in November, 1700. The grandson of the powerful Louis XIV promptly ascended the throne as Philip V, first of the new Bourbon line.

---

[25]Arriola to the Viceroy, June 4, 1700, in *A. G. I., Audiencia de México*, 61-6-22 (Dunn Transcripts).

French encroachments from Louisiana. Numerous were the weighty problems which called for an immediate solution by the new ruler, but chief among these was the unsettled question of Pensacola and Louisiana. Recognizing the rightful claim of Spain to the Gulf region, the French court was the first to broach the question with an explanation of its action and a request for a free and unmolested title to the region now occupied. The Duke of Harcourt, French ambassador to Madrid, was sent a lengthy dispatch drawn up by Pontchartrain, on March 23, 1701, in which he frankly stated the position of France with regard to Louisiana. The primary object in encouraging the discovery of the Mississippi had been, he declared, to aid the French settlements in Canada in securing an outlet for trade. He then went on to explain that Iberville's explorations had disclosed the ulterior designs of the English, who had intended to take possession eventually of the rich mines in New Spain. Their powerful and populous settlements in Pennsylvania, New York, and Carolina made such a project feasible, particularly in the face of Spain's inability to protect her extended frontiers. Mindful of this fact and desirous of impeding a scheme so detrimental to the interests of Spain, the king of France had decided to occupy the mouth of the Mississippi and the adjacent territory to protect the frontiers of New Spain, but with no intention of doing anything contrary to the wishes of Spain.[26]

The dispatch was accompanied by a copy of a memorial prepared by Iberville, who pointed out that unless France and Spain joined forces to stop them, the English would eventually seize Mexico. The possession of the Gulf region and the Mississippi by the French, he argued, was the best safeguard for the Spanish dominions in North America. He went so far as to hint broadly that Spain should give up her opposition to the colonization of Louisiana and allow France to occupy Pensacola in the event the fort be abandoned.[27]

The Duke of Harcourt presented the dispatch and attached memorial and map to the young Philip V, who in turn sent the documents to the *Junta de Guerra* with an urgent request for the earliest possible consideration of this weighty matter. On June 6, this body discussed the question at length in view of all the information at hand. Three months before, in February, the *Junta* had received a report of all that had transpired at Pensacola since Arriola's discovery of the French settlement, the dissatis-

---

[26]Pontchartrain to the Duke of Harcourt, March 23, 1701. Translation in *A. G. I., Audiencia de México*, 61-6-22 (Dunn Transcripts).

[27]Margry, *Découvertes et Etablissements*, IV, 543-550.

faction of the troops stationed at that post, and the decision of the viceroy to defer all action against the French until he obtained further orders from the king.[28] After carefully weighing all the circumstances the *Junta* drew up a series of recommendations. With characteristic Spanish courtesy it advised that the king of France should be thanked for what he had done to preserve the integrity of the dominions of Spain, for the extension of the Catholic faith, and for his timely warning of the designs of the English—ignoring, as it did, that the French had used the English flag to cover their own designs; it recommended that Pensacola should be maintained at all costs because of its strategic position; that the governors of New Spain, Florida, Havana and Campeche be ordered to give all possible aid to the garrison; that the offer of coöperation on the part of the French navy to check the English be welcomed; and lastly, that the king of France be asked to instruct his officers in the settlements on the Mississippi River and adjacent territory to secure commissions from the Spanish government, in order that the viceroy of New Spain might be able to give them the necessary assistance in the performance of their duty.[29]

Although courteous, the *Junta de Guerra* was firm in its recommendations to safeguard what it considered the integrity of the Spanish dominions against the encroachments of foreign powers. But these were not accepted without one dissenting vote. The Count of Hernán Núñez upbraided the *Junta* for its impractical recommendations with unaccustomed frankness and severity. He discussed at great length the impossibility of carrying out the suggestions made, and emphatically declared that it was useless to attempt the impossible. "Seldom, if ever, had the dignified *Junta* listened to words of such uncompromising frankness," declares an able historian.[30] He pointed out that if Spain was sincere in her desire to preserve and extend the Catholic faith, she should accept the offer of the French king instead of trying to deceive herself into believing that by the mere promulgation of royal decrees fleets could be built, Pensacola colonized, and other fortifications constructed.[31]

---

[28]Para despachar dos cartas de Dn. Andrés de Arriola sobre Vahía de Pensacola y Poblazión de franceses en aquella costa. *A. G. I., Audiencia de México,* (Dunn Transcripts).

[29]Consulta de la Junta de Guerra, June 6, 1701, *A. G. I., Audiencia de México,* 61-6-35, (Dunn Transcripts).

[30]Dunn, *op. cit.,* 209.

[31]Consulta de la Junta de Guerra, June 6, 1701, *A. G. I., Audiencia de México,* 61-6-35 (Dunn Transcripts).

When the report of the *Junta* reached the king, he was no more pleased or convinced by its arguments than was the critical and matter-of-fact Count of Hernán Núñez. The king thought the report was too brief and not sufficiently clear on a number of vital questions, such as the means with which the recommendations of the *Junta* for the occupation of Pensacola, the establishment of settlements on the Mississippi, and the defence of these new establishments were to be carried out. Consequently, on June 17, he returned the report to the *Junta* with a number of specific questions to be answered in detail.

Taking for granted that the king asked for additional information because he approved the recommendations in principle, the *Junta* replied extensively on June 21. It pointed out that in addition to the regular revenue of New Spain, which could be applied to the project, there were numerous other sources of revenue such as the *medias anatas* of the *encomiendas,* the tax on arms, the bull of the Holy Crusade, the *Alcabalas,* the million of the charitable subsidy granted by the Pope, the profits from quicksilver, and the royal fifths. The actual occupation of Pensacola, as well as the settlement of the Mississippi being now an accomplished fact, the only thing necessary for their maintenance was to issue the corresponding orders to the viceroy in New Spain. It then went on to suggest that in order to check the possible advance of the English, to which Iberville alluded, alliances with the tribes of Apaches, Apalachicolas, Tejas, and such tribes as inhabited Nuevo León and New Mexico could be formed, which would prove an insuperable obstacle to the designs on the rich mines of New Spain. In the course of its arguments in support of the recommendations, the *Junta* declared that the first duty of the Spanish government was to keep the Catholic faith pure and undefiled in the new world, granted to the crown for that purpose.

It should be noted that in giving his vote, Martín de Solís, one time *fiscal* of the Council of the Indies and now a member, specifically suggested that the viceroy of New Spain should be instructed to send special envoys to the Tejas Indians, asking them not to allow the English to pass through their lands while attempting to reach New Spain.[32] The vote of the various members of the *Junta* contain numerous references to the Tejas as a means of blocking the advance of either the English or French to New Spain, a fact which clearly points to the realization of the importance attached to these Indians, and which makes evident the inti-

[32]Consulta de la Junta de Guerra, June 21, 1701, *A. G. I., Audiencia de México,* 61-6-35, (Dunn Transcripts).

mate association that existed in the minds of Spanish officials at this time between the territory occupied by the Tejas and the French settlements on the Mississippi.

The bulky report was sent without loss of time to the king, together with the former recommendations and a French translation of the entire proceedings for the king of France. Philip V, upon receipt of the documents, wrote a letter to his grandfather and forwarded the French translation on July 5, 1701,[33] without writing a word to the *Junta*. Almost a whole year was to elapse before the subject was again brought to the attention of that body by an unexpected coincidence.

Paying little or no attention to the emphatic protest of the Spanish government, as expressed in the lengthy report of the *Junta* transmitted to the French king, Mobile Bay was formally occupied early in 1702. Martínez sent immediately full details of the matter from Pensacola in a letter dated April 14, 1702. Iberville, he explained, had appeared at Pensacola on December 16, 1701, and requested permission to enter. The request was granted in view of the close relations existing between the two crowns. Three days later, Iberville informed Martínez he had orders from the king of France to occupy Mobile Bay "before the English should seize it." In vain did Martínez protest and entreat Iberville to defer carrying out his purpose until he could receive instructions from the viceroy of New Spain. The French commander merely reiterated that his royal master's only desire was "to act for the best interests of both crowns",[34] as he systematically went about the occupation of Mobile and Martínez stood helplessly watching every move.

Upon receipt of this information the *Junta* immediately held a meeting and on August 1, 1702, reported the whole matter to the king. They called his royal attention to the fact that the extension of the French settlements in the coast region was detrimental to the best interests of Spain, that on two previous occasions the attention of the king had been called to these encroachments; and that until he made some decision in the matter, the *Junta* was unable to apply the necessary remedies to preserve the integrity of the king's domains.[35]

The king did not appreciate the zeal of the *Junta* in pointing out the serious consequences of his procrastination. Such frankness shocked the

---

[33]Margry, *Découvertes et Etablissements des Français,* IV, 552-553.

[34]*Ibid.,* 576-580.

[35]Consulta de la Junta de Guerra, August 1, 1702, *A. G. I., Audiencia de México,* 61-6-22 (Dunn Transcripts).

sensitive monarch who, instead of thanking his well-meaning advisers, made the following annotation on the margin of the report:

This notice is incomplete. Since the papers, which the *Junta* says have not arrived, are lacking, this representation is premature, and it is couched in such ill-advised terms that it has displeased me exceedingly, and caused me great surprise that ministers of such experience and high rank should have allowed it to reach my hands.[36]

In the meantime the French continued to establish themselves firmly along the Gulf coast from Mobile Bay to the mouth of the Mississippi and to strengthen their communications along the river as far north as Canada, drawing closer all the time to the Red River and the outskirts of New Spain.

It has been thought erroneously that during the period from the abandonment of the missions in 1693 until the appearance of St. Denis at the Presidio of San Juan Bautista on the Río Grande in 1714, there was little or no interest in Texas either on the part of the French or the Spanish and that the entire province was relegated to the savages. "For more than twenty years its history is almost a blank. The Spaniards in Mexico forgot it in the press of more urgent matters . . . The fear of a French intrusion into Spanish territory, which in the years 1689, 1690, and 1691 had been strong enough to induce the viceroy to send a company of priests and soldiers exploring far into the interior of Texas, grew less and less as the years passed, and no further attempt was made by the French to claim or possess the territory between the Red River and the Río Grande. The rulers of New Spain, satisfied with a potential ownership, fell into a state of indifference toward the northeastern lands," declares Clark.[37] But since the time this statement was made, many new sources have been made available and this period, considered generally a "blank" in our history, has been gradually revealed as one during which activity went on, interest continued, and the determining forces that resulted in the final and permanent occupation of Texas developed. It has been shown how in an effort to forestall the French on the Gulf coast, Santa María de Galve was established, how the French surreptitiously made a permanent settlement at Biloxi, how they had recourse to a subterfuge to keep the Spaniards at Pensacola from discovering their infant colony, and how both the officials in New Spain and in Madrid tried to prevent this intrusion but lacked the means and the moral support of the king to carry out their purpose and safeguard the integrity of the Spanish dominions.

---

[36]*Dunn, op. cit.,* 215.

[37]R. C. Clark, *op. cit.,* VI, 3.

Early activities of St. Denis.   During this period there rises a figure who seems to dominate the stage of French activity on the Franco-Spanish frontier in America, a man who, for more than forty years, was destined to play an important role, and of whom Governor Boneo y Morales said in 1744: "St. Denis is dead, thank God! Now we can breathe easier."[38] Louis Juchereau de St. Denis was a remarkable man in many respects. Shrewd, resourceful, inured to the hardships of frontier life, acquainted with the psychology of the natives from childhood, and with a gift for languages, he was particularly fitted by nature to be the ambassador *par excellence* of the French from the Mississippi to the Río Grande. His father had come to Canada around the year 1675 and by his services to the king, his ability and his courage had risen to the rank of lieutenant general of Montreal. In 1700, he offered the king to colonize the mouth of the Mississippi, confidently affirming "after twenty-five years of experience I should be able to establish a flourishing colony." He received only a concession to establish a tannery in Louisiana, but death, in 1703, while on the way to the Mississippi, prevented him from carrying out his purpose.[39]

His son, a young man of twenty-one, preceded him to Louisiana in 1700,[40] coming down the Mississippi, probably with Tonty. Louis Juchereau de St. Denis immediately became an active and important member of the colony. Iberville recognized at once the natural ability of the young Canadian, and when the new fort on the Mississippi was finished early in 1700, he left his brother Bienville and M. de St. Denis as joint commanders of this important post.[41]

Just when he became commander of the fort of San Juan on the Mississippi, situated forty leagues west of Mobile, is not clear, but he was its commander by 1705, according to his own statement made in Mexico City on June 22, 1715.[42] It is from this declaration that much information is gathered concerning his activities in Texas from 1705 to 1715. At this

---

[38]H. E. Bolton, *Texas in the Middle Eighteenth Century*, 41.

[39]Margry, *Découvertes et Etablissements des Français*, IV. The data concerning Juchereau de St. Denis, father of Louis, are scattered throughout this volume.

[40]Charmion Shelby, "St. Denis's Declaration Concerning Texas in 1717," The *Southwestern Historical Quarterly*, XXVI, 169. At this time St. Denis declared he was 38 years old. That would make him 21 in 1700, the year he arrived at the mouth of the Mississippi.

[41]Margry, *op. cit.*, IV, 399.

[42]Declaración de St. Denis y Medar Jalot sobre su viaje hasta el presidio del Capitán Diego Ramón, in *San Francisco el Grande Archive*, VIII, 27-32.

time he asserted he had been among the Tejas Indians ten years before. According to his statement made under oath, he went at that time (1705) from Mobile to the Choctaws, a populous tribe which he affirmed numbered about 18,000 members. After a visit with them, he went to the Natchez, a nation that lay thirty leagues west quarter northwest from the Choctaws and consisted of eleven pueblos, all of whom had sworn allegiance to his Most Christian Majesty the King of France. From the Natchez he traveled forty leagues in a southwesterly direction to the Nachitos. This nation had also traded with the French since 1701, the chief article of exchange being salt. According to St. Denis, the salt secured from these Indians was whiter and purer than the salt that came from France. The Nachitos were neighbors of the Asinai, commonly called the Tejas, with whom they traded also. It was thus through the Nachitos that the French traders introduced their merchandise among the Tejas in the early years. After a short stay with the Nachitos, St. Denis went on to visit the Tejas Indians and from there—mark this statement—he proceeded over the same route as in 1714, to the Presidio of San Juan Bautista on the Río Grande.[43]

He not only declared he had visited the presidio ten years before but he goes further and explains that the distance by land from Mobile to the Río Grande is two hundred eighty leagues. In his own words: "There are from Mobile to the said presidio two hundred eighty leagues over good and passable ground and the routes so run that they come together at the Nachitos. No mines have been discovered over the entire land route, but there are numerous groves of shade and fruit trees to be found along the road."[44] The two courses referred to here are the all-land and the water and land routes from Mobile to San Juan Bautista on the Río Grande. It was the latter of these two that was followed by St. Denis and his companions in 1713-15, at which time he traveled by water in canoes from Mobile to the Asinai, and from the Asinai to the Río Grande over land. It is worth noting that at the time he made his declaration he also gave the viceroy a map which he made of the country over which he traveled. If this map is ever found, it will be of great interest not only in helping to locate the first route from the Mississippi to the Río Grande but also

---

[43]"La quarta desde aquí hasta Asinay, y de allí el Presidio Español del Capitán Ramón en la Rivera del Río Grande del Norte 160 leguas que es el mismo camino que expreso arriva." *Ibid.*, VIII, 32.

[44]*Ibid.*, VIII, 32.

as one of the earliest maps of Texas drawn by a European from actual observation.[45]

Although in his declaration he was careful not to state that he had visited the Tejas Indians on other occasions, it seems he was in the habit of frequently spending as much as six months at a time among them. One of the dispatch carriers of Diego Ramón on being asked to give testimony on what he had observed and learned from the Indians said that "St. Denis knew their language because he had lived among them on various occasions."[46] This statement is further borne out by the declarations made by Father Olivares who said: "Don Luis de St. Denis was the one whom the Indians respected most because he knew their language, having lived among them four months on one occasion and for shorter periods at other times."[47] In a letter written by Domingo Ramón on July 26, 1716, he states that St. Denis had been very helpful to him because of his knowledge of the habits and customs of the Tejas and of their language, a knowledge which he had acquired while living among them. He affirms that St. Denis spent "six months in the province on two different occasions."[48]

When the Ramón expedition arrived in the country of the Tejas it was noted that the Indians had cloth of good grade, beads, firearms, and trinkets of various kinds. Upon being asked where they secured all these things they said the French from Natchitoches brought them in square boats on the river and gave them to the Indians for horses and skins of animals.[49] All evidences seem to point clearly to the fact that this trade had been going on for years. Ramón himself admits that he noticed while among the Tejas as many as eighteen or twenty long French arquebuses, many beads, numerous trinkets, large knives, pocket knives, pieces of cloth

---

[45]This map is referred to not only in the declaration of St. Denis already cited, but in various documents contained in the same volume of the *San Francisco el Grande Archive*. See Vol. VIII, 32, 34, 39, and 41.

[46]Resumen de los autos sobre noticias, informes, y escritos desde 1688 a 1716 sobre la necesidad de poblar la región, entre Tejas y la Mobila, sobre los Asinai y su conversión, y sobre lo recomendado por el fiscal sobre cada punto. México, Noviembre 30, 1716, in *San Franciso el Grande Archive,* VIII, 126-163.

[47]*Ibid.,* VIII, 148.

[48]Probably in 1705, before proceeding to the Río Grande, and again in 1713-14, while on the way to the Río Grande for the second time. "Acuerdos de la Junta de Guerra y Hacienda que el Capitán Ramón aprehenda los 4 franceses. Diciembre 2, 1716." In *San Francisco el Grande Archive,* VIII, 170.

[49]Resumen General de Noticias . . . in *San Francisco el Grande Archive,* VIII, 141 *ad passim.*

of good grade, particularly blue, and hatchets, all of which the Indians obtained from the French in exchange for cattle and horses.[50]

From the very establishment of the French in Louisiana their main interest and concern had been the extension of trade with the Indians and the discovery of mines. If no mines could be found in the new territory, it seems it was their intention to open up communications with the Spaniards and to reach the rich mines of Chihuahua and Parral. No sooner were the French settled than an expedition was sent out to explore the country to the west and win the friendship and trade of the natives. Led by M. Bienville and Louis de St. Denis, twenty-two Canadians and seven Indians set out in March, 1700, to explore the Red River country. They ascended the river until they came to a village of Indians which they called Yactaches. The natives told them they were but two days journey from the land of the Caddos. There were a few members of this tribe in the village who invited the French to visit them. They told the French that five days journey from their village, to the west, there was a Spanish settlement where men, women, and children lived. For some reason not stated, Bienville and St. Denis did not go in search of the reported settlement but started back to Mobile on May 18.[51]

No sooner did the expedition return than St. Denis was again commissioned, before the end of the month, to proceed westward with twenty-five men in search of the Spaniards. He traveled up the river for a distance of seventy leagues until he reached the village of the Natchitoche Indians, where he spent a short time and then proceeded to the village of the Caddos about a hundred leagues further west. Upon inquiring from these Indians if they had seen any Spaniards in the neighborhood, he was informed that it had been two years since they had seen any. It seems that St. Denis returned to Mobile without making any further efforts to reach the Spanish settlements at this time.[52] But according to his own statement, he undertook a new expedition in 1704 or 1705, at which time he must have visited among the Tejas Indians for a period of between four and six months, before proceeding on his way to the Río Grande which he reached by following the same route taken ten years later.[53]

---

[50]Acuerdos de la Junta de Guerra y Hacienda . . . in *San Francisco el Grande Archive,* VIII, 170.

[51]Journal de Bienville, Margry, *op. cit.,* IV, 432.

[52]Clark, *op. cit.,* VI, 5-6.

[53]Declaración de St. Denis, June 22, 1715, 27-32; also statements of Ramón, Father Olivares, and dispatch carrier of Diego Ramón, *San Francisco el Grande Archive,* Volume VIII.

Aside from his own admission of this visit, no other information has been found concerning the purpose of the expedition or the number who took part in it.

On August 29, 1707, Don Gregorio Salinas Varona,[54] Governor of Santa María de Galve, wrote a long letter to the viceroy of Mexico. In the letter he informed his excellency that he had just heard that on August 22, the Governor of Mobile had sent out an expedition consisting of twenty-five Canadians armed with rifles, one hundred Indians, and two pirogues loaded with merchandise to explore the approaches to the dominions of the king of Spain for the purpose of introducing merchandise and establishing trade with Nueva Vizcaya, Nuevo Reyno de León, and Coahuila, which they called Nueva Estremadura.[55]

Immediately upon receipt of this information a council of war was held in Mexico City and it was decided that the viceroy should send out without delay instructions to the governors and commanders of these provinces to prevent by all means in their power the introduction of goods or merchandise and the entrance of foreigners. They were authorized to use all available forces under their commands to watch all river crossings and mountain passes, and advised to utilize the friendly Indians in keeping a close watch on the movements of the intruders. In case the merchandise had already been introduced before the orders were received, the governors, commanders, and all public officials were instructed to confiscate all such goods wherever they were found and to arrest persons holding said goods or connected in any manner with their introduction under pain of being removed from office.

---

[54]Don Gregorio Salinas Varona was a distinguished Spanish officer of long and varied experience. He had served for more than twenty years in Flanders before coming to New Spain and had been retired with the rank of Captain and a pension of twenty-five *escudos*. He came to Mexico in 1687 in company with a number of retired officers sent to serve under the Count of Monclova. He accompanied De León on his second expedition to Texas in 1690 and on its return was charged by De León to convey to Mexico City the complete *autos* of the expedition of Pierre Meusnier, two boys, and a girl, all French, rescued from the Indians. He was immediately thereafter ordered to accompany the sea expedition of Captain Francisco de Llanos, sent out early in October, 1690, to remove the buoys seen at San Bernardo Bay. He was in charge of the land operations of this expedition. He was appointed by royal patent Governor of Coahuila on August 29, 1690, but did not take possession of his office until January 23, 1693. On May 3 he led a relief expedition to East Texas arriving there on June 8, just in time to save the starving missionaries and soldiers. Dunn, *Spanish and French Rivalry*, 121, 124, 126, 139-142.

[55]Resumen General de Noticias . . . in *San Francisco el Grande Archive*, VIII, 164-165.

The viceroy was further requested to write to the Governor of Louisiana and informed him, without revealing the source, that a report of the attempted establishment of trade with the various frontier provinces of New Spain had been received; that such trade was strictly prohibited by the king of Spain; and that in view of the circumstances, the Governor of Louisiana should warn all subjects of His Most Christian Majesty to abstain from such trade.

Espinosa-Olivares-Aguirre Expedition. Not content with all this, the *Junta* recommended that immediate steps be taken to establish contact with the Tejas Indians and all their neighbors in order that they might be used to prevent the introduction of illicit trade into New Spain. It was this last suggestion that resulted in the Espinosa-Olivares-Aguirre expedition in 1709, which paved the way for the *entrada* of Ramón seven years later. The earlier entry into Texas just mentioned was practically unknown until its recent publication.[56]

In accord with the resolution adopted by the *Junta General* held on August 7, 1708, Captain Pedro de Aguirre, commander of the Presidio of Río Grande del Norte, was ordered by His Excellency, the Duke of Albuquerque, Viceroy of New Spain, to escort Fathers Antonio de San Buenaventura Olivares and Isidro Espinosa, both friars of the Franciscan Order and missionaries of the Colegio de la Santa Cruz de Querétaro, as far as the San Marcos River (the Colorado?), where the Tejas Indians were said to be now congregated. The expedition could not get on its way, however, until April 5, 1709. On this day Captain Aguirre, the two missionaries, and fourteen soldiers crossed the Río Grande, after leaving the Mission of San Juan Bautista, and set out on their lonely quest for the Tejas. Traveling as rapidly as possible they reached the Nueces by the 8th, and arrived in the present site of San Antonio on the 13th, where they named the San Pedro Springs and called the river San Antonio de Padua. Six days later they reached their goal, the Colorado River, but much to their disappointment found no Tejas Indians awaiting them there as they had expected. After a day of fruitless searching for friendly Indians, they discovered a group of Yojuanes. But let the pious Espinosa tell the story himself:

"Seeing that our efforts to reach the arroyo of the Otates in the hope of meeting the Tejas had been fruitless, and knowing that the Indian leader of the Yojuanes, called Cantona, frequents the province of the

[56]Gabriel Tous, T. O. R., "The Espinosa-Olivares-Aguirre Expedition of 1709" in *Preliminary Studies of the Texas Catholic Historical Society*, I, No. 3.

Tejas with his followers, we inquired particularly about the said Indians, and asked if it was true that they had left their territory and had come to settle on the San Marcos River. To this they replied that the Asinai Indians, commonly called Tejas, were in their own country where they had always lived; that they had not moved to the place we inquired about; that only a few were in the habit of going in search of buffalo meat to the Colorado River and its neighborhood. Asked again, if they knew this to be the truth, they maintained what they had said and declared further that Bernardino, a Tejas Indian, who knew Spanish and was very crafty, having lived many years among the Spaniards, was the chief of all the Tejas, and this they knew well. All this caused us sorrow on the one hand, because we wanted to see the Tejas, and joy on the other hand, because it relieved us of the uncertainty under which we had labored concerning the whereabouts of the Tejas. The Indians said also that it was a three-day journey from the place where we were to the village of the Tejas. Not having planned to stay any longer, and the Captain of the military expedition not having instructions to go any farther, and having been told by all, who knew him, that the chief of the Tejas was very adverse to all matters of faith, never having been made to live like a Christian, and that he had escaped from the mission of the Río Grande with some Indian women who had been left there, we decided not to proceed any farther. . . .

". . . Saturday afternoon we made a paper cross, which we painted with ink as best we could, and gave it to the Indian, Cantona, who came with us. We commissioned him to take it to the governor of the Tejas and to tell them how we had searched for them; that they should go to our missions on the Río Grande since they knew where they were; and to show them the cane he had, that they might give credence to his words. He promised to do everything we told him. This being done we started our return march to the Río Grande. . . ."[57]

Although the expedition failed to meet the Tejas Indians, which it went out to contact for the expressed purpose of securing their good will and coöperation to check the activities of the French, nevertheless, it was not a failure, for it made possible a few years later the Ramón expedition. The Tejas Indians, it must be borne in mind, were crafty and astute. They, no doubt, carried word of the visit of the missionaries and the small group of soldiers to their friends in Louisiana. The news of the intention of the Spaniards to establish a mission among them only aroused the cupidity of the French, who saw in the establishment not a hindrance to their designs but an invaluable opportunity to introduce their merchandise farther into the interior by this means without so much danger. In short, the projected settlement of East Texas would bring the Spanish frontier closer to them and make it easier to establish trade.

---

[57]*Ibid.*, 8-10.

Spanish officials aware of French designs. The Spanish officials were well aware of this fact. When St. Denis made his declarations in Mexico, the *Fiscal* was not in the least convinced by the apparently guileless statements. There were too many discrepancies. It may be lightly thought that the French fooled the Spaniards on more than one occasion. This impression is unfounded. It was not because the Spaniards did not understand or realize the true import and intentions of the French that they did not stop their activities or take more aggressive measures. It was that they were powerless to act; first, because the king did not give them the authorization, not even the moral support they deserved for their zeal in protecting his royal interests; and second, because they did not have the resources nor the man power to put into effect a more decisive policy.

Take, for example, the summary of the Texas situation made by the *Fiscal,* Doctor Velasco, in Mexico City, on November 30, 1716. After giving a long and detailed resumé of everything that had taken place since 1689, he draws up his conclusions and analyzes the reasons for the occupation of Texas, revealing with amazing clearness that he understood the motives for the activity of the French and the character of St. Denis.

"Today," he declares, "in addition to the primary purpose for the establishment of the missions, which is the conversion and civilization of the Tejas Indians, there exists a second and very important one of a temporal nature, the need for the friendship and good will of these Indians, who are under the jurisdiction of His Majesty, in order that with their aid the extent of the French conquest may be ascertained. The establishment of a presidio [in their midst] will serve as a defence for the province, it will impede the incursions of the French from Mobile and Canada, and it will be a point of observation which will enable us to learn their intentions in time to check their advance. Should we fail to take these steps, the French doubtless will extend their influence from Natchitoches to Coahuila and introduce their merchandise from that post into the Province of Texas, having already explored the country and being well acquainted with it as far as the Río Grande del Norte." He then goes on to state that a quantity of goods had been introduced at various times from Mobile, where, according to St. Denis' statement there were at this time more than two millions' worth of cloth and other goods. The *Fiscal* wisely observed that the distance from Mobile to Texas is only two hundred eighty leagues over the all-land route; that the country abounds with wild fruits and game, all of which make the cost of transportation much cheaper; and that since the population of Louisiana is small and the amount of merchandise far too great for their consumption, it is evident that the goods are intended for introduction into New Spain.

He points out that St. Denis himself came to the Río Grande for no other purpose, as is shown by the letter sent by the Governor of Santa María de Galve in 1713; that the trader gave notice of his departure from Mobile with six pirogues loaded with merchandise; that he and his companions must have disposed of these goods is likewise proved by another letter of the Governor of Santa María de Galve, who on October 20, 1715, wrote to the viceroy of Mexico that a group of twenty Frenchmen had returned to Mobile and publicly averred they had been to the Nuevo Reyno de León and Coahuila from which places they had brought back large numbers of horses and cattle.[58] The *Fiscal* argues with logic that these two letters of the governor of Santa María de Galve explain some of the obscure points in the declaration of St. Denis. He shows that the date of the first letter coincides with that of the departure of St. Denis, while the date of the second would correspond to the time the twenty companions of St. Denis would require to return, as they did, from Texas to Mobile. Now if St. Denis had traveled directly from the Tejas to the Río Grande, it could not have taken him one year and nine months from Mobile to the presidio. It is clear, thinks the *Fiscal,* that what actually took place was that St. Denis and his companions did stop among the Tejas for a while and with their aid perhaps reached the Río Grande and disposed of most of their goods; that St. Denis sent back his companions with the horses and cattle obtained in exchange, and presented himself with only two or three companions to the commander of San Juan Bautista after the departure of the rest.[59]

"His statement," declares the *Fiscal,* "that he did not stop among the Tejas or ever lived among them is false, for it has been proved that he was among them at various times and learned their language. The assertion that wild horses and cattle are numerous in the province of the Tejas and that these Indians live in pueblos is likewise false, as shown by docu-

---

[58]This deduction of the *Fiscal* is fully borne out by La Harpe, who says: "Saint Denis, after this expedition [to the Asinai], returned to the Natchez, 113 leagues, to the Mississippi, to give an account of his journey to M. de Lamothe. He took in this place the goods of which he had need and, having ascended the Red River with five Frenchmen, returned to the Natchitoches, and thence to the Asinais." La Harpe, in Margry, *Découvertes,* VI, 193.

[59]The *Fiscal* is partly correct in his deductions. As shown in the previous note, St. Denis himself returned to the Natchez before going on to the Río Grande.

ments and reliable sources in the office of the secretary of the vice-royalty, from all of which it appears that these Indians live separately and widely scattered.[60]

"The solicitude of the French in asking that missionaries be sent to these Indians may well be the result of their desire for closer friendship with the soldiers who may be sent as an escort, in order that through these closer relations the introduction of their merchandise may be facilitated. This assumption is founded first, on the fact that St. Denis, or one of his companions, married the niece of the leader of the Texas expedition; the other, that St. Denis went to Mobile to bring back to Texas 18,000 *pesos* worth of merchandise which he had there."[61]

St. Denis' Expedition to the Río Grande. But how did St. Denis come to undertake this expedition to the Río Grande in 1713? To understand the circumstances surrounding this most significant venture, it is necessary to go back a year in the narrative. On September 12, 1712, Louis XIV granted an unrestricted monopoly of the trade of Louisiana for fifteen years to Antoine Crozat. "The object of M. Crozat," declares La Harpe, "was to open trade with the Spaniards in Mexico, and to establish a commercial depot at Dauphin Island, with brigantines to convey merchandise to Pensacola, Tampico, Veracruz, Tuspán, and the coast of Campeche."[62] It is not strange, therefore, to find the new Governor of Louisiana, M. Lamothe Cadillac, instructed to establish posts in the direction of the country of the Illinois, to search diligently for mines, to cultivate friendly relations with the Indians to the west, and to establish trade relations with Mexico. Agreeable to his instructions, just as soon as he arrived, he dispatched the vessel that brought him from France to

---

[60]The subsequent events of the occupation of East Texas bear out this statement. The Texas Indians could not be made to congregate and it was for this reason that Rivera advised the abandonment of the missions in 1728.

[61]Resumen General de Noticias . . . in *San Francisco el Grande Archive*, VIII, 150-153. It is of interest to note the statement concerning the marriage of Diego Ramón's granddaughter. Heretofore there has been no question of her marriage to St. Denis at the Presidio of San Juan Bautista upon his return from Mexico City. But it is no less a person than Father Olivares who casts the doubt. Speaking of her marriage, he says: "Either Medar Jalot or St. Denis married at the Presidio of Río Grande a granddaughter of Diego Ramón, captain of the presidio, who is a niece of the actual commander of the twenty-five men of the expedition, and although I do not doubt that one of the two married the granddaughter of Captain Ramón, I have not been able to determine with any certainty which of the two did." *San Francisco el Grande Archive*, VIII, 148.

[62]French, *Historical Collections of Louisiana*, III, 39-41.

Veracruz with a load of merchandise, which its commander, M. Jonquiere, was to exchange for cattle and other necessaries. M. Jonquiere was particularly directed to try to secure the free entrance of French vessels into the ports of Mexico. But the high hopes of the governor to establish trade relations with New Spain were blasted by the cold reception accorded to his emissary. The French vessel was not permitted to enter farther than the roadstead, where it was allowed to load only such supplies as were necessary for its return trip, while the proposals for reciprocal trade were haughtily rejected, the viceroy declaring emphatically that the ports of New Spain were closed to all foreign commerce.[63]

Having thus failed to open trade by sea, there remained but one other possibility to carry out his instructions. It was at this crucial moment that there came into the hands of the puzzled governor a letter written two years before by an aging but hopeful missionary, who since 1694, had waited patiently on the outskirts of Coahuila for an opportunity to return to the Tejas. Father Hidalgo, despairing of ever being able to arouse sufficient interest among Spanish officials to allow him to go back to his beloved neophytes to reëstablish a mission, decided to write a letter on January 17, 1711, to the Governor of Louisiana, inquiring about the welfare of the Tejas and deftly asking for his coöperation in establishing a mission for these Indians. To make certain that the letter would reach its goal, Father Hidalgo made three copies which he sent by different routes.[64]

No sooner did Cadillac read this curious letter than he saw his opportunity. He was perfectly willing to help the Spaniards establish a mission among the Asinais, if by this means he could secure the greatly needed supplies for the growing colony of Louisiana from northern New Spain. "To secure this desirable end, and to open the way for a profitable traffic in French merchandise with the markets of Coahuila and Nuevo León were the designs of Cadillac in responding favorably to the petition of Hidalgo."[65] No time was lost in organizing an overland expedition osten-

---

[63]The practice of sending a vessel loaded with merchandise and a heart-rending message of distress was common to the French governors and had been tried with little success on three previous occasions, in 1709, 1711, and 1712. When this vessel arrived, the viceroy was particularly sensitive because he had been ordered by royal *cédula* on May 11, 1712, not to allow any foreign vessel under any pretext to enter the ports of Mexico and to give no aid or supplies on any pretext whatsoever. Consulta al Consejo de Indias, April 26, 1712. *A. G. I., Indiferente General,* 136-4-4 (University of Texas Transcripts).

[64]Le Page du Pratz, *Histoire de la Louisiane,* I, 10.

[65]Clark, *op. cit.,* VI, 9.

sibly for the purpose of going in search of Father Hidalgo and to secure some greatly needed cattle and horses for the colony of Louisiana. The leader had, perforce, to be a man of experience, shrewd, tactful, courageous, resourceful, and capable of dealing both with the natives and the Spaniards. There was but one man who possessed these qualifications. The governor called Louis Juchereau de St. Denis, commander of Fort St. John, at Biloxi, to come to Mobile. The young commander was only too glad to undertake the daring enterprise. He immediately entered into a contract with Cadillac by which he agreed "to take ten thousand *livres* of merchandise from the public store, to transport it across Texas to Mexico, and to endeavor there to dispose of it."[66] Armed with a passport which read: "The Sieur de Saint-Denis is to take twenty-four men and as many Indians as necessary and with them to go in search of the mission of Fray Francisco Hidalgo in response to his letter of January 17, 1711, and there to purchase horses and cattle for the province of Louisiana," the adventurous Canadian set out from Mobile in September, 1713.[67]

Going first to Biloxi, he waited there for Penicault and a few companions, who went to secure some Indian guides from a party of Natchitoche Indians who were living on the Mississippi at this time. It seems that unexpected trouble developed with the Indians and it was not until early in 1714 that the party finally set out for the village of the Tonicas, located two leagues above the mouth of the Red River, where they again halted to collect provisions. The chief of the Tonicas was induced to join the expedition with fifteen of his best hunters, and the party now ascended the Red River for a distance of about eighty leagues to a village of the Natchitoches, where they built two storehouses wherein to store part of their merchandise. A guard of ten men was left at this place. Taking thirty braves from the Natchitoches, St. Denis continued overland on his way to the village of the Asinai.[68] Here it seems they stopped for some time, perhaps four or six months, disposing of a considerable amount of

---

[66]*Ibid.*, 9.

[67]The passport was dated September 12, 1713, *San Francisco el Grande Archive*, VIII, 26. But news of the projected expedition leaked out before this date and preparations must have been made much earlier because on August 29, 1713, Salinas Varona, Governor of Pensacola, warned the viceroy in a letter, that twenty-two Frenchmen, fifty Indians and six pirogues loaded with merchandise intended for introduction into New Spain, were about to leave Mobile. *Ibid.*, 143.

[68]The account as here given is based on Penicault, *Relation*, Margry, *op. cit.*, V; Morfi's *History of Texas;* and St. Denis' declaration in *San Francisco el Grande Archive*, VIII, 27-32. The account given by Clark (*op. cit.*) has been carefully studied and a few variants will be noted.

their goods, which they traded for cattle, horses, and buffalo hides. Ramón (in 1716) noted that these Indians had French guns, beads, butcher and pocket knives, and pieces of red and blue cloth of good grade, and when he asked them where they had secured these articles the Indians replied that the French had given these things to them in exchange for hides and horses.[69]

During this time St. Denis, it should be noted, appears to have gone back to the Natchez on the Mississippi to give an account of the success of the expedition to the governor and, perhaps, to ask for further instructions as to whether he should proceed to the Río Grande in search of Father Hidalgo, who was not found among the Tejas as expected, but of whose whereabouts he learned from the Indians, or whether he should abandon this phase of the enterprise. Encouraged by the success of the venture, the governor must have ordered St. Denis to continue on his journey, who, to replenish his depleted stock, took a fresh supply of goods before repairing to the Asinais.[70]

Speaking of these Indians, St. Denis said in his declaration, "Their land was formerly settled by the missionary *Padres* of the College of La Santa Cruz de Querétaro, who abandoned the site twenty-six years ago [he meant 22, from 1693 to 1715]. There are eleven tribes, the chief of which is the Asinai. Their allies are the Navedachos, Nacaos, Namidis, Nacogdoches, Ainays, Nadacocos, Nacitos, and Nachoos. Among them are some who have kept our holy religion, as is the case with their governor, Bernardino,[71] whom they all obey. Their lands are all cultivated

---

[69]Carta de Domingo Ramón to the Viceroy, July 26, 1716, in *San Francisco el Grande Archive,* VIII, 193.

[70]St. Denis, in his declaration, tries to leave the impression that his trip was continuous, he mentions no stops, and does not account for the long time it took him to reach the Río Grande. The *Fiscal* notes this fact, points out he must have spent considerable time among the Tejas, cites Salinas Varona's letters of August 29, 1713, and October 20, 1715, to prove that part of the Frenchmen returned to Mobile with the fruits of their trade, and points to Domingo Ramón's letter of July 26, 1716, as further proof of the extensive trade carried on by St. Denis and his companions among the Tejas. That he went back to the Natchez, La Harpe himself asserts. "Saint Denis, after his expedition [to the Asinais], returned to the Natchez, 113 leagues, to the Mississippi to give an account of his journey to M. de Lamothe. He took in this place the goods of which he had need and, not having ascended the Red River with five Frenchmen, returned to the Natchitoches, and thence to the Asinais." La Harpe, in Margry, *op. cit.,* VI, 193.

[71]Whether this was "the ancient chief" as Bonilla affirms in his *Breve Compendio,* meaning the chief mentioned by De León and Terán is questionable. Four young kinsmen of the old chief decided to accompany De León to visit the viceroy. Two gave up before they reached Coahuila, a third was killed at Querétaro,

and there is no fruit in the world richer than that found here, nor more wonderful grapes of various kinds and colors in such quantities. The bunches are as large as twenty-eight and thirty-pound shot. There are also such extensive fields of such excellent flax that all the fleets of Europe could be supplied with cordage. From the head tribe, this nation occupies an area of forty leagues, all well populated."[72] The Indians earnestly entreated St. Denis to ask the Spanish missionaries to return and establish missions among them. They were particularly anxious for the return of Father Hidalgo, who had lived among them and knew their language, and Captain Urrutia, who had also dwelt with them for ten years. Bernardino and twenty-five of his warriors finally decided to accompany St. Denis to the Spanish settlements.

The party, consisting now of four Frenchmen and twenty-five Tejas braves under the leadership of their chief Bernardino, set out for the Presidio of San Juan Bautista on the Río Grande early in the fall of 1714. They encountered no difficulty in crossing the numerous streams and traveled without mishap until they reached the San Marcos [Colorado], where they were attacked by a band of about two hundred Indians from the coast, "the mortal enemies of the Tejas," declares St. Denis. The fight lasted from eight in the morning until two in the afternoon, and when the battle was over it was found that twelve men and a woman of the enemy had been killed, while of the Tejas only two were wounded. The enemy was pursued to their *rancherías* and there forced to conclude a peace. Not deeming it necessary to continue the journey, twenty-one warriors decided to return home, assuring St. Denis he had nothing to fear from this point to the Spanish settlement. At least, so affirmed St. Denis, although it may well be that he thought it best to arrive at the presidio of Diego Ramón with as small a retinue as possible. At any rate, St. Denis, three Frenchmen, namely, Medar Jalot, Largen, and Penicault, Bernardino, two Tejas captains and one other Indian continued on their way and arrived at San Juan Bautista, located two leagues beyond the Río Grande, late in the fall of 1714.[73] In passing by the site of the San

---

and only the fourth actually reached Mexico City. There he was baptized and given the name Bernardino. It is likely that it was this nephew of the old chief of 1690, who was met by St. Denis. Dunn, *Spanish and French Rivalry,* 124.

[72]Declaración, *San Francisco el Grande Archive,* VIII, 29.

[73]Clark has nothing to say as to the actual number of men who accompanied St. Denis but vaguely hints they were a goodly number. Morfi is very definite on this point and consistent. He says St. Denis started with twenty-two, left ten at the Natchitoches to guard the storehouses, arrived at the Asinai with twelve, lost five

Antonio River, St. Denis remarked how suitable this location was for the establishment of a large settlement and a presidio.

Upon his arrival he presented to the astonished commander of the Presidio of San Juan Bautista his passport, declaring that he had set out from Louisiana to purchase grain and cattle, which were greatly needed at Mobile, from the missions thought to exist among the Tejas; that having found the missions abandoned, and learning from the Indians that the Spanish settlements were not far away, he had continued his march to the Río Grande for the same purpose. Here was a frank avowal of a desire to establish trade with the northern provinces of New Spain. Less than two years before, the viceroy had circulated the strictest orders to all frontier commanders against the introduction of foreign merchandise and the entrance of foreigners under whatever pretext. He had no choice in the matter but to follow the orders received and arrest the intruders, holding them until further instructions were received from the viceroy, to whom, in accordance with the orders issued in 1713, he had to give notice.[74] With characteristic Spanish courtesy, however, the captain placed the Frenchmen under nominal arrest and lodged them in his own house, treating them with the greatest kindness while he awaited the reply of the viceroy.

St. Denis and his companions were still at San Juan Bautista on February 15, 1715. On that date he secretly wrote a letter to the Governor of Louisiana to inform him of what had happened since their arrival on the Río Grande. He explained that the captain of the presidio had been exceedingly kind, that he could escape with ease but preferred to stay. "As seeing a good fortune before my eyes and wishing to put my name in repute, I rejoice at all that may happen, for I fear nothing from these people or from Mexico." He concludes with an appeal to the governor for his patronage. "After the risks I have run and the services which I have rendered to the public, I flatter myself that you will serve as my

---

here who returned to Mobile, left four among the Tejas and continued to the Río Grande with three companions. What source he used, is not known. St. Denis himself declared that twenty-one of the twenty-four who set out with him left him at the Asinai to return to Mobile. This leaves him three companions, as Morfi states. Naturally St. Denis gave no details as to the exact time when the various members of the expedition left him. Clark, *op. cit.*, 12-13; Morfi's *History of Texas*, Paragraphs 192, 194, 195; Declaración, *San Francisco el Grande Archive*, VIII, 30-31.

[74]Recomendaciones del Fiscal, in *Provincias Internas*, Vol. 181, p. 11. *México, Archivo General de la Nación.*

patron, and that you will procure me some employment at Mobile."[75] In the meantime, the viceroy decided to have St. Denis escorted to the City of Mexico for a personal examination. A guard of soldiers was sent by the Governor of Coahuila from Monclova to conduct the Frenchmen to the capital, where they finally arrived early in June, 1715.[76]

What effect was the interrogation of St. Denis and his companion, Medar Jalot, to have upon the subsequent course of the history of Texas? Was Father Hidalgo's dream of returning to the Tejas to be fulfilled at last as a result of his letter of January 17, 1711? The answers to these questions carry us into the next chapter. In closing the narrative of this daring venture of St. Denis it is well to note here its important consequences for the later history of Texas so ably summarized by Dr. Clark: "The real significance of the expedition is that it determined the ownership of Texas. The Spanish established, by the fact of actual possession, their title to the lands east of the Río Grande. The *entrada* of Captain Ramón was followed by others till a line of missions and presidios was established extending from the land of the Ays and Adays to the Río Grande; and the western limit of Louisiana was fixed at the Sabine. But for the menace of Saint-Denis' presence . . . it is probable that the movement to occupy Texas would not have come until much later . . . and, if we venture to speculate upon what might have happened, the whole course of history in the Southwest would have been changed."[77]

---

[75]Letter quoted by Clark, *op. cit.*, VI, 13-14.

[76]Both La Harpe and Penicault declare that he arrived on June 25, but this is impossible, because he made his declarations on June 22. Le Page du Pratz places the date on June 5, and this is much more likely. Only Medar Jalot accompanied him to Mexico City. Penicault stayed at San Juan but must have left before St. Denis returned, as at that time, when Domingo Ramón listed the men that set out with him on the expedition to Texas there are only three: St. Denis, Medar Jalot, and Pedro Sargen or Largen. Derrotero de Domingo Ramón, *San Francisco el Grande Archive*, VIII, 71.

[77]Clark, *op. cit.*, VI, 26.

CHAPTER II

THE PERMANENT OCCUPATION OF TEXAS, 1715-1716

The arrival of St. Denis and Medar Jalot in Mexico City did not exactly create a sensation, the viceroy and other Spanish officials having been aware of the activities of the French since the time of their departure from Mobile, thanks to the timely warnings sent by the Governor of Pensacola, Don Gregorio Salinas Varona, but fully conscious of the menace which this incursion represented to the interests of the king and the integrity of New Spain, they were prepared to make a thorough investigation of the true motives of St. Denis' expedition before deciding on a definite course of action. The viceroy questioned the prisoners closely on several occasions concerning the object of their mission. In answer to all the questions put to him, St. Denis uniformly asserted that he had been sent by the Governor of Louisiana in quest of Father Hidalgo and to secure some horses and cattle of which the people of Louisiana were in great need and for which they were willing to pay in silver or in merchandise; that not having found the *Padre* among the Tejas as he had expected, and learning that he was at the Río Grande, he had continued his march to that place.[1]

Not satisfied with the verbal reply, the viceroy ordered him to make a formal statement in writing, giving all the details connected with the expedition. This was to be submitted to the *Fiscal,* together with his passport, a map of the country over which he had traveled, and all available information then in the office of the viceroy concerning Texas since 1688. St. Denis made his declaration on June 22, 1715, and that same day, Gerardo Mora translated it, as well as the passport, into Spanish, and sent it immediately, with all the additional material, to the *Fiscal* as ordered.

St. Denis' declaration. St. Denis proved himself a real diplomat in the account of the journey. He declared he was captain of the presidio of San Juan (Biloxi) located on a small stream of that name, which ran from the Mississippi to Lake Pontchartrain; that having been called to

---

[1]Extract from a letter of Cadillac, giving the substance of a report sent to him by St. Denis from Mexico City. Margry, *op. cit.,* VI, 196. St. Denis could not have been very closely guarded as he wrote to Cadillac on at least one other occasion from Mexico to keep him informed of what was transpiring there.

Mobile by the governor, he had been given the commission or patent now in possession of the viceroy; that he left Mobile with twenty-four French Canadians; that twenty-one of these had returned to Mobile from the Asinai; and that he had finally reached the Presidio of Diego Ramón on the Río Grande, a year and nine months, more or less, after his departure. In the course of the declaration he related such events as would not prejudice his cause, describing in detail the different stages of the journey and the physical characteristics of the country visited. He took special care to emphasize the "natural affection" which the Indians had for the Spaniards and their great desire to have the *Padres* return and establish missions among them. He painted in glowing colors the fertility of the country, the richness of its fruit, the abundance of flax, and the admirable qualities of the Tejas Indians. But he failed to account for the year and nine months that it took him to make the trip, or to tell anything of the two storehouses built at the village of the Natchitoches, or the lively trade carried on with the Asinai during the long stop there, or his hurried visit to the Mississippi before continuing the march. He tried, however, to make it appear that the journey had been continuous, and that nothing took place during the entire trip prejudicial in any manner to the interests of the Spaniards.[2]

In transmitting the declaration and accompanying documents to the *Fiscal,* the viceroy said: "In view of all [the facts] presented, you will recommend what you may deem best, keeping ever present the gravity of the matter and the consequences that may follow such *entradas.*"[3] To this the *Fiscal* made a preliminary reply on August 15, in which he declared he had already expressed himself fully concerning the serious consequences of such expeditions, in his opinion given at the consultation held as a result of the letter sent by Governor Salinas Varona a little less than two years before, at which time he had pointed out how the introduction of merchandise into the provinces of Nueva Vizcaya, Nueva Estremadura, and Parral caused a great part of the silver from the rich mines of that region to be diverted with grave detriment to the already diminished trade of those provinces with Spain; that the French, having learned the route to the Río Grande, as shown by their appearance at

[2]Declaración de St. Denis y Medar Jalot. *San Francisco el Grande Archive,* VIII, 27-32. Copy also in *Provincias Internas,* Vol. 181, pp. 3-9. *México, Archivo General de la Nación.*

[3]*Provincias Internas,* Vol. 181, p. 10. *México, Archivo General de la Nación.* Copy also in *San Francisco el Grande Archive,* VIII, 32.

San Juan Bautista, could, with impunity, introduce their merchandise in violation of the orders of the king and much to the prejudice of the trade with the northern provinces; that the map submitted by St. Denis showed a more accurate knowledge of the country between the land of the Tejas and the Río Grande than that acquired by the Spaniards since the time of the first *entrada* of Father Massanet; that His Excellency should, with the approval of the *Junta,* issue similar orders to those decreed as a result of the consultation held after receipt of the first letter of Governor Salinas Varona (August 29, 1713), to the governors of Coahuila, Nueva Vizcaya, and Parral, requesting them to put these into execution under the most severe penalty; that in order to prevent similar incursions on the part of the French, the *Fiscal* deemed it highly advisable and absolutely necessary for His Excellency to issue the corresponding orders at the earliest possible moment for Father Olivares, Fray Francisco Hidalgo and one other religious to proceed to the province of the Tejas without delay, escorted by twenty or twenty-five soldiers, to establish a mission. "By this means," declared the *Fiscal,* "similar incursions will be prevented, and what is more and more important, these Indians will obtain instruction in our holy Catholic faith and the spiritual welfare of their souls, to which the zeal of His Most Christian and Catholic Majesty is so inclined." He then pointed out that the *Junta* of September 10, 1689, had approved sending missionaries from the College of La Santa Cruz of Querétaro to convert the Tejas Indians; that this resolution had been further approved and so ordered by the king in his royal *cédula* of 1690, which order and request was again repeated with great zeal in his *cédula* of December 30, 1692. In consequence of all these facts the *Fiscal,* fully aware of the depleted condition of the royal treasury, asked and requested, notwithstanding, that the means be provided for the mission suggested, the military escort necessary for the trip, and all supplies required for its permanent establishment. Of all the measures taken, His Excellency was to give a complete report to His Majesty for his royal approval and command.[4]

Preparation for the Ramón Expedition. The viceroy now convoked a *Junta General* which met on August 22, 1715. All the members of the royal *Audiencia,* the *Alcaldes* of the Criminal Court, the officers of the Treasury, and other high dignitaries were present at this meeting. The

---

[4]Dictamen del Fiscal, August 15, 1715. *San Francisco el Grande Archive,* VIII, 32-37.

report of the *Fiscal* was read, and after listening to his recommendations, the *Junta* unanimously agreed they should be put into effect without delay. With regard to the first, the *Junta* requested the viceroy to repeat the orders previously issued to the governors of Nueva Vizcaya, Nuevo Reino de León, and Nueva Estremadura, as well as to the captains and commanders of presidios on the frontier, urging them to prevent by all means in their power all commerce and trade in clothes, or goods of any description, whose introduction might be attempted, and to proceed to the confiscation of all such goods wherever found and the arrest of all persons connected with their introduction. His Excellency was to give immediate orders for Father Francisco Hidalgo, Father Olivares, and one other religious of the same Order, to go without delay to the province of the Tejas, escorted by twenty-five soldiers, the selection of the commander of this force being left to the discretion of the viceroy, who was to exercise all care in choosing a man of ability, skill, and experience and one in whom were found the qualities and virtues necessary to aid in founding a mission, in congregating the Indians, in introducing our holy faith, and in procuring the spiritual welfare of their souls. The missionaries and the soldiers were to be provided with everything needed for their *entrada* and permanent residence out of the royal treasury.

The viceroy was requested to urge the missionaries and the soldiers to do their duty in reducing the Indians to civilized life and in establishing settlements, by which means the incursions of the French would be prevented, the introduction of their merchandise avoided, and the observation of the number of French settlements from the Tejas to Mobile and their strength made possible. Keeping in mind that with the pretext of coming for sorely needed supplies of horses, cattle, and other necessaries for the colony of Louisiana, Frenchmen had been in the habit of entering the dominions of the king, the viceroy was advised to instruct the governors of Nueva Vizcaya, Reino de León, and Coahuila, and all commanders and public officers on the frontier not to permit any foreigner to secure either cattle, grain, food, or supplies of any kind, even if they offered to pay in cash for them, but to inform them categorically that only with the expressed consent of the king of Spain could anything be provided, and that under no other condition or pretext were they to be allowed to enter the province.[5]

Presumably at the request of the viceroy, who lost no time in putting into effect the resolutions adopted by the *Junta*, Domingo Ramón pre-

---

[5]Acuerdos de la Junta General, *San Francisco el Grande Archive*, VIII, 37-45.

sented on September 4, a long inventory "of the goods which are necessary to outfit the twenty-five men that are to march to the Province of the Tejas." It seems he had come to Mexico with St. Denis, perhaps in charge of the soldiers who brought the Frenchmen to the capital. That same day, the viceroy ordered the list sent to the factor of the royal treasury, with a request that he report on the portion of the goods that could be bought in Mexico and those that could be secured in San Luis Potosí with an estimate of the cost of each. Ramón had stated, in submitting the list, that in his opinion the goods suggested could be purchased for 5,000 *pesos*. To this amount it was necessary to add, he pointed out, 6,500 *pesos* for the purchase of horses, 11,250 *pesos* for the salary of the twenty-five soldiers at 450 *pesos* a year each,[6] and 2,277 *pesos* for the purchase of gifts for the Indians and the cost of transportation. The list is of great interest for the concrete picture it affords of the supplies that were taken on an expedition of this sort. In addition to the guns, powder, swords, saddles, bridles, necessary clothing, food, and other military equipment naturally included, there are a number of items that appear incongruous, such as one dozen lady's silk hose, twelve bolts of assorted laces, eighteen bolts of various kinds of ribbon, four dozen men's and lady's shoes, and eighteen pair of silk hose for men. But for the Indians, he suggested blankets, tobacco, blue and red woolen cloth, butcher knives, pocket knives, beads of various colors, medals, ribbons and hats. For the mission he listed such implements as hoes, tillers, axes, hack saws, hammers, chisels, cooking pots of various sizes, hand bars, yokes for oxen, and various kinds of seeds.[7]

Within five days, the factor, Ignacio Joseph de Miranda, made his report of the cost of the supplies asked by Domingo Ramón. According to his estimate, based on the current prices in Mexico City, the total amount for equipment of the soldiers, the Indians, and the mission would be 6,166 *pesos,* not including the powder nor the expense of packing and transportation which was estimated at about 1,500 *pesos*. He analyzed the items of the expedition as follows: for the soldiers 5,121 *pesos;* for

---

[6]It is to be noted that Ramón suggests the salary of the soldiers in his estimated cost of the expedition. Up to this time the viceroy had not fixed the actual rate of pay of either the soldiers or the officers of the expedition. This was not done until September 30, when the leader of the expedition was also officially named. See note 10 of this chapter.

[7]Memoria de los generos que son necesarios para el avio de los 25 ombres que Pasan ala probincia de los Texas. *Provincias Internas,* Vol. 181, pp. 25-30. Copy also in *San Francisco el Grande Archive,* VIII, 45-48.

the Indians 910 *pesos;* for one mission 134 *pesos.* It is of interest to note
that in closing his report, Miranda warns the viceroy that there must be
some delay so as to allow a sufficient amount of time for the manufacture
of the twenty-five rifles with the care necessary to insure perfect casting
of the barrels. In the past, because of haste in production the guns proved
defective and caused serious injury to the soldiers.[8]

At this time the number of missions that were to be established was
undetermined and it is for this reason that in making the estimates, the
factor was careful to stipulate the accounting for this purpose was
reckoned on the basis for only one mission. But that same day, September 9, the viceroy, in approving the report and issuing orders to the officers
of the royal treasury to pay over to Miranda the cash indicated for the
purchase of the goods, said, "and the amount stipulated for one mission
is to be understood for four now, and with this understanding let the
necessary supplies for each of the four be bought."[9] Accordingly, on September 12, two orders were issued: one for the purchase of all the goods
listed and one for the delivery of the required powder by the keeper of
the royal arsenal.

It was not until September 30, that the viceroy appointed the commander of the expedition officially and drew up a set of instructions for
the proposed *entrada.* Declaring that the *Junta* had left to his judgment
the appointment of the officers (cavos) and the fixing of the rate of pay
of both soldiers and officers, he now appointed the *Alférez* Domingo
Ramón leader of the expedition with five hundred *pesos* a year, payable
at the office of the treasury in San Luis Potosí; and Luis de St. Denis,
conductor of supplies with the same allowance, payable in the same manner, for such a period of time as his services were required. The twenty-five soldiers were assigned four hundred *pesos* a year each. Joan Medar
(Medar Jalot) was allowed one hundred *pesos* for services rendered in
helping to prepare for the expedition. Domingo Ramón and St. Denis were
to be paid half of their annual salary in advance out of the royal treasury
in Mexico City,[10] notice of this advance to be sent to the office of the
treasury in San Luis Potosí. The soldiers were to be given a full year's

[8]Informe de Ignacio Joseph Miranda. México, September 9, 1715. *San Francisco el Grande Archive,* VIII, 48-52. It should be noted that the guns were made in Mexico City where facilities for casting the barrels existed at this early date.

[9]*Provincias Internas,* Vol. 181, pp. 37-38.

[10]It is to be noted that Clark and all those after him have asserted that St. Denis was paid a full year's salary in advance. This is contrary to fact, as he and Ramón were only paid half a year in advance.

pay in advance, payable at San Luis Potosí, where Domingo Ramón was to present a list of the men, whose pay was to start from the day on which their names were entered on the books at San Luis. The officers of the treasury there were to discount from the total pay of the soldiers 4,962 *pesos* paid by the royal treasury in Mexico City to Domingo Ramón to help him defray the expenses and buy part of the equipment for the soldiers. Orders were likewise issued to the governors and commanders along the route to be followed, instructing them to supply Ramón with horses or any other thing necessary for the expedition. All the corresponding orders in keeping with the wishes of the viceroy were duly issued the first day of October.[11]

St. Denis must have ingratiated himself well into the favor of the viceroy to have been appointed *Conductor de Víveres* of the projected expedition, second in rank only to Ramón and with the same pay. But then, it was not only St. Denis who received money from the Spanish government. Medar Jalot, as will be noted, was also allowed one hundred *pesos* "for services rendered." Unfortunately the documents available give no information as to the life of St. Denis in Mexico. We do not know when he was released after his declaration on June 22, 1715, nor whether he was consulted any further by the viceroy between that time and the day of his appointment. He seems, however, to have kept himself well informed about what was happening, for on September 7, he wrote to the Governor of Louisiana to notify him that the viceroy was about to send a party to establish a mission among the Tejas. At this time the viceroy had not decided on the number of missions. This may explain St. Denis' failure to specify that there would be four missions established by the expedition. He asked that a brigantine be sent to occupy "the Bay of Espíritu Santo, San Luis, or San Bernardo with two purposes in view: one, in order to control all the Indian nations between Mobile and the said bay; the other to make certain to have a depot easily accessible by sea or land wherein to keep our merchandise, near to Coahuila and Nuevo Reyno de León."[12] He is further alleged to have declared in this letter that it would be necessary for the king of France to demand that the boundary of Louisiana be fixed at the Río Grande.[13] It is interesting to

---

[11]Decreto del Virey sobre nombramiento de cavo y sueldo de presidiales para la entrada á Texas. *San Francisco el Grande Archive,* VIII, 53-54.

[12]Resumen de las noticias que desde el año de 1688 . . . se an tenido. . . . *Provincias Internas,* 181, p. 165.

[13]Clark, *op. cit.,* VI, 19.

see how, by this time, he had managed to extricate himself from the embarrassing position in which he was when he first arrived in Mexico, and how he had been able to win the friendship of the Indians, who undoubtedly were deeply attached to him. What influence in his actions his love affair with the granddaughter of Diego Ramón, at San Juan Bautista on the Río Grande, had is difficult to determine, but from the practical character of the man as revealed in all his affairs and the ease with which he adjusted himself to circumstances, it may have been as much a matter of the heart as of good business policy. It has already been fully demonstrated how his mission was purely a commercial venture. His stay at San Juan Bautista and his journey to Mexico City may have opened to him the broad vista of large profits in the rich trade with the northern provinces. By entering the service of the viceroy and marrying into the family of Ramón he had much to gain and nothing to lose in furthering the primary purpose of his real mission, the establishment of trade between Louisiana and New Spain. In these considerations is to be found the true motive for his inconsistent attitudes and deeds during this period of his life.

Religious officials were also interested in the success of the projected expedition. Father Fray Juan López Aguado, Guardian of the College of La Santa Cruz of Querétaro, made a special trip to Mexico City to discuss the matter of the proposed missions. On October 24, he presented a memorial requested by the viceroy, and there mentioned the things that were absolutely necessary for the missionaries who were to enter the province of the Tejas and he made free to offer some suggestions for the success of the enterprise. In the note accompanying the list and the recommendations, the Guardian humbly begged His Excellency to give his immediate attention to his petition, as he was anxious to return to Querétaro as soon as possible, where the friars that were to go on the expedition were awaiting his arrival before setting out. Here is the list of things which he considered essential for the proper administration of the sacraments and for the celebration of the Sacrifice of the Mass:

"First, four sets of ornaments, one for each mission, which consist of an amice, alb, chasuble, burse for corporals, chalice veil, antependium, altar clothes, corporals, and purificators.

"Four chalices with patens,

"Twelve candlesticks of brass—three for each mission.

"Four altar bread irons,

"Four copper holy water fonts,

"Four small bells and four rituals for administration,

"Four towels,

"Four surplices,

"One hundred pounds of wax for [candles during] the celebration of Mass,

"One barrel of [sacramental] wine fram Saltillo,

"Four *cargas* of flour from Saltillo,

"Some oil stocks to carry holy oils."[14]

At the end of the list he added: "And in order that the enterprise may benefit those poor souls, the following recommendations are thought proper, which Your Excellency will prescribe, if he deems it advisable, that they may be put into execution: First, that everything being carried by Captain Domingo Ramón to be distributed among the Indians, as well as the tools for the cultivation of the land, be placed in charge of the religious, that in this manner they be preserved and increased, as in the case of the missions on the Río Grande del Norte under the care of the College of La Santa Cruz.

"That in each of the missions that may be founded, two soldiers be placed to protect the religious, and that these be independent of the governor.

"That the soldiers be not allowed to undertake trips on private business, out of regard for the serious evils experienced [from this practice] in the missions founded heretofore."[15]

The viceroy sent the list and recommendations to the *Fiscal* who, on October 29, replied that since the articles listed were essential for the celebration of the Mass and the administration of the sacraments, His Excellency should order the factor of the treasury to purchase them, requesting him to exercise care to see that they were of good quality as befitted the purpose. With regard to the recommendations he declared that since these were directed to the success and preservation of the missions, the viceroy should issue the corresponding orders to put them into effect. The viceroy approved the report of the *Fiscal* on October 31, and the necessary orders to put it into execution were issued on November 2.[16]

---

[14]Memoria de lo que precissamte. necesitan los Religiosos. *Provincias Internas,* Vol. 181, p. 42.

[15]*Ibid.,* 43.

[16]Dictamen del Fiscal que se remitan los efectos . . . *San Francisco el Grande Archive,* VIII, 56,

Account of the Ramón Expedition. All arrangements having been completed by the viceroy for the expedition to Texas it is well now to turn to the diary of Domingo Ramón for the details of the *entrada.* From Mexico City, Ramón went to Saltillo soon after his appointment as commander, and there recruited most of the mounted soldiers that were to accompany him on the journey. In the meantime, St. Denis and Medar Jalot must have hurried down to San Juan Bautista in advance of Ramón, as there is no mention of either found in the diary until the day the expedition set out from the Río Grande. From February 17, when Ramón started from Saltillo, until April 27, the names of the two Frenchmen do not appear. Clark, without citing his source, declares that St. Denis repaired to San Juan Bautista "to celebrate his marriage with Doña Maria," where "he had time to enjoy but a few weeks of conjugal felicity."[17] Be that as it may, Ramón began his diary the day he left Saltillo, February 17, 1716. "On this day," he declares, "I left the Villa of Saltillo with my whole company, [all] the stock, and the rest of my train." After traveling five leagues to the north he was forced to change his course and go east for eight leagues on account of a very high mountain, resuming then his northerly course, until he arrived at the Nacatas Bridge on February 21. Here he pitched camp to wait for part of his horses and for the arrival of the missionaries who had stayed in Saltillo.[18]

The *Padres* had busied themselves in Saltillo in the collection of alms, in which work they spent ten days. They finally started to join Ramón at Nacatas on March 1, escorted by six soldiers left by him for that purpose. They arrived safely in camp on the 3rd. But the party was delayed further, while provisions and more horses were secured for the expedition. On the night of the 9th, there came to the commander a mestiza named Ana Guerra, to ask him to take her with him to the Tejas, because her master maltreated her. To this petition Ramón readily acceded.

---

[17]Clark, *op cit.,* 20. Concerning the marriage, see chapter I, note 61.

[18]The account of the expedition given here is based on two copies of the diary of Domingo Ramón and of the diary of Father Espinosa. These are to be found in *Provincias Internas,* Vol. 181, pp. 54-88; 95-122; *San Francisco el Grande Archive,* VIII, 63-88; 92-114. Espinosa's and Ramón's diaries have been made available in English by the Texas Catholic Historical Society in its publications. Clark's account, based on a not entirely dependable copy of the diaries found in *Historia,* XXVII, is not as full as it should be, while that given in Bonilla's *Breve Compendio* is even shorter. Morfi, in his *Historia,* not *Memorias,* translated by the writer, gives the fullest account now available in English, but even this is too short to do justice to this important expedition from which dates the permanent occupation of Texas.

Next morning, before setting out, a soldier named Lorenzo Mercado asked Ramón for the hand in marriage of the mestiza woman and he consented, provided the proper practices were observed before the marriage ceremony. Finally the party set out on March 10, and traveling north for a distance of seventeen leagues, arrived at Corral de Piedras on the 14th, where it halted to wait for the horses and stock sent by way of La Culebra.

At the hacienda of Corral de Piedras, Captain Joseph de Villarreal, *Alcalde Mayor* of the district, had built a chapel to St. James. Here the missionaries heard the confessions of all the people during the day. For seven days they waited, until the 21st, when the horses and stock arrived at last. It was here that Ramón learned that four of the soldiers detailed to escort the horses had run away. He immediately reported the matter to the viceroy, pointing out that those men had stolen some of the horses and the one year's salary paid to them in advance. He asked the viceroy to issue orders for their arrest, and suggested that if they were captured they should be made to serve in Texas.[19] Also hostile Indians were reported nearby for the first time, but only the tracks of two Tobosos on foot were discovered in the vicinity.

On March 22, the expedition again resumed its march and traveled fourteen leagues that day on account of the barrenness of the country, before they came to a suitable place to camp. While giving the stock a rest, Father Margil joined the expedition on March 24, bringing some horses and cattle which he was providing for the missions. Continuing in a northerly direction the party arrived at the ranch called Juan Méndez, where they waited six days until March 30, to gather necessary provisions and to give time to Father Margil to bring in some goats which he was taking to the Tejas.

The expedition next halted at El Carrizal on April 1. Here Ramón learned by a messenger sent from the Mission of La Punta that certain Indians had stolen all the horses belonging to that establishment. He became, therefore, alarmed at these depredations so near at hand because some of the stock of the expedition had temporarily been left behind and were in grave danger of loss from thieves. With the help of two cavalrymen he hastily set out in search of the horses, located them, and found them safe in their corrals. The next day he proceeded to La Punta where

---

[19]Ramón to the Viceroy, March 17, 1716. *Provincias Internas,* Vol. 181, pp. 50-51. The names of the runaway soldiers were Diego Alejandro Morales, age 25 years; Jacinto de los Santos, age 30; Joseph Cadena and Joseph García.

he was informed that all mounts there which had been seized by the savages had been recaptured by three men sent in pursuit. After making some inquiries about the route followed by the hostile Indians, the Captain returned to the encampment and resumed his march. Fathers Fray Francisco Hidalgo, Fray Benito Sánchez, Fray Gabriel Vergara, and Fray Manuel Castellanos left the expedition the next day at the Real del Chocolate, and went to the Mission of La Punta to spend Holy Week. Two religious stayed to hear confessions and the entire party availed themselves of the opportunity to approach the sacraments during the next two days they were in camp here.

On April 5, the expedition reached the Conchos River, "so called," says Ramón, "because there are so many shells found in it."[20] Here the travelers halted for five days during Holy Week. A number of wild horses were caught while searching for some of the mules that had been lost.

On the 11th, he crossed the Sabinas at El Paso de los Reineros and there waited for the missionaries who had gone to the Mission of La Punta to spend Holy Week. On the 16th, he crossed Los Juanes Creek, the next day he crossed Amole Creek, and on April 18 he was met, two leagues from the Presidio of San Juan Bautista, by its captain, officers, and men, who lined up on either side of the road and fired a salute when the expedition came in sight. Domingo Ramón ordered his men to do likewise. Father Fray Isidro Felix Espinosa, President of the missions on the Río Grande, came out also, accompanied by three religious, to welcome the party. The men marched past the presidio and pitched camp near one of the missions, where there was plenty of forage for the horses and cattle.

The next day, while Ramón busied himself in assembling provisions and supplies and in making preparations to cross the Río Grande, word came that Father Fray Antonio Margil de Jesús was seriously ill at the Juanes Creek, nine leagues distant. Father Espinosa, accompanied by two friars and two soldiers, set out that night at eight o'clock to bring him to the presidio.

The next day the whole party, with the exception of some of the missionaries, moved the short distance of two leagues to the crossing known as El Paso de Francia, and finding the river unusually low, wasted no time in getting all the equipment and supplies across. More than a thousand

---

[20]This is not the real Conchos. It is a small stream variously known by three names: Sacramento, Nadadores, and Conchos. It flows into the present dam of Don Martín.

head of goats and sheep crossed this day, with the loss of only twelve by drowning. By dusk that evening, "I set up my camp, on the opposite side of the river with a strange feeling of joy," declares Ramón. He was now on the east side of the Río Grande, ready to start on the great adventure and determined to bring to a realization the long cherished dream of Father Hidalgo who, after twenty-three years, was soon to have the pleasure of being put in charge of the reëstablished mission of the Tejas, his beloved neophytes. This was a fitting tribute to his unwavering faith, his ardent missionary zeal, and his incomparable perseverance.

Detained for one reason or another, Ramón stayed in camp here for seven days. A soldier named José Galindo married the daughter of one of the settlers, who was accompanying the expedition, and the festivities celebrating the event consumed two days. The food supply for the missionaries, the equipment for the four missions, and the livestock all had to be crossed, and everything had to be made ready for what may be rightly called the real start of the expedition. On the last day all the missionaries came into camp and early in the morning, on March 27, the members of the *entrada* began to file past Captain Ramón in a long, winding line. "As they marched out," says Ramón, "I made the following list of all the persons that went on the expedition."

At the head of the party, as was befitting an expedition designed for the purpose of establishing four missions among the Tejas Indians and their allies, marched the dignified and resolute Father Fray Isidro Felix de Espinosa, President of the Franciscans from the College of La Santa Cruz of Querétaro. Following him, or perhaps by his side, came the now white-haired Father Fray Francisco Hidalgo, who in his prime had spent almost three years among the Tejas, but who notwithstanding his age, still walked erect, while his countenance glowed with spiritual delight. Then came Fray Mathías Sáenz de San Antonio, Fray Benito Sánchez, Fray Manuel Castellanos. Fray Pedro de Santa María y Mendoza, Fray Gabriel Vergara, Fray Javier Cubillos, a lay brother, and Fray Domingo de Urioste, with the habit of Donado. "And the reason," declares Ramón, "why our Very Reverend Father Fray Antonio Margil de Jesús did not enter at this time, was that his illness became more serious, and with the deepest sorrow and regret on the part of every one, he was obliged to remain at the presidio, while we all lament our misfortune."[21] Had it not

---

[21]He was so ill, that on April 25, all the missionaries at the Presidio accompanied Father Espinosa, who went to administer the Viaticum to the dying Margil. On the eve of the expedition, Father Agustín Patrón, *Procurador,* and Fray Fran-

been for his illness, there would have been nine priests and three lay brothers on the expedition. Before the party reached its destination, however, Father Fray Antonio Margil de Jesús, Father Fray Agustín and Fray Francisco de San Diego, lay brother, joined their companions.[22]

Behind the missionaries, as an evident demonstration of the relative position of the two, came the military, whose purpose was to lend support and aid in the work of congregating the Indians and in teaching them by example the civilized methods of living. There were twenty-five mounted soldiers, besides Captain Ramón, as follows: Diego Ramón, Ensign, Diego Ramón (Jr.), Sergeant Major, Antonio de Espronceda, Francisco de Revilla, Joseph García, Domingo Jiménez, Juan de Zertuche, Nicolás de los Santos Coy, Juan Valdez, Diego Valdez Jiménez, Joseph Galindo, Antonio Flores, Bernardo Prieto, Domingo Flores, Agustín Téllez, Marcial Saucedo, Joseph García (Jr.), Lázaro Chirino, Antonio Cadena, Joseph Cadena, Lorenzo Mercado, Juan de Castro, Manuel Maldonado, Francisco Betancur, and Domingo González, all mounted.

There went also a number of men and women, not enlisted, who came for the purpose of settling in the new country, or perhaps to be on hand in case any mines were discovered or opportunities for profitable trade developed. Among the voluntary settlers were Lorenzo García, retired ensign, with his family—the number of its members is not given— Lorenzo García, former sergeant, Pedro Botello, with his family, number

cisco de San Diego, lay brother, had to stay behind to care for Father Margil at the Mission of San Juan Bautista. He not only recovered, but he actually overtook the expedition before it reached East Texas. *Provincias Internas,* Vol. 181, pp. 96, 122.

[22]There has been considerable conjecture as to the number of missionaries and lay brothers that actually went on this expedition. At the start, as listed by Ramón and confirmed by Espinosa, there were seven priests, all religious, and two lay brothers. Some time before the expedition reached the province of the Tejas, Father Margil and Father Patrón joined their fellow missionaries, as they both signed the report of the establishment of the missions on July 22, 1716. The name of Fray Francisco de San Diego, as well as those of the other two lay brothers, do not appear in this document, but it is safe to assume that Fray Francisco accompanied Fathers Margil and Patrón. It can safely be said, therefore, in view of all the evidence available now, that there were five Querétaran missionaries: Fr. Isidro Felix de Espinosa, President, Fr. Francisco Hidalgo, Fr. Gabriel Vergara, Fr. Benito Sánchez, and Fr. Manuel Castellanos; four Zacatecan missionaries: Fr. Antonio Margil de Jesús, President, Fr. Matías Sáenz de San Antonio, Fr. Pedro de Santa María y Mendoza, and Fr. Agustín Patrón; and three lay brothers, two from Querétaro: Fr. Francisco Javier Cubillos and Fr. Domingo de Urioste, and one from Zacatecas, Fr. Francisco de San Diego. *Provincias Internas,* Vol. 181, pp. 132-135; *San Francisco el Grande Archive,* Vol. VIII, 114-116.

not given, Jacinto Charles, Joseph del Toro, Joseph de la Fuente, Alejandro Morales, and Lucas Castro. Eight married women are listed; that is, seven and one betrothed: María Longoria, Antonia de la Cerda, Antonia Vidales, Ana María Jiménez de Valdez, María Antonia Jiménez, Juana de San Miguel, Josepha Sánchez,[23] and Ana Guerra, betrothed. Three Frenchmen are noted by Ramón: Captain Don Luis de St. Denis, *Cabo Comboyador,* Juan Medar (Medar Jalot), and Pedro Largen. The others listed are two mule drivers: Joseph García and Joseph de Montemayor; ten helpers to drive the stock and conduct the freight: Antonio González, Sebastián García, Valentín Mendoza, Blas Jiménez, Joseph Sáenz, Juan Rodríguez, Juan Pérez, Diego Miguel Pérez, Cayentano Pérez, and Francisco de la Cruz; one negro named Juan de la Concepción; two Indian guides; three Indian goat drivers; one boy six years old and a little girl four years old. When these are added, it will be found there were exactly seventy-five[24] persons.

Although somewhat tedious for the reader, it is important and necessary to follow rather closely the progress made by the expedition almost day by day, as reported both by Ramón and Father Espinosa, in order to get those little details that are essential to make the past live, to get a more realistic picture of the hardships endured by the pioneers of these expeditions, and to determine as nearly as possible the route followed by this truly epoch-making *entrada*. It furnished the trail with some variations for later contacts and communications with East Texas, where the missions were established, when interest of the Spanish officials in Mexico was stimulated and aroused, and when the activities of the French in Louisiana demanded attention. A detailed account reveals with surprising simplicity and incredible vividness the passing emotions, the moods, the whims that moved these men, and the unbounded faith and heroism that prompted the missionaries in their colossal enterprise.

With sixty-four oxen, four hundred and ninety horses and mules, and more than a thousand goats and sheep, in addition to the huge luggage,

---

[23]Could this be María Josepha, or Manuela Sánchez, whom St. Denis is said to have married at the Presidio of San Juan Bautista?

[24]Heretofore, everybody has maintained that there were only sixty-five members in the expedition, but a careful count of those listed by Ramón will show there were seventy-five without counting the families of Joseph Maldonado and Pedro Botello. If we take into consideration that two priests and a lay brother joined Ramón before he reached East Texas, the actual number should be between seventy-eight and eighty persons. Derrotero para las Misiones de los Presidios Internos, *San Francisco el Grande Archive,* VIII, 70-71.

supplies, and equipment for the missions, and gifts for the Indians, Ramón finally set out. But although the long lines hopefully marched five leagues on the first day, they found themselves again on the Río Grande at the end of the journey, at El Paso de Diego Ramón, about three leagues above the starting point. The reason for this was that after following a northeasterly course for three leagues, finding the country exceedingly dry, they turned west for a distance of two leagues and came to the river again. As if this experience were not a sufficient hardship, at about eight that night, just as the *Padres* concluded the evening services, a terrific storm arose "with wind and rain, so fierce and furious, that we felt certain the infernal furies had instigated it. It threw down on the ground the greater part of the baggage and provisions that had been stacked up. Our three tents were in serious danger of being completely ruined, the main pole of one having been broken. But worse yet was what happened to a soldier who was on duty. The wind picked up horse, man, and all and carried them for a distance of three or four *varas* (nine or twelve feet). The horses stampeded, and so did the oxen and the mules, but God granted that they should all be found."[25] The violence of the storm caused the missionaries to fall on their knees and pray to the Mother of Sorrows and all their patron saints for deliverance. Fortunately the wind subsided after a short while.

The next day the expedition reached Cueva de León, about five leagues to the northeast of the river. While traveling, Medar Jalot suffered a severe fall, when his horse stuck its foreleg in a hole and threw him. St. Denis returned to the Presidio of San Juan Bautista for an Indian, and the party moved on towards the Nueces. On April 29, some Pacuache Indians stole twenty horses and started with them towards their *ranchería,* but Lorenzo García pursued them, overtook them about four leagues from camp, recovered the horses, and captured four natives. These were brought to Ramón, who, moved by their frightened condition, decided they had had enough punishment. Through an interpreter, the Indians were told that if they were ever again caught stealing horses, they would be hanged. They were given tobacco and set free. After traveling thirty-three leagues from the Río Grande, in a general northeasterly direction the expedition reached the Nueces River on May 2. Little or no water was found in its bed, and it was necessary to deepen one of the small pools with hoes to permit the horses and cattle to drink. While watering the stock, Ramón counted them and found there were four hundred and ninety head.

---

[25]*Ibid.,* 71. Also Provincias Internas, Vol. 181, pp. 64, 97-98.

The expedition spent Sunday, May 3, at this place to celebrate the feast of the Finding of the Holy Cross. Seven Masses were said; many received Communion; and a procession was formed, during which a cross, made for the purpose and blessed, was carried with great solemnity, while the military fired a salute. Because of this celebration and the fact that the cross was placed in the ground at this spot, the camp was called Encampment of the Holy Cross. The next day the group resumed their march. Before night, Ramón came very near being killed. "There were five falls on this day, the chronicler having been one of those who fell," he records, and then he remarks: "These were all the result of the attempt of a Frenchman to show his skill in picking a hat from the ground while riding." No little amusement and surprise was experienced next day when Diego Ramón, the sergeant major, told how he had caught Joseph del Toro, a runaway soldier. He had gone in search of him accompanied by an unconverted Indian. They found the fugitive hidden in the top of a tree. The sergeant pretended he was going to shoot into the tree, whereupon the Indian begged him, in Gods' name, not to kill the man. In the meantime the soldier descended with all alacrity.

On May 5, the marriage of Ana Guerra, a mestiza, and Lorenzo Mercado, a Spanish soldier, whose banns had been previously published, as requested by the leader of the expedition (who had consented to bring the girl into the company of his family for the purpose), was performed with due solemnity. All the soldiers fired a salute in honor of the newly wedded couple and the missionaries gave them their blessings. It is significant to note this ceremony which, as far as is known, is the first of its kind to take place between the Río Grande and the San Antonio.[26] After a day of rejoicing and feasting, the expedition again resumed its march.

On the 7th, they crossed the Frío River, which they found dry, and two days later went over the Hondo, where a good passageway was found.

---

[26]There were marriages performed in the little colony of La Salle, and no doubt the missionaries that established the first missions in East Texas must have solemnized the marriage of some of the neophytes, but there is no record of a marriage in the country here indicated. It should also be noted that the marriages that took place at the little fort of St. Louis on Garcitas Creek were between Frenchmen, those in East Texas were between Indians, while this was a marriage between a mestiza and a Spaniard, symbolic in many respects of the fusion of the two races and cultures. The marriage was celebrated on the east side of the Nueces, about two leagues southeast of the place where the expedition crossed the river. The marriage of Joseph Galinda, one of the soldiers, took place in Coahuila just before entering Texas.

A religious took an observation and found the latitude was twenty-eight degrees and thirty-nine minutes. The distance traveled from the time they left the Río Grande was forty-eight leagues. On May 13, the Medina River was reached, eighteen leagues from the Frío. When the drove of horses was driven into the river, it seems they lost their footing and started across to a very high bank. Unable to climb, those in the lead turned or fell back and they began to mill in the deepest part. Before they could be driven out, eighty-three were drowned. Undaunted by this unexpected misfortune, the missionaries sang a High Mass the following day to thank God that it was not worse.[27] On the 14th, the expedition resumed the march and reached San Pedro Spring and the San Antonio River that same day, having traveled since their start, seventy-three leagues in a general northeastern direction.

Both Ramón and Father Espinosa remark on the appropriateness of the site for the establishment of a settlement. In describing the San Pedro Spring, Ramón says: "We came to a spring of water on the surface of the ground which we called San Pedro, capable of supplying a city." To this Espinosa merely adds that it was "sufficient for a mission." Speaking of the river, which was explored to its headwaters, Father Espinosa declares "This river is very desirable [for settlement] and favorable for its pleasantness, location, abundance of water, and multitude of fish. . . . Its copious waters are clear, crystal and sweet." At its head waters were found "flax three *varas* long and linen that measured three spans." Here the party decided to halt the next day and Father Espinosa celebrated, with a High Mass, the feast of St. Isidore, his patron saint, with all the missionaries taking part. The soldiers fired a salute.

Continuing the march, they crossed the Salado, and on May 18 reached a river which Ramón at first thought was the Guadalupe, but which was the Comal River.[28] A short distance beyond they came upon the real Guadalupe. On May 20, they reached and named correctly the San Marcos River,[29] and going a little farther, camped on a stream which they called

---

[27]Father Espinosa, in his diary, says that only eighty-two horses were drowned. *San Francisco el Grande Archive*, VIII, 97. Ramón made a list of the owners and offered to pay them out of his own pocket for the loss sustained that they might not be discouraged. *Provincias Internas*, Vol. 181, p. 69.

[28]Ramón passed this river almost at its source, within the present limits of New Braunfels. The river flows into the Guadalupe, which Ramón erroneously called the San Ybon. Hackett, *Pichardo: Limits of Louisiana and Texas*, I, 478, note 7.

[29]Buckley, "The Aguayo Expedition," Texas Historical Association, *The Quarterly*, XV, 37.

San Rafael, present day Plum Creek, across which they noticed two springs to which Ramón gave the names of San Isidro and San Pedro del Nogal.[30] On May 23, the party came upon the Colorado River, a short distance below the present city of Austin,[31] and found this stream was greatly swollen. Unable to find a suitable crossing after exploring its course for four leagues, they camped on its bank. The river subsided about four spans during the night, in spite of a severe thunderstorm, and preparations were immediately made to pass over it without delay. Seven Masses were said, one by each missionary to his own patron saint, invoking divine assistance, while everything was made ready to transfer the baggage and supplies. Before night, the greater part of the expedition found itself safely on the opposite bank. One of the missionaries, Father Manuel Castellanos, almost drowned, however, when his horse was swept off the passageway by the strong current; and one of the soldiers experienced considerable difficulty in getting his horse out of a mudhole where he was held fast. The following day all the goats and sheep were taken across without mishap and the expedition was ready once more to proceed on its march to the Tejas. But it was decided to spend another day here while scouts were sent ahead to reconnoiter the road, which was not well known from this point on. For this purpose *Alférez* Diego Ramón and two soldiers were sent out.[32]

With the information obtained the party now went on and killed on that day, May 27, their first buffalo, and found the meat very much to their liking. The next day they camped on a stream which they named Las Animas, present day Brushy Creek.[33] Again new explorations were undertaken to determine the best route, and while engaged in this work, the tracks of five Indians were discovered. A party was immediately sent after them and two braves were brought before Ramón, one Yerbipiame and one Mescal.[34] They told the leader of the expedition that their

---

[30]These springs have been identified with present day Lytton Springs, Ibid., 37-38.

[31]Hackett, *op. cit.*, 488.

[32]Father Espinosa had made the trip this far in 1709 and it seems Ramón followed the original route closely to this point. Speaking of the number of soldiers sent, Father Espinosa says there were three. Tous, "Ramón Expedition: Espinosa's Diary of 1716." *Texas Catholic Historical Society Preliminary Studies*, I, No. 4, p. 13.

[33]Buckley, *op. cit.*, 38.

[34]The Yerbipiame, or Ervipiame, belonged originally to the Tonkawa group that occupied the territory between the Colorado and the Trinity Rivers, chiefly above the *Camino Real* leading from San Antonio to Los Adaes. They were a highly

rancherías were in the vicinity and that they would be glad to act as guides.[35] Forced to continue the march because of the unsuitable location of the camp, the expedition moved with much labor on May 31, and the missionaries went on "with keen regret since this was the Feast of Pentecost." That night it rained and at dawn the next morning it was still raining. With much difficulty four Masses were said "in which we besought Our Lord to grant us favorable weather." The day cleared by nine and the party marched as far as the San Gabriel River and there stopped next day to celebrate the Feast of Pentecost, being the third day of the octave. A solemn Mass and the *Veni Creator* were sung by all the missionaries, a military salute was fired, and Communion was received by many persons.

From June 3 to June 12, the members of the expedition experienced much trouble in finding their way through the woods and across the numerous streams in their path. They were forced to change their course several times from northeast to southeast. On June 7, they were completely at a loss to trace their course, but on the 12th they came upon a delegation of about forty Indians of various nations, four chiefs among them, who led them to their *ranchería,* where a large *jacal* had been prepared for their reception. One of the chiefs, who had the largest number of followers turned out to be a Yerbipiame who knew Ramón. This Indian had led thieving expeditions to the presidio on the Río Grande many years ago. The natives all showed unmistakable signs of joy and welcomed the Spaniards gladly to their *ranchería.* With well studied tact, Ramón placed his camp about a rifle's shot from the Indian village. He then went to the bower made of leafy branches for his reception. There, about two thousand Indians, men, women, and children, some apostates and others who had never been baptized, came and kissed the hand of Ramón and the missionaries.[36] The rest of the day and all of the 13th, were spent

---

mixed band, wanderers, who planted few crops, but lived upon the buffalo and small game. Bolton, *Athanase de Mézières and the Louisiana-Texas Frontier, 1768-1780,* I, 23.

[35]The version given by Father Espinosa varies considerably and is somewhat more detailed than that of Captain Ramón. "Seeing a smoke," he says, "we investigated it and found six *Yeripiamos* (sic for Yerbipiame) and Mixcales Indians. Two of these were brought into camp that afternoon, one a Christian from the Mission of San Juan Bautista del Río del Norte. The other four went on to notify their chiefs of our approach." Diario y Derrotero . . . *Provincias Internas,* Vol. 181, p. 108.

[36]Father Espinosa says there were about five hundred persons of all ages and fails to mention whether they were apostates or not. According to him the expedi-

in carrying on a lively trade with the Indians, who appeared very good-natured and genuinely pleased with the coming of the Spaniards. It was the Indians who requested Ramón to halt for a day to trade and rest. Ramón warned all the soldiers and members of the expedition to be fair in their dealings with the Indians so that these savages might not get the wrong impression of the Spaniards. The Indians had buffalo and deer skins which they exchanged freely for the things the soldiers had to give them.

That day was also the Feast of St. Anthony of Padua, and the missionaries took occasion to celebrate it with a High Mass, offered for the success of the expedition. During the celebration, the soldiers fired a salute and the numerous Indians were deeply impressed with the ceremony. A feeling of good comradeship prevailed throughout the day, even the dogs of the Indians jumped "among the goats to have sport with the kids." The Indians ate heartily of the food that was given them and the other delicacies for which they traded their skins.

The following day the main stream of the Brazos, which they called Río de la Trinidad, was reached, but finding it impassable on account of the high water, only the smaller stock was that day transferred to the opposite bank. "Sixty Indians took the goats across, one by one, for which [service I ordered] two goats and an ox killed for them," says Ramón. Just a short distance beyond this point, not more than a league, the expedition came upon the second branch of the river which, although not so wide, was found to be deep. It became necessary to make barges, but these were quickly built with the help of the numerous Indians that now accompanied the party. Ramón states that "the Indians were delayed [in their work] a short while, by an alligator that seemed ready to swallow one of them, a common occurrence, for which the natives fear the reptile very much. I relieved this anxiety by shooting the alligator through the eye, as this is the only vulnerable spot. The Indians were greatly impressed with my marksmanship." By the 18th the expedition reached a small stream which was named Corpus Christi. There the group met four Tejas Indians and two women, buffalo hunters, who expressed great joy at seeing the Spaniards and threw their arms around them. The happiness of these inhabitants became even greater when they were

---

tion first met a delegation of Indians on June 10, when a group of Yervipiame, Ticmamaras, Mesquites, and one Teja came into camp. He says that in addition to the tribes mentioned, there were found at the *ranchería* some Pamayas, Payayas, Cantonas, Mescal, Xarames and Sijames. Tous, *op. cit.*, 16-17.

told that the strangers were coming to stay permanently among them.[37] Some of the Indians now accompanied the expedition as guides, and on the 20th, they came to a small Indian village where a number of Tejas were found. They all evinced the same demonstration of joy and gave the newcomers green ears of corn and watermelons. Taking up their march again, on June 22, they reached the present Trinity River, which they called Río de San Juan Bautista, and about a league beyond, they came upon a creek so deep that a bridge had to be built across it. Here they camped on the 24th to celebrate the Feast of St. John. Six low Masses and one High Mass were said; some persons received Communion; and that evening the soldiers amused themselves by holding horse races, during which each one bet on his particular horse.[38]

The expedition waited here another day for the return of the son of Captain Ramón, who had been sent out with St. Denis a few days before to inform the Tejas of the gradual approach of the party. He did not arrive until late in the afternoon, when he showed up with a Tejas Indian, and brought news that all the Asinai were assembling to greet the Spaniards. It should be noted that St. Denis did not return at this time but stayed among the Tejas.[39] The next day, June 26,[40] in the afternoon "there came to my presence Captain Louis de St. Denis," says Ramón, "who is liked by these people because he has some knowledge of their language. He was accompanied by more than twenty-five Indians, most of them chiefs. I ordered some blankets to be spread on the ground for them to sit down. Before arriving in our camp, at about a gun's shot distance, those who came on horseback dismounted and all formed in

---

[37]Father Espinosa, relative to this meeting, says: "Here on the way we met three Tejas Indians who were out hunting for bison, and about noon two women also came and more Indians, about a dozen. They made peculiar demonstrations of pleasure." Tous, *op. cit.*, 18.

[38]As far as the writer knows, this is the first reference to horse racing and betting in Texas.

[39]Neither Ramón nor Father Espinosa give the date when St. Denis and Ramón's son set out for the Asinai. The fact that St. Denis did not return at this time is significant for two reasons. It shows the great power he had over these Indians, his presence being necessary to assemble them to welcome the Spaniards; and it gave him time to communicate secretly with his friends at Natchitoches and indirectly through them with the Governor of Louisiana, all in anticipation of the arrival of the expedition in East Texas.

[40]Father Espinosa says the 27th. The two dates can be reconciled by the fact that Ramón had now gone ahead of the main expedition and probably met St. Denis, as he says, on the afternoon of the 26th, while the *Padres* did not see him until the next morning. *Provincias Internas,* Vol. 181; Tous, *op. cit.*, 20.

single file, with St. Denis at their head. Among these Indians I noted nine long arquebuses, all of French make."

Arrival in the country of the Tejas. Ramón then ordered his soldiers to form in single file on either side of the road, and he, accompanied by all the missionaries, went forth to greet them, carrying an image of Our Lady of Guadalupe and a crucifix. With a great ceremony, amidst the firing of rifles, the Indians entered camp and took their seats on the blankets that had been spread out for them. Each one embraced the Captain and the missionaries before sitting down. Then, "they brought out a large pipe, used only to make peace. Each one took a portion of tobacco, which they have in abundance and, filling the bowl [with it], they lighted it and began smoking. The captains smoked first in this manner: the first puff of smoke was blown to the sky, the second to the East, the third to the West, the fourth to the North, the fifth to the South, and the sixth to the ground, these being the signs of lasting peace. The pipe was adorned with white feathers, attached from one end of the stem to the other, the stem being more than one *vara* in length." When the chiefs finished smoking, the pipe was passed to Captain Ramón, who in turn passed it on until every man and woman present had smoked it. The chiefs now took out more tobacco from their pouches, piled it in the center, and invited Ramón to take some. After accepting their gift, he had some of his tobacco distributed among the Indians and gave orders for a young bull to be killed and fed to them. "All the ceremony took place amidst general contentment, because this people are very happy, carefree, and pleasant, particularly with the Spaniards, whom they seem to have known for many years," declares Ramón.

This ceremony was repeated, with few modifications, on June 28, when as before, St. Denis went out to form the Indians. He acted as their leader so that he might set an example for their proper conduct. About one hundred and fifty[41] came into camp on this occasion. Many shots were fired both by the soldiers and the Indians, the *Te Deum Laudamus* was sung, and after the solemn procession they all sat in a circle. The Indian women then brought green ears of corn, watermelons, melons, *tamales,* and beans cooked with corn and nuts. All these things were piled in the center for Ramón and his men to take. To show his appreciation the Captain ordered one hundred *varas* of flannel, forty light

---

[41]Father Espinosa says ninety-six. It is curious that in this instance as in the preceding one he should state the number was so much smaller than that given by Ramón. *Provincias Internas,* Vol. 181, pp. 116, cf. 83.

blankets, thirty hats, and three bundles of tobacco distributed among the Indians. The Spaniards were much impressed with the fairness with which all these things were distributed by the Indians, noting that those in charge of the distribution had nothing for themselves when they finished.

When all the Indians were gathered that day, Ramón, through an interpreter, addressed them, explaining to them the purposes that brought the Spaniards to their land, which were the salvation of the souls of the natives and the teaching of our holy faith. He told them that all the gifts they had just received had been sent to them by the king through the viceroy, the Duke of Linares, by whose orders he had come, as proof of His Majesty's great love for them, to whom they owed their allegiance. He then pointed out that for their better government and welfare it was necessary that they should recognize one of their chiefs as captain general, and he advised them to elect freely whosoever they wished. The Indians talked among themselves for a while and then elected as captain general a young chief, the son of the *Capitán Grande,* appointed by the Spaniards.[42] It seems that it was their custom to elect a young chief to the highest office in order that his rule should last longer. Ramón now gave him the batón, as the symbol of his office, and presented him with one of the best coats in his own wardrobe. All of these deeds seemed to please everybody.

The expedition remained in camp the next day in order to celebrate with proper ceremony the Feast of St. Peter and to wait for other Indians of the Nasoni and Nacogdoche nations who had promised to come. In the morning a High Mass was sung by all the missionaries, which was attended by a multitude of Indians. In the afternoon eight chiefs,[43] with many followers of the nations expected, assembled and the previous ceremony was repeated. Gifts were then distributed among them and that night, a short distance away, the natives celebrated with dances and great rejoicings the return of the Spaniards.

The expedition had attained its goal. It was now in the land of the Asinai, just a few miles from the Neches River and not very far from

---

[42]The exact words in the Spanish diary of Ramón read: "Luego salio un mozo hijo menor del Capn Grande que elijieron los Espanoles por que siempre elijen el menor porque dure mas su gobierno." From the text it seems the chief chosen was the youngest son of old Chief Bernardino, who in turn may have been the nephew of the Bernardino met by De León and Terán. *San Francisco el Grande Archive,* VIII, 86. *Cf.* note 71, Chapter I.

[43]Ramón does not say how many in this instance. *Provincias Internas,* Vol. 181, p. 85.

the chief village of the Tejas. On June 30, the party went forth to find a suitable location for the establishment of a presidio, and, after traveling about four leagues, came to a small clearing by the edge of a lake, on the west side of the Neches. Here Ramón decided to establish his headquarters temporarily. "We came to a plain," says Father Espinosa, "which seemed to our Captain to be a suitable place, for the time being, to establish his presidio, which was at the margin of a very large lake and not far from the medium sized river."[44] With the aid of the Indians, who proved to be not only willing but skillful workers, a large and comfortable structure was quickly made out of the plentiful timber found everywhere in the region. By the end of the first day they had finished everything but the roof, and on the second they quickly topped it with grass. "These two days were spent," declares Ramón, "in making for me a very comfortable house. All the Indians, who are very handy and like to work, spent about nine hours on the task, thanks to their ability and the abundance of the timber."

While the headquarters for the Captain were being built, the missionaries were not idle, nor was the main purpose of the expedition neglected. The very day the site for the temporary quarters for the military operations was chosen, Ramón and the missionaries, in company with several Indians, among them the old chief of the Tejas, crossed the Neches and went to look for a place wherein to reëstablish the first mission. The *Padres* and the Indians agreed on a spot in the middle of the Neche village, located from two to four miles from the river crossing, close to the mounds.[45] This was four leagues farther east than the original location, the mission being intended for the Naiche or Neche, Nabeitdache or Nabedache, Nacona, and Cacachau,[46] all neighboring tribes, located at a reasonable distance from the place chosen.

---

[44]Espinosa's Diary, *Provincias Internas,* Vol. 181, p. 117. Three weeks later he was still there. *Ibid.,* 89. From the temporary location of the presidio on the west bank to the new location of the reëstablished Mission of San Francisco there was approximately one league or about two and one-half miles.

[45]After a careful study of the original diaries of Ramón and Father Espinosa, the Diary of Aguayo's expedition, and that of Rivera, Dr. Bolton reached this conclusion concerning the exact location of the reëstablished mission of the Neches. See "The Native Tribes About the East Texas Missions," *The Quarterly,* XI, 261-263. Since then Dr. Bolton confirmed his opinion and came to the conclusion, after a personal examination of the ground, that the mission was doubtless on Bowles Creek, not far from the present crossing of that stream by the old San Antonio Road.

[46]Representación hecha por los Padres Misioneros a su Excelencia dando noticia. *San Francisco el Grande Archive,* July 22, 1716, VIII, 114-116.

The following day, while the work on the captain's house went on, the missionaries busied themselves sorting out from the baggage, supplies and equipment that were intended for each one of the missions. On July 2, while still waiting, the *Padres* undertook to write notes on the language of the Asinai. Through St. Denis, who acted as interpreter, they reached an agreement with the Indians as to the proper location for all four missions. Taking advantage of an Indian woman who understood Spanish, having been brought up in Coahuila, the missionaries explained to the natives the purpose of their coming and gave them to understand they should congregate in pueblos and live near the missions. "From that moment, they told us they could not congregate until their crops were gathered."[47]

Founding Mission San Francisco de los Tejas. On July 3, all the missionaries, the captain, and the greater part of the Indians, crossed the river and went to the location chosen for the reëstablishment of the first mission, which was about a league from the temporary camp. The Indians lost no time in building a house, while the missionaries fixed up a temporary shelter of leafy branches where they spent the day. Next morning they all said Mass, and the house having been finished, although poorly, "like a field shanty," they moved into it and made formal distribution of the equipment and supplies provided for each one of the four missions. Everything was now ready for the official reëstablishment. On Sunday, July 5, Domingo Ramón formally appointed a *Cabildo* for the Indian pueblo and gave official possession of the mission to Father Fray Isidro Felix de Espinosa, President, in the name of His Majesty, the King. The happiest moment of his life now came at last for Father Fray

---

[47]This statement is significant in view of the subsequent difficulties experienced by the missionaries in trying to get these Indians to live in the missions.

The woman referred to here by Father Espinosa is no other than the famous Angelina. Speaking of the river of this name, Morfi declares in his *Memorias*: "It took its name from an Indian maid of the Tejas nation who had been baptized and reared in the Mission of San Juan Bautista, on the Río Grande in Coahuila, who, after having returned to her country, proved very useful to the Spaniards, because of her knowledge of the language and her good services in winning the good will of her people for the Spaniards." Morfi, *Memorias*, MSS. It is interesting to note that the association of this woman's name with that of the river, attributed to Bolton by Buckley (*op. cit.*, 42) was known to Morfi. St. Denis and his companions met this woman in 1713, who proved helpful to them. Later in 1720, Bell-Isle who had deserted off the coast of Texas, was befriended by this same woman, who nursed him and sent her two sons to guide him back to Louisiana. Aguayo also met Angelina during his expedition to East Texas. Margry, *op cit., II*, 262-263; Morfi, *Historia*, paragraph 54.

Francisco Hidalgo, who was solemnly appointed, by Father Espinosa, minister of the first reëstablished mission, after waiting for this moment twenty-three years. The new mission was named Nuestro Padre San Francisco de los Tejas. Father Fray Manuel Castellanos was appointed his companion and entrusted with the spiritual care of the soldiers at the presidio. All these ceremonies took place amidst the firing of salvos and the frank delight of the Indians. When the formalities of the occasion were over, Captain Ramón had the gifts, brought for the neophytes of this mission, distributed and then set out for La Purísima Concepción.

Founding Mission La Purísima Concepción. This mission, the second to be established by Ramón, was located about eight or nine leagues northeast of the Mission of San Francisco de los Tejas, just beyond the Angelina River, in the middle of the chief village of the Ainay (Hainai), a mile or two east of the place where the highway crosses the Angelina, near two springs, not far from present day Linwood Crossing.[48] Captain Ramón was truly impressed with the fertility of the land in its neighborhood and the variety of products raised by these Indians. He declares that in their pueblo there was an incredible number of *ranchos* with cultivated fields of corn, watermelons, beans, melons, tobacco, and a pointed flower, which the Indians relished greatly. On July 7, all preparations having been completed, Ramón gave official possession of the mission to Father Espinosa, with the same formalities as before, appointed a governor for the Indian pueblo, named *alcaldes,* and distributed gifts. Father Espinosa named Father Fray Gabriel Vergara, minister of the mission. The Indians now busied themselves in building a dwelling for the *Padres,* and Ramón left in company with the missionaries from the College of Our Lady of Guadalupe of Zacatecas, for the village of the Nacogdoches, to establish there the third mission.

Founding Mission Nuestra Señora de Guadalupe. This mission, founded for the Nacogdoches and designated as the head of the missions to be established by the friars from Zacatecas, was located about nine leagues east-southeast of the Mission of La Purísima Concepción of the Aynai (Hainai), on the present site of the city of Nacogdoches. A temporary log church was quickly built here by the Indians and temporary dwellings for the *Padres* were erected. On July 9, Captain Ramón gave formal possession of the Mission of Nuestra Señora de Guadalupe to

---

[48]*Provincias Internas,* Vol. 181, pp. 86-87; 119; Bolton, "Native Tribes," *Quarterly,* XI, 261-262.

the Reverend Father Fray Antonio Margil de Jesús, President of the Zacatecas missions, appointed the governor of the Indians and other officials, and distributed gifts. The next day he left to establish the Mission of San José. Father Margil stayed at Nuestra Señora de Guadalupe with the three missionaries from the College of Zacatecas: Fathers Fray Matías Sáenz de San Antonio, Fray Pedro de Santa María y Mendoza, and Fray Agustín Patrón, this being the only mission established at this time by the Zacatecan friars. It was twenty-three leagues farther east than the first mission founded by the Spaniards in 1690.

Founding Mission San José. The Mission of San José, founded for the Nazoni and Nadaco tribes,[49] in the village of the first of these, was located on an arroyo that flowed north, about fifteen or sixteen miles northeast of the Hainai village, where the Mission of La Purísima Concepción was established, on present day Bill's Creek, near the north line of Nacogdoches County.[50] Ramón and Father Espinosa went to the village of the Nazoni by different routes. The former started from Nuestra Señora de Guadalupe and the latter from Concepción Mission. Ramón says he traveled ten leagues west-northwest from the village of the Nacogdoche to the Nazoni, over a country thickly settled by Indians, who welcomed him with great joy and gave him presents of all the things they had. Father Espinosa, in company with St. Denis who had stayed behind at the Hainai, traveled seven leagues, going northeast from this village to reach the site of the new mission. Like Ramón, he found many *ranchos* on the way and numerous streams suitable for settlement. Arriving a day before Captain Ramón, he had time to choose the site of the new establishment with Father Fray Benito Sánchez, minister of this mission. A governor for the Indian pueblo was named, *alcaldes* and *regidores* were chosen, and gifts distributed, while the Indians began immediately to build a church and dwellings for the *Padres*.[51] Ramón remarks that the Indians of this nation have particularly pleasing features. Having

---

[49]Letters of Father Hidalgo to Father Mezquia, Oct. 6, 1716. *Provincias Internas,* Vol. 181, p. 215.

[50]Bolton, "Native Tribes," *The Quarterly,* XI, 267-268; Buckley, *op. cit.,* 48.

[51]Ramón in his Diary, says: "On the 11th, steps were taken to build a church and dwellings and I proceeded to appoint a *Cabildo.*" He does not say when he put the missionaries in possession but Father Espinosa clearly states in his Diary, entry for July 10: "The Captain gave me possession of the Mission of San José," and this being the last entry, implies he was put in possession on this day. *Cf.* Diaries of Ramón and Espinosa in Provincias Internas, Vol. 181, pp. 87, 120; also *San Francisco el Grande Archive,* VIII, 88, 113.

established this, the last of the four missions, agreeable to his instructions, he now returned to his temporary camp, *gustoso* (filled with joy) because he saw how gladly the Indians had welcomed the *Padres* and the Spaniards. Here he arrived alone, for the horses of his companions became exhausted on the way. Father Espinosa returned to the Mission of La Purísima Concepción, where he made his headquarters together with Fray Gabriel Vergara.[52] In summing up the activities of the religious on the expedition, Ramón declares: "Up to this day (July 2) more than three hundred low and high Masses were celebrated at different places along the route, more than thirty sermons were preached, and more than ten large crosses were erected along the road, all feasts and days of obligation having been observed." The primary purpose of the expedition had been accomplished, four missions were now established, but this was just the beginning of the real work of evangelization and civilization in Texas.

Reasons for settling East Texas. Why had the Spaniards chosen for the base of their activities a location so far removed from the frontier settlements of New Spain? Why had they not settled nearer to the place where La Salle had attempted to found his colony? Why did they fail to send Captain Urrutia, who knew the Indians of the region so well, to offset the influence of St. Denis and the French? To answer these questions would take us too far from the natural sequence of our narrative. Suffice it to say that from the very beginning, Spanish officials both in Spain and in America, realized logically that the Asinai group represented the strongest, best organized, and most influential tribal organization between the Red River and the Río Grande. By gaining control and extending their influence through the work of the missionaries, over this group, the authority of Spain in this vast region could be better established, the activities of the French checked, and the weaker tribes that roamed over the prairies converted to Christianity. The importance attached to these Indians has already been pointed out. But their proximity to the French subjected them to contrary influences and the missionaries soon realized that the relatively weaker but much farther removed tribes

---

[52]The missionaries placed in charge of the three missions founded by friars from the College of Querétaro were: at the Mission of Nuestro Padre Señor San Francisco de los Tejas, Fathers Fray Francisco Hidalgo and Fray Manuel Castellanos; at the Mission of La Purísima Concepción, Father Fray Gabriel Vergara and Fray Isidro Felix de Espinosa; at the Mission of Nuestro Señor San José de los Nasonis, Father Fray Benito Sánchez. All the friars from the College of Zacatecas stayed at Nuestra Señora de Guadalupe for the remainder of 1716.

that centered around the San Antonio River offered a much more fertile and favorable field for their work of evangelization. The location of La Salle's colony, although much more accessible both by land and sea than East Texas, had the great disadvantage of being surrounded by the fierce and much more barbarous Karankawan tribes, who proved hostile to both the French and the Spaniards and who had little or no influence over the other tribes, being hated by all alike. The country was barren and unhospitable. Only the possibility of the Bay of San Bernardo being used as a base for French incursions prompted the king to order its occupation in 1718,[53] which resulted in the establishment of a presidio at La Bahía del Espíritu Santo by Aguayo.

Why Urrutia did not accompany Ramón. As to Urrutia, St. Denis had faithfully conveyed the message of the Tejas and informed Spanish officials that they wanted Father Hidalgo and Captain Urrutia to be sent to them. The *Fiscal* in his recommendations of August 15, 1715, advised that Urrutia be sent along with the missionaries. But when the expedition set out Urrutia was not among its members, nor Father Olivares,[54] who was also supposed to go. On February 26, 1716, Father Margil wrote an interesting letter to the viceroy from Boca de Leones in Nuevo León. After thanking him for having asked the friars from the College of Zacatecas to take part in the expedition and assuring him that the *Padres* would all work together for a single purpose, "the salvation of souls," he says: "The reason for troubling Your Excellency with the present [letter] is that all those who, because of their experience, consider without passion this *entrada,* realize how much Captain Joseph Urrutia will be missed. Having been reared with the Tejas, and knowing their language, they love him as if he were their father . . . It is necessary, in the opinion of many, that Your Excellency be pleased to order said Captain to enter on this occasion, giving him some title, such as Sergeant Major, or Protector, without this affecting in any way Captain Domingo Ramón. . . . He will be a great help to him for many reasons . . . The French, who have the Indians very much on their side, resenting the loss of their

---

[53]Real Cédula de Junio 11 de 1718. *In Reales Cédulas, 1678-1772, México, Archivo General* (Bolton Transcripts, University of Texas).

[54]Father Olivarez did not go, because he asked his superior to excuse him on account of his age and infirmities. There is no foundation for the story that he refused to go because of animosity against Father Espinosa and the machinations of St. Denis. See letter of Father Diez to the Viceroy, February 10, 1717. *Provincias Internas,* Vol. 181, p. 220.

trade, can do us a bad turn, without showing their face, merely by insti-
gating the Indians . . . But if Urrutia goes, nothing can be done or
planned either by the French or the Indians which the Tejas will not
communicate to him. If the French, because of their following, can raise
a thousand [men], Urrutia can raise ten thousand." The viceroy transmitted this letter to the *Fiscal* for his opinion, who promptly returned it
to His Excellency on April 23, with a strong recommendation that orders
be issued to Urrutia to go with Ramón.

The viceroy now turned both the original letter of Father Margil and
the recommendation of the *Fiscal* to Francisco Barbadillo, *Alcalde of the
Real Camara del Crimen,* who had recently been entrusted with the pacification of the Indians in Nuevo León. On May 19, he replied that
Urrutia had been appointed protector of the Indians in Nuevo León in
view of his great experience in dealing with them; that the work of
pacification having just been started, to relieve him from this post in
order to allow him to go to Texas would be highly detrimental; and that
at the present time there was no other man who could take his place.
Considering all these facts, the viceroy, on May 25, decided it was better
to keep Urrutia in Nuevo León than to send him to Texas.[55]

Need for reënforcements and more missions. But let us return to
Ramón and the missionaries in East Texas. The magnitude of the task
dawned immediately upon them. What could a handful of soldiers and
nine missionaries do, more than three hundred leagues from the nearest
outpost of New Spain, surrounded by several thousand Indians, who
although friendly enough now, might be turned against them at any
moment by the enterprising French, and threatened by the fearless and
barbarous nations of the north who were the enemies of the Asinai and
their friends? Fully conscious of their precarious position and the need
for immediate remedy, they wrote to the viceroy on July 22, 1716,
frankly pointing out their needs and holding out the possibilities for
unprecedented achievement if the proper means were furnished.

Ramón explained that a line of missions had been established extending
from the Neches River east for a distance of eighteen leagues, the last
mission being twenty-three leagues farther inland than the one estab-

---

[55]Letter of Father Margil to the Viceroy, February 26, 1716. *Provincias Internas,* Vol. 181, pp. 46-49. In the letter Father Margil also declares that Joseph
Ramón, brother of Capt. Domingo Ramón, before two brothers-in-law and his
own mother, told him that it was essential that Captain Urrutia should accompany
the expedition.

lished in 1690 by Alonso de León; that the Indians had built in a very short time comfortable dwellings for the *Padres* and were actively engaged in building the churches, all of which was made easy by the abundance of timber, the skill of the Indians, their willingness to work, and the joy with which they had received the Spaniards; and that the four missions numbered about four or five thousand persons of both sexes, all of whom understood the same language and were uniformly pleasant and good-natured. Now, if the establishments were to be permanent and to develop as they should, and grow, attracting the numerous and various tribes of this region who were friendly to the Tejas, bringing them all into the fold of the Church and under the authority of the king, the number of soldiers must be increased from twenty-five to fifty and their rate of pay made four hundred fifty *pesos* a year. With the present force it was impossible to reconnoiter or explore the land, there being hardly enough men left, after taking eight to guard the missions, to mount guard at the presidio and to watch the horses. The climate had proved unhealthy and there were a number of men sick, one having died since their arrival. At the present rate of pay the soldiers were unable to get what they needed. The cost of transportation of supplies was enormous, due to the great distance to the frontier settlements of New Spain. It cost fifteen cents to transport one pound of sugar from Saltillo. The situation was made critical, he declared, by the presence of numerous enemies of the Tejas to the north, such as the Apaches, Juanes (Yojuanes), Chanes, and others.

In order to keep the friendship of the Indians and win other neighboring tribes, it was necessary, in his opinion, to appropriate at least six thousand *pesos* a year for the purchase of suitable gifts. These pleased the Indians greatly and inclined them towards the Spaniards, making them more amenable to the efforts of the missionaries. Not only must sufficient gifts be provided for the Indians, but the missionaries themselves should receive proper attention and care. Because of their isolation, there was no opportunity for them to secure alms, gifts, or offerings from the faithful, nor were they able as yet to raise sufficient crops to supply their immediate needs and those of the neophytes. It was highly important, therefore, that the king should assign them the necessary aid to meet their needs so that they might live in frugal comfort. He related how he had been obliged to pay out of his own pocket the wages of six men, in addition to the twenty-five soldiers, to bring the goats and other offerings given to the *Padres* in Saltillo. He had likewise paid the cost of transportation of seven women, a young boy and girl, provided the animals for them to ride, cared for their baggage, and had given them the necessary food, all of this in order to convince the Indians that the Spaniards had come to stay. To illustrate the hardships of the journey he declared that out of the sixty-four oxen with which he started from Saltillo for the missions, only thirty-four arrived. The others died or became exhausted on the long road of more than four hundred leagues.[56]

To all of this the *Padres* testified, and in their report they added that three of the four missions were along the road to the Nachitos (Natchitoches), by which the French had been in the custom of entering the province from Louisiana; that many more Indians like the Asinai, were expected soon to congregate; and that they had great hopes that this country would become a "Nueva Philipina." It was the declaration of the missionaries that the natives, because of their docility and willingness, deserved the liberality of the King who, like a father, should treat them as children of our faith, provide the means with which they should cover their nakedness, cultivate the fields and raise their own sustenance. The careful and impartial distribution of whatever was sent them was but a duty that the *Padres* would gladly perform. They joined Ramón in his request for sorely needed aid for themselves, pleading they were unable to get any help from their friends at this distance. They further stated that an agreement had been reached between the friars of the two Colleges of *Propaganda Fide* of Querétaro and Zacatecas, whereby the land and the fields of activity had been divided for the purpose of the conversion of the Indians. The College of La Santa Cruz was to labor among the nations that occupied the territory to the north, east, and west of the present missions along the road to Natchitoches, in a direct line with the country of the Cadodachos, which in time might be extended to meet New Mexico. The College of Nuestra Señora de Guadalupe of Zacatecas was to work in the region to the east, south, and west of the present line of missions, extending in time as far as Tampico. Great indeed, they affirmed, was the yield to be expected, both sections being peopled by many nations. With more diplomacy than Ramón displayed, the missionaries hinted that there were rich mineral deposits to be found in the land, according to the opinion of those who knew. Should mines be found, they said, the settlement of civilians would be made easier. But in such an eventuality they hoped that His Excellency would see that all those who came were of exemplary habits; that no one should

---

[56]Ramón to the Viceroy, July 22, 1716. *Provincias Internas,* Vol. 181, pp. 89-93.

be sent to Texas who was serving out a sentence, or who was of ill repute; because "the good or bad habits and customs of our people are transmitted imperceptibly to those of the land."[57]

Founding Mission San Miguel de Linares.   Pursuant to his instructions, Ramón reported, soon after his arrival, what he had been able to learn concerning the presence and activity of the French in the region. After affirming emphatically that St. Denis had been obedient and loyal in the performance of his duties and of great help to him because of his knowledge of the language and customs of the Tejas, he stated that he had noticed eighteen or twenty French guns, beads of various colors, knives, cloth, coats, and hatchets among the Indians, all of which had been introduced by the French and exchanged for horses and cattle on the various occasions they had entered the province. Not a single Frenchman had been seen in the neighborhood up to this time but some Natchitoches who came to his camp on July 23 told him there were four living among them in a large house. These Indians were friends of the Tejas and appeared to be gentle and friendly. Their land, declared Ramón, was about sixty or seventy leagues away on the road to Mobile and it was his intention to visit the Natchitoches the following month in order to report his personal observations. "Of one thing I am certain," he said, "and that is that this conquest and conversion will be memorable and [may prove] a second New Spain, if the proper measures are adopted."[58]

Just when he undertook the visit to the Natchitoches is not clear, but by October he had gone to inspect the rumored establishment of the French and found it to be only too true. On a small island in the center of the river, he discovered a well-built house with a stockade. Here two Frenchmen informed him that ten men were expected to reënforce them shortly from Mobile. Captain Ramón, who was accompanied on the expedition by Father Margil and the missionaries of the College of Zacatecas, ordered the French to erect a large cross and, in the presence of numerous Indians, Mass was celebrated. Observing that the French had already acquired considerable influence over the Indians in the neighborhood, Ramón and the missionaries decided to stop on the way back among the Adaes nation, who lived about eight or nine leagues from the Natchitoches. The Adaes received the party with marked signs of welcome and

---

[57]Espinosa to the Viceroy, July 22, 1716. *Provincias Internas,* Vol. 181, pp. 122-24.

[58]Domingo Ramón to the Viceroy, July 26, 1716. *Provincias Internas,* Vol. 181, pp. 52-53. Copy found also in *San Francisco el Grande Archive,* VIII, 62-63.

asked the missionaries to establish a mission and to come to live among them. Captain Ramón gladly acceded to their petition and appointing as governor the principal chief of this tribe, immediately gave possession of the new mission to Father Antonio Margil de Jesús, as President of the missions to be founded by the friars from the College of Zacatecas, which was named Misión de San Miguel de Linares. All this was done with the accustomed solemnity and copies of the official *Act of Possession and Establishment* were given to Father Margil. This mission, founded in the fall of 1716 and not in 1717, as generally believed, was located near the bank of present day Arroyo Hondo, seven or eight leagues from Natchitoches and about a league from Spanish Lake. The place has been identified with the site of modern Robeline, Louisiana.[59]

Founding Mission Dolores de los Ais. From here Ramón and Father Margil went to the country of the Ais, located about half way between the first four missions established among the Tejas and the Mission of San Miguel just founded. The Indians were friendly and numerous, and like the Adaes, asked Ramón to establish a mission among their people. They declared they liked the Spaniards and wanted them to come and live among them. Ramón readily agreed to establish a mission and, with similar ceremonies, appointed a governor for the Indians and gave possession of the new establishment to Father Margil in the name of His Majesty. The mission was named Nuestra Señora de los Dolores de los Ais. Father Margil took charge of it, selecting it as his headquarters because of its location between Mission Concepción and Mission San Miguel. Thus two additional missions were established by Ramón, with the help of Father Margil and the missionaries of the College of Zacatecas before the end of the year, making a total of six missions, as Father Morfi declares in his *Historia.*[60]

The work of conversion made small progress at first. At the time of

---

[59]Buckley, *op. cit.*, 53. For the account as here given of the establishment of this the farthest east of all the missions the following letters were used: Hidalgo and Castellanos to Fr. Pedro Mezquia, October 6, 1716; Fr. Margil to the Viceroy, February 13, 1718; Diego Ramón to the Viceroy, February 2, 1718, all in *Provincias Internas,* Vol. 181; and Ramón to Alarcón, May 21, 1717, in *The Gulf Region,* 1713-1721 (Dunn Transcripts).

[60]Castañeda, *Morfi's History of Texas,* paragraph 204. It has been stated, without foundation, that these two missions were established in 1717. The facts are that some time in August Ramón went to the Natchitoches, as promised in his letter of July 26, and on his way back founded the missions as stated here. Father Hidalgo refers to Ramón's trip in his letter of October 6, and says he found two Frenchmen at the big house on the island. St. Denis, in his declaration on Sep-

the arrival of the missionaries in East Texas most of the Indian tribes that made up the Asinai confederacy were out hunting or gathering their scattered crops, each Indian family or group living in its own *rancho*. They welcomed the Spaniards and were friendly enough to them, but they were not ready to be congregated at this time. Sickness also diminished the actual number of missionaries who were able to work effectively, as it did the garrison. Father Hidalgo was one of the first to be stricken with illness. From his description of the ailment it seems to have been malaria, for he refers to "chills and fever." From July until almost October, he was unable to do much, and no sooner did he get on his feet than Father Castellanos, left in charge of the spiritual needs of the garrison, fell ill. The Indians, he declared, were friendly but they were idol-worshipers and had special temples where they kept up perpetual fires. The regular teaching of the *doctrina* had not been started as late as October because the houses of the Indians were so far apart. Efforts were being made to induce them to move nearer to the missions, but before this could be accomplished three idols and their temples would have to be destroyed and this could not be done in safety, nor could the natives be made to acknowledge the sovereignty of the king, without at least a garrison of one hundred men. To the north there were numerous other nations among whom the French were actively working and it was essential that more soldiers and missionaries be sent, if the occupation of the province of the Tejas was to be permanent.[61]

Such were the conditions facing the discouraged missionaries and the greatly reduced number of soldiers, who had established their presidio about a quarter of a league from the Mission of San Francisco de los Tejas, in the fall of 1716. The Indians had reported the presence of

tember 1, 1717, stated he had helped to found two missions, one named San Miguel and the other whose name he had forgotten, and although he does not say when, it is evident from the context it was before his departure for Mobile. Father Margil, who gives the most detailed account (February 13, 1718) relates that the missions were founded on the first visit of Ramón to Natchitoches on the return trip, mentioning the establishment of San Miguel as having taken place before that of Nuestra Señora de los Dolores, indicating clearly they were coming from Natchitoches to Concepción Mission. It is to be doubted that St. Denis had anything to do with the founding of these two missions, as neither Ramón in his letter to Alarcón of May 21, 1717, nor Father Margil in his more detailed account of February 13, 1718, mention him. Father Margil would certain have mentioned this fact as he was anxious at this time to help clear St. Denis.

[61]Father Hidalgo to Father Mesquia, October 6, 1716. *Provincias Internas*, Vol. 181, pp. 215-218.

Frenchmen among the Natchitoches and their intention of establishing a post among the Cadodachos.

Many of the military guard had run away, others had fallen ill and four of them had died. The fugitives had taken the best mounts, naturally, to make their getaway safer, and as a result of this desertion Ramón had lost more than forty horses.[62] Unless the officials in New Spain took immediate action to reënforce the insufficient garrison, to supply the missionaries with the most indispensable necessities, and to encourage settlers to come to Texas, the possession secured at such a sacrifice would be lost and the conversion of the Indians would have to be abandoned a second time as in 1693. It had become evident that a halfway station between the Río Grande and the new presidio and missions was essential to the maintenance of this remote establishment. Spain could not afford now to neglect this distant outpost of its colonial empire, nor could the hardships and disappointments suffered discourage the fervent zeal of the determined sons of Saint Francis. The means to hold securely what had been gained so painfully and to extend the work of evangelization and civilization would have to be found.

---

[62]Domingo Ramón to Martín Alarcón, May 21, 1717. *The Gulf Region*, 81-84 (Dunn Transcripts).

CHAPTER III

THE FOUNDING OF SAN ANTONIO AND THE EXPANSION OF MISSIONARY ACTIVITY, 1716-1719

With the coming of the Marquis of Valero to succeed the aging Duke of Linares as viceroy of New Spain, the desire to strengthen the claim to Texas, to put an end to the illicit trade of the French from Louisiana, and to extend the missionary efforts of the Franciscans became the paramount object of the government. Evidence of the widespread activity of the French and the great influence they had acquired over the various Indian nations that occupied the vast region between the Mississippi River and the Río Grande had been transmitted both by Ramón and the missionaries. It was publicly known, by the fall of 1716, that extensive preparations were being made in France to reënforce the settlements on the Mississippi and that tradesmen and soldiers were being enlisted to establish a new colony on the mouth of the river. The new viceroy was officially informed by the *Fiscal* that these preparations could have no other purpose than the desire of the French "to penetrate from there into the country of the Tejas in order to dispose of their goods in the said provinces [of Nueva Estremadura, Reynos del Nuevo León, Nueva Vizcaya, and Parral]."[1] The difficulties of preventing smuggling and of keeping the Indians friendly with the reduced number of soldiers now in East Texas and the scanty supplies at their disposal, coupled with the troubles of transportation, made it evident that a halfway station between the remote missions and presidio established among the Tejas and the Río Grande was indispensable.

Father Olivares' proposals for new missions. When Father Fray Antonio de San Buenaventura Olivares arrived in Mexico late in September with a letter from the Guardian of the College of Querétaro, Father Fray Joseph Diez, to report what was needed for the maintenance and development of the new missions, he found an interested listener in the new viceroy. Father Olivares was an experienced missionary who for many years had been in Coahuila and had come in contact with some of the Indians that visited the outposts on the Río Grande. In 1709 he had accompanied Father Espinosa in his expedition to the San Marcos

---

[1]Dictamen del Fiscal, *Provincias Internas*, Vol. 181, p. 137.

(the Colorado River) in search of the Tejas Indians. Ever since that time, he had nursed a hidden desire to found a mission at the head-waters of the San Antonio River, where he and Father Espinosa had observed how suitable the location was for this purpose. Before going to Mexico City, he had studied with care and much profit, as his report shows, all the data sent by the various missionaries and officials who had visited the country since the time of De León and Father Massanet, concerning the habits and customs of the numerous tribes of the region, the character of the land, the fertility of the soil, the abundance and variety of edible fruits and game, and the possible presence of rich minerals, all of which he used to advantage in convincing the viceroy of the urgent need of taking appropriate measures to strengthen the hold already gained in this important area by extending the missionary activities of the Franciscans. By these means many new friends and loyal subjects could be won for the king and thousands of souls saved from eternal damnation.

Deeply impressed by the earnestness of the aged missionary, the viceroy, after a number of verbal conferences, ordered him to reduce to writing everything he knew about the Indians of the province of the Tejas and their land. "It is impossible," declares Father Olivares, "to exaggerate the pleasant character, the beauty, and the fertility of the province of the Tejas (or Asinai) from the Río Grande, where our missions begin, to the [location] of the new ones which the zeal of Your Excellency desires to establish." He then described vividly the untold quantity of flax that grew there, the richness of the grapes of all kinds, the quality of the mulberry trees which surpassed those of Murcia and Granada, the abundance of nuts, more tasty than those of Castile, and with shells so thin that the Indians cracked them with ease, the variety of birds of all classes and colors, and the large number of wild turkeys and deer, to say nothing of the herds of numberless buffalo. More than fifty different Indian tribes were known to the Spaniards and missionaries, and there were numerous others with whom they had had no dealings. The majority of those known were of pleasing appearance, being kind and willing to help the *Padres* and to share with them whatever they had. They were very fond of Spanish goods and liked Spanish clothes in particular. On numerous occasions they had expressed a desire to become Christians; they had no serious vices; and they showed many virtues that would make their conversion to our holy faith relatively easy. With tact and shrewdness, he pointed out that there were many indications of rich mineral deposits in the land, such as the silver mountain *(Cerro de la Plata)*, the tracings of gold found in some of the rivers, and the heavy green rocks used by the natives to make green paint, which were evidently silver and copper alloy.[2]

Proposed mission on the San Antonio.   This report, in which there is evident exaggeration in spite of the assurances to the contrary by Father Olivares, who allows himself to be carried away by his enthusiasm and missionary zeal, was ordered transmitted to the *Fiscal* for his study and consideration on November 20, 1716. But it must have been in the hands of the viceroy long before this time, because on that same date, Father Olivares handed him another report and a long list of everything needed for the establishment of a mission on the River San Antonio de Padua (present San Antonio River), of which Father Olivares himself was to be the founder. It is safe to say then, that subject to the approval of the *Real Acuerdo,* that is, the council of all the principal government officials with whom the viceroy had to consult before acting in a matter as important as this, he had in fact decided upon the establishment of the mission proposed by Father Olivares verbally, as there is no mention of the plan in his first report. It seems most probable that after his first report he was called by the viceroy to discuss the subject more in detail and that at that time the enthusiastic missionary had seen his opportunity to put into effect his long cherished dream of a mission on the San Antonio River.[3]

The plan as proposed by Father Olivares and approved in principle by the viceroy was to move the few remaining Jarame Indians of the Mission of San Francisco Solano, founded by the same missionary on the Río Grande near the Presidio of San Juan Bautista,[4] to the San Antonio River. The neophytes of San Francisco Solano would serve as teachers,

---

[2]Informe de Fray Antonio Olivares sobre las naciones y lo que hay en tierras de la Provincia de Texas. *San Francisco el Grande Archive,* VIII, 117-120. A copy is also found in *Provincias Internas,* Vol. 181, pp. 127-130.

[3]The exact words of Father Olivares' second report are: "Mandame Vexa. le diga los menesteres y Cossas nesesarias que son Conduzentes ala fundazon. de la Mision del rrío de Sn. Antto. de Padua; en que manda Vexa. sea mi Ynutil persona; fundador Yo mismo de ella." *Provincias Internas,* Vol. 181, p. 131.

[4]The Mission of San Francisco Solano was founded in 1700 by Father Olivares on the Río Grande near the Presidio of San Juan Bautista and the mission of that name. The Indians congregated for the purpose were Jarames, Payaguas, Papanacs and Siaguans. The *Acta de Fundación* is found in *Provincias Internas,* Vol. 28 (Bolton Transcripts, University of Texas).

it was pointed out, for the new Indians to be congregated there, knowing well how to till the soil and to do many other useful things learned in their mission life. It is to be noted that in making this suggestion Father Olivares was following an old custom established in the early days of the conquest. The Indians who had become civilized in the older missions were frequently used to help train those more recently congregated. It is thus that we find Tlaxcaltecan Indians in almost all the missions of the northern frontier. From Saltillo, where the town of San Esteban of the Tlaxcaltecos was established, they were taken as far as Monclova and it was even proposed on several occasions to bring them to Texas.

But let us return to Father Olivares' proposals. He pointed out that a pueblo of about three or four thousand Indians could be established near the new mission when the Payayas, Sanas, Pampoas, and the other neighboring tribes were congregated on the San Antonio River. The location, he assured the viceroy, with pardonable ignorance of the country, was about twenty-five or thirty leagues from the Bay of Espíritu Santo and bordered on the north with the country of the Apaches. It would be necessary, therefore, that ten soldiers be assigned to the new mission for his personal safety until he was able to gather all the Indians to form the new pueblo. It would be highly advisable to induce some civilians to form a settlement in the same locality by offering them lands and water rights, the river being sufficient to supply a whole province.[5]

Report of the Fiscales.   The two reports of Father Olivares, together with the recent communications received from Captain Domingo Ramón and the missionaries were all sent to the *Fiscales* who were asked to make such suggestions and recommendations as they deemed best. Ten days later, on November 30, the *Fiscal Civil* Espinosa and the *Fiscal de Hacienda* Velasco made separate reports to the viceroy on the subject. The first of these recommended that everything needed for the proposed establishment of a mission on the San Antonio River should be furnished to Father Olivares without delay, this being in accordance with the orders of His Majesty and his great zeal for the conversion of the natives. But Velasco took occasion to make a long, detailed, and lucid summary of everything that had transpired in Texas from 1688 to November 30, 1716. After having summarized the various measures adopted by the colonial government for the suppression of illicit trade

---

[5]Father Espinosa to the Viceroy, [November 20, 1717]. *Provincias Internas,* Vol. 181, pp. 131-133.

on the part of the French and the repeated orders of the king for the establishment of missions among the Indians, he concluded that His Majesty had approved and recommended the occupation of the Province of the Tejas and the conversion of these Indians and all others that might be induced to accept our holy faith; that large sums of money had been spent in pursuance of this object; that the only purpose of His Majesty in ordering that missionaries be sent, escorted by soldiers, was the conversion of the natives and their reduction to civilized life; that the reasons why the desired end had not been obtained up to this time were the failure to congregate the Indians in pueblos where they could be instructed in the doctrine of our faith and the customs of civilized life, the bad conduct and abuses committed by the soldiers entrusted with the care of the missions, and the insufficient force placed in each of the establishments; that now, in addition to the primary object there was a second and very important one of a temporal nature, the winning of the friendship of the numerous nations in that region to check the activities of the French, observe their movements, and stop their illicit trade; that to establish a presidio at Natchitoches or among the Cadodachos as suggested by Ramón and the missionaries, without first taking possession of the Bay of Espíritu Santo, could not put a stop to the commercial activity of the French, while the failure to occupy Espíritu Santo might prove a serious danger to the missions already established.

He then went on to point out some material considerations that made the holding of Texas important and indispensable. By gaining control over the Tejas and their allies, the Cadodachos, who were their neighbors and lived to the north in a rich beaver country, could be brought under the dominion of the king, extending thereby the possessions of His Majesty and winning thousands of souls from perdition. The land was rich in flax, valuable woods, and perhaps in minerals, products that would be of great value to the commerce of Spain. According to Don Gregorio Salinas Varona, Governor of Pensacola, direct communication might be established between the outposts on the Río Grande and Florida through the Tejas and their neighbors. Governor Salinas Varona had just celebrated a peace with the Chief of Cavite who ruled fifty-eight different nations from Florida to the tribes beyond the Mississippi, some of whom were neighbors of the Tejas. If these could be brought under the dominion of Spain by the extension of missionary work, they would afford a means of safe communication between the two remote areas. This may appear as a far-fetched plan, but it is of interest in showing the wide scope of the considerations taken into account by the officials of New Spain, often thought to have been narrow-minded and provincial in their general policies.

Turning again to the question of the Bay of Espíritu Santo, the *Fiscal* declared that its occupation was essential to hold Texas and to cut off effectively all French trade in that province. It would prove of great value, furthermore, in reducing the cost of transportation of men, equipment, and supplies for the distant garrison. From Veracruz to Espíritu Santo it was only two or three days sail, and from this bay to the Tejas, according to all the information available, it was only fifty or sixty leagues. The reduction in the cost of transportation of supplies would make it possible to effect a corresponding saving in the pay allowed to the soldiers, while the relatively shorter distance and less time required to reach the country of the Tejas would make it possible to send timely reënforcements and heavy artillery in case of war or hostilities, a thing that was impossible under present conditions.

He now turned to the question of the proposed mission on the San Antonio River which was the occasion for his long report. Whatever the considerations already presented, he stated, the establishment of the mission suggested by Father Olivares was highly advisable. The location chosen, as pointed out by the *Padre,* was between the Bay of Espíritu Santo and the province of the Tejas and it was well suited for the purpose. The Indians of that region were fond of this missionary, who had visited and talked to them on various occasions and understood their language. Furthermore, the mission would be a valuable link between the Tejas and the Bay of Espíritu Santo when this important point was occupied. But should it become impossible to occupy the bay at this time, the mission on the San Antonio River would be all the more important, as a watch could be kept from this point on any attempt made by the French to take possession of the bay or to land goods there for introduction into the northern provinces of New Spain. If Father Olivares succeeded in establishing a large settlement on the San Antonio River, as he expected, the Bay of Espíritu Santo would serve as a very convenient port for the various supplies needed, and artillery, should it be necessary for its defence, could be sent this way much more easily than overland from Coahuila.

Plans for a new expedition. For the success of the missions already established and in order that other nations might be brought under the influence of our holy religion, it was necessary, he explained, to send a person as leader of the new expedition, who was known to be zealous both for the royal service and the conversion of souls, who had had experience in dealing with the Indians, who was liberal and tactful, and who would protect them against all abuses. Great care should be exercised in sending only married soldiers on this expedition to avoid the excesses committed in the time of De León and Terán. The families of the soldiers, who could be transported at royal expense, would form the nucleus of a settlement that would induce others to establish themselves in this remote region and would set a good example to the Indians and convince them of the permanence of the missions. It would be well to take a number of old mission Indians, skilled in the cultivation of the soil, to help in teaching those newly congregated how to plant crops. A master carpenter, a blacksmith, and a mason should also be sent at royal expense that they might help build the churches and dwellings and teach these trades to the Indians. It was particularly important that a good weaver should accompany Father Olivares, who could teach the Indians how to weave the flax, the wool, and the goat hair into cloth.

Turning to the military aspects of the expedition, he suggested that not less than sixty soldiers be sent in order that at least twenty-five could be left as a garrison after an adequate guard was placed in each one of the missions. These men should be stationed at a convenient place that might be considered the capital or headquarters of the new establishments. A sufficient and adequate number of soldiers was essential for the success of the efforts of the missionaries in congregating the Indians. With a competent force, the judicious distribution of gifts and fair treatment of the natives, they could be more easily gathered into pueblos and induced to observe the regulations of mission life without giving occasion for them to become insolent as they did in 1693. It would be well for the soldiers to be all of pure Spanish stock, no *mestizos, coyotes,* or mulattoes to be included. In order to cause no added expense to the already depleted treasury, he was of the opinion that as many as ten men be dropped from the payroll of a certain number of presidios from New Mexico to Sinaloa, their allowances to be used for soldiers sent to Texas. He argued in support of this plan that most of the presidios listed were located among peaceful Indians, and that in all probability the persons dropped from the military payroll would remain at the presidios as civil settlers. For the escort of ten men asked by Father Olivares, he advised that eight be taken from the Presidio of San Juan Bautista on the Río Grande and two from the Presidio of Coahuila. These soldiers would not be missed, he thought, because most of the Indians who troubled the presidios on the Río Grande would soon be congregated at San Antonio by Father Olivares.[6]

The detailed recommendations of the *Fiscal de Hacienda* are important and interesting because they may rightly be called the genesis of the founding of San Antonio de Valero, the first mission on the present site of San Antonio, and the beginning of the civil settlement of San Fernando de Béjar, to be reënforced in 1731 by families brought specially for the purpose from the Canary Islands. It is significant that in this report, while keeping ever present the urgent need for putting a stop to the commercial activity of the French and extending the dominions of the King of Spain, the real motive for the occupation of the San Antonio River was a deep and sincere desire to convert the natives to Christianity. Father Olivares does not refer to the French either in his first or his second report, but he stresses the opportunities for missionary work among the thousands of Indians that lived in the neighborhood of the San Antonio River. The reports of Ramón and the missionaries do not stress the danger from the French either, but they point out that, if the efforts to win the friendship of the Tejas and their neighbors are not supported by the government, if more soldiers are not assigned to afford adequate protection and inspire respect to the Indians, the French may use them for their selfish interest in promoting illicit trade and turn them into enemies of Spain. They showed the need of supplies and the difficulty of securing them from the frontier outposts of Coahuila, thus hinting indirectly at the necessity of a halfway station and preparing the ground unintentionally for a favorable reception of Father Olivares' suggested establishment.

Olivares responsible for mission on the San Antonio. St. Denis and his new attempt to introduce merchandise into the northern provinces of New Spain had no influence whatsoever upon the decision to occupy the San Antonio River, for when he arrived for the second time in Mexico City, in June, 1717, and even before the viceroy had heard through Diego Ramón at San Juan Bautista of the seizure of his goods, the *Real Acuerdo* had approved the recommendations of the *Fiscal;* Martín de Alarcón had

---

[6]Resumen general de los autos sobre noticias, informes y escritos desde 1688 a 1718 . . . Velasco. November 30, 1716. *San Francisco el Grande Archive,* VIII, 126-163; copy also in *Provincias Internas,* Vol. 181, pp. 139-180.

been appointed leader of the expedition, Father Olivares had been fully authorized to found his mission, and all preparations had been made and approved for carrying out the establishment. Interesting and romantic as this new episode of the colorful French adventure is, it has no relation with the founding of the Mission of San Antonio de Valero and consequently forms no part of our narrative. The reasons for the founding of a mission and the establishment of the nucleus for a civil settlement on the San Antonio River are to be found in the reports of Domingo Ramón and the missionaries and in the efforts of Father Olivares, who may justly be called the true father of the idea. It was he and no other who conceived the plan, succeeded in winning the approval of the viceroy, and was instrumental in obtaining the final authorization of the project. Ever since 1709 he had longed for an opportunity to put his plan into execution and his singleness of purpose, as in the case of Father Hidalgo, was at last to result in the establishment of a new center for missionary activity.

The reports of the *Fiscales* were presented to the *Junta General* convoked by the viceroy on December 2, 1716. By a majority of the members present, it was decided that the recommendations concerning the immediate occupation of the San Antonio River be put into effect by the viceroy and that the necessary expenses be paid out of the royal treasury, from such funds as His Excellency might designate. No action was taken by the *Junta,* however, on the more extensive recommendations of Velasco concerning the fitting out of a large expedition to reënforce Ramón, the appointment of a governor, the settlement of La Bahía del Espíritu Santo, and the founding of a capital for the new establishments.

Alarcón appointed leader. The viceroy, however, took upon himself to act on these recommendations independent of the opinion of the *Junta,* a thing which was entirely proper when, as he stated, it was "to the better interests" of His Majesty. Consequently, on December 7, he proceeded to appoint Don Martín de Alarcón, Knight of the Order of Santiago and Governor of Coahuila, Captain General and Governor of the Province of the Tejas and such other lands as might be conquered.[7]

---

[7]Martín de Alarcón was a typical soldier of fortune. He had seen service at Orán, had been in the royal navy, had a commission as Captain of infantry in Valencia from the Count of Cifuentes, and since his arrival in Mexico early in 1690 had held a number of distinguished positions; such as *Alcalde Mayor* of Tacona and Zamora, protector of the Indians of Mazapil, and *Sargento Mayor* of militia in Guadalajara. On August 5, he had been appointed Governor of Coa-

He was to enjoy the same preëminence, honors, and pay as Don Domingo Terán, who had held the same position in 1690. He was ordered to pre-pare himself to take possession of his new post as soon as possible and to select fifty soldiers at his discretion, provided they were, as nearly as possible, all Spaniards and married men. For the transportation of their families the royal treasury would provide the necessary funds for the purchase of horses. One year's pay in advance was to be given to him and to the soldiers and he was to observe religiously all instructions given him. He was to secure a master carpenter, a blacksmith, and a mason, who were to be enlisted and paid four hundred *pesos* a year the same as the soldiers.[8] Although the order and appointment was given on the 7th, the official commission was not issued to Alarcón until December 8.

Having appointed a governor and outlined in a general way the require-ments for the military expedition, he immediately issued the corresponding orders to furnish Father Olivares all that was needed for the founding of the mission on the San Antonio River, as approved and recommended by the *Junta*. He stipulated that a guard of ten soldiers be placed at this mission, eight from the Presidio of Coahuila. Don Martín de Alarcón, the newly appointed governor, was to select the most capable and worthy of the ten and make him *Alférez* (ensign or commander). Four or six of these men, accompanied by friendly Indians, were instructed to visit the Bay of Espíritu Santo once a month and in case they found the French or any other nation had landed there or that the intruders intended to make a settlement, they were to inform the aliens that the region was already occupied by Spain.[9]

Departure of Father Olivares.   Father Olivares had asked for every-thing needed for the celebration of Mass, the administration of the sacraments, the building of a chapel and dwellings, tools for the culti-vation of the soil, kitchen utensils, provisions for missionaries, gifts for the Indians, and cattle, sheep, and goats for the missions, in his report of November 20. He now asked that eight yoke of oxen, thirty cows,

---

huila. A complete record of his services is found in *San Francisco el Grande Archive,* IX, 8-21.

[8]Decreto del Virey, December 7, 1716. *Provincias Internas,* Vol. 181, pp. 199-200.

[9]Decreto del Virey, December 7, 1716. *Provincias Internas,* Vol. 181, 201-202. It is to be noted that the appointment of Alarcón and the orders for the establish-ment of the mission were issued on the same date but separately.

three bulls, one hundred head of sheep and one hundred goats be sent for the mission herd. For the construction of the chapel and dwellings he listed numerous tools used by carpenters and stonemasons and stipulated that a number of locks and keys and one thousand round-headed nails be included. For the Indians he asked two or three bolts of common Mexican cloth, some blue and green material for skirts for the women, rosaries and beads, ribbons, hats for the chiefs, blankets, baskets, and tobacco. For the chapel he wanted a good picture of Saint Anthony, two *varas* in length if possible. For the missionaries he asked common sack-cloth, a box of soap to wash their clothes, a ream of paper, a dozen shaving knives, chocolate, and two guns which might come handy for the defence of the mission.

He was very anxious to start immediately. Within two weeks after the orders for the supplies were issued by His Excellency, he was ready to set out. On December 28, he petitioned the viceroy to give him a patent for the governors, chief justices, and captains of presidios along the road, which he was to follow, that they might give him all help needed and furnish the necessary escort for the safe conveyance from town to town of all the supplies he was taking for the new mission. He also wanted the governor of the Tlaxcaltecan Indians of San Esteban, in Saltillo, to be instructed to give him one master carpenter and one master mason. Lastly he wanted the soldiers in Nuevo León to escort him as far as the Presidio of San Juan Bautista on the Río Grande to protect him, his companions, and the supplies against the well known dangers of this part of the road.[10] Explicit orders, as requested, were issued that same day and the *Padre* left Mexico City soon after, going by way of Querétaro in order to take two other missionaries with him.

He did not wait for Alarcón, but set out ahead of him. The Guardian of the College of Querétaro, Fray Joseph Diez, notified His Excellency that Father Olivares left Querétaro on February 9, 1717, "with two companions selected by himself, and fully equipped with everything necessary for the founding of the desired mission on the San Antonio River." He expresses regret at the unavoidable delay that has kept the governor from setting out, but declares that on account of the advanced age of Father Olivares, it was best for him to start immediately. By March 24, he was in Saltillo, where he presented his patent from the viceroy and was duly attended by Martín de la Peña, *Alcalde Mayor* of the villa.

---

[10]Peticion del Padre Olivares, *Provincias Internas,* Vol. 181, p. 214.

From there he went on to Monterrey, where he secured an escort to accompany him from this point to the Presidio of Coahuila.[11]

He arrived in the missions of the Río Grande on May 3, and lost no time in presenting the order of His Excellency to Governor José Músquiz of the Presidio of Coahuila and to Captain Diego Ramón at San Juan Bautista, asking them to let him have the ten soldiers that were to serve as an escort for his train from here to the San Antonio River and to act as guard for the new mission. But neither one of these officials complied with the order. They stated they would have to consult with the viceroy about the matter because of the reduced condition of the garrisons of their respective presidios. Much as he wanted to continue his journey without delay, the old and experienced missionary knew better than to march unguarded with a train of supplies and Indian gifts from the Río Grande to the site of his cherished mission. Convinced of the unwillingness of these officers to help him, he decided to wait as patiently as he could, until the new governor arrived with the remainder of the expedition to the Tejas. He retired from the Presidio of San Juan Bautista to the Mission of San José, about four leagues distant, "to avoid the thefts which the soldiers commit in the neighborhood of the presidio."

Alarcón's preparations.   While the *Padre* waits here, let us return to Martín de Alarcón in Mexico City. On December 11, he asked the viceroy for two hundred cows, two hundred oxen, one thousand sheep, five hundred *fanegas* (Spanish bushels) of corn, fifty axes, fifty hoes, some clothes, sackcloth, woolen cloth, fifty plows, six large bundles of tobacco, four packages of beads, three hundred horses for the transportation of the soldiers' families, fifty guns, and three boxes of powder. These, he declared, were indispensable for the expedition and the establishment of a warehouse *(almacen)* in the province of the Tejas to supply the missions. He also asked that Francisco Ugarte be ordered to turn over to him the thirty guns for the Presidio of Coahuila, which he now had in his possession.[12] Four days later he specified in a short note that in purchasing supplies one thousand *varas* of wide sackcloth, one dozen half bolts of red woolen cloth, and one thousand blankets—five hundred *pastoras* and five hundred *mestizas*—be included.

---

[11]Fray Joseph Diez to the Viceroy, February 10, 1717, *Provincias Internas*, p. 219; Despacho del Sor. Marqués de Valero, y certificaciones, Querétaro, México. *Archivo del Colegio de la Santa Cruz* (Dunn Transcripts, University of Texas).

[12]Martín de Alarcón to the Viceroy, December 11, 1716. *Provincias Internas*, Vol. 181, p. 115.

On this same date he addressed a long communication to the viceroy explaining his purpose of leaving without delay to carry out his instructions. It was his intention to go immediately to the interior provinces to recruit there the fifty soldiers he was to take on the expedition, declaring that it was best for the success of the expedition to take men who had had experience in dealing with the Indians. The engineer, the master carpenter, the blacksmith, and the mason he would take from the city. In order to recruit the men and equip them without delay, he had obtained on his own credit, the money necessary, equivalent in amount to one year's pay for himself and all the men. In view of this fact he asked His Excellency to order that the officers of the treasury in Guanajuato pay him one year's salary in advance. This, together with one year's pay for the soldiers and tradesmen and the four thousand *pesos* allowed by His Excellency to aid the establishments in Texas and to provide for incidental expenses of peace and war, would amount to twenty-eight thousand one hundred fifty *pesos*. Since the officers at Guanajuato, he pointed out, had been instructed to send all royal funds to Mexico City by Christmas, he suggested that the viceroy order the royal treasurer in the city to pay this sum to him out of the funds sent from Guanajuato. It was his intention to start immediately to execute the command of His Excellency, and he asked that his pay and that of the men already recruited or enlisted should begin in January, 1717. To all of this the viceroy agreed and ordered the sum to be paid as suggested.[13]

Just when Alarcón left Mexico City is not clear, but he was busily engaged in Saltillo by June, 1717, in making an investigation of the activities of St. Denis and the complicity of the whole Ramón family in the introduction of French merchandise. He even suspected Dr. Codallos, a cleric of prominence and the administrator of the estate of the Marquis of Aguayo, of being an accomplice.[14] St. Denis, who arrived at the Río Grande on April 19, had gone to Mexico soon after to remonstrate before the viceroy against the seizure of his goods at the Presidio of San Juan Bautista. "It is necessary," declares Alarcón, "that St. Denis be not allowed to return but that he be kept safely there." He says he is going to send his wife, who is now with her grandfather, Diego Ramón, senior, to Mexico. In his opinion both Diego Ramón, senior, and Diego

---

[13]Alarcón to the Viceroy, December 14, 1716. *Provincias Internas,* Vol. 181, pp. 206-208. The order for payment was issued the following day.

[14]His full name is José Codallos y Rabal. He accompanied Aguayo in his expedition to Texas and there is no foundation for the suspicion cast upon him by Alarcón.

Ramón, junior, should be taken away from Coahuila. The latter accompanied St. Denis to Mobile and seemed to have profited considerably, judging from his opulence since his return from East Texas.[15]

Upon his arrival in Saltillo, he found a letter from Father Olivares waiting for him. After wishing him divine guidance in the great undertaking entrusted to him, and assuring him it would be a pleasure to carry out any instructions he might give him, the disappointed missionary goes on to say that he arrived at the Mission of San Juan Bautista on May 3, with the intention of continuing on his journey to the San Antonio River without delay for the purpose of planting crops immediately. The Río Grande was very low at the time and could have been crossed with ease, but the governor of Coahuila and the Captain of San Juan Bautista failed to give him the escort ordered by the viceroy. Captain Ramón refused to let him have the eight men because he claimed he could not spare them, nevertheless he took a larger number and went to the Presidio of Coahuila just to see a bullfight. Father Olivares paints a gloomy picture of conditions at the Presidio of San Juan Bautista. "I have witnessed and experienced all that these holy religious in charge here suffer as a result of the negligence of Captain Ramón and the haughtiness of the Indians, who, encouraged by the captain, have lost all respect for the soldiers as well as for the *Padres*. The whole country from Coahuila to the Tejas is in revolt *(alsada)* and there is no nation we can trust. . . . Your Lordship will see for himself how the Indians steal from the Spaniards and will notice many articles which they have exchanged with those of Nadadores and Parral." The French come and go freely, he declares, and three were actually digging a mine at Coahuila, while four were at that time at the Presidio of San Juan Bautista. He closes by earnestly entreating Alarcón to enlist his men somewhere else than in Coahuila, as the people of this region are not dependable.[16]

Without answering the letter, Alarcón proceeded to the Río Grande and reached the Presidio of San Juan Bautista on August 3, 1717. Two days later he took possession officially of the government of Coahuila and was duly sworn into office by the *Cabildo* of the Villa de Santiago de la Monclova, the capital of the province.[17] Here, while making an extensive

---

[15]Alarcón to the Viceroy, June 27, 1717, *A. G. I., Audiencia de México*, 61-6-33 (Dunn Transcripts).

[16]Father Olivares to Alarcón, June 5, 1717. *A. G. I., Audiencia de México*, 61-6-35 (Dunn Transcripts).

[17]Certificación del Cabildo, Justicia y Regimiento de la Villa de Santiago de la Monclova, August 6, 1717, *Provincias Internas*, Vol. 181, p. 221; Alarcón to the

investigation concerning the introduction of merchandise by the French, in which he questioned the soldiers as well as the missionaries and the settlers, he carried on active preparations for his *entrada* into Texas. He was able to discover little or nothing of value to incriminate either St. Denis or the Ramóns. The French who were at the presidio fled upon his arrival. With much disgust he declares that in the Presidio of San Juan Bautista there are only Frenchmen and sympathizers of the Ramóns, which association, in his opinion, was one and the same thing. He is glad to report, however, that he has enlisted thirty-two soldiers, all of whom are in the villa ready to start; that seven of these are married and have families; that he has received a letter from Captain Domingo Ramón stating that he has twenty-five men now in Texas; that he (Alarcón) has succeeded in gathering one hundred and fifty *cargas* (equivalent to about one hundred pounds each) of flour, one thousand sheep, a number of oxen, and two hundred cows. But he informs His Excellency that he is still waiting for the three hundred horses he was to secure in Saltillo.[18]

The soldiers enlisted for the expedition, according to Alarcón, were: Francisco Hernández, *Alférez,* who was going with his family; Diego Escobar, with his family; Francisco Barreyro, engineer, who was put under arrest September 20, for complicity with Diego Ramón; Miguel Martínez de Valenzuela; Diego de Zárate y Andizávar; Juan Barrera; Cristóbal Carvajal; Joseph Flores Quiñones; Juan Valdés; Joseph Gaona, with his family; Juan de Castro, with his family; Nicolás Hernández and Francisco Hernández, sons of the *Alférez;* Joseph de Neira; Joseph Velásquez; Francisco Menchaca; Lázaro Joseph Chirino, with his family; Gerónimo Carvajal; Sebastián Peniche; Antonio Guerra; Francisco de Escobar; Domingo Flores, with his family; Cristóbal de la Garza; Sebastián González; Joseph Plácido Flores; Joseph Jiménez; Manuel Maldonado; Manuel de Vargas; Pedro Rodríguez; Francisco Juan de la Cruz, master mason; Santiago Pérez, carpenter; Joseph Menchaca; Antonio Menchaca; Vicente Guerra, and Cristóbal Barrera.[19] When added, the list will be found to consist of thirty-five instead of thirty-two men. But although the *Cabildo* testified to the correctness of the statement of

Viceroy, September 20, 1717, *A. G. I., Audiencia de México,* 61-6-35 (Dunn Transcripts).

[18]Alarcón to the Viceroy, September 20, 1717. *A. G. I., Audiencia de México,* 61-6-35 (Dunn Transcripts).

[19]Certificación del Cabildo de la Villa de Santiago de la Monclova. September 18, 1717. *San Francisco el Grande Archive,* VIII, 192-193.

Alarcón with regard to the soldiers enlisted, a check of the names dis-
closes that five of them cannot be considered as such because they had
either run away from the presidio established by Domingo Ramón or
had overstayed their leave. They had not only taken the best horses, but
they owed the royal treasury for the year's pay they had received in
advance. These were Juan de Castro, Manuel Maldonado, Domingo Flores,
Juan Valdés, and Lázaro Chirino. Furthermore, Francisco Hernández,
the *Alférez*, who had been sent by Ramón with a message to Alarcón,
was still a member of the garrison of the Presidio of los Tejas, and owed
Domingo Ramón five hundred twenty-three *pesos* for advances made to
him.[20] Consequently only twenty-nine of the men listed were really new
enlistments. It is well to keep this in mind to form a correct opinion of
the character of the leader of this *entrada,* who was rightly accused by
the missionaries of having violated his trust and of being responsible to
a large extent for the failure of the expedition. Although this project
cost the royal treasury more than that of Domingo Ramón, it produced
much less satisfactory results.

Difficulties between Alarcón and Father Olivares.   Soon after Alarcón's arrival in the Presidio of San Juan Bautista, Father Olivares
went to him and again explained how important it was for him to proceed to the San Antonio River without delay. Three months of waiting
had naturally made the *Padre* impatient and he now urged the new governor to let him have the ten men which the *Junta* had approved and the
viceroy had ordered as a guard for the projected mission. Far from
obtaining satisfaction and being allowed to go in advance of the main
body to establish the mission which would have been of great service as
a halfway station to the expedition, the good *Padre* was put off with flimsy
excuses. As requested, Alarcón had eight men transferred from the Presidio of San Juan Bautista to him, but instead of turning them over to
the missionary he gave these men strict orders in writing to take commands from no one but himself. "He did not even give them instructions," declares Father Olivares, "to watch the king's property which was
in my care at the Mission of San José. . . . During the eight months
that this gentleman [Alarcón] was in Coahuila, they [the eight men]
did no service for His Majesty. They could have saved the expense of
having to hire persons to take care of the stock for the new mission

---

[20]Ramón to Alarcón, May 21, 1717. *A. G. I., Audiencia de México,* 61-6-35,
p. 81 (Dunn Transcripts).

which was kept at San José, where there was not a single mission Indian."[21]

"In the meantime," he says, "numerous Indians came to see me and captains of different nations, all from among those that live in the region of the San Antonio River. I told them the purpose of my coming; I explained and extolled to them how greatly the king and Your Excellency desired their conversion and that they should live according to the law of God and the customs of civilized men, and that Your Excellency had provided me with the necessary means for that purpose. To convince them, I showed them the supply of clothes, tobacco, and other things which Your Excellency placed under my care and in order that they might not think my words were but an empty promise, I distributed some of these goods among them. The number who came to see me was over one hundred and fifty, many of whom were captains of different nations, and they all gave me their word they would wait for me on the San Antonio River."[22]

As time went on and Alarcón still postponed his departure, there grew a misunderstanding between him and Father Olivares. The governor encountered greater difficulty in getting started than he had expected, and as winter drew near, he must have followed the advice of those who had had experience in the country and decided to wait until spring. Provisions had to be collected, more men enlisted, and families induced to accompany the expedition; the horses, so essential for the soldiers and the transportation of the families, had to be secured; and the stock had to be brought together. But Father Olivares thought the delay was inexcusable and, as far as he was concerned, he could not understand why he was not allowed to go on. About the middle of September, after having seen that Alarcón did not have the required number of soldiers, nor the families necessary to proceed to Texas, he wrote a letter to him again urging to be allowed to go alone, and pointing out the many inconveniences that would result from putting off carrying out the orders of His Excellency. To this Alarcón replied that it was impossible for him to start now, that he could not spare the ten men for the new mission, and that he could not permit the *Padre* to proceed alone, that he would have to wait a little longer.

These continued denials had exhausted the patience of the enthusiastic

[21]Father Olivares to the Viceroy, June 22, 1718. *San Francisco el Grande Archive*, VIII, 205-212.

[22]*Ibid.*, 205-212.

missionary who now assumed a supercritical attitude. He called Alarcón's attention to the fact that most of the men he had enlisted as soldiers were not married, contrary to the express command of the viceroy, that their character was not of the best, and that many of them were not of Spanish blood. This exasperated Alarcón, who appears to have been naturally hot-tempered. He replied that unfortunately he did not have an Apostolic College from which to recruit his men, that in the Province of Coahuila there were only *Mulatoes, Lobos, Coyotes,* and *Mestizos.*[23] "Such people," exclaims Father Olivares, "are bad people, unfit to settle among gentiles, because their customs are depraved, and worse than those of the gentiles themselves. It is they who sow discontent and unrest among them and come to control the Indians to such an extent, that by means of insignificant gifts they make them do what they please. When it is to their interest, they help the Indians in their thefts and evil doings, and they attend their dances and *mitotes* just to get deer and buffalo skins from them . . . It is with this sort of people, Your Excellency, that he wishes to settle the new site on the San Antonio and the Province of the Tejas."[24] There was little hope of coöperation between the two leaders of the expedition from this time on.

Reason for delay on Río Grande.   It has been said that the chief reason for Alarcón's delay at the Río Grande was the lack of instructions, but that as soon as he received these, he lost no time in starting.[25] The fact is that the instructions drawn up by the viceroy on March 11, 1718, did not reach Alarcón until a week after he had departed from San Juan Bautista. By this time he had already crossed the Nueces and was planning to proceed to San Antonio as rapidly as possible. In view of the orders received, which he misinterpreted, he changed his plans and decided to go first to La Bahía del Espíritu Santo.[26] The instructions were most

---

[23]A *lobo* was the offspring of a negro and an Indian, a *coyote* was the offspring of a *mestizo* and an Indian, and a *mestizo* the offspring of a Spaniard and an Indian.

[24]Father Olivares to the Viceroy, June 22, 1718. *Provincias Internas,* Vol. 181, 250-251.

[25]Clark, *The Beginnings of Texas, 1684-1718,* 85-86.

[26]The details of the Alarcón expedition can now be determined, thanks to the finding of his long lost Diary by Señor Vito Alessio Robles, of Mexico City, who discovered it in 1933 among the 3000 volumes in the *Seccion de Tierras,* of the *Archivo General de la Nación.* He presented a typewritten copy of this important document to the University of Texas and it is this copy which was used in the writing of this chapter. References to the Diary will be made frequently in the remainder of the chapter. The diary has been published as Volume V of the Quivira Society *Publications.*

carefully drawn and provided for every possible contingency. The stress placed in these secondary instructions on the fear of French aggression is the result of St. Denis' presence, imprisonment, and release in Mexico City from where he later fled, and a number of subsequent letters received from Diego and Domingo Ramón, as well as from the missionaries in East Texas, all of which magnify the activities of the French since the first establishment of the six missions and the presidio among the Tejas. Alarcón's investigation on the Río Grande added somewhat to the apprehension and to this, no doubt, is due the importance given in the final instructions to the immediate exploration of the Bay of Espíritu Santo and the strengthening of the presidio and missions in East Texas. There is no question that the missionaries had become anxious for relief in the fall of 1717, and this may account in part for the changed note in their communications concerning the French. In their first reports the fear of French aggressions was very vaguely suggested, but later it is played up considerably and the idea is left that they are at the mercy of the French, who may stir up the Indians at any time. They knew full well that this was the infallible bug-a-boo that would bring about immediate action, but they were ignorant of the fact that strenuous efforts had been made to send them relief in the winter of 1717, that this had been accidentally detained by the swollen condition of the rivers, and that Alarcón's delay in setting out was not due to any lack of interest on the part of the officials. As a natural result of these conditions the idea of establishing a mission and a civil settlement on the San Antonio River had become clear and definite.[27]

Alarcón's instructions. Before proceeding to the founding of the Mission of San Antonio de Valero it will be well for us to make a brief summary of the instructions which Alarcón received on April 16. Their purpose is clearly stated at the outset. They were to guide him in the introduction of the relief supplies and equipment and the establishment of the missions and towns thought most advisable for the conversion of the natives and the propagation of our faith, as well as for the extinction of French settlers and the promotion of the trade with New Spain.

[27]The facts briefly summarized in this paragraph are to be found in the following documents: Hidalgo to Mesquia, October 6, 1716, Espinosa to the Viceroy, February 28, 1718, Diego Ramón to the Viceroy, May 8, 1718, also May 30, 1718, *Provincias Internas,* Vol. 181; Diego Ramón to the Viceroy, May 2, 1717; Salinas Varona to the Viceroy, February 15, 1717, Olivares to Alarcón, June 5, 1717, *A. G. I., Audiencia de México,* 61-6-35 (Dunn Transcripts).

Having assembled all the soldiers, families, and other persons who were to accompany the expedition on a previously agreed day, and having put in readiness for the start all the supplies, cattle, stock, and equipment at the Presidio of San Juan Bautista on the Río Grande, the governor should set out at the earliest possible date, this being the most opportune season of the year for the expedition. The various members were to keep together and travel in a body in sight of the supply train of mules and the stock and cattle, maintaining always an advance guard of at least four soldiers who, with the aid of reliable Indian guides, were to explore the country and keep ahead of the expedition. The daily journeys were to be reasonably short and the camping site for each night was to be chosen by the advance guard. Alarcón was to make a careful check of the members of the expedition, the supply trains, the stock and cattle, and the equipment each night and to recheck them each morning. He was to follow closely the established route as far as the San Antonio River and to try to the best of his ability to reach this point with his entire group and all the supplies, exercising great care to see that the stock and cattle suffered no diminution while *en route*. Careful diaries of everything that happened and everything that was observed on the road were to be kept by various members of the expedition and sent back when opportunity offered.

When the San Antonio River was reached one or two missions were to be established "at the best and most suitable location on the said river" for the conversion of the Indians and the propagation of the faith. All this was to be done with the approval of Father Olivares and his two companions to whom Alarcón was to furnish all the means necessary for the purpose; such as, some cattle, oxen, sheep, goats, seed for planting, tools, and other things required to cultivate the land and to establish the pueblo or pueblos formed by the congregated Indians. The natives were to be treated kindly, without violence, and to be presented with blankets, cloth, beads, and other gifts, all of which were to be distributed by the *Padres* or through the Indian chief chosen as governor. The Indians were further to be excused from the payment of all tribute for a period of ten years, but the missionaries were to induce them to work in the cultivation of the land, the improvement of their pueblo, and the building of a church, all of which was for their spiritual and temporal welfare.

Given the important location of the site proposed for the mission by Father Olivares on the San Antonio River, within easy reach of the coast, it was highly advisable that the governor should establish on the banks of this river, near the mission, a settlement of Spaniards with at least thirty families from among the soldiers and those who accompanied the expedition. Such as chose to settle were to be given all the rights and privileges accorded by His Majesty to first settlers, and they were to receive lands, water rights, and wood rights as provided by law. The number was to be increased later to one hundred families, which was considered the minimum required for the firm establishment of this important post. The men who now chose to establish themselves as permanent settlers with their families were to be allowed their full pay as soldiers "for the very just reason of being engaged in an actual military expedition and obliged to be always ready for military service, exposed to the possible invasion of enemies who may attack them by land or sea, and particularly to the barbarous nation of the Apaches that infests that region . . . as a result of which they must always be prepared for defence." The settlers were to court the friendship of all the Indians in the neighborhood so that in case of attack by either foreign invaders or the Apaches, they could have the support of the well-disposed tribes.

After establishing the mission or missions and the civil settlement on the San Antonio River, Alarcón was to proceed as rapidly as possible to the presidio and missions established in East Texas, where with the advice and approval of Father Fray Antonio Margil de Jesús and his companions, he was to leave as many soldiers and families to assist the missionaries in congregating the Indians in the missions already founded and in erecting such new ones as were deemed necessary. The soldiers that were to be left among the Tejas should be chosen from those who had families, to avoid the troubles experienced in the past and the complaints of the Indians. All the soldiers left to guard the missions were to be under the orders of Father Margil and his missionaries. Here, as in San Antonio, kindness and gentleness were to be the means of congregating the Indians, whose friendship was to be won by fair treatment and timely gifts. Every effort was to be made to prevent the extension of French influence among them. Throughout the instructions the military members were subordinated entirely to the missionaries. It was clearly the intention of the authorities that the soldiers should aid and lend their support to the religious instead of hindering their work. The primary purpose of this expedition was to foster missionary activity and to win the respect and confidence of the Indians.

When the objects of the expedition as outlined were attained, when the new mission and settlement on the San Antonio River had been accomplished, and the presidio and missions of East Texas had been supplied and reënforced, Alarcón was to send immediately a full and complete report of everything that had been done and observed from the time the expedition left the Río Grande until it reached the missions in the Province of the Tejas. If any Indian chiefs wished to visit the viceroy, or if it was thought advisable to send a soldier who could give a verbal account as an eyewitness of everything that had taken place, these need not travel as fast as the couriers. They could make the trip by easy stages after the Río Grande was reached. It was important, however, that the written report or reports reach the viceroy as soon as possible.[28]

Although in the instruction it was suggested that the Bay of Espíritu Santo be examined and that its distance from the location of the new mission on the San Antonio River be determined, as well as the character of this stream and that of the Guadalupe, there is nothing to indicate that this was of primary importance. It is difficult to understand why, in view of these orders, Alarcón should have changed his route and attempted to reach the bay before going to San Antonio. But let us return to the governor and the expedition at the Río Grande where early in April he was still completing his arrangements to set off.

Founding of San Antonio de Béxar. On April 9, 1718, the entire expedition crossed the Río Grande and started on its journey to found a mission on the San Antonio River and to reënforce the presidio and missions in East Texas. There were seventy-two persons in all, including the mule drivers and the families.[29] Unfortunately, Alarcón was not as careful as Domingo Ramón and failed to make a list of all the persons. There were, besides the soldiers, missionaries, and families, seven droves of mules loaded with the clothes, provisions, and supplies; a considerable number of cattle and goats; some hens; and five hundred and forty-eight horses. Three hundred of these were furnished by the Marquis of Aguayo, who also gave from his *hacienda* most of the cattle for the expedition.

---

[28]Directorio que ha de observar, y ordenes que ha de Practicar el Sargento Mayor Don Martín de Alarcón. *Provincias Internas,* Vol. 183; a copy also in *San Francisco el Grande Archive,* VIII, 217-225. The copy in *Historia,* XXVII, is defective and undependable.

[29]The number of persons has been a question of conjecture, but the Diary now available has cleared all doubt and the number is further confirmed by the statement made in the *Relación de Servicios* of Alarcón. *San Francisco el Grande Archive,* IX, 201. See *Diario y Derrotero* of Alarcón, 1. (All references are to the typewritten copy presented by Señor Alessio Robles to the University of Texas.)

On the 15th, they crossed the Nueces River at about the same place that Ramón did two years before, and that evening a courier, with the detailed instructions already summarized, overtook the governor at his camp, six leagues beyond the passageway. The next day he changed his course in order to go directly to East Texas by way of Espíritu Santo, but he became so tangled with the numerous streams and heavy timber encountered by the new route, that on the 23rd he again changed his course and struck out for the Medina and the San Antonio Rivers. Just where he forded the Medina is not clear, but from that point to León Creek the distance was three leagues and from there to the San Antonio River three more.

He arrived at the present site of San Antonio on April 25. "There is a spring of water which is about three-quarters of a league from the main stream," declares the chronicler of the expedition, referring to San Pedro Spring. "On the site, where the *Villa de Béjar* was located, there is opportunity for opening one irrigation ditch with ease and no more. At the head of the said spring there is a thick wood of various kinds of trees, such as elms, poplars, hackberry trees, oaks, and many mulberries, all of them being thickly covered with wild grapevines." Governor Alarcón stayed here for ten days engaged in founding the mission and establishing the location for the new settlement. "The fifth day of May the governor took possession of the site called San Antonio in the name of His Majesty. After the celebration of Mass by the Father Chaplain, he had the royal standard brought forth and placed there with the corresponding solemnity. It was called *Villa be Béjar*. From this time the said place was designated as the site where the settlers and soldiers were to be established. At the same time [he chose] a site about three-quarters of a league down the creek, whereat he founded the Mission of San Antonio de Valero."[30] From this description it is not clear just where the first site designated for the civil settlement was located. But since the mission stayed at its first location, we know that the chronicler meant river where he says creek. This puts the original location of the temporary settlement and first presidio three-quarters of a league from the mission, on the west side of the river, and not far from the present site of San Pedro Spring, where it remained until 1722, when the Marquis of Aguayo moved it to a place almost across from the Mission of San

---

[30]*Diario y derrotero of Alarcón's Expedition*, 6 (Alessio Robles Transcript). In all documents of 1718 and 1719 the civil settlement is referred to as *Villa de Béjar* with reference to *San Fernando*.

Antonio de Valero, two hundred *varas* from the river and thirty from San Pedro Creek.[31]

A few more details concerning the founding of San Antonio are gathered from a letter written by Alarcón to the viceroy on September 28, 1718. He declares that he left ten families there with a sufficient guard of soldiers; that there were many Indians at the Mission of San Antonio de Valero; and that the reason why the thirty families were not settled as stipulated by His Excellency was that the swollen condition of the Río Grande did not permit the passage of families. Later, in his statement of *Services Rendered,* he claimed to have established the thirty families required and the presidio. "He likewise succeeded," declares the document, "in establishing a Spanish villa and presidio in the valley of San Antonio, with thirty families, in the most pleasant spot to be found in the entire Province where [they] enjoy the greatest advantages and facilities anyone can desire. He also founded a mission there under the appellation of Mission of San Antonio de Valero."[32]

Founding of San Antonio de Valero (The Alamo).   Let us now go back and follow the movements of Father Olivares from the Río Grande to San Antonio. Impatient as he had been to start, it seems that he became so disgusted with the conduct of Governor Alarcón, that he refused to accompany him and traveled by himself, with one or two companions and the stipulated guard of soldiers. He did not leave the Mission of San José on the Río Grande until April 18, nine days after Alarcón left the Presidio of San Juan Bautista. He does not say how many were in his party, nor does he state when the Jarame Indians of the old Mission of San Francisco Solano were moved to the new site on the San Antonio River. But it does not seem, however, that there were any Indians left to move, because Mission San José was the original San Francisco Solano, the location of which was changed twice before Father Olivares decided to transplant it to Texas and by that time he himself admits there was not a single mission Indian.[33] He did not meet Alarcón on the way because the governor had left the main road in an attempt to reach Espíritu

---

[31]Buckley, "The Aguayo Expedition," *op. cit.,* 55; Bolton, *Texas in the Middle Eighteenth Century,* map following Table of Contents.

[32]Alarcón to the Viceroy, September 28, 1718; Relación de los empleos, meritos y servicios de Don Martín de Alarcón, January 18, 1721. *San Francisco el Grande Archive,* IX, 1, 19.

[33]Olivares to the Viceroy, June 22, 1718. *San Francisco el Grande Archive,* VIII, 205-212. In the first page of the old mission record book it is stated that San Francisco Solano was moved first in 1703 to San Ildefonso and later to San

Santo, consequently he did not see him until May 1, after he arrived at the San Antonio River. Contrary to the statement made in the *Diary* of the expedition previously cited, however, Governor Alarcón gave possession of the site for the new Mission of San Antonio de Valero to Father Olivares in the name of His Majesty, on May 1, 1718. This is confirmed by Olivares' statement of the facts in his report to the viceroy and by an entry, in his own handwriting, made on that date, in the records of the old mission still preserved in San Fernando Cathedral. One reads here on that day, official possession was given to the venerable missionary, and that the new mission was founded by the express order of the Marquis of Valero.[34] Thus the Mission of San Antonio de Valero was formally founded five days before the Villa de Béjar.

With three Indians who accompanied him, and who were particularly devoted to him because he had raised them from childhood, Father Olivares soon succeeded in erecting a temporary *jacal*[35] in which to celebrate the Holy Sacrifice of the Mass. Here the old missionary and his companions lived and waited for the Indians to come. According to Father Olivares there were six missionaries here in June, but unfortunately he did not give the names and hence we are unable to tell who they were. The provisions were duly stored and the ground in the vicinity of the new mission was plowed and made ready for planting. While waiting, many new plows and other tools necessary for the cultivation of the soil were provided by the *Padres*. The Indians appear to have been slow in coming into the mission. This failure to congregate may have been the result of the long wait from the middle of May, 1717, when various chiefs visited Father Olivares at the Río Grande, to May, 1718, when he at last arrived, or it may have been due to the fact that in the summer most of these tribes went long distances in search of different wild fruits and prickly pears. But Father Olivares blamed the governor for their absence. "The Indian whom this gentleman brought as a guide from the Río Grande ran away after his arrival in San Antonio, impelled by the

José, from where it was moved to the new site on the San Antonio River. *Mission Records,* San Fernando Cathedral, San Antonio, Texas.

[34]*Libro en que se Assientan los Bautismos de los Indios de esta Misión de S. Ant. de Valero,* 11. Mission Records, San Fernando Cathedral, San Antonio, Texas. Olivares to the Viceroy, June 22, 1718. *San Francisco el Grande Archive,* VIII, 205-212.

[35]A structure made out of brush, mud, and straw. The walls are made by putting together slender poles and brush and filling the cracks with mud which the sun bakes soon after. The roof is made out of straw.

bad treatment accorded to him, and he went to the meeting of the nations.[36]
Fears may well be entertained, because he was an intelligent Indian who
had followers. When the Indians get together afterwards, they add more
[to their grievances] than they actually are, and they do not say this
or that Spaniard dealt with me unfairly, but declare the Spaniards maltreated me. In truth, this Indian had reasons [for running away]. When
asked if the Indians would come to the missions or not, he replied that
he could not say, but that he would talk to them about it and would try
to induce them to come. To this [statement] Governor Don Martín de
Alarcón replied that if they did not come, he would [go in search of them]
and put all of them to the sword. [This threat is] more than sufficient
reason why not an Indian stayed in this neighborhood and for leagues
around. Imagine, Your Excellency, such a method of congregating
Indians and settling the land!"[37]

In spite of the disappointments of Father Olivares and the undeniable
animosity that existed between him and the governor, by the end of the
winter of 1718, numerous Indians of the Jarame, Payaya, and Pamaya
tribes had come to the mission and with unprecedented willingness,
accepted the new order of things. When on January 12, 1719, Governor
Alarcón returned from East Texas to San Antonio, he found the number
of Indians now living at the mission was such that he thought it best
to proceed to the formal organization of the Indian pueblo that had
grown up around the mission center. With the consent and approval of
all the Indians congregated, he appointed a governor, selected *alcaldes*
and *regidores* from among the principal leaders, and formally organized
them into a self-governing community under the direction and care of
the missionaries. He then distributed presents among them, giving them
clothes, blankets, tobacco, and pieces of cloth of various colors. The Indians
had made considerable progress by this time under the patient and able
direction of the missionaries, and the governor was moved to remark how
edifying it was to watch the natives attend prayers at the ring of the bell.
He declared that they came quickly and with apparent eagerness, and
that they inspired great hope in the Spaniards by this excellent beginning
of order and good conduct.

---

[36]The Indians became suddenly hostile early in 1718, and a general uprising
was feared even before the expedition left the Río Grande. Olivares to Alarcón,
June 5, 1717. *A. G. I., Audiencia de México* (Dunn Transcripts).

[37]Olivares to the Viceroy, June 22, 1718. *San Francisco el Grande Archive*, VIII,
210.

Determined to make the new establishment self-supporting as soon as possible, the whole month of January was spent in the construction of irrigation ditches to facilitate the cultivation of the presidio and mission lands. Besides securing watermelon, pumpkin, chile, and melon seed to plant, vine and fig tree cuttings were brought from Coahuila, and an abundant crop of corn, beans, and grain was confidently expected from the early sowing. A new supply of cattle, sheep, and goats was obtained, and boars were brought to breed pigs. Everything looked promising. The mission and settlement seemed to be well supplied in the spring of 1719 with all they needed to insure their steady growth and development into a prosperous settlement.[38]

Hardships of the missions in East Texas. But let us turn to the presidio and missions in East Texas. By the spring of 1718, they had been reduced to dire distress and it seemed as if the reoccupation was to be ephemeral. Soon after Captain Domingo Ramón reached the country of the Tejas, he moved the temporary location of the presidio from the west side of the Neches to its permanent location, a quarter of a league from the Mission of San Francisco de los Tejas.[39] The country in the neighborhood appears to have been unhealthy, for shortly after the little band of soldiers and missionaries settled itself in its new surroundings, illness confined many of them to bed. Ramón, the leader, took ill immediately after his arrival, and by May, 1717, four of his best men had died with malaria. The garrison had been further reduced by seven soldiers who had either run away or overstayed their furloughs. It is true that most of these men had been replaced by those who had accompanied the expedition as supernumeraries, but the little group had dwindled perceptibly. The first winter was particularly severe, and with no relief having arrived throughout 1717, the condition of the disheartened garrison of Ramón had become almost desperate by the time Alarcón at last reached East Texas in November, 1718.[40]

Such was the condition of the garrison sent to protect the missionaries and help them congregate the Indians into pueblos. The missionaries

---

[38]Diary of the expedition of Martín de Alarcón, 42. (Vito Alessio Robles Transcript, since translated by Fritz Hoffman and published by the Quivira Society as Volume V of its publications.)

[39]For the location of this mission see Chapter II, pp. 57-58.

[40]Hidalgo to Fr. Mesquia, October 6, 1716; Domingo Ramón to the Viceroy, February 29, 1718, *Provincias Internas*, Vol. 181, pp. 215-218, 226-227; Ramón to Alarcón, May 21, 1717. *A. G. I., Audiencia de México*, 61-6-35 (Dunn Transcripts).

MISSION OF SAN ANTONIO DE VALERO, LATER KNOWN AS THE ALAMO, LOCATED AT SAN ANTONIO IN 1718

themselves had fared no better. Father Hidalgo, who had so enthusiastically taken up his work at San Francisco de los Tejas, fell ill in July,
1716. He was hardly out of bed when his companion, Father Castellanos,
fell a victim to the same malady. They both had severe chills and fever.
More distressing to these men than their physical ailments was the fact
that the Neche, Nacachau, and Nacono nations for which the mission
had been refounded had not been congregated, and Father Hidalgo sadly
admits that "it will be difficult" to do so. The members of these tribes
had been found to be idolatrous and nothing could be done to force them
to abandon their evil practices with the reduced number of soldiers now
under the command of Captain Ramón. By the fall of 1716, three months
after their arrival, the missionaries had not started the formal teaching
or *doctrina* to the natives, because of the long distances that separated
the various *ranchos*. It was necessary, furthermore, to destroy the temples
of their idols, a thing the *Padres* did not dare to undertake without a
more competent garrison to protect them. A year after their arrival, in
the fall of 1717, they were in actual need of clothing and food. "To the
lack of clothes and food," declares Father Espinosa, "has now come the
lack of the very essentials for the celebration of the Holy Sacrifice of
the Mass. Although we are, thanks to God, happy to suffer all privations,
this last must of necessity reach the ear of Your Excellency." A serious
epidemic broke out during the winter of 1717 and the spring of 1718,
and the labors of the missionaries were redoubled. They had to travel
long distances over icy and muddy roads and cross the swollen streams
to take the last Sacraments to the hundreds of scattered Indians, all
because it had not been possible to induce them to come and live in the
missions. More than a hundred Indians had been thus baptized and saved
from eternal loss of their souls, affirms one of the *Padres* in triumph. A
few natives were living in the missions, but the majority, and there were
thousands of them, had not formed pueblos as had been expected.[41]

The spirit of the missionaries in the midst of adverse conditions and
growing difficulties was really heroic. Almost with the same breath they
described their misfortunes, they gave expression to their imperishable
faith. "We are all in good health and very happy, glory be to God,
working in His vineyard, which although [it is] so cultivated, has

---

[41]Hidalgo to Fr. Pedro de Mesquia, October 6, 1716; Espinosa to the Viceroy,
February 28, 1718, Espinosa to Fr. Diez, February 28, 1718, Hidalgo to the
Viceroy, April 8, 1718, *Provincias Internas*, Vol. 181, pp. 215-218, 225, 228-
230, 231-232.

supplied us with more than one hundred baptisms *in articulo mortis*. With the epidemic, the knowledge of our Lord has spread and the party of Satan has suffered much." Touched by the superhuman efforts of his fellow-missionaries, Father Espinosa asked the Guardian at the College of Querétaro to thank each one personally for the splendid work they were doing among the Tejas, "for with the exception of myself," he declared with true Christian humility and charity, "all are exerting themselves to the limit of their strength . . . I hope our good Jesus will strengthen us in this enterprise." Although the *Padres* had waited patiently almost two years for all the Indians to follow the example of the few and to come and live in the missions, they still had implicit faith in the ultimate success of their efforts. "The Indians are very well pleased with us and give good reason to hope that they will congregate. The only thing lacking is a suitable leader who will sponsor the cause." Ramón was doing everything he could and was coöperative, declared Father Espinosa, but he lacked vigor in his efforts because he was expecting to be removed in the near future. He pointed out that from the faded color of the ink, it was easy to infer how badly he needed a piece of huisache and some copperas to make new ink. The best antidote for the prevailing sickness of this region, Father Espinosa had found, was cassia fistula and tamarind. He pleadingly asked the Guardian of the College to send a supply of these two remedies with the messenger.[42]

Attempts to relieve the missions.   Why had the supplies ordered to relieve the distress of the garrison and the missionaries been delayed? Before Alarcón left Mexico City in December, 1716, he had been provided with the sum of four thousand *pesos* to satisfy the requirements for the missions of East Texas. This sum was in excess of the amount ordered for the equipment and establishment of the mission of Father Olivares on the San Antonio River. But being slow and dilatory, and hoping, perhaps, to set out sooner than he did, the new governor did not decide to send a relief party to remedy the acute situation until November 17, 1717, at which time he began preparations to dispatch a group of fifteen soldiers and Father Fray Miguel Núñez de Haro of the College of Zacatecas, to conduct a train of supplies to East Texas.[43] It was December when the detachment finally left the Río Grande. Winter

---

[42]*Ibid.*

[43]He so declared in a testimony sent to the viceroy (Directorio que ha de observar . . . *Provincias Internas*, Vol. 183), but in the *Diary* it is stated that the party with the supplies did not leave until December. *Diary of Martín de Alarcón*, 5.

had set in and the cold northers and frequent rains made travel both slow and difficult. Painfully, the small group with its precious cargo made its way with untold hardships as far as the Navasoto River. Just beyond this stream they were forced to halt on January 28, on the banks of Lake Santa Anna, unable to proceed farther on account of the swollen streams. From here Father Núñez sent back eleven soldiers for help, while he remained with four companions to watch the cargo and to wait for an opportunity to proceed on his errand of mercy. They stayed there doggedly waiting for the rains to cease and the rivers to subside until March 30. At first, some of the Tejas Indians in the neighborhood gave them corn, then others gave them different kinds of edible roots on which they subsisted, but at last all the friendly Indians had to go away to sow their crops. In vain did Father Núñez try to get someone to swim the lake and the streams beyond to carry word to the distressed missionaries in East Texas. Finally in despair the four men hid the cargo in a thick wood, covered it with a tent, and gave letters to a Tejas Indian for the *Padres,* explaining to them where the supplies were hidden. After leaving instructions for the delivery of the message at the first opportunity, they started back to report to Alarcón.

The governor had tried on two previous occasions to send help to Father Núñez, but the men had been unable to cross the Colorado River. One time four men were sent and on another occasion thirteen, but all to no avail. It was not until April 21, that Father Núñez and the four soldiers met Alarcón, about six leagues west of the Medina River, and acquainted him with their misfortunes. The missionary did not need to tell him how much he had suffered. His appearance was a silent testimony of the hardships he had undergone. He was pale, sickly, and emaciated. A new cargo was ordered from the Río Grande and on June 27, the President of the Missions at San Juan Bautista set out with instructions to search for the cargo left at Lake Santa Anna, referred to from this time as *Laguna de las Cargas,* and if not found, to continue to East Texas with the new shipment of goods.[44]

By a strange coincidence, that same day, unaware of the action taken by the governor, but moved by the urgent appeals received from the missionaries, the viceroy called a meeting of the officers of the treasury to determine the action to be taken in view of the loss of the goods sent to East Texas. The *Junta de Hacienda* advised the viceroy to send immediately a new relief cargo and authorized the expenditure of another

[44]*Ibid.,* 13.

four thousand *pesos* for the purpose. In their opinion, a thorough investigation of the circumstance attendant upon the loss of the first cargo
should be instituted at once by the governor of Coahuila, and a full
report of the findings made to His Excellency. Agreeable to the recommendations of the *Junta,* the viceroy immediately issued the necessary
orders to put into execution the measure suggested.[45]

Two months later, on August 27, Alarcón learned of the success of
the President of the Mission on the Río Grande in finding the lost cargo.
Father Espinosa, Captain Ramón, and the President, accompanied by nine
soldiers, arrived in San Antonio that day and told how the party that set
out on June 27, had traveled as far as Lake Santa Anna, where it arrived
on July 21. Looking around for the supplies left there since March 30,
they found the cargo intact and in perfect condition, notwithstanding the
heavy rains and the fact that the Indians were on the warpath. Filled
with joy, the soldiers fired a salute and were very happy at what appeared
to them a miracle. Four days later, while waiting to reload the goods
found, Father Espinosa arrived in company with Captain Ramón. The
letters left with the Tejas Indian had been faithfully delivered to the
proper persons after overcoming many difficulties, and a group had lost
no time in going after the sorely needed supplies. Having sent these on
to the missions, the captain and Father Espinosa decided to proceed to
San Antonio, in company with nine soldiers, to welcome the new governor
and accompany him to the country of the Tejas.[46]

With the party now came the chiefs of twenty-three nations who had
been in revolt. They came to offer their allegiance, having been won over
peacefully by the bountiful gifts given to them by Captain Ramón in
the name of the governor. They gladly pledged loyalty and obedience to
the king of Spain and were warmly welcomed by Governor Alarcón. This
filled the missionaries with joy since "shortly before the natives were so
rebellious to our Holy Mother the Church and the royal crown because
the devil had led them astray."[47]

Alarcón's exploration of Espíritu Santo. With the mission and settlement on the San Antonio River well established and supplied, Alarcón
continued his journey to East Texas, where the relief supplies had at last
arrived as reported by Father Espinosa and Captain Ramón. There being

---

[45]Acuerdo de la Junta de Hacienda, June 27, 1718. *San Francisco el Grande
Archive,* VIII, 203-205.

[46]*Diary of Martín de Alarcón,* 5, 13, 14.

[47]*Ibid.,* 14.

no longer any rush, and having unsuccessfully attempted twice to explore the Bay of Espíritu Santo, the governor now decided, after consulting with the missionaries and officers, to proceed to the exploration of the bay first, and afterwards to go from there to the missions in East Texas. He concluded that traveling together the group would be safer.

Preparatory to leaving, on September 5, Alarcón officially appointed a prominent chief, generally called *El Cuilón,* governor and captain general of all the nations found on the road to the Tejas. In an impressive ceremony, the Indian governor was baptized and given the name of Juan Rodríguez. Alarcón then gave him his own *batón* as a symbol of his new office, and all those present appeared to be well pleased. This chief was highly respected and well liked by all the Indians. It will later be seen how hard he tried to congregate several nations to found the short-lived and almost forgotten Mission of San Francisco Xavier on the San Antonio River.[48]

According to Alarcón, he set out from San Antonio for the Bay of Espíritu Santo that same day (September 5, 1718). He had twenty-nine persons in his party and there were seventeen others with Father Espinosa, but as agreed, they all traveled together. In addition to Father Espinosa, there were two other religious in the group: Father Fray Joseph Guerra, of the College of Querétaro, and Father Fray Francisco de Celis, Chaplain and Chronicler of the expedition and missionary in charge of the Mission of Santísimo Nombre de Jesús del Peyote in Coahuila. They took along twenty-eight loaded mules, sixteen of these with goods and supplies for East Texas and twelve with provisions and gifts for the Indians of Espíritu Santo. There were two hundred and nineteen horses in all. Because of the numerous streams and heavy woods they had to cross, it took the expedition almost three weeks to reach the first destination.

Alarcón and a small group of soldiers, together with the three missionaries, left the main body of the expedition on the Guadalupe, about twenty leagues before reaching the coast and proceeded to explore the

---

[48]The mission was founded by Aguayo in 1722, two years after San José was established, but for various reasons the Indians failed to congregate and it was abandoned in 1726 before permanent quarters had been erected. *Mission Records,* San Antonio, Texas. From here on the account is based entirely on the heretofore unknown *Diary* of Alarcón. The statement of facts has been checked as near as possible with all other documents available on the subject and found to be correct. Allowances must be made only where Alarcón speaks of *his* accomplishments, which he naturally tends to over-emphasize.

bay. It seems they struck the coast at a point somewhere between the present town of Prague and Port O'Connor, in Calhoun County, judging from the rather detailed and vivid description of the locality. They arrived at the bay on September 23. "Having reached its shore, we followed the coast for about two leagues in a general southwestern direction to a point opposite a small island which seems to be about a quarter of a league long and a little more than a gun's shot distance in width. There are some cacti, mesquite trees, and oak groves upon it. On its shore is a very thick beam stranded in the sand and a little beyond this one there is another much smaller. Both are in the water but they can be seen at low tide. . . . There is about a quarter of a league from the mainland to the island. . . . The bay runs from north to southwest and forms a semicircle, closed by a small island that lies from east to south for a distance of about three leagues. Beyond this lies the high sea. Along the arm of the sea that runs to the north-northeast there is a passage to the sea.[49] The Bays of Todos los Santos and San Bernardo, formed by different lakes which we explored the day before, are navigable and in canoes one can go to the rich and level lands that border them."[50]

Alarcón's visit to East Texas. Alarcón and his little group now returned to the main body of the expedition. After sending a complete report of everything he had done and his observations on the Bay of Espíritu Santo, the governor at last departed for the Presidio de los Tejas, on September 28, 1718. A short distance beyond the point where he crossed the Guadalupe, about twenty leagues from the coast, he was met by a large delegation of Indians who came to ask him to establish a mission for them. There were six nations represented: Xanac, Emet, Too, Mayeye, Huyugan, and Cumercai. Presents were distributed among them and they were assured that a mission would be founded as soon as possible. The Indians said they had selected a place for it on a small hill near the river, where there was a little spring. The spot was marked by a cross and the expedition continued its march.

With bells ringing, the missionaries and Indians of the Mission of Nuestro Padre San Francisco de los Tejas welcomed the new governor with undisguised joy, on October 14, when he at last arrived in East

---

[49]This is evidently Pass Cavallo, off Port O'Connor. The description given here cannot fit any other section of the coast, because present Espíritu Santo Bay is the only locality where there are three small islands—one extremely small as described here—at such a close distance from shore.

[50]*Diary of Martín de Alarcón,* 21-22.

Texas, six months and five days after he left the Río Grande the first time. The Indians brought their humble offerings of corn and beans, wild nuts and skins and received from the governor clothes, beads, knives, and many trinkets of different kinds. Alarcón then called all the natives together and made a long talk to them. He explained the zeal of His Majesty in making them Christians and helping them live as civilized men. He urged them to congregate about the mission and form a pueblo. To all the Indians agreed, but said they could not congregate at this time because many of their people were out hunting buffalo. With those who were at the mission the governor reorganized the pueblo and now called it San Francisco Valero. He inspected the records of the mission and found that up to this time there had been twenty baptisms performed.

The next day he went to Concepción Mission on the Angelina River, where he was met by Captain Ramón, Father Espinosa, a number of soldiers, and the mission Indians drawn up in line to welcome him. Father Espinosa had left the main expedition four days before and hurried to Concepción Mission to arrange for the reception of the governor. A salute was fired, the bells rang merrily, and all the Indians cheered and presented their gifts. Then followed a curious ceremony. The Asinay Indians adopted the new governor as a member of their tribe and initiated him with great solemnity. That evening Alarcón rode his horse to a large straw hut which had been built specially for the occasion by the Indians. When he arrived, several chiefs came out to receive him. He was first helped down from his horse, then a chief took his sword and pistols, another took him up on his back, and a third held his feet. In this manner they carried him into the hut. At the door they gently washed his face and hands and dried them with a piece of cloth. With a chief on each side, their hands on his shoulders, Alarcón was escorted to a seat prepared for him. After he sat down, the principal chief gave him the peace pipe which he smoked and then passed to the others. After they had all smoked, several Indians rose and with expressive gestures made known to the governor their great pleasure at his coming, to which he replied by explaining to them the pious zeal of His Majesty, who had sent him and all the missionaries to help them and instruct them in our holy faith and defend them against their enemies.

The governor decided to make Concepción Mission his headquarters while in East Texas and asked the Indians to build a shelter for him, which they did promptly. This was a circular structure with walls made of branches and the roof covered with grass, in the shape of a rounded dome. To celebrate the completion of the house and to honor Alarcón the Indians held a native dance. At this celebration the initiation of the governor was completed. The Indians came decked in bright feathers and dressed in skins. They built a large fire in front of the hut, placed a special seat near it, and spread a number of buffalo skins on the ground in place of rugs. The principal chiefs then entered the house, where the governor was and adorned him carefully with white feathers plucked from the breasts of geese, which they placed on his head after their own fashion. They then painted a broad black stripe upon his forehead, which came down each side of his face to about the middle of his cheeks. He was now taken before the fire, made to sit down on the buffalo skins and to lean back on one of the chiefs who sat on the specially prepared seat and placed his hands upon the governor's shoulders. The ceremony had thus far been conducted in silence. Now they began to beat on a big drum made out of an old kettle partly filled with water and covered with a piece of wet rawhide. The beating of the drum was accompanied by the swish of rattles. The Indians all sat on the ground and arranged themselves in groups, the men, women, and children each seated separately. When the drum began to beat and the rattles to swish, they all began to sing in unison. Four additional large fires were now built and the leaders, who held lighted torches made out of bamboo, diligently went about the crowd to keep order. From time to time the din ceased and one chief or another would stand before the governor and make a long talk with forceful gestures. They declared they were glad the Spaniards had come back, that they considered the new governor one of their own, that he was their *Caddi,* or chief, that they would always be friendly to him and his people and that they wanted him to help and to protect the Indians against their enemies. Alarcón replied to these manifestations of attachment by declaring he would help and protect them, but they must swear allegiance to the king to whom they should always be grateful for all he had done, for it was he who had sent the soldiers to shield them, and the missionaries to instruct them in our holy religion. The ceremony lasted until three o'clock in the morning, according to the chronicler.

Alarcón remained at Concepción during the next thirteen days, making an inspection of the mission and planning the organization of a pueblo for the Indians that were now living there. A large delegation of natives from San José Mission arrived on October 18. They marched in perfect order and fired a salute which was answered by the garrison, but it was noted that the Indians had more guns than the soldiers. Father Espinosa

counted on this occasion as many as ninety-two.[51] A number of Cadodachos came with these Indians. They were all welcomed and feasted by
the governor. Next day three children were baptized with much ceremony, Alarcón serving as godfather. It was found that sixty-two baptisms
had been performed up to this time. In the Indian quarters of the mission
there were five houses. The influential Angelina was induced to come and
live in one of them and the pueblo was reorganized and named Concepción de Agreda.[52]

On October 29, the chief of the Biday nation, accompanied by a number
of women and children, came to pay his respects to the governor and to
ask for a mission in their *ranchería*. This was a numerous nation that
lived, according to the chief, about three days' journey to the south of
Concepción Mission and occupied the territory from there to the coast.[53]
The chief expressed a desire to visit the viceroy, but he changed his mind
before Alarcón was ready to return to San Antonio.

From Concepción Mission, Alarcón went to visit San José on October
31. He spent four days inspecting the mission, distributing presents, and
reorganizing the Indian pueblo, which he called San José de Ayamonte.
Accompanied by Father Espinosa and eight soldiers he resumed his march
to Nuestra Señora de Guadalupe on November 4, where he found the missionary in charge seriously ill. His assistant welcomed the governor by
ringing the bell, and a salute was fired by the Indians. He inspected the
mission and found that twenty-seven baptisms had been celebrated since
its establishment. He now named the pueblo Nuestra Señora de Guadalupe
de Albuquerque, and proceeded on his tour of inspection to Nuestra Señora
de los Dolores. Here he was given a warm reception on November 6 by
Fathers Espinosa and Margil, who came out to meet him with a large
group of Indians. The *Te Deum* was sung by the missionaries, and, upon
inspection of the records, it was found that twenty baptisms had been
performed. The Indian pueblo was named Nuestra Señora de los Dolores
de Benavente.

He then journeyed to San Miguel de los Adaes where he arrived on

---

[51]Espinosa, *Chrónica Seráphica de Todos los Colegios de Propaganda Fide*, 451.

[52]This was very appropriate, for these were the Indians to whom Mother María
de Agreda is said to have appeared almost a century before as the "woman in blue."

[53]This tribe occupied the region between the Hasinai Confederacy and the Gulf
of Mexico. They lived on both sides of the lower Trinity and were closely related
to the Arkokisas and Deadoses. They represent a somewhat higher degree of
advancement than the Karankawas, who lived west of them on the coast. Bolton,
De Mézières, I, 20.

November 10. The Indians welcomed him with much joy and the missionaries again sang the *Te Deum*. The pueblo was now named San Miguel de Cuellar and, upon examining the records, it was found that seventeen baptisms had been performed in this the farthest east of all the missions. Being so near to Natchitoches—only seven or eight leagues— the governor sent a sergeant and a soldier on November 11 to visit the French post and report on the condition of the fort. While the two men went on this mission to the Red River, Alarcón explored a large lake (Spanish Lake) which was about two leagues above Natchitoches and found it was navigable, that it was surrounded by rich and fertile lands, and that it was about fifty leagues in circumference. On the shores of this lake lived the Cadodachos.[54]

The soldiers sent to Natchitoches returned November 12, and reported that the French had a well built stockade and houses made out of timber, roofed with the bark of trees. The garrison consisted of twenty men, most of them young boys. The Spaniards learned that there were two Frenchmen in the country of the Cadodachos. Governor Alarcón conceived the idea of driving the French out of Natchitoches, thinking his force sufficient to accomplish his purpose, but the missionaries warned him that such an act might endanger the peace between the crowns. Alarcón learned that the French were in the habit of buying young Indian boys and girls to serve as slaves, from the Cadodachos, giving them in exchange guns, powder, and ammunition, which they prized highly. As a result of this infamous trade, declared Alarcón, these Indians were constantly at war with their neighbors in order to capture prisoners to sell into slavery. It was also learned from the Indians that the French had a mine about two hundred leagues to the north, near the point where the Missouri River entered the Mississippi. They offered to take him there if he wanted to visit it.[55]

---

[54]This was one of the chief tribes of the Caddo group, which was a division of the great Caddoan linguistic stock. They lived on both sides of the Red River above Natchitoches, and were similar in culture to the Hasinai, their languages being much alike. Bolton, *op. cit.*, I, 21-22.

[55]In connection with this visit it may be noted that Ramón had visited Natchitoches early in 1718. On February 28, he reported to the viceroy that he had gone to Natchitoches to observe personally conditions there. He found the garrison consisted of twenty-five men; that a guard was kept night and day; that they had a good stockade and plenty of powder and balls. About thirty persons were living at this place, and the commander informed him he was expecting fifty men who were on the way with the inspector of frontier posts, twenty-five of these for Natchitoches and twenty-five for the new post to be established among the

To celebrate the completion of his journey a Solemn High Mass was sung by the missionaries on November 21, in honor of our Lady, the Virgin Most Holy. A large number of Indians attended this ceremony which marked the close of Alarcón's mission to East Texas. While there he had a number of conferences with the missionaries to determine the best measures to be recommended to the viceroy for the extension of missionary work and the establishment of a firmer hold on Texas. He then began to make preparations for his return to the San Antonio River but before he reached the Villa de Béjar he stopped at the old site of the first mission of 1690 and found there a bell that weighed six *arrobas* (about one hundred fifty pounds). He decided to take this to the Mission of San Antonio de Valero.[56]

Disappointment of missionaries.   The missionaries were frankly disappointed in the new governor and the momentary joy caused by his belated arrival was soon dissipated. He had failed to bring the families recommended by the viceroy; he had not recruited the fifty additional soldiers and, as a consequence, he had been unable to increase the number of guards at each mission as instructed and to reënforce the garrison of the Presidio de los Tejas; very few of the soldiers were married and fewer still brought their families; he had done nothing to help the missionaries congregate the Indians other than distribute gifts with little discretion, and he had by his overbearing nature and boastful spirit antagonized many Indians and aroused the fears of the French, who now began to think seriously of asserting their claim to the country of the Tejas. The missionaries realized better than anyone else the influence which the French had upon the natives. The easy morals and good-natured comradeship of the French with the Indians made them much more popular than the Spaniards. "I warn Your Excellency that the French have a complete hold upon the Indians and have subjected them entirely to their will by means of gifts and flattery," declares Father Olivares. The Indians had been won over by the generous manner affected

Cadodachos. Domingo Ramón to the Viceroy, February 28, 1718, *Provincias Internas,* Vol. 181, 226-227.

[56]Diary of Martín de Alarcón, 15-40. It is interesting to note how the bell of the first mission was brought to San Antonio. Here are some additional facts about the mission bells of San Francisco de los Tejas and Santísimo Nombre de María. Ramón reported he had found three bells of good quality and size and an anvil that weighed over a hundred pounds, where the old missions of 1690-93 had stood. He asked the viceroy for instructions as to their disposition. Ramón to the Viceroy, February 28, 1718, *Provincias Internas,* Vol. 181, 226-227.

by these neighbors and by the fact that they literally "take the shirts off to give them to the Indians," the *Padres* asserted. The attention of the viceroy was called to the dangers resulting from an insufficient force, now that the French were rapidly supplying the natives with guns in addition to their arrows.[57]

Alarcón seems to have been interested to a considerable extent in making the most out of his new position. Although sincere, perhaps, in his desire to extend the dominions of the king, he was more interested in his own political advancement and for this reason wished to increase the military contingent of the province. After his return to San Antonio, the governor in his report to the viceroy told all he had done and what was needed to carry out the full intent of his instructions, and asked for one hundred and seventy-five additional soldiers. The repeated complaints of the missionaries, who vehemently clamored against him as they saw their work menaced by his indiscretions, especially by his attitude towards the French, caused the viceroy and his advisors to doubt the sincerity of Alarcón's petition for more soldiers and supplies. The refusal to grant his request brought about the governor's resignation. He realized only too well that he had lost the confidence of the viceroy. His decision to retire from the governorship was promptly accepted early in 1719, but he continued in office until December.[58]

If the results of this new attempt to extend the missionary activity of the Franciscans and to strengthen Spain's uncertain hold on the vast territory from the Río Grande to the Red River are summarized it will be found that little or nothing was accomplished. The only tangible result for this very expensive expedition was the establishment of a mission and a small presidio on the San Antonio River. But this weak post was shortly to prove its worth. Had it not been for its establishment, the Spaniards might have been forced to continue in their precipitate retreat all the way to the Río Grande in the fall of 1719, when the French surprise attack on San Miguel de los Adaes took place. The affront by the

---

[57]Father Olivares to the Viceroy, June 22, 1718. *Provincias Internas,* Vol. 181, p. 251.

[58]Alarcón to the King, November 3, 1721. *San Francisco el Grande Archive,* IX, 21-25. He experienced considerable trouble collecting part of his salary and expense account. The king ordered the viceroy to settle with him on October 27, 1722, but it was not until April 9, 1723, that the viceroy finally gave orders to pay him. The facts summarized in this paragraph are found in the following documents: Alarcón to the Viceroy, September 28, 1718; November 7, 1718; Olivares to the Viceroy, June 22, 1718; Royal Cédula, October 27, 1722. *San Francisco el Grande Archive,* Volumes VIII and IX.

French to the power of the king was to be the occasion for a much more formidable expedition and a much better planned attempt to reëstablish the title of Spain to the territory on a solid basis and to extend the missionary endeavors of the devoted *Padres* among the numerous tribes that inhabited the land, many of whom had become truly attached to the Spaniards and sincerely desired to be Christianized. Each successive effort carried a knowledge of the Gospel to new tribes and brought the natives more and more under the civilizing influence of the missionaries.

CHAPTER IV

The Aguayo Expedition and the Founding of San José Mission, 1719-1722

Conditions in Texas in 1719. Conditions in Texas were rapidly approaching a crisis in the spring of 1719. The failure of Alarcón to strengthen the hold of Spain upon the province and to expand the missionary activities of the Franciscans was to prove a serious blow to Spanish interests. In spite of the earnest efforts of Spanish officials to widen the sphere of influence among the numerous tribes, to increase the military force, and to encourage civil settlers to establish themselves in the new land, the missions were no better off at the close of 1718 than they had been when founded two years before. The military garrison of the Presidio of los Tejas was weaker, the number of families had remained stationary, and the Indians still found one excuse after another to postpone their being congregated at the missions.[1] The garrison of the presidio had, in fact, become the laughing stock of not only the French but of the Indians themselves. There were less than twenty-five soldiers and most of them were mere boys, poorly clad, and without mounts or arms.[2] The new mission on the San Antonio had a few more Indians and promised to be a greater success, but the number of soldiers was insufficient to afford it adequate protection against the Apaches, which were beginning to appear in its vicinity, and Governor Alarcón had neglected to bring the thirty families which the viceroy had recommended.

The missionaries had clearly foreseen the unavoidable failure of their efforts unless the government gave them more material and intelligent support. As early as May, 1718, they had begun to give serious attention to the advisability of presenting their case to the viceroy. Before Alarcón arrived in East Texas, when they were reduced to the direst need and even the essentials for the celebration of the Holy Sacrifice of the Mass had been exhausted, they held a meeting, at the suggestion of Father Margil, to discuss their plight. Six religious attended this meeting held at the Mission of Dolores. After due deliberation, it was decided to send two representatives to Mexico, one from each college, to appeal per-

---

[1] Espinosa, *Chrónica Seráphica,* 443-445.

[2] Letter of Fathers Espinosa and Margil to the Viceroy, July 2, 1719. Buckley, "The Aguayo Expedition," *Southwestern Historical Quarterly,* XV, 7.

sonally to the viceroy and acquaint him with the true situation that faced the *Padres* in Texas. President Espinosa was chosen to represent the Querétaran friars and Father Matías Sáenz de San Antonio to represent those of Zacatecas. Setting out immediately, they hurried to San Antonio where they met Governor Alarcón in August, 1718. Father Espinosa now decided it would be best for him to accompany the new governor on his tour of inspection of the missions. He asked Father Sáenz de San Antonio, therefore, to hasten on to Mexico City, where he was to represent the interests of the two colleges.

It was November before the emissary arrived in Mexico City. He remonstrated to the viceroy that the Province of the Tejas was in imminent danger of being lost; that the French were penetrating the country of the Cadodachos where they had already established a post;[3] that the Mississippi was being rapidly settled in force; and that "it was to be feared on good grounds that they would attach the Tejas Indians to their side, because they fondled them much, giving them firearms in exchange for horses."[4] He pointed out that the establishment of civil settlements in the vicinity of the missions to set an example to the natives and to increase the number of Spaniards was of the utmost importance, and that more adequate supplies, until crops could be successfully raised, were also essential. But with the characteristic inability to seize an opportunity and act promptly, the viceroy confined himself to the issuance of orders to seek new families to be sent to form villas and to collect the alms set aside by the king for missionaries. No action was taken, however, to put these directions into effect, and the good friar finally departed from Mexico City, in February, 1718, disgusted and disappointed at the failure of officials to realize the full significance of his pious mission.[5]

French opposed to Spanish settlement. The habitual procrastination and slow measures adopted by the viceregal government were soon to disclose how timely the warnings of the missionaries were and how their fears of French designs were not mere figments of the imagination. Contrary to the general opinion that the French in Louisiana were primarily interested in trade and that they saw the establishment of mis-

---

[3]This is an evident exaggeration, as La Harpe did not establish a post there until the spring of 1719. Margry, *op. cit.*, VI, 260-261. Since 1716, however, there had been two or three traders living among the Cadodachos.

[4]Espinosa, *Chrónica,* 450.

[5]*Ibid.,* 450.

sions and a presidio by the Spanish in the Province of the Tejas with gratification, the truth is that, regardless of St. Denis' attitude, the representatives of the French crown were opposed from the beginning to the Spanish settlement of Texas. They resented it as an encroachment upon territory to which France had acquired a legal claim by the efforts of La Salle. St. Denis, it is curious to observe in this respect, had been careful to take formal possession of the country of the Asinais in 1714, while on his way to the Río Grande, even as La Salle had done almost thirty years before.[6] A well posted authority, in discussing St. Denis' expedition to Mexico (1713-1715), voices his disappointment with its outcome, saying, "He had to submit to conduct to the Asinais missionaries and troops which were being sent to establish a post . . . Thus not only were all hopes founded on St. Denis' expedition destroyed, but the Spaniards, disturbed by the first attempt, put themselves in position to forbid us access to this territory."[7] Governor Cadillac, who dispatched St. Denis on the expedition, was of the same opinion and not only saw an obstacle to future expansion in the newly established missions but he feared the possible descent of the Spaniards to the Mississippi by way of the Red River. It was because of this fear that he ordered a fort to be erected among the Natchitoches.[8] It is further to be remembered that St. Denis wrote Cadillac from Mexico City in December, 1715, urging him to take possession of the Bay of San Bernardo immediately, before the Spaniards did. Referring to this incident, the governor declared in a report: "The Spaniards are going to occupy it in order to exclude us, and Sieur Saint Denis' letter makes known their alarm, to which Sieur Saint Denis has contributed much by not having followed his instructions." But he goes farther to state that he "will give orders to Sieur Saint Denis to engage all the savages on Red River to oppose the establishment of the Spaniards."[9] The French, it is evident, did not regard the occupation with favor and were willing to tolerate it only until an opportunity offered to dislodge the Spaniards. In the meantime, they were actively enlisting the help of the Indians to discourage their permanent stay.

The loud threats made by Alarcón that he would drive the French out of Natchitoches and his much talked of plans to occupy the country of

---

[6]Margry, *op. cit.*, VI, 193.

[7]Heinrich, *La Louisiane sous la Compagnie des Indes, 1717-1731*, lxv.

[8]Margry, *op. cit.*, V, 535.

[9]*Ibid.*, VI, 198-199.

MISSION OF SAN JOSÉ Y SAN MIGUEL DE AGUAYO, FOUNDED BY THE VENERABLE PADRE FRAY ANTONIO MARGIL DE JESÚS IN 1720

the Cadodachos, only served to arouse the apprehension of the French to a high pitch. As a result, La Harpe made all haste to forestall the contemplated advance of the Spaniards and established a post among the Nassonites early in 1719. Bienville, who was now governor of Louisiana, ordered St. Denis to instigate the Indians secretly to refuse help in the way of maintenance to the Spaniards and to intercept any aid coming to the Asinais.[10] In view of these instructions the alleged meeting of the Indian nations in the spring of 1718, to which both Alarcón and Father Olivares refer in their communications to the viceroy, take on added significance. The repeated warnings of the missionaries that the French were diligently working to turn the natives against the Spaniards become, when these facts are considered, more than a clever ruse to frighten Spanish officials into taking action to support their earnest endeavors to win the friendship of the Indians through their pious work of conversion and civilization. It is of interest to note in this connection that the French felt confidently sure of their hold upon the Indians and their ability to drive the Spaniards out at any time. Speaking of the establishment in East Texas, Governor Cadillac assured his home government that it would remain only as long as the French wished, "for it will be easy to destroy or appropriate it."[11]

Before the middle of 1718, the French were already seriously contemplating the occupation of the Bay of Espíritu Santo, considered the key to the Province of Texas. On February 20, and again on April 25, the viceroy wrote to the king to inform him of the designs on this coveted bay. In his first communication he stated that he had been warned by Governor Salinas Varona of Pensacola, that the French in Louisiana had received orders from the Duke of Orleans, now Regent of France, to take possession of a port on the Mexican Gulf "if necessary by force of arms." On receipt of this disquieting information, the viceroy had convoked a general council of war to which Governor Salinas Varona was invited out of regard for his varied experience and his knowledge of the Gulf Coast. The council discussed at length the menace that threatened the sovereignty of the king. It was finally decided that before a course of action looking to the occupation of the Bay of Espíritu Santo could be adopted, it would be best to send Salinas Varona to explore the Bays of Espíritu Santo and San Bernardo. The council ordered that two

[10]*Ibid.*, VI, 224-225.
[11]*Ibid.*, 198-199.

ships be made ready without delay for that purpose.[12] The careful and detailed instructions, for the exploration of the first of these bays given to Alarcón on March 11, 1718, are significant when considered in the light of this consultation.[13]

In the second letter of April 25, the viceroy informed the king that the governor of Pensacola, pursuant to his orders, had sent Captain Juan Manuel Roldán, who spoke and understood French, to Mobile to observe secretly the purpose which had brought three armed vessels to that port. This officer had found out that a new company had been organized in France to foster and promote trade in the Indies; that the three vessels had brought many soldiers and munitions of war for the colony of Louisiana; and that two other vessels were expected with settlers. All of this information pointed clearly to the ulterior designs of the French upon New Spain, the viceroy noted in transmitting this information, together with another letter from the commander of Veracruz, on the same subject.[14] These letters were submitted by the king to the Council of the Indies on March 27, 1719, with a request that this body make such recommendations as it might deem proper.

Attack on Pensacola. It is not strange, in view of the antecedents just summarized, that when Governor Bienville received word of the declaration of war on Spain, in April, 1719, he should lose no time in preparing to attack the Spaniards both at Pensacola and Los Adaes and in trying to gain possession of the Bay of Espíritu Santo. War between Spain and France had broken out on January 9, 1719, as a result of Spain's occupation of Sardinia and the invasion of Sicily.[15] Bienville was immediately ordered by the Company of the Occident, to which Louisiana had now been granted, to attack Pensacola without delay.[16] But Spain seems to have neglected to inform the viceroy of Mexico of the outbreak of hostilities. He was not to learn of the situation for some time. The first intimation of hostilities which the Spaniards had was the unexpected

---

[12]Satisfacción a la orden de V. M. . . . . *A. G. I., Audiencia de México*, 61-6-35.

[13]Directorio que ha de observar, y ordenes que ha de Practicar el Sargento Mayor Don Martín de Alarcón. *Provincias Internas*, Vol. 183; a copy also in *San Francisco el Grande Archive*, VIII, 217-225. The copy in *Historia*, XXVII, is defective and undependable.

[14]Satisfaciendo á la orden de V. M. con q se sirvio Remitir tres Cartas y vn testo. del Virrey de Na. Espa. y Corregor. de la Veracruz. *A. G. I., Audiencia de México*, 61-6-35.

[15]Hassall, *The Balance of Power, 1715-1789*. Ch. II.

[16]Heinrich, *La Louisiane sous la Compagnie des Indes, 1719-1731*, p. 55.

attack of Pensacola on May 14. The capture of this fort came as a distinct surprise, but the history of its two subsequent recaptures by Spanish and French forces alternately has no bearing on our narrative. Our chief concern is with the attack on Los Adaes.

Attack on East Texas missions.   About a month after the capture of Pensacola, some time between June 16 and June 22, M. Blondel, commander of the post at Natchitoches, suddenly appeared at the Mission of San Miguel de los Adaes. There was a flurry and a scurry of chickens, as the little French band of seven men triumphantly took the two solitary occupants, a lay brother and a ragged soldier, prisoners. In the confusion caused by the unexpected resistance of the chickens, who lustily flapped their wings in protest, the lay brother escaped while the soldiers attended the commander, who had been thrown off his horse by the commotion created. The *Padre* in charge of the mission was absent at the time of the attack, having gone on a pious errand to Mission Dolores with the other soldier, and thus he was saved the mortification of being captured by the enemy.[17] It has been asserted that the force under Blondel was composed of soldiers and Indians, but all contemporary accounts agree that no Indians took part in the attack.[18] Satisfied with the success of the expedition, Blondel took all the sacred vessels, ornaments, and fixtures of the mission and leisurely retired to Natchitoches.

In the meantime the lay brother made his way to Nuestra Señora de los Dolores as fast as he could travel, arriving there on June 22. It seems the good brother had time to talk to the French soldiers before he escaped. He learned from them of the capture of Pensacola, the declaration of war, and the intention of the French to drive the Spaniards out of Texas. He was told that one hundred soldiers were on the way from Mobile, and that the only hope for the Spaniards was to retreat as rapidly as possible to the Río Grande. Father Margil was surprised to hear all this, but although he was impressed he did not give credence to the entire story. With only two soldiers to defend the mission and a few faithful Indians, however, he realized that it would be best to abandon the place and take refuge at Mission Concepción, where there was a larger miltary force. He quickly buried the tools and all the heavier articles, packed the ornaments and sacred vessels, and hurried to Concepción.

---

[17]Arricivita, *Chrónica*, 100.

[18]Espinosa, *Chrónica*, 451; Letter of Margil and Espinosa, July 2, 1719, in Buckley, *op. cit., Southwestern Historical Quarterly*, XV, 15.

Retreat from East Texas.   But news of the French attack had preceded him. By the time he reached his goal, panic had seized the little garrison. The soldiers under Captain Domingo Ramón were ready to retreat. Through the efforts of the missionaries, a hurried consultation was held. The officers, the priests, and some of the families discussed the situation. The majority of the missionaries emphatically were for staying a while longer to ascertain the real force of the enemy and their designs. But the women—there were eight—were for immediate abandonment. They were willing to risk the perils of the wilderness and the danger from hostile Indians, if allowed to go to the San Antonio River with two soldiers as an escort. In vain did the *Padres* point out there was no immediate danger and that the French were more than one hundred leagues away. Fear being unreasonable, panic spread with the unfounded rumors of French activity; and the families, soldiers, and some of the religious to whom the spirit of fear had been communicated, decided to withdraw without further delay as far as San Francisco Mission on the Neches.[19]

That the labor of the missionaries had not been entirely in vain is brought out in the critical situation that now faced them. The Indians, who had become sincerely attached to the missionaries, earnestly entreated that they be not left alone at the mercy of the French. They offered to put out scouts to warn the Spaniards of the first approach of the enemy, and agreed to help them in case of a fight. Father Espinosa assured them that the Spaniards were not abandoning their country, but were merely withdrawing temporarily and would return with reënforcements soon. In order to quiet them, he stayed at Concepción for a few days, but hearing that Ramón and his group were about to retreat farther, he decided to go to San Francisco and try to use his influence to persuade them to remain. The Indians now became truly apprehensive, and although the *Padre* told them he was leaving some of the furnishings of the mission in their care to convince them of his return, they, too, decided to follow the missionary to San Francisco de los Tejas. They were determined that the Spaniards should not withdraw.

After holding a new consultation at the camp on the east bank of the Neches River, it was decided that everybody, with the exception of

---

[19]The details of the retreat are based on two accounts, one by Fathers Espinosa and Margil, given in their letter of July 2, 1719. (Buckley, "The Aguayo Expedition," *Quarterly* XV, 11-14) the other found in Espinosa's *Chrónica,* 453-455. Arricivita, in his *Chrónica,* gives a briefer account on page 100.

Fathers Margil and Espinosa, might retreat to the farthest ranches of the Tejas on the Trinity River, where they were to wait for reënforcements. In the meantime the two presidents were to return to Concepción and stay there to appease the Indians. Captain Ramón hesitated to carry out this decision for fear of punishment. But the two missionaries gave him a written statement to relieve him of all responsibility, in which they declared they were staying voluntarily.

While the disheartened band made its way to the Trinity River, Fathers Margil and Espinosa bravely retraced their steps to the now deserted Mission Concepción. Here they remained hoping against hope for reënforcements to arrive. On July 2, they dispatched a letter to the viceroy from the Angelina River, giving the details of the attack on Mission San Miguel and of the measures adopted in view of the contingency. This account written at the time of the events described is an invaluable source for this truly pathetic episode. The missionaries were too human not to take this opportunity to tell the viceroy they had previously warned him. They pointed out that their former petitions, warning the officials of the danger from the French, had been disregarded; that their request for fifty men to settle the Cadodachos had been ignored; that their present plight was the direct result of Alarcón's failure to carry out his instructions; and that while the French had steadily advanced during the last three years the Spaniards had made no progress because of the failure of the government to support the missionaries properly in their labors. The crops had given greater promise this year than any other, but were now to be left to the ravages of the disappointed Indians. The letter closed with a passionate appeal that the viceroy "remembering the blood of the Son of God, shed for these poor gentiles, will moisten his pen in it to write with his own hand what may be best for the good of their souls, the service of the King and Lord, and the consolation of these afflicted missionaries."[20] They also sent an urgent call for help to the captains of the presidios of Béjar and Río Grande and to the Governor of Coahuila, stating that if reënforcements were sent, the missionaries would return to their missions and the soldiers would repair to the presidio. Hearing that Captain Ramón and the rest of the party, now encamped near the Trinity, were about to retreat farther, the two *Padres* at Concepción were forced to follow them regretfully.

By the middle of July the two presidents had joined the rest of the fugitives. The party doggedly remained in camp on the Trinity until

[20]Quoted by Buckley, *op. cit.*, XV, 13.

almost the end of September. But seeing that no help came, the little band of disappointed settlers, soldiers and missionaries was forced to retire to the new establishment on the San Antonio River. It is evident that the retreat, then, was not precipitate, for in spite of the natural fear they harbored, they waited more than three months on the limits of the Tejas country. This was surely a reasonable time. The missionaries tried in vain to dispel the fears entertained by the soldiers and the families and to appease the Indians. Only when they became convinced that no help was forthcoming, were they willing to abandon at last, with deep regret, the land of their beloved Tejas Indians. Conclusive evidence of the slow retreat from Concepción Mission to the Trinity River is afforded by the corporal who was sent by La Harpe to report on what had happened at Los Adaes. Corporal Saint François was ordered by La Harpe on June 20 to observe the movements of the Spaniards and to report on what had actually taken place at San Miguel Mission. Saint François went from the Nassonites to the Amediche Indians, a tribe that has been identified with the Nabedache, for whom the Mission of San Francisco was founded. Here he stayed until almost the end of July, returning to the post among the Nassonites, August 1. He informed La Harpe that Blondel had driven the missionaries out of Los Adaes and that all the Spaniards had retired for fear of the French soldiers and their savage allies first to the Neches and later to the west bank of the Trinity River, where they had camped and were staying at the time of his departure.[21]

The camp on the Trinity must have been abandoned early in October. Winter was approaching, no news of help had been received, and the limited supplies were practically exhausted by this time. "We suffered many hardships," declared Father Espinosa, "for although we had meat, we lacked salt altogether, and a small portion of flour which we had left had so many husks and was of such poor quality, that only in a place such as we were, could we stand it."[22] There was nothing to do but try to reach the settlement on the San Antonio River before the northers blew and the winter rains made the roads and the streams impassable. By December, the party was already in the Villa de Béjar and the Mission of San Antonio de Valero.[23] Here they were to wait anxiously for the arrival of reënforcements and supplies to return to East Texas.

---

[21]Margry, *op. cit.*, VI, 280.

[22]Espinosa, *Chrónica*, 454.

[23]Father Margil wrote the Marquis of Aguayo on December 26, 1719, from San Antonio de Valero. Margil to Aguayo, December 26, 1719, in Testimonio de la possn. y missn. de Sn. Joseph. *A. G. I., Audiencia de Guadalajara*, 67-3-11.

The patient work of three years had been wiped out. The unexpected appearance of M. Blondel and seven French soldiers had caused the Spanish settlements among the Tejas Indians to collapse as if struck by lightning. The oft-repeated warnings of the missionaries had at last become a sad reality. Not a single man had remained from San Antonio to Red River to defend Spain's title to this vast territory. The relatively large sums spent in the enterprise and the great sacrifices of the missionaries had been of little or no avail in bringing this territory under the power of the king or the civilizing influence of the sons of Saint Francis. But neither Spain nor the missionaries had any intention of definitely abandoning Texas. This bold affront to Spanish honor and dignity, this telling blow to the patient efforts to Christianize the Indians and bring them into the fold of the Church was to spur the viceregal government to a more vigorous effort, and to steel the determination of the *Padres* to spread the Gospel among the thousands of unredeemed souls that roamed the wilderness, at the cost of their lives if necessary.

The King's plan to reënforce Texas. While still ignorant of the attack on the Mission of San Miguel and the subsequent abandonment of the Province of the Tejas, the viceroy received, on May 29, 1719, an interesting *cédula* which had been issued almost a year before on June 11, 1718. From the instructions given in this instrument concerning Texas, one is tempted to believe that the king and the Council of the Indies were gifted with prophetic insight, for the *cédula* covered every phase of the emergency which now faced the viceroy, with surprising accuracy. After commanding the viceroy to issue strict orders immediately to all governors of ports against the admission of French vessels and to all commanders of presidios on the frontier against permitting expeditions from Mobile to enter New Spain on whatever pretext, the king declared that it was his royal will that the viceroy "dedicate himself with the greatest application and care to foment and maintain the missions established in the Province of the Tejas. Placing a convenient guard of soldiers in each one of them, you will take steps to see that the mission on the San Antonio River is provided with as many missionaries as necessary, this being the nearest to the Bay of San Bernardo. On this bay you will cause a fort to be erected on the same spot where M. de la Salle established his in the past." In order to save both time and expense, the viceroy was to send all the materials and supplies necessary for the erection of the fort and the establishment of a settlement by water from Veracruz, using two ships for this purpose.

The measures suggested were considered of utmost importance to the service of the king and the safety of his dominions in America and were to be put into execution without delay. To increase the military guard of the new missions, agreeable to the wishes of the king, the viceroy was empowered to recruit whatever number of soldiers he deemed necessary, taking for this purpose six, eight, or ten men from such presidios in the interior as in his judgment could spare them. In order that more missionaries be sent to care for the numerous tribes that were being congregated, he was to follow the same practice and take them from such missions as were ready to be turned over to seculars. Great care was to be exercised in the appointment of a governor for the province and in selecting the commander for the new post to be established on the Bay of Espíritu Santo. These men were to be cautioned, particularly, not to allow the French from Louisiana to secure horses in the Province of Texas. Should any attempt be made to penetrate the province, the leader was to be arrested and sent to Acapulco and all persons accompanying him were to be sent to work in the mines, as had been done in the past with Englishmen.[24]

Plans for a new expedition. The Marquis of Valero was already contemplating the sending of a new expedition to Texas. He had not as yet learned, however, how urgent it was for him to take immediate action as ordered by the king. Almost three months were to elapse before he heard of the abandonment of the greater part of the province as a result of the attack of Blondel on the Mission of San Miguel. When the order of June 11, 1718, arrived he had not yet heard of the declaration of war by France on Spain. The king did not send him official notice of the outbreak of hostilities until January 30, and the *cédula,* instructing him to put all forts and ports on a war footing to prevent a surprise by the enemy, did not arrive in Mexico until July 13, 1719.[25] By that time the viceroy was straining every nerve to dispatch a maritime expedition to recapture Pensacola. But in spite of the many weighty problems that made a demand on his time, he was giving due consideration to the

---

[24]Royal *Cédula,* June 11, 1718. *Historia,* Vol. 289. The *Cédula* was received in Mexico on May 29, 1719.

[25]Royal *Cédula* of January 30, 1719. *Historia,* Vol. 298.

Texas question, unaware of the seriousness of the situation. The messenger despatched by Fathers Margil and Espinosa on July 2, 1719, finally arrived in Mexico early in August. This afforded the viceroy the first detailed information of what had happened and caused him to hurry the preparations for a new expedition which he now realized was imperative and of paramount importance.

Appointment of Aguayo.   Orders were at once issued to raise as large a force as possible in the Nuevo Reyno de León, Parral, and Saltillo. To take charge of recruiting the men and equipping them with all haste, the viceroy appointed the Marquis of San Miguel de Aguayo, who was residing in Coahuila at this time. The choice proved a happy one. The full name of the Marquis was Joseph Azlor Virto de Vera. Before coming to America in 1712, he had seen service in Spain, where he had equipped at his own expense fifty men during the campaign of 1704. The next year he saw service in the Kingdom of Navarre with a group of mounted men, similarly recruited and equipped at his expense. After his arrival in Coahuila, where he made his residence in the Hacienda de Patos, he had taken an active part in the defense of the frontier against the Indians until the time he was called to take charge of the force being equipped to recover the lost Province of Texas. He came from a distinguished family who had rendered loyal service to the king from time immemorial, both in Spain and in America. His grandfather, Don Martín de Azlor, who was Maestro de Campo, died at the siege of Barcelona in 1656. His brother, the Count of Guara, who had been field marshal and commander on the frontier of Aragon, was killed in action in the year 1705. On the side of his wife, her forefathers had seen service in the army in Catalonia and in Flanders, coming later to America where his wife's fourth grandfather had been one of the conquerors of New Spain. His family owned a vast estate, which included almost half of Coahuila.[26]

Previous to his appointment in 1719, he had shown interest in Texas as early as 1715, when he wrote to the viceroy urging that Joseph Urrutia be commissioned to discover and conquer the mythical kingdom of La Gran Quivira. Urrutia, as it will be remembered, had been in Texas with De León and Terán, and when the missions were abandoned in 1693, he was one of those who remained for several years among the Indians.

---

[26]Satisfacción a una real orden del rey Nuestro Señor. *A. G. I., Audiencia de Guadalajara,* 67-1-37.

Father Margil had urged the advisability of sending Urrutia with Domingo Ramón on the expedition of 1716 because of his knowledge of the customs and habits of the Tejas Indians and their language, but this petition was refused because Urrutia was at that time employed as Protector of the Indians in Nuevo León. La Gran Quivira was thought to be located somewhere near the country of the Tejas and Aguayo believed that Urrutia was the man best suited to discover it because of his intimacy with these Indians. This proposal was unfavorably considered by the *Fiscal* who thought it impractical, but when presented to the *Junta de Guerra* on July 13, 1715, it was thought of sufficient importance to ask Aguayo and Urrutia for more details concerning the projected expedition. The Marquis of Aguayo made a report on the nature and character of La Gran Quivira on November 2, 1715, based on such information as he had acquired from Urrutia, the Tejas Indians, and others who had been to their country. But since Urrutia, who had a first-hand acquaintance with the country, failed to report, the whole matter was dropped on January 11, 1716, with a recommendation that Urrutia be again requested to report.[27]

Pursuant to the orders of the viceroy, Aguayo quickly enlisted and equipped eighty-four men as instructed, gathering at the same time the necessary supplies of flour, corn, and meat for one year. The men were marched to Santiago de la Monclova, the capital of Coahuila, from where they were sent to the Presidio de Béjar on September 4. Aguayo, in reporting his activities to the viceroy, offered him his life and fortune for the service of the king, whereupon the viceroy appointed him governor and captain general of Coahuila and the Province of the Tejas and New Philippines. Aguayo had pointed out to the viceroy that the men enlisted were insufficient, that a larger force was required for the emergency, but that since men were scarce on the frontier, they would have to be recruited elsewhere. Fully impressed with the magnitude of the enterprise, the viceroy ordered five hundred additional men recruited in the districts of Celaya, Zacatecas, San Luis Potosí, and Aguascalientes. For the immediate expenses of the proposed expedition thirty-seven thousand *pesos* were appropriated and Aguayo was given the equivalent of one year's salary at the rate of four hundred and fifty *pesos* for each man

[27]Autos sobre el descubrimiento de La Gran Quivira segun lo consultado por el Marqués de San Miguel de Aguayo, Superior Govierno, Ano de 1715, Texas, No. 2, in B. Ms. Cited by Buckley, *op. cit.*, 21. Copies of these documents are also found in the *San Francisco el Grande Archive*, Vol. VIII.

enlisted. He had already spent out of his own purse over nine thousand *pesos* in raising the first contingent of eighty-four men which had been sent to San Antonio.[28] He assumed the office of governor of the two provinces in October, 1719, at Monclova.[29]

Father Espinosa's plans for civil settlements. While preparations are carried on for the new expedition, let us see what was being done by the missionaries in San Antonio. Shortly after the arrival of the fugitives, some time early in November, 1719, Father Espinosa went to the Río Grande, where he was informed by Father Pedro Múñoz, president of the missions in the vicinity of San Juan Bautista, that the Marquis of Aguayo had been appointed governor to replace Alarcón and that he had been put in charge of the organization of the new expedition now being planned to recover Texas. Father Espinosa asked Father Múñoz to go to the Hacienda de Patos to inquire from the new governor what his plans were. He seems to have been particularly anxious to know how soon aid for the reoccupation of East Texas could be expected. Being of a restless nature, he could not wait at San Juan Bautista, so he traveled to Monclova. He there conducted a mission, preaching for a week, and had the pleasure of seeing in the audience the two governors, Alarcón and Aguayo, who were then in Coahuila. Learning that Aguayo was not to start for some time, and feeling that it was highly important for him to speak to the viceroy, if possible, before the expedition set out, Father Espinosa left immediately for Querétaro to consult with the Father Guardian of the College of La Santa Cruz. After a short stay in Querétaro, he went on to Mexico City, where he interviewed the viceroy early in 1720, and discussed "the state of the poor province of the Tejas," not only with His Excellency but with some of the members of the *Audiencia*.

He declared to the viceroy and to such officials as cared to listen to him, that it was the unanimous opinion of all the missionaries, and particularly of Father Margil, that the success of their work in Texas depended greatly on the character of the soldiers that were sent to guard

---

[28]The details summarized in this paragraph have been gathered from various sources, the principal ones being Testimonio a favor de Nicolás Flores, *Provincias Internas*, Vol. 32; Peña, *Diario y derrotero,* original draft, *San Francisco el Grande Archive;* Diferentes Autos y otres providencias dictadas por el Gobernador Marqués de San Miguel de Aguayo, 1719-1720. *Saltillo Archives,* Vol. I, 178-192.

[29]Buckley says "He apparently took possession of his office December 19, 1719, giving as a reason that Alarcón went out of office on this day, but Aguayo himself says that he took possession in October. Testimonio a favor de Nicolás Flores, *Provincias Internas,* Vol. 32.

the missions. Instead of conscripts, married men with families, who desired to settle in the province and make it their permanent home, should be sent. Indigent families who were unable to make a comfortable living in the city should be encouraged to go to Texas. The heads of such families could be enlisted and paid the same salary as the soldiers. These men should be given the equivalent of two years' pay in advance, and their wives and children over fifteen years of age should be paid half as much. By advancing them the cash, they could buy and transport, at their own expense, all they needed to establish their permanent settlement in Texas. Upon arrival in the province they should be assigned land and given full rights to will their property to their children. This would naturally prove a great incentive to the new settlers, who would cultivate and improve their land for the benefit of their children. Furthermore, Father Espinosa pointed out that children born and reared in Texas would come to regard it their country. There were many mechanics and tradesmen living in Mexico City and other large centers, he observed, who were unemployed and who were barely able to subsist. These would be more than glad of the opportunity to make a new start in a new land.[30] The officials listened with interest to his proposals but, as usual, did little to put them into effect. In the instructions for the enlistment of men for the new expedition it was urged, as in the past, that they be married men as far as possible. Nothing else resulted from the earnest efforts of Father Espinosa to promote the building up of substantial civil settlements near the missions.

Margil offers to found San José mission. While Father Espinosa was on his way to Mexico, Father Margil, who remained in the Villa de Béjar, was not idle. Consumed by a desire to preach the Gospel and bring into the fold of the Church the hundreds of Indians with whom he came in contact, it grieved him exceedingly to see so many tribes come to San Antonio in quest of missions. On December 26, 1719, he wrote a long letter to the Marquis of Aguayo, congratulating him on his appointment as governor. After the customary courtesies, he explained to the new governor, who was an old friend of the saintly missionary, that the friars from the Colleges of Querétaro and Zacatecas were working in perfect harmony with but one end in view, the salvation of souls. He related how each had founded three missions in East Texas and how they had

---

[30]Father Espinosa, *Chrónica*, 455-456. It is interesting to note the arguments advanced by Father Espinosa in an effort to solve the question of unemployment at that time.

been forced to fall back to the San Antonio River as a result of the French attack. Here there was but one mission, which had recently been founded by Father Olivares from the College of Querétaro. The friars from the College of Zacatecas were in great need of establishing a mission located somewhere between East Texas and Coahuila that would serve them as a base and a halfway station. The College of Querétaro had a mission at La Punta, three at San Juan Bautista, and one at San Antonio, while the College of Zacatecas had none, and its friars were obliged to be the guests of the Querétaran missionaries all the way from Coahuila to East Texas. The members of the Pampopa nation, who were friendly to the Spaniards but greatly feared by other Indians for their prowess, had come to San Antonio and expressed to him their willingness to be congregated. There were other nations who were asking to be placed in missions at this time. The beautiful crop of corn raised at San Antonio de Valero, Father Margil observed, had inclined many Indians in the vicinity to look with favor upon the idea of living in pueblos under the care of missionaries.

Father Margil had been greatly impressed with the advantages offered by the site on the San Antonio River. "According to what we have seen," he declares, "this site on the San Antonio and its vicinity, where we wish to establish the mission, is destined to be the heart, as it were, from which we are to branch out in our work of founding missions, one group in one direction and the other in another as agreed in [the country of the] Tejas. The [friars of the college of] Querétaro are to extend northward to New Mexico and we southward to Tampico." He pointed out to Aguayo that it was not necessary to wait for the ornaments and supplies usually required for the establishment of a new mission, because he already had a statue of Saint Joseph, which had been given to him by Captain Gaspar Larranaga at the time of his death in Zacatecas, with the request that it be used for the founding of a mission under the advocation of San José. For the celebration of Mass and the administration of the Sacraments he had all that was necessary, having brought these things from the abandoned missions. These could be replaced later when the viceroy approved the establishment and furnished the customary aid in the name of the king. With great tact and a profound knowledge of human nature, he suggested that the new mission could be named San José y San Miguel de Aguayo, provided it met with the approval of his Lordship. Through the kindness of friends he had in his possession a quantity of trinkets, beads, and clothes that could be used to attract the

Indians and win their friendship. The only thing needed was the approval and authorization for the founding of the new mission. If his Lordship approved the idea, he could issue orders to Captain Juan Valdez, now in San Antonio, to select a suitable site for the new establishment and to give possession of it, in the name of His Majesty, to Father Margil, as representative of the friars from the College of Zacatecas. This had been the procedure followed in East Texas by Ramón. It would be well to send, he suggested, a few oxen and some corn seed. Two or three yokes of oxen from those destined for the soldiers of the Presidio of San Antonio could be used temporarily to plant a crop as soon as possible after the establishment of the new mission. He closed the letter by declaring that it was his cherished hope that the proposed Mission of San José y San Miguel de Aguayo might be the first which his Lordship founded in the Province of the Tejas.[31]

Margil's letter found a favorable reception. The idea of establishing a mission so soon after his appointment both pleased and flattered Aguayo. He immediately gave orders, therefore, for the founding of the proposed mission to Captain Juan Valdez, his lieutenant in San Antonio. In a long decree the new governor explained that the propagation of the Catholic faith had always been the chief concern of the king, who, in the case of the Province of the Tejas, had issued special instructions directed to this end. The governor had been informed by Father Margil and other persons worthy of credit that "in the vicinity of said Villa [de Béjar] and farther inland, there are many nations of peaceful Indians, docile and friendly to the Spaniards, who live in the wretched night of heathenism, clamoring for missions in order that the beautiful day of evangelical truth may dawn upon them," and that among these were the Pampopas, an Indian nation of about two hundred members who lived near the San Antonio River. In view of these facts he had seen fit to order, in the name of His Majesty, "that a mission be founded and built under the advocation and patronage of San José y San Miguel de Aguayo, in the vicinity of the said Villa of San Antonio, and that the most suitable, fertile, and convenient site [for the purpose] be chosen." Unable to be present in person, because of his many duties in connection with the enlistment of men and the purchase of supplies, such as arms, horses, munitions of war, provisions, and all those things necessary for the expedition entrusted to him by the Marquis of Valero to reëstablish the power

<hr/>

[31]Father Margil to Aguayo, December 26, 1719, in Testimonio de la Possessión y Missión de San José. *A. G. I., Audiencia de Guadalajara,* 67-3-11.

of the king over the Province of the Tejas and Nuevas Philipinas, he explained that he was obliged to give full authority to his Lieutenant General, Captain Juan Valdez, to act in his name and that of the king. Captain Valdez was instructed to select the place that seemed to him best suited for the purpose, exercising due care to see that there were abundant water and fertile land for good farms and pastures for all kinds of stock. He was to found there a mission to be called San José y San Miguel de Aguayo, and to give possession of it to Father Antonio Margil de Jesús of the College of Zacatecas, who was to have charge of the new establishment. All this was to be done with "the solemnity prescribed by the royal laws." These orders were immediately transmitted to San Antonio.[32]

Opposition of Father Olivares. When Father Olivares heard of the plans of Father Margil to establish a mission on the San Antonio River, he was much perturbed. Accompanied by Bartolomé Lorenzo, *alcalde;* Manuel, *alguazil;* and Agustín Solano and Baltazar Valero, *regidores,* all Indians from the Mission of San Antonio de Valero, he appeared before Captain Valdez on February 23, 1720, to protest against the establishment of the proposed mission and to present the reasons why, in his opinion, it was not advisable to permit it. In the petition presented it was declared that the Pampopas and Pastias, who were to be congregated in the new mission, were traditional enemies of the Indians now living in San Antonio de Valero; that their establishment such a short distance away might result in serious trouble between the neophytes of the two missions; that the Marquis of Valero had granted the site originally to Father Olivares; and lastly, that the laws of the Indies provided that new missions had to be at least three leagues distant from those already founded.[33]

In reply to this protest Captain Valdez informed the petitioners that he had received orders from the Marquis of Aguayo, Governor of the province, to select an appropriate site for a mission whereon to establish the Pampopa, Suliajame, and Pastia nations, who had requested through Father Margil suitable lands and sufficient water for irrigation to form a pueblo. He assured the petitioners that in carrying out his orders he would observe the laws of the Indies with all care, and that he would

---

[32]Decree of Aguayo for the establishment of San José, January 22, 1720. In Testimonio de la Possessión y Misión . . . *A. G. I., Audiencia de Guadalajara,* 67-3-11.

[33]Oposición a la fundación de la Misión de San José del Río de San Antonio. In *Archivo del Colegio de la Santa Cruz, 1716-1749.*

respect the rights of all parties concerned. He thereupon immediately
summoned Father Olivares, the Indians from the Mission of San Antonio
de Valero, Father Margil, the Indians of the Pampopa, Suliajame, and
Pastia nations, Captain Cárdenas, who was now in San Antonio with
eighty soldiers, Nicolás Flores, and Captain Lorenzo García, the last two
having had experience in such matters.[34]

Founding of San José Mission.   When all the parties summoned had
assembled, Captain Lorenzo García, who understood the language of the
natives, acted as interpreter. He told the Indians who were about to be
congregated, that they were going to receive the land and water from His
Majesty who expected them to live in the new mission. He then explained
to them the routine of mission life and all their different rights and
duties. Both Fathers Olivares and Margil witnessed the explanation.
Captain Valdez now invited all the persons present to go with him to
select a site for the new establishment in accord with the orders of
Governor Aguayo and the laws of the Indies. Father Olivares, who was
old and sickly, asked to be excused, and sent Father Fray Joseph Guerra
to represent the interests of the College of Querétaro.

Captain Valdez, Fathers Margil and Guerra, *Alférez* Nicolás Flores,
and Captain Alonso Cárdenas and Lorenzo García, followed by a group
of Indians, made their way along the river until they came to a spot
where Father Margil thought an irrigation ditch could be dug. Here
they were met by Fathers Fray Agustín Patrón and Fray Miguel Núñez
de Haro, who had built a hut of straw at this place, which had been
chosen by the missionaries and the Indians for the proposed mission.
Here they met also the chiefs of the three nations that were going to
be congregated. Joining Captain Valdez's group, they all walked through
the fields for a distance of about three-quarters of a league, along the
route where the irrigation ditch or *acequia* was to be constructed. "And
seeing how all the fields were covered with grass, heavy timber, and
firewood, with the river close at hand affording good watering places for
sheep, goats, cattle, and horses; and everybody having agreed that the
best location for the church of the new pueblo was on an elevated, spacious,
and very level plain just traversed, I asked all those who were accompanying me how many leagues it was from here to the Mission of San
Antonio Valero and all answered by saying that it was a little more
than three leagues. Knowing this to be true, I alighted from my horse

[34]*Ibid.*

and called Captain Lorenzo García, who in the presence of the missionaries and all those present, explained to the Indians all the requisites for the act of possession. Having listened to everything, the Indian chiefs declared they have desired and do desire to be given land and water in order to live as Christians; that they will work to build an irrigation ditch and will cultivate the soil; that they will teach their children to do these things; that they wish to live according to the law of God; that they and their children will always obey the missionary fathers; and that they will observe and cause to be observed whatever they, the *Padres,* order for the service of God.[35]

He then took the Indian chiefs by the hand and led them over the fields. The Indians pulled grass, scattered rocks and dirt over the land, cut branches of trees, and did other things in evidence of ownership. Captain Valdez now gave them possession, in the name of His Majesty and the governor, of all the lands necessary for the new mission, and the right to irrigate them by drawing water from the river, as well as to use the woods and timber. A place was selected on which to build the pueblo and on this was marked where the church, the cemetery, the hospital, the jail, and the *plaza mayor,* or public square, were to be located. The last was to be one hundred and twenty *varas* square. The houses were to be arranged along streets and these were to be of uniform width. The Indians were told they were to build their own houses and make their furniture under the direction of the missionaries, and they were to be allowed to raise chickens and other yard animals.

Having placed the Indians in possession of the lands for the new mission, Captain Valdez proceeded to the election of officers. Juan, Chief of the Pampopas, was made governor of the new pueblo; Nicolás, Captain of the Suliajames, was appointed *Alcalde;* and Alonso, Chief of the Pastias, was made *Alguacil.* Francisco, a Pampopa Indian, and Antonio, a Suliajame, were chosen *regidores.* Captain Valdez, through his interpreter, Lorenzo García, explained to each one of them their respective duties and enjoined them to try to live as Christians and to cause all orders and regulations to be obeyed. The new establishment, after being officially named San José y San Miguel de Aguayo, was placed under the care of Father Margil, as president of the missions established by the friars from the College of Zacatecas in the Province of Texas. Fathers Miguel Núñez de Haro and Agustín Patrón were left in charge of the

---

[35]Auto de Possessión. In Testimonio de Possessión y Missión . . . *A. G. I., Audencia de Guadalajara,* 67-3-11.

new mission by Father Margil, and a copy of the act of foundation and possession was ordered sent to the governor of Coahuila for him to forward it to the viceroy for his information. The certified copy of the proceedings was sent by the Marquis of Aguayo to the viceroy on March 13, 1720, but the mission itself was officially established by Captain Valdez on February 23, 1720.[36]

Organization of Aguayo's Expedition.   But let us return to Aguayo in Coahuila. As usual, the preparations for the expedition into Texas were delayed for various reasons. In spite of the sincerity of the Marquis and his strenuous efforts to start as soon as possible, a whole year elapsed before he was ready. With unusual vigor and diligence, he began to collect the provisions and supplies necessary early in the fall of 1719. To prevent the dissipation of the resources of Coahuila, he issued an order on December 7, 1719, prohibiting the inhabitants of the province from selling their corn and other products to anyone other than the governor or his representatives. Any Spaniard violating this order was to pay a fine of fifty *pesos* for each *fanega* sold and to suffer the loss of all his corn. If the transgressor was an Indian, a mestizo, or a negro he was to suffer the loss of his corn and to receive one hundred lashes. The governor assured the people that the current market price would be paid them for such supplies as were needed for the expedition into Texas.[37] His difficulties increased considerably when early in 1720, the Indians of the Hacienda of Santa Rosa became dissatisfied and deserted the mission. As they were committing numerous depredations in the vicinity, the Marquis of Aguayo was now not only forced to suspend active preparations, but to recall *Alférez* Nicolás Flores from San Antonio, who came to his aid with eighteen men in March, 1720. Fortunately, on April 14, the rebellious Indians were overtaken and cornered at Nadadores, where the new governor, with the aid of Flores and a hastily recruited force, succeeded in killing about half of them and taking the rest prisoners.[38] This left him free once more to turn his attention to the Texas expedition.

The five hundred men enlisted in the districts of Celaya, Zacatecas, San Luis Potosí, and Aguascalientes, agreeable to the orders of the

---

[36]Testimonio de possessión y missión de San José en el Río de San Antonio. *A. G. I., Audiencia de Guadalajara,* 67-3-11.

[37]Diferentes autos y otras providencias dictadas por el governador Marqués de San Miguel de Aguayo, in *Saltillo Archive,* Vol. 1, 175-177.

[38]Testimonio a favor de Nicolás Flores, *Provincias Internas,* Vol. 32.

viceroy, started for Monclova in April, with about three thousand six hundred horses. When they reached their destination, on June 23, they had only five hundred sixty horses. As a result of the severe drouth and the intense heat of the season, almost three thousand five hundred had died or had been left on the road to die. Aguayo immediately dispatched messengers to all the haciendas in the neighborhood and succeeded in purchasing three thousand four hundred additional horses to replace those that had been lost, but on account of the weather these did not arrive in Monclova until late in September.[39] The men, who were now waiting in Coahuila to enter Texas, grew restless and began to desert in great numbers. Aguayo had to take severe measures to put a stop to this serious evil that threatened the success of the expedition. Notice was given that any soldier who deserted would be tried by court-martial and if convicted would be shot. This warning was disregarded, however, until on August 2, 1720, he issued a proclamation stating that José Chavez and Juan Castillo, deserters, had been duly tried, found guilty, and convicted by a court-martial to be shot. These men were to be executed publicly on the main plaza three days hence and due warning was given to all those incurring in the same transgression.[40] This harsh means seems to have accomplished the desired result, for desertions decreased notably.

It was not until October, that the Marquis of Aguayo was at last ready to start. Early this month six hundred mules, loaded with clothes, arms, munitions, and six fieldpieces arrived in Monclova from Mexico. These supplies had been ordered by Aguayo and he had been anxiously waiting for them to start. The new governor had by now succeeded in assembling six hundred *cargas* of supplies, four thousand horses, six hundred head of cattle, nine hundred sheep, and almost eight hundred mules.[41] This was the most formidable attempt ever made to establish the king's dominion over the Province of Texas. The five hundred men were divided by Aguayo into eight companies and formed into a battalion of mounted infantry, which he called San Miguel de Aragón. In accord with the authority given him by the viceroy he appointed Fernando Pedro de Almazán, later to become governor, his Lieutenant General, and he made Tomás Zubiría, Miguel Colón, Manual de Herrera, Francisco Becerra,

---

[39]Castañeda, *Morfi's History of Texas.*

[40]Public proclamation of Aguayo, August 2, 1720. *Saltillo Archive,* Vol. I, 187-189.

[41]Aguayo to the King, June 13, 1722. *Archivo de la Santa Cruz de Querétaro, 1714-1729.*

Luque, Gabriel Costales, Joseph de Arroyo, Pedro Oribe, and Juan Cantu captains of the eight companies. Three standards were blessed with great ceremony, one consisting of the picture of Our Lady of Pilár, San Miguel, and San Rafael, bearing the motto *Pugnate pro Fide et Rege;* the second having a picture of Our Lady of Guadalupe, San Miguel, and San Francisco Xavier; and the third was the image of the patron saint of Spain, Saint James.

Equivocal policy of Spain towards the French. Just as Aguayo was about to depart, he received a communication from the viceroy on October 5, 1720, giving him detailed instructions for the expedition and the general policy he was to observe towards the French. He was to proceed to the reoccupation of the Province of Texas and New Philippines without delay; to restore the religious to their missions; to occupy the Bay of Espíritu Santo and to erect a fortification there; and to establish a post, if possible, in the country of the Cadodachos. In carrying out these instructions he was not to use force of arms unless he found the country occupied by the enemy and resistance was offered, as news had just been received in Mexico that a truce was being negotiated between the two crowns. Agreeable to the wishes of the king, Aguayo was further instructed to welcome all those who wished to enter the service of Spain or to establish themselves in the Spanish settlements in Texas.[42] The Marquis was frankly disappointed with the idea of waging only a defensive campaign, for he had hoped to drive the French not only out of Texas but out of Louisiana as well. He was thoroughly disgusted with the order to receive French deserters in the Spanish service and to allow French settlers to establish themselves in Texas. Nevertheless, with a gesture of supreme resignation, he declared to the viceroy that he was willing to make this "sacrifice as evidence of my blind obedience" to the orders of His Majesty.[43]

Council of the Indies first to recommend civil settlement. The king seemed to be undecided for some time as to the policy toward the French in Louisiana, hence the contradictory character of the orders received by the viceroy. Soon after the outbreak of hostilities the king issued a *cédula* on April 22, 1719, which was immediately sent to New Spain. This was

---

[42]Castañeda, *Morfi's History of Texas,* 1673-1779; Peña, *Derrotero, San Francisco el Grande Archive,* 217.

[43]Peña, *op cit.;* Autos fechos en La Bahía de el Espíritu Santo sobre dos muertes. . . . *Provincias Internas,* Vol. 181.

the result of a series of recommendations made by the Council of the Indies on March 27, in reply to the king's request for advice concerning two letters recently received from the viceroy, warning him against the intention of the French to take possession of a gulf port "by force of arms if necessary." Among other things the Council recommended that in so far as regarded the Bay of San Bernardo, commonly known to the Spaniards as Espíritu Santo, it was urgent that a ship of medium draft be dispatched immediately to reconnoiter the bay and report if the French had already occupied it. If found unoccupied, the ship should remain to guard the bay until measures for the construction of a fort were adopted. It further recommended that a number of settlements should be established between the San Marcos and the Guadalupe Rivers, both of which emptied into the bay, in order to prevent the introduction of French merchandise through these rivers into the Province of Texas and hence into the Reyno de Nueva Vizcaya, Province of Coahuila, and the Nuevo Reyno de León. Of particular interest in connection with the proposed settlements is the fact that in these recommendations is found the first mention of the idea of settling families from the Canary Islands or Galicia in Texas. "It is advisable that Your Majesty," declares the Council, "issue orders to the officials in the Canary Islands and the Kingdom of Galicia for two thousand families to be transported by way of the city of Veracruz. . . . It will also be greatly to the advantage of the royal service for one hundred Tlaxcaltecan families, skilled in farm labor, to be sent to Texas that they might help to teach those newly converted how to cultivate the soil . . . Master carpenters, blacksmiths, and masons should also be sent to help build the settlements that are to be established."[44] Following the general recommendation of the Council, the king repeated the instructions of June 11, 1718, which covered fully the question of French trade. He then urged the viceroy to take possession of the Bays of San José (near Pensacola) and San Bernardo, declaring that no foreigner was to be permitted to enter or settle within his dominions. With regard to the establishment of settlements on the Guadalupe and San Marcos (Colorado) Rivers with families from Spain, he did not believe the suggestion was practical. He ordered the viceroy therefore to select the most suitable sites in the vicinity of the Bay of San Bernardo and settle them with families from New Spain because

---

[44]Satisfacción á la orden de V. M. con que se sirvio Remitir tres cartas . . . March 27, 1719. *A. G. I., México*, 61-6-35 (Dunn Transcripts, University of Texas).

their transportation would be less expensive and more convenient than if these were taken from the Canary Islands.[45]

The viceroy had informed the king in a long report sent on March 10, 1719, of the measures he had adopted to prevent the introduction of French merchandise. He assured the king that immediate steps would be taken to put into effect the orders of June of the previous year; that a fort would be built on San Bernardo Bay as soon as possible; and that orders had already been given for the establishment of a post among the Cadodachos. He offered to drive the French out of Louisiana if the king so desired, and asked that a large number of families be sent from Spain to replace the French.[46] By his *cédula* of November 1, 1719, the king approved all that had been done and the measures now being contemplated to prevent the French from occupying any part of the Gulf coast or penetrating his dominions. Due to the war, it was impossible at this time, he declared, to send the families suggested, but this matter would be given due consideration as soon as the war was over. He closed the order by saying that "since Mobile, Massacra, and the rest of the territory belonging to my royal crown is now occupied by the French with no right whatsoever, you, the viceroy, shall make the necessary provisions to cause them to abandon it, dislodging them from it."[47] But soon after, the king changed his mind, it seems, and ordered the viceroy not to attack the French in Louisiana but to confine himself to the reoccupation of the lost Province of Texas. French deserters were to be admitted into the royal service and settlers who swore allegiance to the king were to be allowed to establish themselves in the Spanish settlements. It was these last instructions that caused the viceroy to modify his orders to Aguayo at the last minute. In a letter to the king, sent on August 17, 1720, the viceroy told him that although the suspension of arms had altered the intent of previous orders, he had, nevertheless, instructed the Marquis of Aguayo to establish a presidio among the Cadodachos, to increase the forces in Texas, and to occupy the Bay of San Bernardo.[48] On March 16, 1721, the king approved everything the viceroy had done and the instructions given Aguayo as reported on August 8, 1720, adding that notwithstanding the peace negotiations, if the French made any movement

---

[45]Royal *Cédula* of April 22, 1719, *Historia.* Vol. 298.

[46]This report was based chiefly on the accomplishments of Alarcón as reported by him immediately after his return to San Antonio early in 1719.

[47]Royal *Cédula* of November 1, 1719. *Historia,* Vol. 298.

[48]Royal *Cédula* of March 16, 1721. *Historia,* Vol. 298.

in pursuance of their designs, he was to expel them from Texas by force of arms. But on May 16, 1721, a treaty of peace having been concluded, he again addressed the viceroy, commanding him to suspend the execution of the orders of November 1, 1719, and March 16, 1721, with regard to the use of force in driving out the French. He declared, however, that this order did not affect the instructions given for the establishment of a presidio among the Cadodachos, the increase of the number of missions on the San Antonio River, the occupation and fortification of the Bay of Espíritu Santo, nor the reënforcement and increase of the garrisons or presidios in Texas.[49]

Aguayo sets out from Monclova.   The Marquis of Aguayo, having received his final instructions and completed his preparations for the expedition, finally ordered his men to set out on November 16, 1720, under the command of Lieutenant Governor Almazán. At the head of the column was placed a picket of veteran soldiers who were familiar with the road and had had experience in fighting Indians, then followed the equipage, behind which came the eight companies in order of seniority, followed by the baggage, provisions, and munitions of war. In the rear came the droves of animals.[50]

It was now winter. The rivers were swollen and the road was difficult. The expedition was delayed several days at the Sabinas River and did not reach the Río Grande until December 20. According to the official diary the river carried so much water that it was more than one and one-half rods in depth and more than a gunshot in width. The Marquis of Aguayo, who had remained behind, joined the expedition before it crossed the river. With him came Father Espinosa. A few days later Dr. Joseph Codallos y Raval, who was sent to Texas as Vicar-General of the Bishop of Guadalajara, arrived in camp. At San Juan Bautista the group was joined by Father Benito Sánchez, a missionary who entered Texas with Domingo Ramón in 1716, and who had been stationed at San José de los Nazonis until the French attack in 1719. There was one other cleric who accompanied the expedition, Father Juan Antonio

---

[49]Royal *Cédula* of May 26, 1721. *Historia,* Vol. 298.

[50]Peña, *Derrotero, San Francisco el Grande Archive.* For a detailed account of the progress of the expedition see Buckley, *"The Aguayo Expedition," Southwestern Historical Quarterly,* XV, 165. This splendid study of the route followed by Aguayo is invaluable.

Peña, the official chaplain and chronicler, to whom we are indebted for the detailed and careful diary of this important undertaking.[51]

While still on the Río Grande, Aguayo received news from Captain Matías García, of the Presidio of San Antonio, that St. Denis was holding a convocation with many Indian nations on the Brazos River and that he intended to attack the presidio. Greatly disturbed by this information, the Governor called a council of war to discuss the situation. It was decided to send one hundred and sixteen men at once to the aid of the threatened post on the San Antonio River with Captains Tomás Zuribía and Miguel Colón, under the command of Lieutenant Governor Almazán.[52]

Ramón sent to occupy Espíritu Santo. At the same time Aguayo ordered Captain José Domingo Ramón to set out with forty men to occupy the Bay of Espíritu Santo in order to prevent its falling into the hands of the French. Both parties seem to have traveled together as far as San Antonio, from where Ramón set out on March 10, 1721, to carry out his orders. Three and a half weeks later, the very day the Marquis of Aguayo entered San Antonio with the main body of the expedition, Ramón took official possession of the bay and all the surrounding country in the name of the king. This was on April 4, 1721. When Aguayo learned of the accomplishment of one of the chief aims of the expedition, he celebrated the news with great joy on April 18.[53]

Fathers Margil, Gabriel Vergara, Joseph Guerra, and Joseph Rodríguez and Brothers Joseph Albadejo and Joseph Pita,[54] who had been anxiously awaiting the arrival of Aguayo in San Antonio in order to return to the abandoned missions in East Texas, lost no time in joining the expedition immediately upon its arrival. The rumors of St. Denis' activities had been found to be unworthy of credence and the men being in need of relaxation before continuing their march, Aguayo decided to stay in San Antonio for a while to give them a rest and permit the proper observance of Holy Week. During his stay he was not idle. He inspected the

[51]Peña, *Derrotero*, 2-3.

[52]*Ibid.*, 3.

[53]*Ibid.*, 6.

[54]Brother Pita was killed by a party of Apaches before the expedition reached East Texas. He was with a detachment escorting a supply of provisions at the time it was surprised by a group of hostile Indians. Aguayo to *Auditor de Guerra* in Autos sobre diferentes puntos consultados por el Governador de la Provincia de los Texas . . . *Año 1724*.

presidio and the missions, he sent out exploring parties to locate possible sources of salt, and he actively attended to the many details of the expedition. On April 26, he sent a messenger to the viceroy with a detailed report on the occupation of the Bay of Espíritu Santo. He informed His Excellency that he was now ready to continue his march to the country of the Tejas, but he pointed out that it was extremely difficult to keep his men properly supplied from his base in Coahuila, which was about four hundred leagues distant. He suggested that if His Excellency was willing, a ship should be permitted to ply between Veracruz and Espíritu Santo by means of which the necessary supplies could be transported with a great saving in time and cost. He offered to defray the expenses for this experiment and, taking for granted that the permission would be given, he wrote to his agent in Mexico City that same day to charter or purchase a vessel for the purpose and to secure the needed provisions.[55]

March from San Antonio to the Neches.   Delayed for various reasons, the expedition did not resume its march until May 13, 1721. It was decided to follow a more northerly course than that previously taken by others, in order to avoid the large and flooded streams encountered along the lower road. Under the guidance of an Indian chief from La Ranchería Grande, Juan Rodríguez, who offered his services on condition that Aguayo establish a mission for his people upon his return from the country of the Tejas, the expedition reached and crossed Comal River, near present New Braunfels, on May 17. That same day the Guadalupe was crossed, and by the 20th the men camped beyond the San Marcos. The new route took the expedition dangerously near the country of the Apaches, but a strict watch for enemies was kept constantly and every precaution was taken to prevent a surprise. The Colorado River was safely crossed on May 23, 1721. From here to the Brazos progress became increasingly difficult because of the numerous small streams and it was not until June 19 that the latter river was crossed near the present site of the city of Waco. Aguayo was somewhat perplexed to find no Indians along the road. Not until July 8, when the vicinity of the Trinity River was reached, did the expedition meet any natives.[56]

---

[55]Peña, *Derrotero,* 6.

[56]Peña, *Derrotero,* 11-13. For a detailed account of the route followed by the expedition see the splendid study of Miss Eleanor Buckley, "The Aguayo Expedition," *Southwestern Historical Quarterly,* XV, 33-45. The official text of this important expedition has been translated and critically edited by Rev. Dr. Peter

A short distance beyond the road a *ranchería* was now discovered and here Aguayo found all the Indians from La Ranchería Grande, together with a number of Bidais and Deodosos. These and other Indians had come perhaps to the convocation called by St. Denis.

This explains why Aguayo did not see any natives before. The bugles sounded and the drums rolled as the royal standards were unfurled and the whole expetdition marched into the Indian camp to be welcomed, much to their surprise, by the natives who formed in perfect order and came out to meet them, bearing a large, white taffeta flag with blue ribbons which had been given them by the French. The Spaniards further noticed that they were all well supplied with rifles and ammunition. These were mute but eloquent evidences of the work of the French among them. Aguayo pitched camp here and asked all the Indian chiefs to come to see him next day. The following morning, after declaring that the Spaniards had been sent by the king to protect them against their enemies and to instruct them in the Christian faith, he distributed gifts and promised the chiefs of Ranchería Grande that he would found a mission for their people near the San Antonio River if they would return to their country.[57]

The march was then continued to the Trinity. Extreme difficulty was experienced in crossing this stream. For sixteen days the expedition struggled to gain the opposite bank. On July 25, 1721, the last man and piece of baggage were finally taken safely across the river. A short distance beyond, the expedition was met by the chief of the Aynay tribe, who was recognized as the head of the Asinai Confederacy. He came, accompanied by eight chiefs and four women, one of whom was the famous Angelina,[58] to welcome the Spaniards. With tears in his eyes he assured them he had become so impatient at their long delay that he had decided to go in search of them. Aguayo was touched by the sincerity of the faithful chief. He welcomed him in the name of the king and appointed him Captain and Governor of the Tejas, presenting him with a silver-headed cane as the insignia of his office. There is no doubt that the Tejas Indians were truly glad to see the Spaniards again. They brought flowers, corn, beans, and watermelons in token of their joy. Aguayo ordered that presents be distributed and they were all given clothes and trinkets of various kinds. As usual, the Marquis assured them

P. Forrestal in *Preliminary Studies of the Texas Catholic Historical Society,* II, No. 7.

[57]Peña, *Derrotero,* 13.

[58]See p. 58.

the king had sent his soldiers to protect and defend the Indians against their enemies, and the missionaries to instruct them in the Christian faith. He declared that the Spaniards had come to stay among them permanently and urged them to congregate in pueblos.[59]

Accompanied by the Tejas Indians, the expedition resumed its march to the Neches River. On the 27th of July, Father Espinosa left the main body and went in advance of Aguayo with the chief of the Tejas and his followers to gather the Indians at the site of the first Mission of San Francisco de los Tejas[60] and make arrangements for its reëstablishment. When the expedition came up on the following day, it was greeted by a large number of Indians,—men, women, and children,—all of whom brought gifts to the Spaniards and seemed genuinely happy at their return.

Among those who welcomed the Spaniards was a chief of the Neche tribe, who, with sixty followers,[61] marched into camp in perfect order and fired several salutes. Aguayo was impressed by this demonstration and, after smoking the peace pipe, listened to their manifestations of loyalty and joy. He assured them he had come at the command of the king to protect them against their enemies, asked them to return to their village, gave them provisions, and promised to distribute gifts upon his arrival.

The guns and the military formation observed by these Indians, as they came into camp, were expressive evidence of the activity of the French during the absence of the Spaniards. At this very time, St. Denis, who had been appointed commander of Natchitoches on July 1, 1720, and had assumed his post early in 1721,[62] was but a short distance away, at the site of the abandoned Mission of La Purísima Concepción. He now dispatched a messenger to solicit an interview with the Marquis in orders to acquaint him with the instructions he had recently received

---

[59]Peña, *Derrotero,* 14-17.

[60]This was the original mission founded by De León in 1690. It was located about four and a half miles from the mouth of a small stream called San Pedro and seven or eight miles west of the place where the road crossed the Neches River. The site was about ten miles from the Neche village, which was located a short distance beyond the river. Bolton, "The Native Tribes about the East Texas Missions," *Quarterly,* XI, 265; Buckley, "The Aguayo Expedition," *Quarterly,* XV, 43, note.

[61]Peña, in his *Derrotero,* gives the number as sixty, although it has been stated there were seventy in the group. Buckley, *op. cit.,* Peña, *Derrotero,* 15.

[62]Margry, *op. cit.,* VI, 220-224.

from the Governor of Louisiana. The courier came into camp that same
day, at sunset. After making known his mission to Aguayo, he was
assured that St. Denis could come at his pleasure with perfect safety.[63]

Leisurely, the expedition continued its march. They were now approaching the heart of the Asinai Confederacy. Passing by the first site of the
Presidio de los Tejas, where Ramón established his camp temporarily in
1716, before crossing the Neches River, they halted on its right bank, a
short distance from the old fort.[64] Here a large delegation, about one
hundred Indians of the Nacono nation, came to pay their respects to
Aguayo on July 30. Their chief, now a very old man, had blinded himself
in order to become their high priest, this being an old and well established
tradition in the tribe.[65] With pathetic gestures, he tried to express his
great joy and that of his companions at finding the Spaniards among
them once more. Aguayo was as profuse in his expressions of appreciation and his promises of protection. He enjoined the Indians to congregate in a pueblo and live together in order that the missionaries might
better be able to take care of them. All this he made clear through Nicolás
de los Santos, a former soldier of Domingo Ramón, who had learned
the language of the natives and was very skillful in its use.[66] The following day gifts were exchanged, the Indians bringing tamales, fresh
ears of corn, watermelons, and other presents and receiving knives,
scissors, combs, beads, and other trinkets which they valued highly.

Interview of Aguayo and St. Denis. While Aguayo was still encamped
on the west bank of the Neches, St. Denis arrived and presented himself
to the Marquis, after swimming his horse across the river. The usual
courtesies having been exchanged, the French commander of Natchitoches,
who seems to have been anxious to talk privately to his friends, the missionaries, begged Aguayo to excuse him and permit him to retire for
the night to rest from the fatigue of his journey. "This seems to suggest

---

[63]Peña, *Derrotero*, 15.

[64]Ramón established a temporary presidio on a small plain, a few miles west of
the Neches and from there went with the missionaries to select suitable sites for
the missions. It was not until three months later that he moved the presidio to
the vicinity of Concepción Mission. The site has been identified with that of present
day Douglas, on Thomas Creek. Bolton, "The Native Tribes," *Quarterly*, XI, 260;
Buckley, "The Aguayo Expedition," *Quarterly*, XV, 47.

[65]In speaking of this chief, Peña says: "After having led them for many years,
he put his eyes out, as is customary among these Indians, in order to be their high
priest." *Derrotero*, f. 15 vuelta.

[66]*Ibid.*, f. 15 vuelta.

that St. Denis did not feel exactly safe among the Spaniards," declares Miss Buckley, with much reason.[67] It is to be remembered that he had fled from Mexico City; that orders had come from the king for his deportation to Guatemala, together with his wife; and that he was suspected of the attack on Los Adaes.[68] He was naturally uneasy of the reception that might be accorded him by the Spaniards and seems to have desired an opportunity to talk confidentially to Father Espinosa and the other missionaries who had always been his friends. From them he must have found out that night what had transpired in the last few years in Mexico. Perhaps he became convinced of the determination of Aguayo to demand that the French evacuate the province of Texas.

The following morning, on August 1, the Marquis of Aguayo called all the captains and other officers together for a council of war in his tent. St. Denis was sent for and asked to state frankly the purpose of his visit. He replied that he was now the commander of the post at Natchitoches; that he had received information from Mobile that a truce had been negotiated between the two nations and that a conclusive peace had been signed; that he wanted to know if His Lordship intended to observe peace, in which case he, St. Denis, would do likewise. To this Aguayo answered that in accordance with the instructions given him by the viceroy, he was resolved to observe the truce faithfully, provided St. Denis and his men immediately evacuated the entire province of Texas and retired to Natchitoches, without impeding or trying to impede, directly or indirectly, the reoccupation of all that had been previously possessed by His Majesty, the King of Spain, up to and including Los Adaes. In view of the firm purpose of the Spanish commander, St. Denis reluctantly agreed to abandon Los Adaes. In vain he tried to discourage the Spaniards from establishing at Los Adaes, pointing out the unhealthfulness of the climate and the poor quality of the soil. The superior force of Aguayo, however, left him no choice. For three days he tarried among the Indians, seven leagues beyond Concepción Mission, after he had promised Aguayo to retire immediately to Natchitoches. At this time he had a considerable number of Cadodacho Indians "whom since winter he had gathered to go to take possession of the Bay of Espíritu Santo."[69] But his schemes were frustrated by the quick action of the Marquis, who

---

[67]Buckley, "The Aguayo Expedition," *Quarterly*, XV, 44, note 3.

[68]See p. 88.

[69]Peña, *Derrotero*, 17; Buckley, *op. cit.*, XV, 45; Castañeda, *Morfi's History of Texas*, Paragraph 245.

even before he reached San Antonio, dispatched a force to occupy this important site.

The expedition crossed the Neches on August 3 and on the 5th reached the site selected by the missionaries for the reëstablishment of Mission San Francisco de los Tejas, which was now located on the east bank of the river, in the Neche village, close to the mounds, and about three miles from the crossing. The mission was now renamed San Francisco de los Neches.[70]

But the reëstablishment of the East Texas missions will be the subject of the following chapter. There, full details will be given of each one of the missions. The narrative in the remainder of this chapter will be confined to the principal events of the Aguayo expedition until it reached Los Adaes and its return to Coahuila.

March from the Neches to Los Adaes. From San Francisco de los Neches, Aguayo sent out a small detachment to Mission San José de los Nazonis. On the 13th, having been notified that everything was in readiness, he immediately set out with a part of his troops, leaving the main body of the expedition to rest at Concepción, and proceeded to reëstablish this mission on its new location, about fifteen miles northwest of Concepción, near the north line of Nacogdoches County. Upon his return to Concepción, he officially installed Captain Juan Cortinas and a company of twenty-five soldiers in the old Presidio of Nuestra Señora de los Dolores, situated about a league from the mission. On the 15th of August he set out with the entire expedition for Nacogdoches, where on the 18th he reëstablished the Mission of Nuestra Señora de Guadalupe. From here he proceeded without loss of time to refound the Mission of Nuestra Señora de los Dolores, and, after three days of travel, camped on a spot one-fourth of a league beyond where the former mission had stood. On the 21st he established the mission on this spot, which has been identified with that of modern San Augustine.

Three days later Aguayo started for Los Adaes. After six days' travel in a general east-northeast direction, he camped half a league beyond the site of the old Mission of San Miguel. The place was deserted and not an Indian was anywhere in sight. Scouts and messengers were sent in different directions to call the Indians. On September 1, they

---

[70]Dr. Bolton, after a personal investigation on the grounds, reached the conclusion that the mission was doubtless located on Bowles Creek, not far from the present crossing of that stream by the old San Antonio Road. Buckley, *op. cit.,* XV, 45, note 3.

began to arrive. They told a pitiful tale, how the French had driven them from their lands because of their friendship for the Spaniards, and how they had taken their women and children as slaves. It was because of the cruel treatment to which they had been subjected by the French that they had been obliged to abandon their homes and take refuge in the more inaccessible country higher up.[71]

French protest against establishment of Los Adaes. But it was not the Indians alone who had heard of the arrival of the Spaniards. The same day the natives began to assemble, there came a messenger with a letter from M. Rerenor, the French commandant at Natchitoches. He informed Aguayo that St. Denis had departed for Mobile immediately upon his return from his interview with the Spaniards. As in the meantime M. Rerenor had received no instructions to permit the Spaniards to settle, he asked the Marquis to abstain from acting until St. Denis returned. To this Aguayo replied that he was determined to carry out the orders he had received from the viceroy and that he was going to erect a presidio wherever he thought it best to the interests of His Majesty. He decided to send his reply with Lieutenant Governor Almazán and Captain Costales in order that they might observe closely the condition and location of the French fort.

The two officers reported on their return that the fortification consisted merely of a square stockade, about forty *varas* on each side, without any redoubts; that the garrison consisted of fifty soldiers and five civilian settlers. On another island in the river, near the one on which the fort was located, a number of Indians armed with rifles and skilled in the use of firearms, was kept, but the French relied for their defence mainly on the river itself, which formed a moat around the two islands. When they explained to M. Rerenor the instructions which the Marquis of Aguayo had received to reoccupy the entire province of Tejas and made clear his determination to carry them out, he replied that he had no orders either to oppose or consent to the settlement or occupation of Los Adaes and consequently would take no action. He wrote a letter to Aguayo, which he sent with his two messengers, in which he now offered him his full coöperation and placed his person and his goods at

---

[71]The narrative is based mainly on the official diary of the Aguayo expedition written by Peña. The location of the mission given herein is that determined by Bolton after a careful study of the sources, all of which were rechecked by the author.

his command. He even asked for permission to present his respects to the Spanish commander. Eight days later, M. Rerenor made a courtesy call on Aguayo, who entertained him at dinner. M. Rerenor brought a dozen chickens, some melons, and some vegetables as a peace offering and Aguayo gave him some much needed wine and brandy, to take back to Natchitoches. Aguayo, in his report to the viceroy, is emphatic in stating that he had made it clear to M. Rerenor that there would be no more trade in merchandise or supplies.[72]

But in spite of his strong protestations to the contrary, he goes on to say that due to unexpected delay caused by the flooded conditions of the rivers, he was obliged soon after to ask two French settlers who lived on the side of the island nearer to Los Adaes to sell him or let him have fifty or sixty *cargas* of corn, which they agreed to do on condition that the Marquis sent for them after dark in order that the French commander might not find out about the purchase. Thanks to this arrangement, Aguayo declares, he was able to keep his troops supplied until the arrival of provisions from La Bahía and the Río Grande.[73]

Founding of Los Adaes. From September 1 until November 4, Aguayo busied himself with the selection of a suitable location for a presidio and its construction. After a careful exploration, he chose a site half a league beyond where the old mission had stood, near a spring of water, which flowed down the side of a small hill. Here the presidio was stoutly built with a stockade of pointed logs two and three-quarters *varas* high all around it. The presidio was hexagonal in shape with three bulwarks placed on alternate corners, each protecting two sides. A garrison of one hundred men was placed in charge of the presidio which was officially named Presidio of Nuestra Señora del Pilár. Twenty-eight of these were married men and all were fully equipped with arms and horses. Six brass fieldpieces brought from Mexico were placed in the presidio and the necessary powder and balls supplied. The French post of Natchitoches was seven leagues from the new fort intended to hold in check all future attempts of the French to penetrate the Province of Texas. To guard this important post Don Joseph Benito de Arroyo

---

[72]Aguayo to the Viceroy, November 7, 1721. In this letter Aguayo transmitted the one he received from M. Rerenor and his reply. *A. G. I., Audiencia de México,* 61-2-22 (Dunn Transcripts, 1713-1729, University of Texas).

[73]*Ibid.*

was appointed captain by Aguayo and formally placed in command of it, November 4, 1721.[74]

A little more than a month before, on September 29, and not on October 12, as Peña says in his *Derrotero,* the Mission of San Miguel de los Adaes was officially ordered reëtablished in a formal celebration held at the presidial chapel. Father Margil was given authority to erect a mission on a suitable site tentatively selected opposite to the presidio, about one-quarter of a league beyond, across a small creek. The mission itself was not established at this time, because the Indians who had been forced to abandon their homes had not returned with their families. They had promised to congregate in the new mission early in the spring.[75]

Celebration of Aguayo's accomplishment.   With the construction of the fort and the site of the new mission selected, the purpose of the expedition had been accomplished. The French had been driven out of Texas without firing a shot, the Indians had been reassured of the protection of the Spaniards, and French prestige among the natives had undoubtedly suffered a severe blow. To celebrate the accomplishment of their task, the soldiers held a big celebration on October 12, the feast day of Our Lady of Pilár, after whom the presidio was named. There were dances and masquerades. But more strange and significant still was the presentation of several plays.[76] The virgin forest of East Texas became the stage for the first dramatic representation on Texas soil only three years after the first play was given in Williamsburg, Virginia.[77] The natives must have gazed in amazement at the performance, so different and yet reminiscent of their pagan festivals. Unfortunately the chronicler does not record the name of the pieces presented, nor does he give any details. But the practice of using dramatic representations as a means of propagating the truths of the faith was common in Mexico ever since the beginning of the sixteenth century. Perhaps the plays were

---

[74]Auto de Fundación del Presidio de Nuestra Señora del Pilár de los Adaes. November 4, 1721. *A. G. I., Audiencia de México,* 61-2-2 (Dunn Transcripts, University of Texas).

[75]Buckley says the new church and presidio were dedicated on October 12, but the presidio was not finished until November 1. The official *autos* of the dedication of the presidial chapel and of the reëstablishment of the mission have come to light since. *Ibid.* (Dunn Transcripts, 1713-1722, University of Texas).

[76]Peña, *Derrotero,* 22.

[77]For a summary of the early development of the theatre in America and the earliest dramatic representations, see Castañeda, "The First American Play," *Catholic World,* January, 1932.

autos or miracle plays designed specially for the benefit of the large number of Indians who gathered on this occasion for the celebration.[78]

Return to San Antonio. With winter almost upon him, Aguayo was anxious to start back to San Antonio, but lack of supplies made it impossible for him to leave. On October 20, a portion of the flour and corn which had been brought by a vessel from Veracruz to La Bahía, arrived at Los Adaes. At the same time the first two droves of sheep and cattle ever to be driven across Texas from the Río Grande to the Red River came into camp. One consisted of four hundred sheep and the other of three hundred head of cattle. They had been directed over a distance of about three hundred forty leagues, from the frontiers of the kingdom of Nuevo León to the Red River. No expedition before had brought so large a flock or herd. These were the forerunners of the cattle droves that were to play so important a role in the later history of the State.[79]

With the arrival of these supplies, the Marquis definitely set the date of departure for November 12, but a severe sleet and hailstorm on the day before, followed by unusually cold weather, made him postpone the start until the 17th. The bitter cold caused many horses, and not a few mules, to die, so that with much difficulty the expedition started back on its long march to San Antonio. By the time it reached Mission Dolores, many of the soldiers had to travel on foot. The horses and mules continued to die and part of the provisions had to be left on the road with a guard of twenty soldiers. Messengers were dispatched to San Antonio to hurry the provisions, and even the Marquis was obliged to walk at times after the expedition left the Presidio de los Tejas. The weather became more severe as the army proceeded on its way, but the men, Aguayo remarks, seemed to grow healthier and hardier with the hardships of the journey. He did not lose a single person during the march.

The expedition at last reached San Antonio on January 22, 1722. Out of four thousand horses,[80] only fifty returned, and of eight hundred mules only one hundred remained. Aguayo immediately busied himself with the founding of the promised mission to Chief Juan Rodríguez of Ranchería Grande, the removal of the old presidio founded by Alarcón, and the general improvement of the irrigation ditches of the Mission and Presidio of

---

[78]*Ibid.*

[79]Peña, *Derrotero,* 22.

[80]Peña says that the number was almost five thousand but this is an exaggeration. Aguayo, in his letter to the king, declares it was 4000. Peña, *Derrotero,* 23; Aguayo to the King, June 13, 1722 (Bolton Transcripts, 1716-1749).

San Antonio. He dispatched messengers to Coahuila and Nuevo León to secure, in the meantime, horses, mules, and provisions for the return to the Río Grande. The old presidio was defenceless and the soldiers' quarters were thatched-roof huts. He had adobe bricks made, selected a new site between the San Pedro and the San Antonio Rivers, two hundred *varas* from the latter and thirty from the former, and there erected the new presidio, a square structure with four bastions. In a letter written to the king, he declares that the new location is much better and that he placed a garrison of fifty-four soldiers in the new presidio.[81]

Establishment of the Presidio and Mission at Espíritu Santo.   As soon as horses arrived from the Río Grande, early in March, Aguayo dispatched Captain Gabriel Costales to La Bahía with fifty picked men to reënforce the forty sent previously under the command of Captain Ramón. On March 16, Aguayo set out with forty men for the purpose of personally attending to the construction of an adequate fort and the official establishment of the Presidio and the Mission at La Bahía del Espíritu Santo. Illness prevented him from doing anything the first week, and the Easter season having arrived, he postponed action until after Easter week. On April 6, 1722, the foundations for the new presidio were begun on the very spot where La Salle had built his fort in 1685. Nails, firelocks, and other fragments of guns were dug up as the work proceeded. It took fifteen days to finish the foundations. The fort was an octagon, with a moat all around it and four bastions, to which a tower was to be added for a lookout. Each side was forty-five *varas* long. But as the time was short, Aguayo could not wait until the building was completed. After officially founding the Mission of Espíritu Santo de Zúniga, he placed José Domingo Ramón in command of the reënforced garrison, which consisted of ninety men, and taking his departure, arrived in San Antonio on April 26. During the time he was at La Bahía del Espíritu Santo and after his return to San Antonio, Aguayo was in ill health.

During his absence nothing had been done to complete the Presidio of San Antonio. The heavy rains had prevented the men from working and had ruined over thirty thousand adobe bricks which had been made. Aguayo immediately gave orders for twenty-five thousand more to be made and paid forty laborers out of his own pocket to finish as much of the projected fort as possible.

---

[81]Aguayo to His Majesty, June 13, 1722, *Archivo de Santa Cruz de Querétaro, 1716-1749* (Bolton Transcripts, University of Texas).

Significance of Aguayo's Expedition. A fresh supply of horses arrived in San Antonio from Coahuila on April 30, and the Marquis began active preparations for his start back to Coahuila. On May 5, having left a garrison of fifty-four men in San Antonio he set out for Coahuila, where after some hardships, he arrived with his men on May 25. In obedience to orders received from the viceroy, he paid and disbanded his troops on the 31st, giving each man provisions to make the trip home.[82]

"The Aguayo Expedition," declares Miss Buckley, "the last of its kind into Texas, exceeded all others in size and results. It was perhaps the most ably executed of all the expeditions that entered Texas, and in results it was doubtless the most important. It secured to Spain her hold on Texas for about one hundred and fifteen years . . . When Aguayo retired from Texas he left ten missions where before the retreat there had been seven, four presidios where there had been two, two hundred and sixty-eight soldiers instead of some sixty or seventy before, and two presidios were for the first time erected at the points where danger from foreign aggression was most feared—Los Adaes and Espíritu Santo."[83]

[82]The summary given above is based in the main on Peña's *Derrotero* and Aguayo's letter to the king of June 13, 1722, found in *Archivo de Santa Cruz de Querétaro,* 1716-1749 (Bolton Transcripts).

[83]Buckley, *op. cit.,* XV, 60-61.

CHAPTER V

REËSTABLISHMENT OF MISSIONS AND THE FOUNDING OF SAN FRANCISCO
XAVIER AND ESPÍRITU SANTO, 1721-1722

One of the two objects of the Aguayo expedition was the reëstablishment of the missions in East Texas after their forced abandonment in 1719, as a result of the attack of the French. It was with this end in view that ample supplies had been taken along on the march and that the Franciscan missionaries, both from the College of the Holy Cross of Querétaro and the College of Our Lady of Guadalupe of Zacatecas had accompanied Aguayo. The interest of the King and other Spanish officials in the conversion of the natives was genuine. In the royal orders and in the instructions of the viceregal officials we find this sentiment repeatedly expressed in the most emphatic and pious manner. But whatever was the real attitude of the officials, the motive that prompted the unselfish sons of St. Francis are beyond a doubt. It was their desire to spread the Gospel, to bring the thousands of erring and untamed Indians into the fold of the Church, to teach them the manners, the customs, the industries, and the arts of civilized life. No love of glory, no spur for fame, no lure of earthly profit moved the brown-robed Franciscans in their endless toils, their painful journeys over untracked wilderness, their supreme sacrifice for the salvation of souls which many of them were called to make in the course of their missionary endeavors in far-away Texas. The fickle nature of the natives, the rigors of the climate, the privations of the pioneer, the unfounded accusations of officials, born of lack of sympathy, all of these and much more they endured with Christian patience and labored on with unshaken faith and unflinching courage. When despair gripped the heart of officials, when it seemed all labor was in vain, it was the missionaries who never lost hope and slowly, patiently, with love and understanding, laid the foundations of civilized life deep in the soil of Texas.

Refounding of San Francisco de los Tejas. While still camped on the west bank of the Neches River, Aguayo sent a detachment of soldiers with Father José Guerra, on August 2, 1721, to go to the old site of Mission San Francisco de los Tejas to rebuild the church and dwelling place of the priests and make the necessary arrangements for reëstablishment. The little group swam their horses across the stream and after

[149]

traveling a few miles came upon the abandoned mission.[1] This was located in the village of the Neche tribe, close to the mounds, about three or four miles from the crossing. The location has since been definitely identified as being on Bowles Creek, not far from the present crossing of that stream by the old San Antonio road.[2] On August 4, after Aguayo had crossed the river, he sent another detachment of soldiers to help the missionary get everything ready for the next day.

The eight companies of the battalion of San Miguel de Aragón were drawn up in military formation on August 5, before the temporary church which had been hurriedly built for the occasion. High Mass was sung with all solemnity by the Reverend Father Antonio Margil de Jesús and a salute was fired by the troops at the proper time. The bells pealed a joyous welcome to the amazed Indians who came in great numbers to witness the ceremony, while the trumpets blew and the drums rolled. After the ceremony the Marquis and officers retired together with the missionaries to the priests' quarters, where over one hundred and fifty Indians of the Neche tribe had gathered to witness the formal act of taking possession of the mission. The Reverend Father Isidro Felix de Espinosa, President of the missions in the Province of Texas placed under the care of the College of the Holy Cross of Querétaro, now appeared before His Lordship and requested to be placed in charge of the mission which was about to be reëstablished by order of His Majesty and the instructions of the viceroy.

Espinosa, as superior of his group of missionaries and in behalf of the Neche tribe and such others as might be congregated in this place, requested His Lordship that he be installed as the authorized spiritual director and that the Indians be given land and water nearby to sow crops and raise cattle. But the President stipulated that he wanted it clearly understood that if after the mission was established here, and after the Indians were congregated, as they had been urged to do by His Lordship, a more suitable or better location for the mission was found, the present *Act of Possession* would not be invalidated, but would apply to the new site. He said that he was presenting Father Fray Joseph Guerra as resident missionary of the mission to be reëstablished, who would instruct the Indians in the catechism and educate them in the customs and manners of civilized life, ministering to them in all things

---

[1]Peña, *Derrotero*, 16.

[2]Bolton, "Native Tribes," *Quarterly*, XI, 262-263; Buckley, "The Aguayo Expedition," *Quarterly*, XV, 45, Note 3.

spiritual. He further assured the Marquis that he was ready to assign an assistant to Father Guerra upon the arrival of other *Padres* who, according to information received, were now on the way to Texas.

To this Aguayo replied that he was ready to accede to the request of the Reverend Father Espinosa and to grant all that he had asked. He declared that the mission, now to be known as San Francisco de los Neches, was officially placed under the care of the missionaries of Querétaro; that the Indians congregated in the mission were to possess, hold, and enjoy the use of the lands and water necessary to sow crops, raise cattle, and establish a pueblo. In case it was found advisable to move the mission and pueblo to another site, the grant would still be valid, but the missionary in charge at such a time should be instructed, for the sake of information and of permanent record, to notify officially the Captain or *Justicia* of the neighboring presidio regarding the removal. As further evidence of possession, Aguayo took the Reverend Father Guerra by the hand and led him in and out of the church through both doors. He then grasped the hand of the chief of the Neche Indians in like manner and led him in and out of the church around the grounds, causing him to pull up weeds, take up dirt, and scatter rocks to the winds as tokens of occupation.

After this formal ceremony, Aguayo clothed one hundred and fifty-eight Indians, men, women, and children, of the Neche tribe. Through the Reverend Father Espinosa, who knew their language, he explained to them that they had to congregate in a pueblo which was to be known as San Francisco de Valero; he warned them that they must be loyal in their purpose of living near the mission in order that the pueblo might be permanent. The Indians promised they would do all that His Lordship asked just as soon as the crop of corn, which they now had in scattered fields, was gathered.[3]

Refounding of Concepción Mission. The same day that Aguayo sent Father Guerra with a detachment of soldiers to San Francisco, he also sent Fathers Gabriel Vergara and Benito Sánchez with another party of men to proceed to Mission Concepción to make such preparations as were

---

[3]The details of the reëstablishment of the Mission of San Francisco de los Tejas under its new name of San Francisco de los Neches have been gathered from Peña's *Derrotero,* and a copy of the official *Auto de Fundación* contained in Dilixencias Executadas Sobre el restablesimto. de Misiones perthenesientes a la Prova. de los Texas Nuevas Philipinas y Consulta echa a su Ex. por el Marqués de S. Migl de Aguayo y lo demás que dentro se percibe. *A. G. I., Audiencia de México,* 61-2-2 (Dunn Transcripts, 1713-1722).

necessary for its restoration. As soon as the ceremony of refounding San Francisco had been concluded, Aguayo set out with all his troops for the Mission of La Purísima Concepción. He arrived there on August 6 and camped on the site of the Presidio de los Tejas which was abandoned by Ramón in 1719. The diary of the expedition explains what meticulous care the Marquis exercised on this occasion in order to do no damage to the planted crops of the natives. Throughout the entire expedition he had consistently exercised great pains not to antagonize the natives but to win their friendship. The Presidio de los Tejas had been placed by Ramón about four miles from the Angelina River, about a league from Mission Concepción. The actual site of the presidio is just west of the present location of the town of Douglas, on Thomas Creek, while that of the mission, which was about a league southwest of the presidio, is near the present Linwood crossing on the Angelina. The mission was slightly over a mile from the place where the road crossed the river, near two springs, in the middle of the Hainai or Aynay village.[4]

This mission suffered less than any of the others in this region, being the only one that was not completely destroyed. In order to hasten its reëstablishment, Aguayo sent another group of men on August 6 to help complete the work of restoration and construct two dwelling houses for the missionaries. The following day he was notified that everything was in readiness.

On the morning of the 8th, Aguayo and all his troops marched out from their camp on the site of the old Presidio de los Tejas and made their way to Mission Concepción. Here they were met by a large number of Aynay Indians. To impress the natives, Aguayo now presented his best suit, expensively tailored and beautifully trimmed with gold braid, to the captain of the Tejas. He also gave him another jacket adorned with gold and silver cloth. This not only flattered the old chief but greatly pleased all the Indians. The battalion was now formed in three files in front of the church and the six pieces of field artillery were placed between the troops and the church. As at San Francisco de los Neches, High Mass was sung by the Reverend Father Antonio Margil de Jesús, and during the ceremony several salutes were fired by the musketry and the artillery. This made a deep impression upon the Indians who had never witnessed so great a display of military force. The sermon was preached by the Reverend Father Isidro Felix de Espinosa who, according to the chronicler, pronounced "a very eloquent and touching discourse,

---

[4]Peña, *Derrotero,* 17; Bolton, "Native Tribes," *Quarterly,* XI, 269.

for he rejoiced to see the reëstablishment of the mission and the Catholic Faith."

Among those who came to witness the events at Mission Concepción were about eighty Cadodachos. These Indians lived in territory controlled by the French and were under their influence. They were invited, however, by the chief of the Tejas, with whom they were on friendly terms. The large number of troops and the completeness of their arms and equipment made a profound impression also upon these visitors, according to the chronicler.

When the ceremony at the church was over, the chiefs of the various tribes and other Indians who had assembled went to one of the two dwelling houses of the *Padres* to meet the Marquis. The women brought in as gifts their favorite articles of food. When all had assembled, one of their spokesmen told Aguayo that the Indians feared that the Spaniards would abandon them again as in the past. He reassured them of the firm intention of the Spaniards never to forsake them again, explaining that a sufficient number of soldiers would be left among the natives this time to protect them against their enemies. Singling out Chief Cheocas, of the Tejas nation, which he knew was one of the strongest and most influential, he requested him to gather all his people because he, Aguayo, wanted to give them presents and explain why the king had sent so many Spaniards to their land. The chief replied that his people were then scattered but he promised to bring them together soon. The Marquis then ordered dinner to be served to all the captains and the *Padres* and the great feast was enjoyed by all.

After dinner the Reverend Father Espinosa appeared before Governor Aguayo and requested, as had been done at San Francisco de los Neches, to be given possession of the mission in the name of the College of the Holy Cross of Querétaro and on behalf of the Indians of the Aynay nation and such others as might be congregated. The President stipulated, as in the previous case, that if a more suitable location was found later for the mission and the proposed pueblo, the act of possession would not be invalidated by this circumstance, and he declared that the Mission of La Purísima Concepción would again be designated as the capital or head of all the missions placed under the care of the College of Querétaro in the Province of the Tejas. He presented Father Fray Gabriel Vergara as the resident missionary who, together with the petitioner, would instruct the natives in the catechism and educate them in all things pertaining to mission life. Upon hearing the petition, the governor declared that, in accordance with the instructions received from the viceroy, he placed the mission now being reëstablished under the care of the College of the Holy Cross of Querétaro and that he gave the Indians now congregated, and such as might be congregated later, all the necessary lands and water for them to sow crops, to raise cattle, and to build a pueblo. He then took the missionary by the hand and led him in and out of the church as he had done at Mission San Francisco performing the same ceremony with the chief of the Aynay Indians. All the natives who had assembled for the reëstablishment of the mission then took the customary oath of obedience to submit to the missionaries in all things. Chief Cheocas having been officially chosen governor of the mission Indians, was formally given a silver-headed cane as the insignia of his office and dressed in a new suit of blue cloth, resplendent with gold and silver braid. Many gifts and especially articles of clothing were distributed to about four hundred Indians.[5]

Refounding of San José de los Nazonis. After the reëstablishment of the Mission of Nuestra Señora de la Purísima Concepción, Aguayo and the troops retired to their camp, which was about three miles distant. The following day a detachment of soldiers under the command of a lieutenant was ordered to go with Father Fray Benito Sánchez to Mission San José de los Nazonis to rebuild the old church and dwelling house of the missionaries. This mission was about seven or eight leagues to the northeast of Concepción. Its location has been identified as having been on one of the tributaries of Shawnee Creek, near the north line of Nacogdoches County. This tributary is now known as Bill's Creek.[6]

On August 12, Aguayo, hearing that everything was ready, set out from his camp at the old site of the Presidio de los Tejas. He took along only one company of soldiers in order to give the remainder of the expedition an opportunity to rest in camp while he proceeded to refound the third Querétaran mission in East Texas. By the time he arrived, the Nazonis had been called together by the missionary and the church and dwelling houses had been rebuilt. The Indians welcomed Aguayo with unfeigned demonstrations of joy and appeared to be truly happy at the return of the Spaniards.

On August 13, 1721, the formal reëstablishment of Mission San José de los Nazonis took place. High Mass was sung by the Reverend Father

[5]Peña, *Derrotero*, F. 17 vuelta; Dilixencias Executadas sobre el restablesimto . . . *A. G. I., Audiencia de México*, 61-2-2.
[6]Bolton, "The Native Tribes," *Quarterly*, XI, 263.

Espinosa. The company, which was drawn up in front of the church, fired repeated salvos during the ceremony. After the celebration of Mass, Aguayo addressed the Indians,—there were three hundred present. Through an interpreter, he explained to them the purpose of the expedition and he urged them to congregate in a pueblo and live under the tender guidance of the missionaries. He told them, as he had done before on similar occasions, that the Spaniards had come to protect them against their enemies and to instruct them in our Holy Faith and in the ways and customs of civilized life.

Father Espinosa then asked for possession of the mission for his College and for the Indians of the Nazoni nation under the same conditions as were stipulated in the two grants previously made, to all of which the Marquis acceded. After going through the usual ceremonies observed in placing the missionary and the Indians in possession of a new mission, Aguayo gave a full dress of blue cloth to the chief of the Nazonis who had been chosen governor of the proposed pueblo to be founded as soon as the crop was gathered. He was also given a silver-headed cane as the insignia of his office. To the three hundred Indians, Aguayo gave articles of clothing and other presents. Father Fray Benito Sánchez, who had charge of this mission from the time of the Ramón Expedition until its abandonment in 1719, when he had been forced to retreat to San Antonio, was again appointed as pastor. With the refounding of this mission, Aguayo completed the restoration of the three establishments originally founded by Ramón and placed under the care of the missionaries from the College of the Holy Cross of Querétaro.[7]

Refounding of Nuestra Señora de Guadalupe. Aguayo returned on August 14 from the Mission of San José de los Nazonis to his camp at the site of the Presidio de los Tejas, which he used as a base for his operations during the first two weeks in August. Four days before, on August 10, he had dispatched from here a detachment of soldiers with the Reverend Father Antonio Margil de Jesús and two other missionaries to rebuild and make ready the Mission of Nuestra Señora de Guadalupe of the Nacogdoches. This foundation was eight leagues east-southeast from Concepción and was located on the present site of the city of Nacogdoches.[8]

---

[7]Peña, *Derrotero*, 18; Dilixencias Executadas Sobre restablesimto . . . *A. G. I., Audiencia de México,* 62-2-2.

[8]Bolton, "The Native Tribes," *Quarterly,* XI, 258.

Aguayo started with the whole expedition from his camp at Presidio de los Tejas on August 15, after celebrating in a becoming manner the Feast of the Assumption. He did not reach Mission Guadalupe of Nacogdoches that day. As the church and dwelling house for the *Padres* had not been completed by the detachment of men sent six days before, the Marquis ordered more workers to speed up the restoration, on the 17th, and thus he succeeded in getting everything ready for the reëstablishment on the following day.

The Very Reverend Father Antonio Margil de Jesús had the holy joy of celebrating, on August 18, High Mass at the site of this mission which he had founded five years before and which he had been forced to abandon so reluctantly in 1719. During the celebration of Mass the entire battalion of San Miguel de Aragón, organized into eight companies, was formed in front of the church and fired repeated salutes. The Reverend Father Isidro Felix Espinosa, who came up with Aguayo, preached an eloquent sermon and enjoined the Indians to congregate in a pueblo where they should live as Christians. When the Mass was over, the Reverend Father Margil de Jesús, President of the missions in the Province of Texas in charge of the College of Nuestra Señora de Guadalupe of Zacatecas, appeared before the Marquis and requested to be placed in possession of the restored mission for the Zacatecan friars and in behalf of the Indians of the Nacogdoche tribe, and such others as might be congregated here later. He asked that these be given sufficient land and water to enable them to sow their crops, to raise their cattle and to establish a pueblo. He stipulated that if in pursuance of the injunction of His Lordship to the Indians to form a pueblo, a better site for this purpose was found, the grant made now should not be invalidated by this circumstance. He presented Father Fray Joseph Rodríguez as resident missionary and declared he was ready to assign him an assistant upon the arrival of other missionaries who were now on their way to the Tejas. Father Rodríguez would teach the catechism to the Indians in the meantime and instruct them in the arts of civilized life. Aguayo readily acceded to the request of Father Margil, stating that in case the mission should be moved to a better location, the matter should be reported, for official record, to the Captain or *Justicia* of the neighboring presidio. He then took the missionary by the hand and led him in and out of the church, and, doing likewise with the chief elected governor by the Nacogdoche Indians, he gave them sufficient lands and water for the sowing of crops and the raising of cattle.

The Indians were earnestly entreated by Aguayo, as they had been by Father Espinosa, to form a pueblo and live there in order that the *Padres* might be better able to instruct them in the faith and to care for them. To the chief who was chosen as governor of the mission Indians he gave a full dress of English cloth and the customary cane with a silver head as the insignia of his office. There were three hundred and ninety Indians present at the ceremony and all of them were given articles of clothing and presents of various kinds. To conclude the occasion, the Marquis ordered a great banquet to be served to the missionaries, officers, and chiefs of the Indians. In this manner was the first of the Zacatecan missions officially restored by Aguayo.[9]

Refounding Mission Dolores. From Guadalupe, Aguayo continued his march to Mission Dolores. After going six leagues to the east-north-east, the expedition halted at Lake San Bernardo. From here the Venerable Father Fray Antonio Margil de Jesús went ahead with a detachment of soldiers to undertake the work of restoration. Because of difficulties encountered in crossing the numerous streams and in making their way through wooded areas, it was not until the 21st that the main body of the expedition reached the site of the former mission. This had been completely destroyed and not a trace of it was left. When this vanguard arrived, camp was established about half a league from the original site. But not pleased with the former location, Father Margil had, in the meantime, selected a new one. He chose a place beside a stream, near a beautiful spring, on a high slope of clear ground from which a plain well suited for planting extended all around. The stream described in *Peña's Diary* has been identified as Ayish Bayou. The site of the mission itself was on a conical slope, about half a mile south of the present city of San Augustine, on the old King's Highway, at the edge of the bayou.[10]

The following day, the church which Father Margil had started to rebuild was partly finished with the help of the whole battalion and everything was made ready for the restoration of the old mission on the next day. On August 23, High Mass was celebrated with all solemnity and, after the customary speech by the Marquis, possession of the new Mission Nuestra Señora de los Dolores de los Ais was given to the Very Reverend Father Antonio Margil de Jesús as representative of the College of Zacatecas. At the same time the Indians who had gathered for the

[9]Peña, *op. cit.,* 18 vuelta; Dilixencias Executadas, *Audiencia de México,* 62-2-2.
[10]Buckley, *op. cit.,* XV, 50.

occasion occupied the mission lands and were urged to congregate in a pueblo. The usual formalities were observed as in the previous reëstablishments. After the official Act of Possession had been concluded, the Reverend Father Margil presented Father Fray Joseph Albadadejo as the resident missionary and promised to give him an assistant upon the arrival of the missionaries who were now on the way to Texas. The Indians then elected a chief to be the governor of the mission Indians and the Marquis presented him with a new suit of fine cloth and the customary cane with a silver mounting as the insignia of his office. After these ceremonies, clothes and gifts were distributed to one hundred and eighty Indians. As the church and the dwelling house of the missionaries had not been completed, Aguayo left a detachment of soldiers to help finish them, while he continued on his way to Los Adaes.[11]

Refounding Mission San Miguel.   After six days travel the expedition reached the site of the old Mission of San Miguel de los Adaes, but finding it undesirable, pitched camp about half a league beyond, at a spring that flowed through a spacious plain. Aguayo was somewhat perplexed to find no Indians present. Scouting parties were sent out in different directions, but it was not until two days later, on August 31, that news of their whereabouts were obtained. The scouts reported that they had found the *rancherías* of the Indians about ten or fifteen leagues away; that they had welcomed them with much joy; and that their chief, on hearing of the arrival of the Spaniards and their intention to restore the Mission of San Miguel, had promised he would call his people together and would come to see the Marquis as soon as possible.[12]

On September 1, the chief of the Adaes nation came into camp accompanied by many Indians. They all assured Aguayo they were very glad to see the Spaniards return. The old chief told a sad story of how the French had cruelly treated them because of their friendship with the Spaniards, and how the enemy had taken many of the Indian women and children captive to sell them as slaves. He said that his people had been forced to abandon their homes and to move to a more distant site because of the hostility of the French and their allies. Aguayo assured him the Spaniards had come to protect them against their enemies. He told them that a large number of soldiers were going to make their home in this region and that the Adaes should gather in the new Mission of San

[11]Peña, *Derrotero,* 19; Dilixencias Executadas, *Audiencia de México,* 62-2-2; Espinosa, *Chrónica,* I, 443.
[12]Peña, *Derrotero,* 20.

Miguel which was going to be reëstablished for their benefit in the vicinity of the new presidio which he was about to build. The Indians promised they would congregate in the new mission as soon as they harvested their crops.

In spite of their promises and apparent joy at seeing the Spaniards back, a whole month passed, during which the new Presidio of Nuestra Señora del Pilár was almost completed and a presidial chapel was built, without sufficient Indians appearing there to start the proposed mission on the new site. Finally, on the Feast of the Archangel St. Michael, September 29, it was decided to declare the establishment, this being the day of its titular saint and patron. The ceremony took place in the presidial chapel. After the celebration of High Mass, during which salvos were fired by the entire battalion and the six fieldpieces of the expedition, the Reverend Father Antonio Margil de Jesús, President of the missions of the College of Zacatecas in the Province of the Tejas, declared that not being able to establish at this time the proposed Mission of San Miguel de Cuellar de los Adaes because the Indians, who were to be congregated in this mission, were now living ten to fifteen leagues away and would not be able to come together until the spring, he requested, nevertheless, that a place be designated for its establishment at a later date, with sufficient lands and water to raise crops and cattle and to found a pueblo, and that these allotments be granted for that purpose. In the meantime, he, Father Margil, promised to care for the Indians of the Adaes nation in the presidial chapel and to visit them and minister to them in their distant *rancherías* as well as circumstances permitted. He agreed to assign another missionary to this mission upon the arrival of those who were now on their way to Texas. Upon hearing the petition of the Very Reverend Father Margil, the Marquis granted everything he asked, selected a spot, and gave possession to him and to such Indians as might be congregated later. This mission, which was not erected at this time, was located about a mile from the new Presidio of Nuestra Señora del Pilár, which for fifty years was to be the residence of the governors of the province until the office was moved to San Antonio in 1772. Its location has been definitely fixed about two miles from the present town of Robeline, Louisiana.[13]

San Francisco Xavier Mission in San Antonio. With the nominal reëstablishment of the Mission of San Miguel de los Adaes, the last of

---

[13]Peña, *Derrotero*, 22; Buckley, *op. cit.*, XV, 52-53; *Dilixencias Executadas, Audiencia de México*, 62-2-2.

the three Zacatecan missions had been restored. It had the distinction of being the most advanced outpost of the Spanish possessions in Texas. It was located about a mile beyond the presidio on the road to Natchitoches. Aguayo had now attained the two main objects of his expedition. He had established a strong military defense with a garrison of one hundred men within seven leagues of the most advanced French outpost, and he had restored the six missions of the two colleges of Querétaro and Zacatecas, which the missionaries had been forced to abandon in 1719. He was now ready to start back to San Antonio.

Setting out from Los Adaes on his return march on November 17, 1721, Aguayo finally reached his destination on January 23, 1722, after many hardships, as a result of the inclement weather and the flooded stage of the rivers. True to his promise made to Chief Juan Rodríguez over a year ago he immediately took steps to found a new mission for the Indians of Ranchería Grande. As it will be remembered, their chief had acted as a guide for the expedition on its way to East Texas, leading Aguayo and his men by a new route higher up than the road that had been followed by previous *entradas*. As early as 1720, before Aguayo set out from Coahuila, Chief Rodríguez had visited him in January of that year, to ask that a mission be founded for his people. He had explained at that time that his nation comprised about six hundred Sana Indians, all of whom were anxious to be congregated in a mission. With the promise that upon the arrival of the Marquis in San Antonio action would be taken for this establishment, he returned to his followers whom he had left there and awaited word from His Lordship for more than a year.[14]

When Aguayo reached San Antonio the first time, on April 4, 1721, the faithful Chief Rodríguez was among the first to welcome him and to remind him of his promise. Aguayo suggested that the Indians from Ranchería Grande join those already congregated in the Mission of San Antonio de Valero. But Chief Rodríguez declared this was not possible because, in the first place, his nation was too numerous, and in the second place, they were not on friendly terms with those already living there. He expressed his fear that they would not get along well with the other tribes and explained that he preferred to wait until a new mission could be established for his people, separate from that of Valero. After Aguayo returned to San Antonio for the second time, early in 1722, Chief

---

[14]Testimonio de la Misión de San Francisco Xavier, *A. G. I., Audiencia de Guadalajara*, 67-3-11.

MISSION OF NUESTRA SEÑORA DE LA CONCEPCIÓN DE ACUÑA, LOCATED AT SAN ANTONIO IN 1731

Rodríguez immediately went out to Ranchería Grande and brought back with him fifty families for the new mission. He again petitioned the Governor to found the new establishment as he had promised. Desirous of fulfilling his pledge His Excellency summoned Father Fray Joseph González, resident missionary of San Antonio de Valero, all the captains of the battalion of San Miguel de Aragón, and all the Indians interested to appear before him on March 12.[15]

On the appointed date, when all had assembled, Aguayo went out with them to choose a suitable place for the new mission. The site selected was on a beautiful plain, about one league to the south of the Mission of San Antonio de Valero. Water could easily be obtained to irrigate the lands either from the ditch that carried water to Valero or directly from the San Antonio River. It was the opinion of all those present that the location offered was the most satisfactory for the proposed mission. The Marquis gave formal possession of the site in the name of the king to Father Fray Joseph González, of the College of Querétaro, and to Chief Juan Rodríguez and all the Indians present. The lands of the new mission were bounded on the west by the San Antonio River and on the north by the area already granted to the Mission of Valero. "In evidence of real possession His Lordship took the Indian Juan Rodríguez by the hand and led him to a high prominence found on the site, near a natural clearing. Walking over the ground he caused the chief to pull up weeds and grass and pick up dirt which he scattered to the four winds. He then appointed Chief Juan Rodríguez governor of the mission [which he named San Francisco Xavier de Nájera], entreating him to comply with his duties. Father Fray Joseph González promised His Lordship he would take charge of teaching the doctrine of our Holy Faith to the Indians until a missionary came from his College, destined for that purpose." He assured His Lordship that he knew that a missionary would come as soon as the report of the establishment of the mission was made known, because the Very Reverend Father Fray Felix de Espinosa, Guardian of the College, gave him this assurance.[16]

A copy of the proceedings was sent immediately to the viceroy for his approval and another one to Father Espinosa that he might send a missionary for the purpose specified. The act was witnessed by Captains Tomás Zubiría, Miguel Colón, Gabriel Costales, Manuel de Herrera, Francisco Becerra Luque, Pedro de Oribe, Juan Cantú, and Matías García

---

[15]*Ibid.*
[16]*Ibid.*

and Father Fray Joseph González. Thus was the Mission of San Francisco Xavier de Nájera formally established on March 12, 1722, subject to the approval of the viceroy, as a result of the unwavering faith of Chief Juan Rodríguez, of Ranchería Grande. The foundation, however, was destined to have a precarious existence for a few years before its disappearance, as will be shown by subsequent events.

When the report of the establishment of this new mission reached the viceroy with a request for the royal aid usually granted on such occasions, which consisted of all the things necessary for the furnishing of the chapel and a liberal supply of grain, cattle and tools for the same Indians, he was in no frame of mind to regard the proposal with favor. The new Viceroy Casafuerte had but recently arrived in Mexico with special instructions from the king to curtail all expenses possible. At this time, he was already contemplating drastic measures to correct the serious abuses of all the frontier presidios of New Spain which were the chief source of drain upon the royal treasury. The Aguayo expedition had already cost the king over two hundred thousand *pesos,* and with the danger of the French apparently removed, the viceroy did not see why the expense for the establishment of a new mission so near to those of San Antonio Valero and of San José was necessary. He consequently curtly informed Father Espinosa that the royal treasury was unable to supply the customary aid for the new mission of San Francisco Xavier de Nájera, or to pay the usual stipend allowed the missionary. Under the circumstances, Father Espinosa replied to the viceroy that the College of Querétaro could not undertake to bear the financial burden of the foundation; that such Indians as wanted to join either of the other two missions already established would be welcomed and would receive instruction in the *doctrina* the same as all others.[17]

In the meantime, true to his promise, Father González tried to take care of the Indians of Ranchería Grande until a new missionary arrived. A special record of baptisms and burials for these Indians was kept in the Mission of San Antonio de Valero, until the new mission was established, in order that they might be transferred at that time.[18] But years passed and nothing more was done. Father González lost interest in the work as the result of misunderstandings with the captain of the presidio and many of the followers of Chief Juan Rodríguez became tired of the

---

[17]Fray Pedro Pérez de Mezquia to the Viceroy, June 22, 1725. *Archivo de Santa Cruz de Querétaro* (Dunn Transcripts, 1716-1749).

[18]Bolton, "Spanish Mission Records at San Antonio," *Quarterly,* X, 297-308.

temporary arrangement, grew dissatisfied with mission life, and went back to their *ranchería*. The Marquis of Aguayo, who had been deeply touched by the fidelity of the old chief, had furnished the Mission of Valero, out of his own pocket, supplies to keep him and his followers until the new mission was permanently provided with the necessities and he had asked his successor, Governor Pérez de Almazán, to do likewise.[19]

Three years later in 1725, when the Marquis of Aguayo learned that nothing had been done in the matter, he pointed out in an interview with Viceroy Casafuerte the importance of establishing the mission for the Indians of Ranchería Grande and promised His Excellency that he was ready and willing to contribute all the things necessary to furnish the new chapel and supply the Indians with the required tools, cattle, and grain. He said that a new missionary was not necessary because the location of the proposed mission being only a quarter of a league from San Antonio de Valero, one of the two friars stationed there could be assigned to take care of the new mission without inconvenience. It seems that the viceroy was under the impression that the Fathers of the College of Querétaro had refused to take charge of San Francisco Xavier and were still of the same mind. In view of this fact, Aguayo communicated with the Guardian and made an agreement with him in writing in which the Marquis listed the various supplies, provisions, tools, and grain he would furnish for the establishment of the mission, if the College undertook to order one of the missionaries of San Antonio de Valero to take charge, and the viceroy gave his approval.[20] He offered to supply one red vestment, corporals, burse, amice, pall, and antependium; one surplice; one manual; one bell; twelve oxen; eight young bulls, three or four years old; two bulls for breeding; ten cows, three or four years old; eight bulls seven or eight years old to feed to the Indians; eight carders and plows to cultivate the mission farms; eight new axes; six dozen large knives; six dozen pocket knives; six bundles of beads; two iron bars, one twenty and one twenty-five *varas* long; two saws, one large and one small; two chisels, two bits, one large and one small; one adze; one compass; one paring chisel; two planes, one small and one large; one bolt of blue woolen cloth; one-half bolt of cotton goods; one bolt of red woolen cloth; two bundles of tobacco; fifty blankets; two brass pots; two copper kettles;

[19]Aguayo to the Viceroy, February 26, 1725. *A. G. N., Provincias Internas,* Vol. 32, Part 2, 1725-1731.

[20]*Ibid.;* also Fray Pedro Pérez de Mezquia to the Viceroy, June 22, 1725, *A. G. N., Provincias Internas,* Vol. 32, Part 2.

one large copper spoon; four brass candlesticks; one lamp and wick; one rug or mat to place before the altar; four *metates* with eight pestles to grind corn; four cooking pans; and four hundred *pesos* in silver to purchase corn. The Marquis declared that the mission already had a large painting of San Francisco Xavier with a beautiful gold frame as well as a chalice, paten, little spoon, wine and water bottles of silver, and a white vestment. The Guardian now petitioned the viceroy to allow the College of Querétaro to begin operations, and informed His Excellency of the readiness of Aguayo to furnish all the necessary supplies and provisions. The viceroy quickly consented to the request and issued a decree ordering the immediate formal establishment of the new mission for Chief Juan Rodríguez and the Indians of Ranchería Grande, which was to be founded on the site chosen by Aguayo in 1722, and cared for by one of the missionaries now stationed at San Antonio de Valero without expense to the royal treasury. Father Mezquia, the Guardian of the College, upon receipt of the viceregal decree instantly instructed the Father President of the mission in San Antonio to proceed with the foundation.[21]

By the time the viceregal decree arrived in San Antonio, Father González was no longer there. It fell to Father Fray Miguel Sevillano de Paredes, the newly appointed President of the missions of the Querétaran College in Texas to carry out the instructions of the Guardian and the orders of the viceroy. In a long report written in January, 1726, shortly after his arrival he gives in detail the reasons why he was unable to comply with the orders received for the formal establishment of the Mission of San Francisco Xavier de Nájera. Three or four days after his arrival, he called Juan Rodríguez and all the Indians of Ranchería Grande in San Antonio at that time to appear before him. Great was his surprise when only twelve warriors, and not all of them with families, came in response to his call. Agreeable to the order of the viceroy of July 2, 1725, and the instructions from the Guardian of the College, he informed the Sanas he was going to provide permanent quarters for them. He explained to them, through an interpreter, their duties and pointed out the advantages of mission life. He told them that the establishment was going to be founded at their request, and that they could choose between himself and Father Fray Joseph Hurtado, the other missionary

---

[21]Order of the Viceroy for the establishment of San Francisco Xavier, July 2, 1725. *Archivo de la Santa Cruz de Querétaro*, 1716-1749 (Dunn Transcripts, University of Texas).

at San Antonio de Valero, whomever they preferred as their pastor. But his surprise at the small number of Indians present was surpassed by that of the reply which Chief Juan Rodríguez made to his announcement.[22]

He declared that he and his people no longer desired a separate mission; that they preferred to stay in San Antonio de Valero; that they were too few to live in a separate district so far from the presidio; that the Apaches, who were their bitter enemies, would most assuredly kill all of them in the new abode. Father Sevillano de Paredes asked Chief Rodríguez to go to Ranchería Grande to bring others of his tribe in order that the mission might be founded. But to this he replied that he had recently seen them and that they had all declared not to accept the proposals made in their behalf. He said that he and his companions would rather live with the Xarames in the Mission of San Antonio de Valero.

The next day, Father Sevillano de Paredes, unable to believe his eyes or his ears, asked Chief Juan Rodríguez and his followers to appear before Nicolás Flores, the Captain of the Presidio of San Antonio de Béjar, that he might bear testimony to their determination of not being placed in a separate mission. Asked in his presence if they desired to have a mission established for them, separate and distinct from that of Valero, they again affirmed their wish to remain there. They stated that the rest of their friends had become discouraged by the long delay and believed they had been deceived.

As Governor Pérez de Almazán was in Saltillo at this time and intended to bring the supplies and provisions offered by Aguayo for the Mission of San Francisco Xavier, on his return, a messenger was dispatched to him with all haste, asking him not to ship them as they were not necessary in view of the refusal of the Indians to be congregated as originally planned. Governor Almazán informed Aguayo of the changed opinion of Chief Rodríguez and left the supplies in Saltillo to await further news from San Antonio.

In the meantime, Father Sevillano de Paredes called seven chiefs of the Sana nation, who were at Ranchería Grande, to see if he could get them to come and live in the proposed mission. They all came along with Chief Marcos, bringing a number of warriors and women. After three days of feasting, during which they were urged to congregate in the new location, they became angry at the insistence and said: "The Span-

---

[22]Representación sobre dificultados para llevar a efecto la orden. . . . Por Fray Miguel Sevillano de Paredes, January, 1726. *Archivo de la Santa Cruz de Querétaro*, 1716-1749 (Dunn Transcripts).

iards want us to work for them; we want to be their friends and to fight
no more; but to live near them, or to be placed in a mission, we do not
want even to speak of it." Father Miguel frankly confesses that he did
everything *usque ad ultimum potentis* to attract the Indians, but all in
vain. He says that Fray Juan de los Angeles, who knows the language
of the Tejas and is very skillful in the use of signs, tried to convince
them but failed, and that Chief Rodríguez had tried the same persuasion
without results.[23]

But the enthusiastic missionary would not be discouraged in spite of
the circumstances. In his report he goes on to explain that he is going
to make one more attempt. He says that he has arranged for Chief
Rodríguez to accompany Governor Almazán on his return to East Texas
and that the two of them will stop at Ranchería Grande in a last effort
to get some of the chiefs of the Yerbipiames to come to live at the proposed mission of San Francisco Xavier. He points out that this end is
greatly to be desired because the Indians of Ranchería Grande have
always had a bad influence upon those congregated in the missions of
East Texas. Most of the Yerbipiames are apostate Indians, he says, who
visit the others frequently and cause them to become dissatisfied with
mission life. He expresses the fear, however, that all the endeavors to
bring them to the new mission will be unsuccessful.

If this last attempt failed, he promised the Guardian of the College of
Querétaro that he would go in person to the *ranchería* of the Paquache
nation on the upper Nueces and try to convince these Indians to congregate in the new mission. He said he was hopeful of success because these
Indians had suffered two severe attacks recently from the Apaches, and
as a result of these misfortunes they were more likely to be willing to
listen to his proposals to come and live under the protection of the Spanish
garrison on the San Antonio. He closed his report by assuring his superior
that he would try to establish the Mission of San Francisco Xavier as
ordered by the viceroy with one or the other tribe, or with both.[24]

It seems that his efforts to carry out the belated establishment of the
Mission of San Francisco Xavier de Nájera proved useless. The result of
Father Miguel's negotiations with the Paquache was never reported. After
1726, the separate record kept by the missionaries at San Antonio de
Valero for the Indians of San Francisco Xavier was discontinued. Thus
this mission never became a reality in spite of the persistence of Chief

[23]*Ibid.*
[24]*Ibid.*

Rodríguez from 1720 to 1722 and of the Marquis of Aguayo and the missionaries of the College of Querétaro, manifested in the several earnest attempts of Father Miguel Sevillano de Paredes to carry out the vice-regal decree for its establishment.

Founding of Nuestra Señora del Espíritu Santo. But let us now turn to the founding of the Mission of Nuestra Señora del Espíritu Santo. It is necessary to go back in our narrative to the beginning of the Aguayo expedition. While he was still on the Río Grande, early in 1721, the Marquis sent a detachment of forty men under command of Captain José Domingo Ramón, to occupy the Bay of Espíritu Santo which was being threatened by the French. This detachment traveled with another group of one hundred soldiers sent to San Antonio under the command of Lieutenant General Almazán.[25] On March 10, Ramón and his detachment continued their march to Espíritu Santo, accompanied by the enthusiastic missionary Agustín Patrón, who had originally entered Texas in 1716 and had been forced to retreat to San Antonio in 1719. The party arrived on April 4, 1721, and after taking formal possession of the bay in the name of His Majesty, reported the occupation of this important post to Aguayo, who had arrived in San Antonio on the same day. Father Patrón, who had been instructed to found a mission for the coast Indians in the most suitable location near the proposed presidio, lost no time in sending word to the Indians to come to see him. A month after his arrival a number of Indians of the Coco nation visited him and the Spaniards. To this tribe the good friar explained the desire of His Majesty the King to congregate them in a mission, where they could be instructed in the word of God and where they could be taught to live as civilized men. Through an interpreter, Francisco El Sixame, an Indian from the Mission of Dulcísimo Nombre de Jesús, of Coahuila, who knew the language of the coast tribes well, he pointed out the advantages of mission life as compared with their wandering ways. They listened with interest and replied that they would go back and tell their friends all they had heard and that they would try to bring many others to form a pueblo around the mission the *Padre* was going to found for them. By the next moon, they came back, led by all the chiefs of the Coco and the Cujame nations, followed by all their women and children. Father Patrón had succeeded too well. Here were two populous nations ready to be congregated, but there were not enough supplies to feed the Indians of the mission until they

---

[25] Peña, *Derrotero*, 6.

could raise a crop of their own. With deep regret, the zealous missionary was forced to inform them that they would have to return to their *rancherías* until he could get the necessary provisions and the seed required for planting.[26]

Father Patrón lost no time in notifying the Marquis of Aguayo of the success he had met with in getting the coast Indians to agree to be congregated in a mission. He asked for His Lordship's authorization to start a foundation for these Indians and he suggested that, if the plan met with his approval, he might issue the corresponding orders immediately to Captain Ramón that he might assign the necessary lands close by. Without delay Aguayo sent orders to Captain Ramón from Peñuelas, while en route to East Texas, to select a suitable site for the new establishment and to give formal possession, in the name of the king, to Father Patrón and the Indians who might come to live there. But the arrangement could not be carried out because the corn and cattle which the viceroy graciously granted for the purpose were delayed many months on the road as a result of the high stage of the rivers. It was not until early in March, 1722, that a portion of the supplies arrived. Captain Ramón, agreeable to the instructions received from Aguayo, immediately sent word to the Coco and the Cujame nations to come, as everything was ready to found a mission and pueblo for them. By the 16th, when Aguayo arrived at La Bahía del Espíritu Santo from San Antonio, many Indians had already come with their families and many others had gone in search of their friends to bring them to the new mission. Aguayo, who was anxious to win their friendship, distributed gifts to them, giving them cotton and woolen goods, skirts, blankets, butcher knives, pocket knives, mirrors, beads, and tobacco. He gave presents to the men and the women alike, treating them with sincere kindness. The lands selected by Father Patrón were plowed and made ready for the sowing of the crops, and everything was prepared for the official establishment.[27]

The location selected by Father Patrón for the new mission was on the bank of the stream that flowed by the presidio, and this rivulet has been definitely identified as Garcitas Creek. It was about three-fourths of a league from the fort. Here there were good farm lands near the fresh water and hence the farms were capable of being irrigated without much trouble, Father Patrón requested Aguayo to give him possession of the

---

[26]Testimonio de la Misión de Nuestra Sra. de Loreto. *A. G. I., Audiencia de Guadalajara*, 67-3-11 (Dunn Transcripts, 1710-1738).

[27]*Ibid.*

site chosen in order to safeguard the rights of the Indians who had already been congregated thereon. Much pleased with the progress made by the indefatigable missionary in getting the coastal tribes to agree to form a mission and establish a pueblo, the Marquis ordered that possession be given to Father Patrón, as representative of the College of Zacatecas, and to the Indians of such lands as were necessary for the erection of a church, the founding of a pueblo, and the establishment of farms where they might raise their own food. The governor fixed the date of the ceremony for April 10, 1722, and summoned Father Patrón, the mission Indians already congregated, and Captains Tomás Zubiría, Miguel Colón, Gabriel Costales, and Manuel Herrera for that day.[28]

Father Agustín Patrón gathered all the Indians of the Coco and Cujame nations on the site selected for the proposed mission, which was about two miles from the very spot where the unfortunate La Salle had originally established Fort St. Louis. Here the captains, already mentioned, also came to witness the formal ceremony of transfer. When all had assembled, the Marquis of Aguayo in person gave possession of the chosen site to Father Patrón and the Indians, designating the place where the church was to be built, and granting them all rights to the use of the lands and the water necessary for the planting and raising of crops, all in the name of His Majesty the King. Father Patrón entered the temporary church and made other demonstrations to show possession. Aguayo took the chiefs of the assembled Cocos, Cujames, and Carancahuas (Karankawas) by the hand, led them into the church and out again and then over the fields. After the ceremony was over, he appointed the chief of the Cocos as governor of the Indian pueblo nearby and ordered that a copy of all these proceedings be sent to the viceroy. To all of the transactions Father Patrón and the captains present gave testimony. The new foundation was officially named Mission Nuestra Señora del Espíritu Santo de Zúñiga and the zealous *Padre* was left in charge of the new establishment.[29] It remained at this site but four years, and was moved in 1726 to the Guadalupe River.

When Aguayo returned to San Antonio on April 26, 1722, he could claim with reasonable pride that he had successfully accomplished the purpose of his expedition. He had not only refounded the original seven missions, but he had added three: San José, San Francisco Xavier de Nájera, and Nuestra Señora del Espíritu Santo de Zúniga. The first

---

[28]*Ibid.*
[29]*Ibid.*

of these was destined to become the queen of the frontier institutions, and although San Francisco Xavier was never to be realized, that of Espíritu Santo, in spite of many changes of location, developed into one of the most successful undertakings in the coastal region of Texas. These ten centers of civilization, for each mission was truly a center, where the Indians were not only instructed in our Faith but also in the customs, the manners, the industries, and the arts of social development and the cultivation of the fundamentals of self-government, were in time to exercise a far-reaching influence. It is no exaggeration, therefore, to say that the missionaries, through their unselfish endeavors for the spread of the Gospel, planted the seeds of civilization deep in the virgin soil of Texas.

CHAPTER VI

The Organization of Mission Life, 1722-28

After thirty-two years of untiring and persistent efforts, in spite of numerous vicissitudes and frequent French intrusions, the missionaries of the two colleges of Propaganda Fide of Querétaro and Zacatecas saw their dream realized at last. In 1722, when the Marquis of Aguayo left Texas, the missions were permanently established under adequate protection for the first time. Upon his retirement from Texas in 1694, Father Massanet, disillusioned and truly saddened by his experiences with the fickle nature of the natives, was forced to admit that missionary endeavors without proper military backing were useless. But it had taken twenty-eight years and the French threat of 1719 for Spanish officials to come to a realization of this fact. The Franciscans had consistently urged that a sufficient military guard should be provided to command respect by the Indians.

Now the Presidio of San Antonio had a garrison of fifty-four men to protect the Missions of San Antonio de Valero, San José, and San Francisco Xavier; the Presidio of Nuestra Señora de Loreto at La Bahía had ninety soldiers under the sway of Captain José Domingo Ramón, to safeguard the new mission of Nuestra Señora del Espíritu Santo; the Presidio de los Tejas had twenty-five men to afford adequate protection to the Missions of San Francisco de los Neches, Concepción, and San José de los Nazonis; and the new Presidio of Nuestra Señora del Pilár de los Adaes counted on a garrison of one hundred men with which to defend the Missions of Nuestra Señora de Guadalupe, Nuestra Señora de los Dolores, and San Miguel. It is true that the purpose of these garrisons was not solely the protection of the missions from foreign aggression which was the particular objective of the military posts placed at La Bahía and Los Adaes. The chief duty of the soldiers, however, was to coöperate with the spiritual authorities in the vicinity in congregating, converting, and civilizing the Indians. The officials of Mexico, as well as those of Spain, fully realized the importance of winning the friendship of the natives and were unquestionably moved in the establishment of these presidios by an ardent desire to help the zealous Franciscans in their worthy endeavors. The early misunderstandings between the various commanders and the missionaries during the period under discussion was due largely to the failure of these officers to understand the relation which the king and the viceregal officials intended should exist between the two pioneer institutions, which in coöperation with one another formed the very body and soul of the frontier system of Spain in America.

Fernando Pérez de Almazán becomes Governor. While at Los Adaes, Aguayo wrote a significant letter to the viceroy on November 7, 1721, just ten days before his return march to San Antonio. After giving many interesting details of what had been accomplished by the expedition placed under his care and the many difficulties which had been overcome, he declared that he was going to leave his Lieutenant-General Don Fernando Pérez de Almazán in command of the entire province upon his withdrawal. He assured His Excellency that no one was better able to carry out the reorganization of the Province of Texas just recovered from the French than Don Fernando, whose noble parentage, distinguished services, unquestioned ability, unselfish devotion to duty, and great zeal fitted him particularly for this important work. In discussing the vital question of the administration of the vast territory, he pointed out that he had come to the conviction that it was not possible for a single man to govern efficiently the two provinces of Coahuila and Texas. In support of the opinion he alleged that the distance from the Presidio de Coahuila to Los Adaes was fully three hundred fifty leagues and that the road was intercepted by numerous rivers and streams, many of which were impassable during the greater part of the year as a result of the heavy rains. He stated that the governor of the Province of Texas would naturally be forced to divide his time between Los Adaes, San Antonio, and La Bahía, each of which he should visit frequently. These tasks would be impossible if he had to reside in Coahuila. "If the government of the two provinces is not separated, it is my humble opinion," he declares, "that the fruits of this expedition will be seriously jeopardized." In view of the facts stated, he concluded that the government of the two provinces should be separated for the best interests of the king and the provinces themselves.[1]

Should his recommendations meet with the approval of the viceroy, he suggested further that in selecting a governor for the province, Don

---

[1]Aguayo to the Viceroy, Los Adaes, November 7, 1721. *A. G. I., Audiencia de México,* 61-2-2 (Dunn Transcripts). It is worth while noting the arguments advanced by Aguayo in 1722 in support of a separate political government from Coahuila for Texas, which are surprisingly similiar to those advanced in 1833 for independent statehood.

Fernando be given preference. To send someone else might cause dissatisfaction among the Indians and make them distrust the Spaniards. This would give the French an opportunity to regain their influence at a time when the natives had just been weaned from their tutelage. In support of his judgment in this matter he declared that Don Fernando was well liked by the Indians, who had become much attached to him; that the soldiers had a high opinion of his ability and obeyed him willingly; and that the missionaries looked upon his possible appointment with favor, particularly the Reverend Father Margil, who had asked the Marquis to request his appointment. As he was on the eve of setting out for San Antonio, from which place he would proceed to La Bahía to establish there officially the presidio and to reënforce its garrision as ordered by the viceroy, Aguayo asked that the appointment of Pérez de Almazán as governor be sent to him at La Bahía, that he might turn the government over to his Lieutenant-General before leaving the province.[2]

When Aguayo arrived in San Antonio in January, 1722, he was sick. The hardships of the expedition had undermined his health. It will be remembered, however, that in spite of his illness he went on to La Bahía in March, where he had to spend over a week in bed before he could officially establish the presidio and the mission. But as soon as he returned to Coahuila, he immediately resigned as governor of both Coahuila and Texas.[3] The viceroy accepted his resignation and Don Fernando Pérez de Almazán was accordingly appointed Governor of the Province of Texas as suggested by Aguayo. The new governor immediately took up his residence at Los Adaes, which being the most advanced post in the direction of the French frontier and having the largest garrison, naturally came to be regarded as the capital of the province.

Conditions in San Antonio and Los Adaes.   Next in importance, not so much because of the number of soldiers stationed in its presidio, but because of the number of missions in its vicinity and the growing number of unofficial civil settlers, was the Presidio of San Antonio de Béjar. Upon his return from East Texas, Aguayo had appointed Matías García, an experienced officer and Indian fighter, captain, but he was soon afterwards named by the viceroy protector of the mission Indians of Coahuila. To fill the vacancy created, the Marquis of Aguayo now appointed Nicolás Flores y Valdez to this important position. He had begun his service as a

---

[2]*Ibid.*

[3]Aguayo to the King, Coahuila, June 13, 1722. *A. G. I., Audiencia de Guadalajara,* 67-3-11 (Dunn Transcripts).

soldier in 1693, by joining an expedition organized by Governor Gregorio de Varona Salinas to take supplies to the missions in Texas. When in 1701 the garrison of San Juan Bautista was established, he was one of the first to enlist. He continued to serve here for fourteen years, beginning as a private soldier and being promoted first to sergeant and later to *Alférez,* the highest rank next to the captain in the absence of a lieutenant. From here he went to Texas on September 4, 1719, with the detachment of eighty-four men organized by Aguayo at the request of the viceroy, serving as lieutenant under Captain Cárdenas. When in March of the following year the Indians of Santa Rosa de Nadadores revolted, Aguayo asked Flores to bring as many soldiers as possible from San Antonio to enable him to put down the uprising, with which request he complied and succeeded in joining Aguayo in time to help him defeat the Indians in April. During the expedition to Texas, he acted as scout or explorer and was of great assistance not only in the reëstablishment of the missions, but in securing supplies from San Antonio on various occasions. When Aguayo went to La Bahía, he was left in charge of the construction of the new presidio outlined by the Marquis. During this time he discovered a new source of salt for the garrison. Shortly after the return of Aguayo, five Apache Indians stole fifty horses. Flores immediately set out in pursuit with ten men and, after an exciting chase, succeeded in recovering the stolen horses, bringing back to Aguayo as gruesome evidence of his triumph the heads of four of the Indians.[4]

After the departure of Aguayo and his large expedition, things settled down to the same slow pace as before, and hunger, want and sickness visited the struggling missions once more. "Although for a while the poor missionaries saw many companies in Texas," exclaims the Reverend Father Espinosa, "they did not have the pleasure of seeing their missions increased by a single extra guard, nor did they receive any additional help in sowing the scanty grains which are essential for their sustenance." In vain they tried to make their needs heard, he declares, by word of mouth, by letters, and by reports, explaining what the country needed in order that it might prosper. But the chief interest of the governor and the captains of the various presidios had never been to take a real interest in the conversion of the natives, he goes on to explain, sadly observing that the military have always left everything for the mission-

[4]Appointment of Nicolás Flores y Valdez as Captain of San Antonio de Béjar, April 30, 1722; Certificación de servicios del Capitán Nicolás Flores. In *A. G. N., Provincias Internas,* Vol. 32, Part 2, 1725-1731.

aries to do and have placidly expected that the missions should grow and develop, without their putting forth the slightest effort.[5] Although this view of conditions may seem somewhat exaggerated, it is corroborated sufficiently by contemporary reports of military officials to justify the disillusionment felt by this zealous missionary, who had labored so faithfully and so long in Texas.

Governor Pérez de Almazán, who was in actual distress, came to San Antonio in search of supplies. Here he wrote a letter to the viceroy on March 24, 1724, in which he gives a vivid account of conditions in Texas during the two years immediately following the withdrawal of Aguayo. Both during the summer of 1722 and 1723, the crops planted at Los Adaes and La Bahía proved dismal failures and the grain harvested was insufficient to supply the needs of the presidios and missions. There were several contributing factors. The rains had come too late and the excessive heat had caused much sickness. In vain, he goes on to explain, that he tried to secure supplies and provisions at this time from either San Antonio or Río Grande. During the preceding year, a train of flour and a drove of cattle sent from San Juan Bautista for the presidios and missions of La Bahía and Los Adaes had been detained on the road seven months as a result of the heavy rains and the high stage of the numerous rivers that intercept the three hundred fifty leagues that lie between the Río Grande and East Texas. Almost the entire shipment of flour which consisted of one hundred *cargas,* had spoiled before it reached its destination, and many of the cattle were lost in the long delays at the different rivers, some animals had run away and others were drowned in crossing the streams. Aware of the obstacle presented by the rivers, he said that he had placed rafts at the most difficult intersections, but these conveyances seemed to have done little or no good.[6]

The captain of the Presidio de los Adaes, José Benito de Arroyo, took seriously ill early in the preceding summer and the governor was unable to go in person after the sorely needed supplies because there was no one to remain in charge. With the approach of winter, Captain Arroyo asked leave to go to Saltillo for treatment and Governor Almazán was obliged to grant the request, being forced to remain at Los Adaes until December 29, 1723, before necessity forced him to start in the middle of winter for San Antonio. He explained to the viceroy that it was his plan to buy

[5]Espinosa, *Chrónica Apostólica,* I, 457.

[6]Fernando Pérez de Almazán to the Viceroy, San Antonio, March 24, 1724. *San Francisco el Grande Archives,* Vol. X, 110-115.

a supply of corn at the Río Grande from the Mission of San Juan Bautista and to secure the flour from Saltillo. If he succeeded in obtaining these provisions he intended to bring them by mule train to San Antonio, and from there he would send what was needed to both La Bahía and Los Adaes.[7]

Conditions at Espíritu Santo. Bad as conditions were at Los Adaes, they were even worse at La Bahía. The Governor said that the inefficiency of the acting captain, Diego Ramón, was responsible for the extreme need experienced at the Presidio of Nuestra Señora de Loreto. He declared that Diego's father had exerted himself in securing the necessary supplies, but that the son had completely neglected his duties and had even failed to make an official report to his superior regarding the death of his father, the former captain of the presidio, or about the recent attack made by the former mission Indians. If Governor Almazán had not come to San Antonio, La Bahía might have been abandoned without his knowledge as a result of the dire need to which it had been reduced by the neglect of its commander to secure supplies in time. Upon learning of the great suffering of its garrison, he despatched one hundred *fanegas* of corn without delay to relieve their immediate want, and he was now making active efforts to send additional provisions at the earliest possible moment.[8]

He promised the viceroy to make an official inspection of the presidio at La Bahía in the immediate future in order to correct the flagrant abuses which now existed, and he declared most emphatically that Diego Ramón was incapable and unfit to hold the position of captain. Because of the continued illness of Captain Arroyo, the governor had sent to Saltillo for José Lobo Guerrero, a soldier of experience and courage, who knew how to deal with the Indians, and he planned to appoint him captain of Los Adaes. All these acts were subject to the viceroy's approval. He suggested that if His Excellency decided to remove Ramón from La Bahía, it would be well for him to consider José de Urrutia, now living in San Antonio, for this important position.[9]

French and Spanish relations in Texas. Early in April, 1723, three Frenchmen, who claimed to be fugitives from justice, had come to Los Adaes and requested the governor to give them a pass so that they could

[7]*Ibid.*
[8]*Ibid.*
[9]*Ibid.*

MISSION OF SAN FRANCISCO DE LA ESPADA LOCATED AT SAN ANTONIO IN 1731

proceed to La Bahía del Espíritu Santo where they intended to embark for Veracruz. They were Pedro Rosel, former ensign of one of the companies stationed in Louisiana; Pedro Barroy, former paymaster of troops in New Orleans, and Francisco Martín, a former ensign in Flanders and more recently secretary on board one of the French company's ships. Permission was accordingly granted to them on April 8, to proceed without molestation.[10] Just why it took them almost four months to travel from Los Adaes to La Bahía is not clear, but on August 24, 1723, the three Frenchmen presented themselves with their passports to Captain Domingo Ramón, who was then still living. He informed them that there would be no vessel in port for ten months. Unwilling to wait that long they decided to proceed to Mexico City overland. The next place they went seems to have been Mazapil, and from there they traveled to Monclova, on September 13. Governor Blas de la Garza Falcón, who suspected them of being spies, sent them under guard from there to Mexico City. They reached Saltillo on October 25, and finally arrived in Mexico City on December 18, 1723.[11]

Aguayo, who was in Mexico City at the time, had been notified in advance by Captain Nicolás Flores regarding the Frenchmen who were on the way to the capital. On November 23, 1723, the Marquis made a long report to the viceroy on various matters concerning Texas and referring to the Frenchmen among other things, he stated that in his opinion they were spies or traders who had stealthily introduced themselves into the province. The dilatory and aimless manner in which they traveled from Los Adaes to Mexico seemed to lend color to this suspicion.[12] When the matter was referred to the *Auditor*, Juan de Oliván Rebolledo, he suggested to the viceroy on January 27, 1724, that efforts should be made to ascertain the character of the Frenchmen and to determine their purpose. He also recommended that it would be well for the viceroy to order that they be formally examined and if guilty of espionage, that they be sent to Spain by the first vessel sailing from Veracruz. In the meantime he advised that the prisoners, for such they were now, be placed in one of the cells of the *Cabildo*.[13]

---

[10]*A. G. N., Provincias Internas*, Vol. 181.

[11]*Ibid.*, Vol. 181, 275-278.

[12]Summary of Aguayo's report, November 23, 1723. *A. G. N., Provincias Internas*, Vol. 181.

[13]Opinion of the *Auditor*, January 27, 1724. *A. G. N., Provincias Internas*, Vol. 181.

Although the examination of the prisoners did not disclose anything of importance, it furnished the occasion for the viceroy to issue strict orders to Governor Almazán with regard to the precautions which he should take to prevent all possible communication with the French. In the instructions sent him, he was told that deserters from the French army should be welcomed into the royal army, but that sharp, unceasing and stern vigilance must be exercised to prevent all trade of whatsoever description between the French in Louisiana and the Province of Texas; that there must be no intercourse between Los Adaes and Natchitoches; and that foreigners must not be allowed to enter the province under any pretext.[14]

In reply, Governor Almazán assured the viceroy that the orders he had just received with regard to relations with the French would be faithfully observed in the future. He explained that until the receipt of the instructions there had been friendly and polite intercourse between the settlers of Los Adaes and Natchitoches. During the last two years the presidio and missions had frequently been obliged to appeal to the French for needed supplies. The failure of crops and the long delay experienced in securing provisions from the Río Grande made this traffic with aliens imperative. He hinted that had it not been for this timely relief the soldiers, the missionaries, and the mission Indians would have fared much worse. As the French had no priests at Natchitoches, the missionaries were in the habit of visiting them to administer the Holy Sacraments and regularly went over to say Mass for them on feast days. All this, he declared, the French appreciated highly and seemed to be very grateful for the services rendered.[15] But in view of the orders of His Excellency these relations and courtesies would cease immediately.

In the fall of 1724, Almazán received additional instructions from the viceroy, dated April 25 and May 25, concerning the treatment of the Indians, the policy which he was to observe with regard to the Apaches, and the necessity of preventing a possible alliance between these Indians and the French. He took advantage of the opportunity to state that he was ready and willing to observe all the instructions just received, but that it was extremely difficult, in view of the previous orders of His Excellency which strictly prohibited all communications with the French,

---

[14]Report of Governor Almazán to the Viceroy, March 24, 1724. *Archivo San Francisco el Grande*, Vol. 10.

[15]Governor Almazán to the Viceroy, March 24, 1724. *Archivo San Francisco el Grande*, Vol. 10.

for him to find out what relations existed between them and the Apaches. Through the country of the Cadodachos, the French could communicate with these Indians and negotiate an alliance with them without the knowledge of the Spanish governor. In the past he had been able to find out what they were doing and ascertain their intentions, thanks to the friendly intercourse that had existed between the two presidios, but since this had ceased, he knew little or nothing of what they did or planned. He suggested that if His Excellency would allow courteous relations to be reëstablished as in the past, it would be an easy matter to learn what contacts were being made with the Apaches.[16] But the question of permitting trade with the French, which is what the suggestion of mutual exchange of services meant, was a matter so strictly prohibited by royal *cédulas,* that Governor Almazán was not even given an answer on this point at issue.

Indian depredations at Espíritu Santo.   Let us now turn to note conditions at La Bahía. A glimpse of what had been transpiring there had been revealed first in the reports of the governor made on March 24, as previously cited. Diego Ramón, now acting captain of the Presidio of Nuestra Señora de Loreto in place of his deceased father, Domingo, wrote a letter to the viceroy informing him directly of the murder by Indians of the messenger sent by His Excellency to La Bahía. This attack occurred a short distance from San Antonio. The captain stated that he had previously informed the viceroy about the revolt of the mission Indians and the death of his father. He next gave a brief account of a charge by a band of natives on the presidio January 31, 1724, at which time two soldiers were killed and a number of horses stolen. Since the abandonment of the mission the Indians of the coastal region had been committing petty depredations and repeatedly threatened the destruction of the military post. When in need he had requested help from Captain Nicolás Flores, stationed at San Antonio. The latter replied that he was unable to spare any of his men and that moreover he had instructions from the governor which prevented the transfer of soldiers. Ramón now had great fear and worry that the Spanish establishment at La Bahía might experience the same fate as that of the unfortunate La Salle. Ramón's bitter complaint was that the garrison lacked military equipment, that the horses were insufficient in number and in poor condition and that the food supply was almost exhausted. What made the situation desperate,

---

[16]*Ibid.*

however, was Captain Ramón's inability to get help anywhere. Had it not been for thirty mules loaded with provisions which his deceased father had ordered brought to the presidio at his expense early the year before, they all would have perished. He informed the viceroy that a few days before writing, he had received one hundred *fanegas* of corn purchased from Mission San José in San Antonio, which Governor Almazán had forwarded, but that this shipment would last perhaps fifteen or twenty days, after which they would have nothing to eat.[17]

In the fall of 1723, the Presidio of La Bahía had furnished ten men to Captain Flores of San Antonio for a campaign against the Apaches. It was because of this fact that Diego Ramón resented the refusal of aid to him now. Since the revolt of the mission Indians, they had become so insolent and threatening that the garrison was unable to do guard duty along the bay as instructed. The Karankawas, Cojames, and Guapites must be reduced by force, he said, before the Presidio of La Bahía would be able to perform any service in guarding the coast against possible foreign aggression.[18] But he failed to tell why the mission Indians had revolted and had become so hostile, or to relate in detail the circumstances of his father's death.

The cause of Indian hostilities at La Bahía was disclosed, however, by the visit of the governor. Agreeable to his promise to the viceroy, Governor Almazán made a personal inspection of the presidio shortly after his report of March 24. Upon his arrival, he found conditions as bad as he had anticipated. Gambling was rampant, the soldiers were in rags, their arms were unfit for service, and there was little or no discipline. Captain José Domingo Ramón had been as careless as his son Diego, the governor surmised, because the state of affairs he found could not have developed in the three months since the death of Domingo. In his report to the viceroy on the inspection, he explained that the Marquis of Aguayo had left the garrison fully equipped and well armed in 1722. Fourteen months after his departure a vessel came from Veracruz with additional clothes for the men, thirty new rifles, and as many new swords. Notwithstanding these facts, half of the rifles in the hands of the soldiers were worthless, and many of them had not been cleaned since they were received.

The stockade built at the time of the establishment of the presidio was

---

[17]Diego Ramón to the Viceroy, March 24, 1724, *Archivo San Francisco el Grande,* Vol. 10.

[18]*Ibid.*

almost gone. The logs had rotted in some instances, but more frequently they had been deliberately pulled out and used for kindling and firewood by the soldiers themselves. It was evident that the officers in command had made no protest against this unpardonable abuse. He recommended that the fortification should be rebuilt in its entirety out of brick, as wood did not last in this locality on account of the humidity of the sea breeze, and stone was too far away to bring it for that purpose.

As to the men, he found some were supremely happy because of the absolute lack of discipline and employment; while others were disgusted with their idleness and the inefficiency and the languor of martial spirit of the commander. He sent to the viceroy, together with his report of the inspection, a petition drawn up by a number of the soldiers, asking His Excellency to remove Diego Ramón from command and place a more capable man in his place.[19]

Death of Captain Ramón.   Having completed the inspection, Governor Almazán proceeded to hold an investigation into the death of Captain José Domingo Ramón. After examining a large number of witnesses, all of whom testified to the principal facts without contradiction, he found that the trouble began on December 15, 1723. An Indian from the mission entered the house of a soldier in the presidio, where a cow had just been killed and was being butchered. While waiting for a portion of meat, the native decided to shake the dust off his blanket. Unfortunately, the particles fell in a cloud upon the corn which the wife of the lieutenant of the presidio was grinding on a *metate*. This enraged the woman, who called her husband and asked him to drive the Indian out of the presidio. He was accordingly ordered to depart, but he refused to leave without a piece of meat, whereupon a scuffle followed and the Indian was obliged to take refuge in the pueblo of the mission. The officer in charge sent two soldiers to bring him back in order to whip him, but he attempted to escape. They pursued him, overtook him, and one of them wounded him with a knife. The rest of the tribe became alarmed. About forty warriors took up their bows and arrows and attacked the soldiers, wounding many of their horses. In the meantime the whole Indian population became aroused, but fearing the consequences of an encounter with the garrison, the natives fled to the woods.

Captain José Domingo Ramón was at a ranch two leagues from the

---

[19]Fernando Pérez de Almazán to the Viceroy, May 1, 1724. *A. G. N., Provincias Internas,* Vol. 181.

presidio at the time of the disturbance. Word was sent to him, that all the Indians had run away. He mounted his horse and, accompanied by a few soldiers, went in search of them. He overtook them a short distance away and after talking to them for a while he succeeded in quieting their fears and in persuading them to return to the presidio and mission. It grew dark before he reached La Bahía and many of the Indians, who did not entirely trust Captain Ramón, took advantage of the opportunity which night afforded them to steal away, so that when he arrived at the post only about half of the men were left, although most of the women and children were still present. He ordered all that remained to be placed in a small hut, and from this overcrowded prison they were to be summoned, a few at a time, to meet their doom. Ramón commanded the slaughter of a bull apparently to supply these Indians with meat, but in reality the butchered animal was provided to entice the savages to the place where the cannon of the fort might be trained on the victims with deadly effect. This was the original intention for the cowardly trick, according to the majority of witnesses examined. One soldier, however, declared that he had been ordered by the captain to gather up all the rope in the presidio to bind and hang these poor defenceless Indians.

Whether the tribesmen became suspicious because of the sinister preparations that they saw going on around them, or whether they understood what the real intentions of the captain were, they refused to leave the hut, even though they were hungry for the meat of the bull which had been killed ostensibly for their benefit. Instead, they tried to break away from the narrow confines where they were held in captivity. When Domingo Ramón noticed this attempt to escape, he called some of the soldiers and with their help forced them all back into the wretched prison. He now entered the hut or was drawn into it by the Indians. He tried to pacify them, assuring them nothing would happen to them. When they became calm, noticing a number of soldiers nearby, he suddenly called out with a loud voice, "At them, friends, and get them!" When the Indians heard him yell these words, one of them approached him and stabbed him in the breast with the blade of a large pair of scissors. The soldiers attacked the Indians, and at the command of the captain, fired a cannon which was trained on the hut. The Indians, with the exception of two, succeeded in escaping unharmed through a hole in the house. A squaw was the only one that they were able to catch and Ramón ordered that she be hanged. Eight days later he died as a consequence of the wound he had received.[20]

Removal of Diego Ramón from command.   As a result of this unfortunate occurrence, the mission Indians abandoned their pueblo and returned to their former haunts. The work of Father Agustín Patrón was thus undone by the imprudent actions of Captain Domingo Ramón. The natives not only abandoned the mission, but to avenge themselves for the insult offered them, they surprised the guards of the presidio and stole a good number of horses. It was to these depredations that Diego referred in his letter to the viceroy. To determine the circumstances of this thievery, Governor Almazán commissioned Manuel Malo de Mendoza, his secretary, to conduct a thorough investigation on March 31. On the following day he opened the formal inquiry at La Bahía. He was to find out if the theft had been committed by the former Indians of the mission, namely, the Cojames, Guapites, and Karankawas; the number of soldiers who were on guard on the night of the attack; the manner in which they were armed; whether they were on foot or mounted; and whether the loss of the horses had been the result of negligence or lack of vigilance. He called as witnesses Nicolás Meave, Francisco Xavier Múñoz, and Bernave de Arce, all soldiers; Juan Rodríguez and Fernando Pérez de León, eyewitnesses; and Diego Ramón, the acting captain of the presidio.

According to the declarations, Manuel de Arce, one of the soldiers, arrived at the presidio late in the afternoon on January 13. He notified the guards that on the way to the post he had seen a lurking Indian spy across the river making what appeared to be a smoke signal. After receiving this warning, Ignacio de la Garza, who was the lieutenant of the garrison, made a hasty reconnoissance, without crossing the stream, to ascertain if Indian prowlers had been in the vicinity of the presidio, and he reported that there was no sign of Indians or Indian smoke. He declared that the soldier who had given the alarm had mistaken a small palm tree for an Indian; and that there were no grounds for fear. Instead of ordering the horses brought into the presidial corral, they were allowed to graze outside. About midnight a party of Indians surprised the guards. There were four in number and all were on foot. It was further disclosed that at the time of the attack one was asleep. Of the four, two were killed, one was wounded, and the other escaped unharmed. Among the four

---

[20]Governor Almazán to the Viceroy, May 1, 1724. *A. G. N., Provincias Internas,* Vol. 181.

guards, it was shown that they had but one useless gun and a short sword to defend the horses and themselves.[21]

In view of the facts revealed by the investigation, Manuel Malo de Mendoza, who conducted it, returned formal charges of negligence against both Diego Ramón and Ignacio de la Garza. The governor reported the whole proceedings to the viceroy, transmitted a copy of the testimony and findings in the case, and informed him that he had suspended De la Garza from his rank as lieutenant until further instructions from His Excellency. The matter was referred by the viceroy to the *Auditor de Guerra,* who rendered his opinion and recommendations on September 4, 1724. He advised that His Excellency confirm the temporary suspension of Ignacio de la Garza, acting lieutenant, and he recommended that since Colonel Olors, whom the viceroy had decided to appoint as Captain of the presidio to replace Diego Ramón, had died, that another man of recognized merit and ability be selected and given instructions to restore the discipline of the garrison. The *Auditor* was emphatic in his condemnation of the treatment accorded the Indians of the mission and strongly urged that the new commander be instructed to do everything possible to reconcile them. On September 17, the viceroy ordered that the recommendations made by the *Auditor* be put into effect without delay, and that a copy be sent to Don Pedro de Rivera for his information.[22]

Appointment of Bustillos y Ceballos as Captain of La Bahía. Acting upon the recommendation of the *Auditor,* the viceroy soon afterwards appointed Don Juan Antonio de Bustillos y Ceballos to replace Diego Ramón as commander of the Presidio of Nuestra Señora de Loreto. Just when he arrived at his new post is not clear, but by the spring of 1725 he was already at La Bahía. As early as October, 1724, Governor Almazán had heard of the appointment, for in a letter written on the 24th of that month he said that on August 2 a ship with provisions, supplies, and arms had arrived at La Bahía del Espíritu Santo, but that these had not been issued to the soldiers because the captain-elect of the presidio had not come. He had ordered the arms to be distributed to the men so that they might be well equipped to defend themselves against the Indians, who, although they seemed to have assumed a peaceful attitude and visited the presidio now and then, could not be trusted. Shortly after

---

[21]Autos fechos en la Bahía de el Espíritu Santo sobre dos muertes que ejecutaron los yndios . . . *A. G. N., Provincias Internas,* Vol. 181.

[22]Opinión del Auditor General. *A. G. N., Provincias Internas,* Vol. 181.

the arrival of the ship, they attacked and killed four sailors one evening as they were coming from the ship to the presidio. The natives not only murdered the seamen, but they stole the boat in which they were making their way to shore.[23]

Removal of Presidio and Mission to the Guadalupe River. Both the missionary and the new captain, after his arrival, must have reported to the viceroy that all efforts to reconcile the Indians and induce them to return to their former mission had proved useless; for on April 15, 1725, he sent detailed instructions to the commander to hold a conference with Governor Pérez de Almazán at the earliest opportunity to discuss the advisability of the removal of the presidio to a more suitable location. If the two agreed, they were instructed to select the site to which the post was to be moved and report the matter to the viceroy for final approval.[24]

Bustillos communicated the orders he had received to Governor Pérez de Almazán, but the latter was unable to hold the conference during that year because he had to go first to Coahuila to secure greatly needed supplies, and after his return, the rains and floods prevented him from coming to La Bahía as requested. In the meantime, Bustillos explored the country and on September 20, he wrote a long letter to the viceroy informing him that although the governor had been unable to come for the various reasons stated, he had explored, in his absence, a site which he thought was suitable for the purpose. It was in a nearby ranch, a league or two from the present location, and offered many advantages both for the presidio and the mission. Impatient at the delay, he again requested the governor in January, 1726, to come as instructed by the viceroy.[25]

It was not until the first week in April, 1726, that Almazán was at last able to make the trip to La Bahía. By this time Bustillos, or rather the missionary, had discovered a much better place than the ranch which had been previously chosen. Accordingly, the governor was taken to a spot on the Guadalupe River, about five or six leagues from the original location on the coast. The new place had much in its favor. It was on the bank of the river, with spacious plains extending back which could

---

[23]Governor Pérez de Almazán to the Viceroy, October 25, 1724. *Archivo San Francisco el Grande,* Vol. 10.

[24]Juan Antonio de Bustillos y Ceballos to the Viceroy, La Bahía, June 18, 1726. *A. G. N., Provincias Internas,* Vol. 236, Part 1.

[25]*Ibid.*

be irrigated with ease. There was abundant timber to rebuild the presidio and stone could be secured if desired from a quarry which Captain Bustillos claimed was found about two leagues away. A quarter of a league from the proposed site was a small creek with abundant water, where the missionary had already started to congregate the Indians for the mission that was to be established there. The irrigation ditch for the farms had been dug and the fields were already plowed and planted.

Here a new nation, the Jaranames, were to be congregated. The members of this tribe were numerous and seemed pleased with the idea of the establishment of the presidio and mission in the midst of their country. Captain Bustillos declared that they came and went all day. He had doubts as to whether all of them could be congregated in one mission, but he said that fortunately, a large creek had been discovered about three leagues on the west side of the river, on the new road he had opened from La Bahía to the Río Grande, with sufficient water to irrigate the broad plains that bordered it. Another mission could be founded at this place, if necessary to accommodate all the Indians. "So many are the natives who live in this region that it moves the most indifferent observer to pity to see so many lost souls, . . ." declared Bustillos in his letter to the viceroy.[26] The former neophytes of Nuestra Señora del Espíritu Santo were no longer hostile and visited the old presidio from time to time peacefully, refusing however, to be congregated again in the former mission now abandoned. Ever since the new captain arrived there had been no depredations committed by the coastal tribes and general tranquility had been observed.

Aside from the natural advantages described, it was reported that the new site was in reality only a league or two farther from the entrance to the Bay of Espíritu Santo than the former had been. If one followed the river, which was navigable to its mouth, the Bay of San Rafael, where it emptied, was only five leagues to the southeast. From here to the Bay of Espíritu Santo it was about eleven or twelve leagues in a general east-southeasterly direction. The difference in the distance from the former location to the entrance to the bay was two or three leagues.[27]

According to the instructions of the viceroy, Captain Bustillos and Governor Almazán were to make separate reports on the findings of the exploration. As Almazán had returned to San Antonio immediately after

[26]Bustillos to the Viceroy, June 18, 1726. *A. G. N., Provincias Internas*, Vol. 236, Part 1.
[27]*Ibid.*

inspecting the proposed site, Bustillos sent his report with a special messenger, who was to stop in Béjar to pick up the letter of the governor and take both, without delay, to His Excellency. On July 4, the governor verified all the details given by Bustillos, adding that the new location was higher and free from marshes and lagoons; that there was abundant drinking water; and that the climate was much better in spite of the short distance from the former site. In describing the old presidio, he declared that it would be advisable to build a new one, as the original consisted of a few miserable huts roughly made of logs and thatched with rushes. The stockade built in the beginning had been almost totally destroyed by time and the soldiers. Timber was so scarce that it was extremely difficult to find the necessary firewood. He pointed out that the fort would afford as much protection in its new location, because the actual distance to the entrance of the bay was almost the same and could be reached with greater ease by the river. He declared that in view of all the facts stated he was of the opinion that the presidio should be moved to the Guadalupe, where the fortification could be rebuilt out of more permanent materials and placed in condition to withstand the attack of foreign aggressors much better; where the climate was much more healthy, and where several missions could be established under proper protection. Subject to the final approval of His Excellency, he had instructed Captain Bustillos to clear the ground and assemble the materials for the construction of the new presidio. It would be highly advisable, he suggested, that the viceroy issue the corresponding orders for the removal as soon as possible, so that this work might be completed before winter set in.[28]

The two reports were received in Mexico in August, 1726, and turned over to the *Auditor de Guerra* on the 9th, for his consideration and opinion. Two weeks later, on August 26, he made a brief summary of the facts presented by the two officers in Texas and recommended that in view of the deplorable conditions of the presidio in its present location and the advantages which the new site offered, His Excellency should issue orders for its immediate removal. Satisfied with the opinion rendered, the viceroy ordered that the corresponding instructions be drawn up and sent in duplicate to Governor Almazán and Captain Bus-

---

[28]Pérez de Almazán to the Viceroy, July 4, 1726. *A. G. N., Provincias Internas,* Vol. 236, Part 1.

tillos, all of which was done on August 29, 1726.[29] The Presidio of Nuestra Señora de Loreto was destined to remain at its new location for twenty-three years, before it was moved for the last time to the San Antonio River in 1749.

Apache hostilities and organization. Although the Presidio of San Antonio de Béjar had not experienced the want and distress which afflicted Los Adaes and La Bahía, chiefly because of its relative proximity to the presidio on the Río Grande and the better organization of the missions founded in its vicinity; nevertheless, the region had not been exempt from troubles of its own. No sooner was this post established than it became the mark of the undying enmity of the Apaches. These Indians were to prove a thorn in the side of the Spaniards in Texas. When the Tejas were befriended and aided in their campaigns against the Apaches, the seeds for their hatred were sown. They never forgot it and continued to pester the Spaniards relentlessly for more than half a century. Before discussing their hostilities during the period under discussion, it will be well to give a brief summary of the nature and character of these fierce tribes.

The Apaches of Texas, more properly referred to as the Eastern Apaches, were a branch of the Athapascan family, the most widely distributed of the North American Indian linguistic groups. Their name was probably derived from *apachu,* the Zuñi name for enemy, applied first to the Navajos of New Mexico. They are in reality a part of the southern division of the Athapascan family, which includes three large groups: the Navajos of New Mexico, just mentioned; the Apaches Carlanes, a number of tribes surrounding the Navajos; and the Texas Apaches proper, or Lipanes.[30] In the early years, however, no distinction was made by the Spaniards between the different tribes or groups and the name was applied in a generic sense to all of them. At the beginning of the eighteenth century they lived far to the north and west of San Antonio, on the upper waters of the Colorado, Brazos, and Red River, but as time goes on, they were slowly pushed south by their invet-

---

[29]Report of the *Auditor de Guerra,* August 26, 1726. *A. G. N., Provincias Internas,* Vol. 236, Part 1.

[30]*Handbook of the American Indians,* Part I; Opinión del Auditor, Juan de Oliván Rebolledo, January 27, 1724. *A. G. N., Provincias Internas,* Vol. 181; W. E. Dunn, "Apache Relations in Texas, 1718-1750," *Quarterly,* XIV, 198-269. The last monograph is a splendid study of the subject and the only one available in English.

erate enemies, the Comanches, and forced to make their home succes-
sively on the San Sabá, Chanas, Pedernales, Medina, Río Grande, and
Pecos Rivers. In the latter part of the century, some of them moved
even farther south and west along the Río Grande. The Texas or Eastern Apaches were not as numerous as originally thought, but being
divided into several bands or tribes under separate chiefs, they moved
with astounding rapidity from place to place, committing depredations
over a vast area.[31]

Through the capture of a number of prisoners in 1723, the Spaniards
learned for the first time the form of their tribal organization. According to the statements made by an Indian woman at this time, they were
divided into five nations, each one governed by a separate chief. All of
these chiefs, however, recognized the authority of a head chief or *capitán
grande* who lived far to the north. When a raid was planned, the five
chiefs came together and each one furnished about twelve men, who
went out to forage and steal. Upon their return the booty was equally
divided and all returned to their respective homes. No chief undertook
a raiding expedition, declared the squaw, without first obtaining the consent of the head chief.[32] The warriors of the tribes were ordinarily well
supplied with a number of additional horses as remounts so that they
could make their raids more rapidly and travel over long distances to
evade their pursuers. They did not ride bareback but had curiously fashioned saddles made of wood, equipped with iron stirrups and painted in
a variety of colors. Like the Arabs, they liked fast horses which were
bridled to keep them under control. They protected their steeds from the
arrows of the enemy by coverings of buffalo skin. The men also had large
shields made of tough hide adorned with pigments of red, white, green
or blue. In the early part of the century the Apaches had not yet learned
the use of firearms. Their weapons consisted of the bow and arrow and
a short or light lance which they threw with great skill while attacking
the enemy. Unlike other Indians, they generally tipped their arrows with
iron instead of flint. They differed from most of the Texas Indians in
their clothing, which was made of buckskin.[33]

When Aguayo set out on his expedition, he had been carefully

---

[31]Dunn, *op. cit., Quarterly,* XIV, 202-203.

[32]Flores to Aguayo, October 21, 1723. *A. G. N., Provincias Internas,* Vol. 181.

[33]Testimony of Flores, *A. G. N., Provincias Internas,* Vol. 181; Declarations
of the soldiers, January 10, 1724; *Archivo San Francisco el Grande,* Vol. 10;
Flores to Aguayo, October 21 and November 2, 1723, *Provincias Internas,* Vol. 181.

instructed to win the friendship of the Apaches and to try to induce them to settle in missions. When he reached Los Adaes, he had to admit, however, that in spite of his efforts he had been unable to contact them. He promised the viceroy that in the return march he would redouble his efforts in regard to this matter. One of the dreads of the viceregal authorities had been the possibility of an alliance between this fierce nation and the French. On this point, Aguayo assured His Excellency, that this danger had been permanently removed by the establishment of the new presidio at Los Adaes, as the only avenue of communication between the French and the Apaches had been through the country of the Cadadachos. He made the significant observation that the haunts of these Apaches were about one hundred and fifty leagues to the northwest of the French frontier.[34]

From the time Aguayo entered Texas, the Apaches taunted him continuously. Before he arrived in San Antonio, they raided the presidio and stole some horses. While in East Texas, they surprised Brother José Pita, a Franciscan friar from the College of Querétaro, who was out hunting buffalo with a companion, and both of them were killed by these savages. Two years later, Captain Flores piously gathered the bones of the friar and brought them back to San Antonio for burial. No sooner had the expedition returned to San Antonio, than five Apaches attempted to steal some horses, but four of the culprits paid with their lives for the affront, as already related.

After Flores became captain of the Presidio of San Antonio it seems the depredations moderated. In a letter to the viceroy he claims that due to his vigilance no horses were stolen by these raiders for more than a year. But on August 17, 1723, a band of the Indians, availing themselves of the darkness and inclement weather of a stormy night, succeeded in breaking one of the gates of the corral where the horses of the presidio were kept and drove off eighty of them, in spite of the ten soldiers stationed there to guard them. As soon as Captain Flores was notified of the occurrence, he set out in pursuit accompanied by a few of his men. He followed the trail until noon of the following day, when he decided it would be better to return to the presidio and organize a regular expedition to recover the stolen animals. Thirty soldiers and as many Indians from the Mission of San Antonio de Valero were made ready, including among the former, eight men from La Bahía. Taking

---

[34]Aguayo to the Viceroy, Los Adaes, November 7, 1721. *A. G. N., Audiencia de México,* 61-2-2 (Dunn Transcripts, 1713-1722).

along only two pack loads of flour and relying on game for the supply of meat on the road, the party set out the following day. It took five days to reach Lomería Alta, a high range of hills to the north of San Antonio. But as the enemy was nowhere in sight, the march was continued for almost a month, over a country which Flores declares was the most beautiful he had ever seen. Finally on September 24, the *ranchería* of one of the Apache bands, which had divided after the raid, was sighted at about eight o'clock in the morning.

The Indians prepared for the attack with alacrity and for six hours the battle raged. Then the Apaches broke and fled down a ravine to a large river which they crossed to avoid pursuit. Upon the field they left thirty-four dead, their chief among them, and the Spaniards recovered not only the eighty horses originally stolen, but about one hundred and twenty others, including some mules. In the abandoned camp they found a large amount of plunder which had been left behind. There were many saddles painted blue, red, green, and white, hats, knives, bridles, iron stirrups, spearheads, ribbons, sugar, corn, *pinole,* salt, buffalo and deer skins, and beads of all colors. Twenty prisoners were captured, all women and children. The total damages suffered by the Spaniards were three soldiers and one Indian slightly wounded in the fight. Mateo Rodríguez received a cut on the thigh; Xavier Múños from La Bahía was bruised in the hand; and Captain Flores lost a tooth which was knocked out by an Apache dart. In a letter to Aguayo he remarked that it hurt him more to see his good horse injured than to have lost a tooth. The location where the battle probably took place has been tentatively identified with the present site of Brownwood.[35]

Efforts to make peace with the Apaches.   On the return march, Captain Flores interrogated one of the prisoners, a squaw about forty years of age, who readily answered the questions put to her through an interpreter. Asked why the Apaches attacked the Spaniards and stole their horses, she replied that her people carried on trade with "other Spaniards" who lived far to the north. It was to these that they sold the horses and captives taken on the raids. She added that the "other Spaniards" came often to see them in their *rancherías.* When asked how far from the haunts of the Apaches these visitors lived, she declared that it was about twelve days' journey from where the battle took place. It was

[35]Flores to Aguayo, October 21, 1723, *A. G. N., Provincias Internas,* Vol. 181; Father González to the Viceroy, January 10, 1724, *Archivo San Francisco el Grande,* Vol. 10; Dunn, *op. cit., Quarterly,* XIV, 208.

this squaw who told Captain Flores how Fray Pita was killed and showed him where his bones were located. She also told him how the raids were organized and how her people were governed. After the party arrived in San Antonio, both Father González and Flores again sought the woman, and questioned her about the chiefs of the five nations and their willingness to make peace. To this she replied she had often heard them say that they wanted to be the friends of the Spaniards, but that many of the Indians were afraid they would be punished for the depredations they had committed in the past. She said that since the location of their *ranchería* had been discovered, her people would be inclined to make peace.[36]

It had been the desire of the Spaniards for a long time to use the Apache prisoners as the means of negotiating an alliance. Aguayo had tried in vain to capture members of this nation for the purpose. Here was the opportunity at last for a treaty. Flores and Father José González explained to the squaw that they wanted her to go back and tell the five chiefs to come and be friends. She was told to make known to them that if they came and made peace, the prisoners now held would all be released. Both the captain and the missionary gave her many presents, furnished her with a saddled horse, and escorted her a whole day's travel. Upon leaving them she agreed to take the message to the head chief and return in twenty days.[37]

True to her word, the squaw returned within the time specified, accompanied by an Apache chief, his wife, and three warriors. When Captain Flores saw them coming in the distance he hastened to greet them. Upon his approach, the chief said "Dios! Dios!" and handed him a silver-mounted cane, the ordinary insignia of his rank. Father González accompanied the visitors to the Mission of San Antonio de Valero, where for three days they were feasted and treated with the greatest kindness. The chief explained that when the woman bearing the message of Captain Flores arrived, he sent word to his four companions to come to hold a council. One of these appeared and suggested that it would be better for just one to go to the presidio to find out if the woman were telling the truth. In the meantime his companion was to call the other chiefs and upon his return they would all go together to make peace. On November 1, the Indians took leave with assurance that it would not be

---

[36]Flores to Aguayo, October 21 and November 2, 1723. *A. G. N., Provincias Internas,* Vol. 181.

[37]*Ibid.*

long before they returned with all their people to live as friends with the Spaniards.[38]

Although it seemed as if the long desired peace were about to be concluded, there was evidence that the negotiations were not entered into with good faith. In a declaration made by an Indian named Gerónimo, who had escaped from the Apaches while in the neighborhood of San Juan Bautista on the Río Grande, he said that the defeat they had suffered had made them very angry; that after the withdrawal of Flores, they had assembled in a council of war and planned to attack San Antonio; that it was at this time that the Indian woman had arrived; and that in view of her message of friendship, they had decided to postpone the attack. With characteristic cunningness, the head chief had explained to the Indians, that they should send a few of their number to secure their relatives, and that when these had been released, they would attack and destroy San Antonio. This story was corroborated by a Spaniard named Juan Santiago de la Cruz, who had been captured by the Apaches and forced to live among them for six years, until his recent escape. He said that these Indians were always ready for war against the Spaniards; that the defeat inflicted by Flores had made them long for revenge; that the letter sent offering them peace was read to the chiefs by two missionaries who were captives in another *ranchería;* and that the motive of the reply sent by the Apaches was cleverly schemed to see if they could obtain the immediate release of the prisoners in San Antonio before an attack would be made.[39] Such then were the true intentions of the Apaches, according to the witnesses examined. Captain Flores, although anxious for peace, doubted the sincerity of their efforts for friendship with the Spaniards, but Father González had taken a great liking to these Indians and had conceived sanguine hopes of being the instrument through which a treaty with them could be soon obtained.

When the natives returned after a delay of almost two months, they were naturally greeted by the captain and the missionary with decidedly different feelings. Late in December, about thirty of them arrived in San Antonio and were welcomed with much enthusiasm by Father González, who took them to his mission. After feasting them as was customary, the *Padre* promised them that he would see that the prisoners would be released to them, if the five chiefs agreed to be friends of the Spaniards. .

---

[38]*Ibid.*

[39]Declaración de Juan de Santiago de la Cruz, July 12, 1724. *A. G. N., Provincias Internas,* Vol. 32, Part 2.

This proposal was made without consulting Captain Flores, who objected, stating that he would not consent to an agreement until the chiefs first came in person. To this demand Father González remonstrated that, perhaps, the rest of the chiefs did not care to come until further proof of good faith was given them. Angry words were exchanged and the discussion became heated before the amazed visitors. The Indians, unable to understand the finer points of the argument, were frightened and decided it was time to leave. Quietly they began to slip out of the mission. One of them clasped a young girl by the hand, and leading her over to Captain Flores said, "take girl." Before the conference ended, the Indians promised to return when winter was over, but they explained that only four chiefs would come with them, because the other did not want to be the friend of the Spaniards.[40]

Misunderstandings of Father González and Captain Flores. Father González was deeply disappointed with the outcome of the negotiations and blamed Captain Flores for it. Ever since the night the horses were stolen the misunderstanding between the two had been growing. Shortly after the incident it seems that Father González complained to the Guardian of the College of Querétaro, that Flores was negligent of his duties and that the garrison was poorly armed for defence. The Guardian reported the state of affairs to the viceroy, who on October 3, warned Flores to be more diligent, hinting that if the soldiers had been properly equipped and the presidio in good condition the Indians could not have stolen the horses.[41] In order to clear himself, Flores appealed to the missionary to make a statement as to the circumstances of the theft and the difficulties and needs of the garrison.

In complying with the request, Father González reaffirmed all he had said before and added to the shortcomings previously enumerated, the grievous offence offered to the Indians during their last visit in December. He declared that the soldiers were poorly armed, that most of them were mere boys, and that half of them were unfit for service. The night when the horses were stolen, he stated, there had been only seven soldiers on guard and these were unable to oppose the raiders because their arms were no good. He pointed out that six, eight and sometimes as many as ten men were always kept busy working on private farms, while

---

[40]Declaration of the soldiers, January 6, 1724; Testimony of Father José González, January 10, 1724, *Archivo San Francisco el Grande*, Vol. 10.

[41]Flores to the Viceroy, undated. *A. G. N., Provincias Internas*, Vol. 32, Part 1.

some others were continuously at Los Adaes or La Bahía. The captain's refusal to release the women and children had been the cause of the failure of the negotiations which would have brought peace with this large and powerful nation.[42]

To this complaint was added the testimony of Father Hidalgo, who supported in every detail the statements already made. He explained that the Apaches could have been converted long ago if the presidios had been rightly managed. In his opinion the poor pay received by the soldiers was responsible for the type of men that made up the frontier garrisons, whose bad habits often caused the loss of their souls and those of the Indians as well.[43]

Not satisfied with what he had already said, Father González made a long report on March 18, 1724, in which he attempted to inform the viceroy of the true state of affairs in Texas and to suggest the remedy for all the ills suffered. The root of many of the existing evils, he averred, was the greed of the commanders of many of the presidios. In those of Coahuila, Río Grande, and San Antonio the soldiers were charged five times the actual cost of the goods supplied to them. As a result they received little or no pay in specie and this practice was responsible in a large measure for the inefficiency of the soldiers on the frontier. The country of the Apaches covered a vast area, extending all the way to the Cadodachos, and was much more fertile than the portion of Texas now occupied by the Spaniards. Through the Cadodachos these Indians had communication with the French who induced them to commit frequent depredations. He praised their skill as warriors and horsemen and said the type of soldiers found in the presidios were no match for the Apaches.

Recommendations of Father González. After giving a summary of the campaign of Flores against the Apaches which resulted in the capture of twenty women and children, he declared that his refusal to treat with them had spoiled all chance of making peace. He accused Flores of having attacked the Indians without provocation, when he invaded their *ranchería,* and of mercilessly killing them from behind as they ran for shelter. He even hinted that the reason why he was opposed to the delivery of the prisoners to the Apaches was that he wanted to keep them as

---

[42]Testimony of Father José González, January 10, 1724. *Archivo San Francisco el Grande,* Vol. 10.

[43]Hidalgo to the Viceroy, January 14, 1724, in *Ibid.*

slaves.[44] As long as he remained in command, there was no hope of reconciling the Indians because he was too harsh with them. For the peace of the province, the salvation of souls, and the progress of the missions, it was imperative that Captain Flores be removed from control. In his place he suggested Mateo Pérez, a soldier of the Presidio of San Juan Bautista on the Río Grande, who feared God and had served His Majesty, the king of Spain, for twenty years.[45]

Having said all he could on conditions at the Presidio of San Antonio de Béjar he now turned his attention to affairs at La Bahía and Los Adaes. The French, he said, had made the Spaniards believe that they were interested in the country surrounding the Bay of Espíritu Santo, but this was only a ruse. The country there was sterile and worthless. By means of this maneuver the French had succeeded in penetrating unobserved, the much richer and more fertile lands of the Apaches by way of the Cadodachos. The presidio at Los Adaes could not prevent these incursions or stop communication between them from its present position. The French could enter the country through the river of the Cadodachos without hindrance. Unless measures were taken to prevent these forays, an alliance could be formed between the two forces which might soon destroy all the missions and presidios in Texas.

But he had a remedy to avoid so dire a calamity. He suggested that an expedition be organized to enter the country of the Apaches. This would not entail any expense to the royal treasury. The Presidios of Coahuila, Río Grande, San Antonio, and La Bahía could furnish ten or fifteen men each to make up fifty or sixty, the number required for the undertaking. The commander should be supplied with gifts for the Indians and he should be instructed not to attack the Apaches, but to try to attract them by kindness. Several missionaries should accompany the party to act as mediators and the women and children now held in San Antonio should be taken along to be released to their relatives. By this means, Father González thought the Apaches could be persuaded to come to live in missions. In order to preclude all future communication between these Indians and the French, it would be necessary, he declared, to establish a presidio on the Cadodachos River by removing Los Adaes

---

[44]Father José González to the Viceroy, March 18, 1724. *A. G. N., Provincias Internas*, Vol. 32, Part 2. The statements in regard to Flores were evident exaggerations. Father González did not go on the campaign and consequently did not see the battle.

[45]*Ibid.*

to this new location, where it could do much more good than at its present site.

Determined to tell the viceroy what to do in every instance, he then took up the matter of the escort furnished at Saltillo to convoy the missionaries and the trains of supplies on the way to Texas. In his opinion this guard, which consisted of nine soldiers, was an unnecessary expense. Ordinarily there were not more than five trips made a year. The time consumed in going and coming was not over a month each time. With one thousand *pesos* a year, a special escort could be hired each time it was needed for the duration of the journey and the royal treasury would save the additional expense of maintaining nine men at Saltillo all the year.

He went on and stated that the position of Protector of Indians was unnecessary. This service could be abolished in Saltillo, Nuevo Reyno de León, and Mazapil, and the duties of the functionary performed just as well by the *Alcalde Mayor*. "The multiplication of offices," he said, "results only in added expense to the king."

He closed his long report, which he said he was making at the request of the viceroy, with the appeal that the commanders of presidios in Texas be instructed to furnish the missionaries the necessary number of soldiers to accompany them when they set out in quest of new converts or runaways.[46]

This long report is significant because in the course of subsequent events, its far-reaching influence over the policies adopted towards the presidios and missions in Texas by viceregal officials, and by Rivera during his inspection three years later, will be evident. In his zeal for the conversion of the Apaches, which he sincerely thought had been thwarted by Captain Flores, the enthusiastic missionary stressed the truth beyond the bounds of common sense and opened the way for evils which were to affect the future development of the missions more than any of those circumstances he described. Many of the recommendations of Rivera, which were to be so strenuously condemned by the College of Querétaro in particular, and which finally resulted in the removal of the three Querétaran missions of East Texas to San Antonio, can be directly traced back to the report of Father González.

Removal of Captain Flores. Agreeable to these recommendations of the *Padre,* it seems, the viceroy ordered, on April 6, 1724, Captain Flores

---

[46]*Ibid.*

to turn over his command to Mateo Pérez and retire one hundred leagues from the Province of Texas. The latter received his commission at San Juan Bautista. Father González was the bearer of these orders from the viceroy in Mexico City.[47]

Upon his arrival he delivered the appointment and notified the viceroy that he made the trip without guard from Saltillo to San Juan Bautista in the company of two other missionaries and two Indians, because the escort was at the Río Grande. The party was attacked at Los Hierros by a band of Tobosos, who killed one of the Indians and badly wounded the other. One of the missionaries was shot in the backbone with an arrow, and although this had been pulled out, the tip, however, remained imbedded in the bone. Father González lost all his baggage and four mules were killed in the encounter. From here he planned to make the journey to San Antonio in company with Mateo Pérez, the captain-elect.

The new officer dictated a letter to the viceroy when he obtained his commission and frankly admitted he had been honored far beyond his deserts. He could neither read nor write, but he had learned to make a scrawl for his signature. After thanking His Excellency profusely for the appointment, he made a strange request. He begged the viceroy that the place left vacant in the garrison of San Juan Bautista by his promotion be not filled so that he could return to it in case it became necessary.[48] Aguayo remarked later that the poor judgment exercised by Father González in recommending Pérez as captain, was very evident when one considered the fact that he had been a private soldier for twenty years without ever having been promoted.[49] On June 17, 1724, Pérez presented his appointment to Flores and was duly placed in command as ordered by the viceroy.[50]

Vindication of Captain Flores. In obedience to the instructions received, Flores retired from San Antonio to Coahuila and from there wrote a long letter in justification of his actions while in charge of the presidio. He said that he had recovered the only horses stolen during his term of office and that for twenty-four years he had served the king in

---

[47]Viceroy's decree; Father González to the Viceroy, June 5, 1724. In *A. G. N., Provincias Internas,* Vol. 32, Part 2.

[48]Mateo Pérez to the Viceroy, June 6, 1724, in *Ibid.*

[49]Aguayo to the Viceroy, February 26, 1725, in *Ibid.*

[50]Testimonial of Mateo Pérez, Captain *ad interim* of San Antonio de Valero, in *Ibid.*

various capacities. Contrary to the statements made by Father González, the garrison was complete, as Mateo Pérez himself testified when it was turned over to him, consisting of fifty-four soldiers. Referring to the campaign against the Apaches, he declared that the Indians had been attacked while trying to run away; that they began the battle and fought stubbornly for six hours before they were overcome. The proposed peace negotiations which followed his return to San Antonio with twenty women and children prisoners, had been a ruse of the Indians to obtain the release of their relatives. This had been shown by the declarations of the Indian Gerónimo and the Spaniard Juan Santiago de la Cruz. Father González did not understand the method of making peace with the Indians. No treaty with them is binding unless made by their chiefs. This was the reason why the Captain had refused to treat with them. In support of his character and veracity, he presented several testimonials from the Marquis of Aguayo, Father Margil, and Father Núñez de Haro. Claiming that an injustice had been committed, Flores begged His Excellency, out of regard for his past record and his family, to restore him to his command.[51]

Aguayo in his representation in favor of Flores said that Father González had always caused trouble wherever he went, that he was of a domineering nature, and that his own College admitted that he was turbulent and unruly. With regard to the supporting testimony given by Father Hidalgo, he stated that it was but a repetition of what Father González had said and that it was evident the former had been unduly influenced by the latter. He praised Flores highly, giving a detailed account of his services in various capacities, and particularly during the expedition in Texas. In conclusion he recommended strongly that he be restored as Captain of the Presidio of San Antonio and that he be given his back pay for the time he had been suspended.[52]

Father Margil affirmed in his declaration that Flores had always served the king with zeal and had consistently given assistance to the missionaries in their labors; while Father Miguel Núñez de Haro, of the Mission of San José, declared he had known Flores for two years, while in San Antonio, and that during that time he had always coöperated with him. He said that the Captain had brought runaway Indians back,

---

[51]Flores to the Viceroy, no date, *Ibid.*

[52]Aguayo to the Viceroy, no date, in *Ibid.* In the long letter of Aguayo refuting the charges brought against Flores, he cites a letter of Father Espinosa as a base for his statements with regard to the character of Father González.

had regularly furnished the soldiers assigned as guards, who helped to instruct the neophytes in their various tasks about the mission farm, and had always been diligent in the performance of his duties.[53]

It would be unfair to Father González not to give some of the circumstances that may account in part for the serious charges brought against him by the friends of Captain Flores. A letter written on July 4, 1724, by the Marquis of Aguayo to the Reverend Father Margil is significant in the light of subsequent developments. After informing him of the replacement of Flores by Mateo Pérez through the intervention of the disturbing *Padre,* Aguayo told Father Margil how that missionary had gone to Mexico and there had spoken ill of everything and everybody in Texas. The Marquis resented in particular a statement ascribed to Father González, declaring that he, Aguayo, had defrauded the royal treasury by collecting the salary of one hundred and thirty men who had not taken part in the expedition entrusted to him. He explained to Father Margil that there had been only sixty-seven deserters, but that all of them had been replaced by men from the company raised by Captain Cárdenas prior to the expedition; that he had personally furnished one hundred and thirty thousand pesos for the undertaking; and that every man had been paid in full for services rendered to May 1, 1722, when the entire troop was disbanded at Monclova. "If Father González says he never heard of it, he is guilty of unpardonable ignorance," Aguayo added. "As for myself, it seems to me hell itself would open to engulf me if I maligned the integrity of my most ordinary fellowman." In closing he asked Father Margil, as Prefect General, therefore, to order the detractor to restore to him his good name before the viceroy in writing.[54]

In vindicating Flores, Aguayo was indirectly striking at the man he believed had attempted to injure his reputation. This accounts for the vehemence with which he attacked the character of Father González. But the testimony of the two missionaries from the College of Zacatecas still remains to be explained. From the beginning, a strong rivalry had always existed between the two colleges of *Propaganda Fide.* Captain Flores naturally had been inclined to favor the Mission of San José, founded by and named after his patron, the Marquis of Aguayo. It

---

[53]Testimony of Fathers Margil and Núñez de Haro, June 14, and July 20, 1724, in *Ibid.*

[54]Aguayo to Father Margil, July 4, 1724. *Archivo de Querétaro, 1716-1749* (Dunn Transcripts).

happened that this mission was in charge of the College of Zacatecas. Captain Flores could, and probably did, coöperate fully with the *Padres* in charge of Mission San José, while failing to give as much help to those of San Antonio de Valero. Keeping these facts in mind, then, we may conclude that the various religious testifiers in the case told the truth so far as it concerned their respective missions, but they committed the serious error of making their statements general instead of specific. This explains to a certain extent the contradictory nature of their evidence.

Father González recalled and Captain Flores reinstated.   Be that as it may, the viceroy turned over the whole matter to the *Auditor* for his consideration and opinion. On May 26, 1725, after having studied all the testimony in the case, he recommended to the viceroy that the Guardian of the College of Querétaro should be requested to remove Father José González from San Antonio, replacing him by a more prudent and peaceful missionary for the sake of harmony. In regard to Captain Flores, he advised that in view of the statements made by the Marquis of Aguayo in his favor and the other testimonials he had presented, His Excellency should order that he be restored to his former command and that Mateo Pérez should return to San Juan Bautista on the Río Grande to his post as a soldier of that presidio. Pérez was to be reimbursed for all expenses incurred by him in going and coming to and from San Antonio. The recommendations were approved by the viceroy on June 2, when the corresponding orders were issued.[55] This lamentable incident was to have far-reaching effects. Many of the accusations and supposed evils presented and described by Father González were to prejudice certain Spanish officials, and these same charges were brought up within five years in justification of the radical curtailment of missionary endeavors in Texas.

Progress made in missions and presidios.   In spite of the dire needs experienced by the soldiers and missionaries of the various establishments during these early times, steady progress was made in laying the foundations for the firm and permanent occupation of Texas. In was during these truly trying years that the temporary and flimsy structures built in the first *entradas* were replaced by more substantial buildings, that the locations of the missions and the presidios were more carefully selected, and that both civil and missionary life slowly became organized. Contrary

---

[55]Opinión de Don Juan Oliván Rebolledo, Auditor General de Guerra, May 26. *A. G. N.,* Vol. 32, Part 2, 1725-1731.

to the general belief that Alarcón moved the Presidio of San Antonio de Béjar to the same side of the river as the Mission of Valero after Father Olivares accidentally broke his leg in crossing over a provisional and unsteady bridge, we find that it was still on the west side of the river in October, 1724. Father González, in his interview with the viceroy and his subsequent recommendations, had strongly urged the removal of the presidio to the Mission of San Antonio de Valero, making one establishment of the two. On April 6, 1724, the viceroy wrote a letter to Governor Pérez de Almazán, consulting him about the advisability of putting this proposal into effect. In reply, Almazán pointed out that it would not be well to move the presidio to the mission. He said that the Indians and the soldiers would not get along if both were made to live in the natural intimacy that would result from the new arrangement. In its present location, between the two streams, it was much more secure against surprise attacks by the Indians than it would be if placed on the east side of the San Antonio River. He was not, however, entirely satisfied with its present place and had been exploring the surrounding country for a better site. He informed the viceroy that he was contemplating moving it nearer to the mission but would still keep it on the west side.[56]

The Presidio of San Antonio de Béjar at this time consisted of one adobe building, poorly constructed, thatched with grass, nearby a number of miserable huts made of brush. Governor Almazán fully realized how inadequate it was to withstand a regular siege or attack and had already begun to gather the necessary materials to rebuild it. It was his intention, as expressed to the viceroy, to select a better site, and to erect a new building of stone and mortar. By means of mules, oxen, and canoes, he had assembled a considerable amount of stone for the new structure. His greatest handicap in carrying out his plans was the lack of men. The work so far accomplished had been done with the aid of those persons he had brought from Los Adaes, but they would have to return to their post soon to escort a train of greatly needed supplies for that presidio. He had tried in vain to get Indians from the missions to help on this project under the direction of the soldiers, offering to pay them wages and give them their meals. Most of the neophytes were busy at this time rebuilding the mission pueblos and tilling their farms, and those that could be spared, worked so slowly, being unaccustomed to regular labor, that little or no progress was made. The garrison was constantly kept

---

[56]Governor Almazán to the Viceroy, October 24, 1724. *San Francisco el Grande Archive,* Vol. 10.

busy watching the presidio horses, assisting the missionaries, and escorting travelers and supplies to and from Saltillo, La Bahía, and Los Adaes. But he was determined to carry out his plans as soon as possible and he promised the viceroy he would return from Los Adaes at the earliest possible moment to rebuild the presidio.[57]

The Mission of San José y San Miguel de Aguayo was now in a flourishing condition. Father Miguel Núñez de Haro had done much to improve the farms and attract new Indians. With the aid of Captain Flores the *acequia,* or irrigation ditch, had been completed. It will be remembered that it was from the granary of this mission that Governor Almazán dispatched one hundred *cargas* of corn to relieve the distress at La Bahía in the spring of 1724. Such neophytes as became tired of regulated life and ran away to enjoy the freedom of the forest, much as school boys are wont to do, were quickly brought back by the diligent Flores. Progress in San Antonio de Valero had been no less satisfactory in spite of the relative indifference of the presidio commander. The irrigation ditch of that mission had been completed also, its farms were just as productive, and the number of Indians who had been brought under the direction of the tireless missionaries may be judged from the fact that Father González was able to furnish Captain Flores thirty Indian warriors, fully equipped, for his campaign against the Apaches.[58]

Aided by Governor Almazán and his lieutenants, the missionaries in East Texas accomplished much. The three missions founded among the Tejas particularly were making satisfactory progress. The temporary churches and the living quarters of the *Padres* so hastily erected in 1722 had been replaced by more permanent structures made of such timber as the country afforded. Stone was difficult to secure and it seems the missionaries were not ready to construct buildings that would withstand the ravages of time and the elements, and they hoped that locations more suitable and convenient to all the Indians might be found later. The various tribes of East Texas had steadily refused to be congregated in pueblos, and only a few had come to live in the missions. Using these as centers, the zealous Franciscans, undismayed by existing conditions,

---

[57]*Ibid.;* also report of soldiers on peace with Apaches, January 6, 1724. *San Francisco el Grande Archive,* Vol. 10.

[58]Aguayo to Father Margil, July 4, 1724; Report of soldiers on Peace with the Apaches, January 4, 1724; Almazán to the Viceroy, October 24, 1724. *Archivo San Francisco el Grande,* Vol. 10.

constantly visited the scattered *rancherías* to minister to the sick and to persuade the more obstinate natives to come to the missions.[59]

The Presidio of Nuestra Señora del Pilár de los Adaes, so carefully delineated by Aguayo and built with a competent stockade, had suffered a fate similar to that at La Bahía. The frequent rains had rotted the logs, and the soldiers' habitation was in such poor condition that it had to be rebuilt. Some time in 1725, Governor Almazán, whose health had been undermined by the unsanitary climate and the many hardships he had undergone since he assumed the governorship, decided to appoint Don Melchor de Mediavilla y Azcona his Lieutenant Governor and to station him at Los Adaes, with the approval of the viceroy. The pending negotiations with the Apaches and the urgent need of supplies, added to the removal of Captain Flores, had necessitated the almost permanent residence of Almazán in San Antonio. Thus it fell to Mediavilla y Azcona to restore the fort at Los Adaes. By July, 1726, he reported that the entire stockade had been replaced and the military living quarters rebuilt of timber.[60]

It is of interest to note at this point the growth of the settlement around the Presidio of San Antonio de Béjar. In 1726, there were forty-five soldiers who garrisoned the fort, the remaining nine being regularly assigned to guard the missions or escort supply trains. In addition, there were four *vecinos,* or settlers. In a letter of Almazán to the viceroy, he declared that these persons, together with their respective families numbered over two hundred souls, including men, women, and children, who were living in the vicinity of the presidio. Because Father Fray Miguel Sevillano, President of the Missions of Querétaro, who resided in San Antonio de Valero, refused to send a missionary on feast days to celebrate the Holy Sacrifice in the presidial chapel, all of them were being deprived of hearing Mass. The governor explained that there was no reason for the *Padre's* refusal, because there were two missionaries at Valero, besides a lay brother, and the distance from the mission to the presidio was very short.[61]

When the matter was reported to the viceroy and turned over to the *Auditor,* he was so shocked at such a state of affairs that he recommended, in the strongest terms, that the Commissary General of the Franciscans be

---

[59]Aguayo to Margil, July 4, 1724; Espinosa, *Chrónica,* I, 457-477.

[60]Governor Almazán to the Viceroy, July 4, 1726. *A. G. N., Provincias Internas,* Vol. 236 (Bolton Transcripts).

[61]*Ibid.*

requested to order one of the two missionaries under oath of obedience to proceed immediately to look after the spiritual needs of the garrison and settlers. But the *Auditor* became so excited that he misread the letter of Governor Almazán which in main dealt with the proposed removal of the Presidio of Nuestra Señora del Loreto at La Bahía to the Guadalupe River, and thinking the reference was to this coastal establishment instead of San Antonio de Valero, he explicitly and emphatically asked that the missionary be sent to La Bahía at once. The viceroy accepted the recommendations and issued the corresponding orders, in the strictest terms, on August 29, 1726. The Commissary General commanded the Father President at San Antonio, under oath of obedience, on December 9 of the same year, to send one of the missionaries to La Bahía without delay, and it took almost a year to correct this oversight of the *Auditor*. Although such an occurrence was not common, it nevertheless illustrates the serious evils which at times resulted from hasty action in Mexico City.[62]

Mission life in Texas.   It is important here to give a detailed account of the trials and the hardships which the missionaries had to endure in civilizing the Indians. Father Espinosa, who for many years labored in Texas, has left us a vivid description of their toils. First and foremost, he declares, was the difficulty of learning the languages of the numerous tribes. The viceroy issued an order at the close of 1724, directing all missionaries to learn the various dialects of the tribes that were congregated in the different missions.[63] This urgent demand was hardly necessary because the *Padres* had striven diligently for the mastery of these Indian tongues, for that was always the first step in the great work of evangelization and conversion. No one realized more than the sons of St. Francis themselves how essential this speaking knowledge was for the teaching of Christian doctrine. This was no easy task for the missionaries. To reduce to writing and to try to systematize the primitive dialects spoken by the natives was much more difficult than to decipher the most intricate modern code. The Indians depended largely on the inflection of their voices and the accompanying gestures for varied meanings of the same sound. "It is necessary to work with our fingers, writing, noting, and

---

[62]Governor Pérez Almazán to the Viceroy, July 4, 1726; Opinión del Auditor, August 19, 1726; Ordén de Fray Fernando Alonso González, Commissary General, December 9, 1726. *A. G. N., Provincias Internas,* Vol. 236, Part 1 (Bolton Transcripts).

[63]Viceregal decree, November 15, 1724. *A. G. N., Misiones,* Vol. 21.

interpreting the signs that we cannot make out with words," says Father Espinosa. This was torture to one's tongue, the good missionary assures us, and he was in position to know, for he mastered several of the languages spoken by the tribes of East Texas. It was necessary to twist and turn the tongue into all sort of shapes, he says, in order to produce the strange and harsh sounds of the natives. There were missions where as many as six and seven different dialects were spoken by the neophytes.[64]

After the difficulties of the languages were overcome it still required infinite patience to train the native sons of the plains slowly to regular habits of industry. Accustomed to a roving life, to move freely from place to place as need or desire prompted them, the Indians experienced great reluctance in adapting themselves to missionary life. "When the poor wretches come into our missions," Father Espinosa observes, "we have to be indulgent with them for a long time in order that they may become accustomed to systematic labor." It was hard for them to realize that they must work regularly day after day. When they were gathered in a mission, one of the first things they were taught was how to cultivate the soil and raise a crop. In their *rancherías* the planting was done in a desultory manner and that burden was placed generally on women. Under the supervision and direction of one of the soldiers assigned as mission guards, the men were taken to the field and patiently taught how to plow and how to sow. The missionary frequently set the example himself, laboring side by side with the neophytes. The necessary tools and seed were furnished by the *Padres* and most of the plowing was done with oxen. When the harvest was gathered it was carefully stored in a common barn, the key to which was kept by the missionary. Throughout the year these supplies were distributed weekly to those who had learned to apportion their daily allowances carefully; but those who did not know how to manage the diurnal rations, were accustomed to present themselves every morning to receive these goods from the commissary. In this way those who had been longer at the mission gradually learned self-control and gained the ability to direct their own affairs.

If at the end of the year there was any grain left, after all the neophytes had been amply supplied and a sufficient amount set aside for planting, this was sold either to the captain of the neighboring presidio or to settlers in the vicinity. The governor of the Indian pueblo and the *alcaldes*, acting as agents for the mission Indians, carried on the negotiations and

---

[64]The foregoing details, as well as those that follow, are taken from the description given by Father Espinosa in his *Chrónica*, I, 475-478.

made the sale. The missionary took part merely as an umpire to protect the interests of the Indians and to see that they obtained a fair price for their products. The proceeds were turned over to him and used to purchase cloth and other things needed for the natives. The amounts received and spent were set down in a book and all the goods purchased were equally distributed among those who needed them. Not a cent was used for the missionary or the mission. The entire sum obtained from such sale was used for the benefit of the neophytes. But when the crops were not abundant and there was a shortage, it was customary for the missionary to use part of his own allowance provided by the king for sustenance, to secure the things most needed by his wards. Not infrequently, particularly in the case of the mission at La Bahía, the neophytes were supported almost entirely by the meager allowance sent to the missionary in charge. As a result of the solicitude of the enthusiastic and industrious *Padres,* by 1730 most of the mission Indians in Texas were well dressed, had a surplus of grain in their barns, owned their cattle and stock, and were enjoying a modicum of comfort which the civil settlers had not been able to attain.

Let us next turn to the spiritual labors. Father Espinosa says: "In all the missions, both on the Río Grande and on the San Antonio River, it is an inviolable custom for all the Indians to attend church in the morning and in the afternoon to say their prayers and receive instructions in the *doctrina.* The method used is for them to repeat the words after the *Padre* and in his absence the *Fiscal,* who is an Indian who has been well trained in the *doctrina."* The exercises were generally conducted in Spanish, Father Espinosa tells us, and the number of the neophytes who could understand and speak this language was truly surprising, he states, particularly among those who had come to the missions while they were still young. As the number of Indians was not stable and there were frequent new arrivals, the unconverted and unbaptized were allowed to attend church with the rest in order that they might begin to learn the catechism and prepare themselves to be admitted to the Sacrament of Baptism.

In the morning, and again in the afternoon, the mission bell rang out its call. The *Fiscal* and his assistant, usually two Indians appointed by the *Padre,* out of those who had been in the mission the longest and knew the *doctrina* best, went from house to house, asking both young and old to go to the mission chapel. No one was excused from attendance unless he was sick in bed. When they had all gathered in the church, just before the missionary began his daily instruction to the neophytes, the

Fiscal informed him how many were absent on account of illness. If one of those who was well failed to appear, he was brought before the *Fiscal* after the *doctrina,* and if he could not give a good reason for his absence, he was taken out to the mission cemetery and there made to kneel before the cross in penitence for his fault as an example and warning to the others who may be inclined to stay away from these exercises. If the offender was in the habit of absenting himself, the *Fiscal* would administer four or five lashes to the culprit while he knelt in the presence of all the other Indians.

Contrary to the general belief that many of the natives were hastily baptized without being first instructed in the fundamentals of our Faith, Father Espinosa declares that particular care was taken to teach all new arrivals the *doctrina* before admitting them to the Sacrament of Baptism. The missionary would take each one of the new arrivals individually, and with the help of an interpreter who was well acquainted with the language, he explained to him the mysteries of our religion. The instruction was continued *largo tiempo* (long time). When the Indian had been taught the *doctrina* and gave evidence of understanding the principles of Christianity, he was asked if he still wanted to be baptized. If he answered in the affirmative, he was then administered this sacrament with all solemnity and the entire mission celebrated the occasion with great rejoicings.

The greatest handicap encountered by the missionaries in their endless toils was the tendency of the neophytes to run away. This tendency was not the result of dissatisfaction with mission life or mistreatment, but rather a desire to return to their former roaming and irresponsible life. When the hunting season approached, all the mission Indians became restless for the chase. They felt an urge that was beyond their power to withstand. Their former friends and companions, and at times their own relatives who had not been congregated, sent word to them regarding the abundance of game or fish. It was then they forgot the security they enjoyed in the mission, the kindness of the *Padres,* the peace and calm of their regulated life. It was then they longed for adventure, for the fierce yell of the hunter, for the orgy and dance that followed the exciting race after buffalo. Two or three families would then get together and plan to leave. They waited, usually, until night. Protected by darkness, they would silently steal away, traveling as fast as they could all night and far into the following day. Not until the faithful neophytes were gathered in the chapel would the runaways be missed. As soon as the zealous missionary learned of their flight, he would set out with a soldier or two as companions, or sometimes alone, and like a true father goes in search of his children, he would travel across plains, over hills, and into the forests until he found them and brought them back. Almost all the missionaries agree that when the neophytes saw the *Padre* after their escapade, they ran to him like lost lambs to the shepherd. Although this was a common occurrence throughout the year, the fickleness of their words did not seem to discourage the missionaries, who, like trusting mothers, constantly forgave their children for the indescribable hardships they had to endure for their sake.

One of the most common and recurring epidemics to which the missions were exposed was smallpox. The natives seem to have been particularly susceptible to the contagion and greatly dreaded the perilous consequences of the disease. In their childish way they believed the malady was an evil spirit that walked from one afflicted person to another. Whenever a member of a tribe became a victim of smallpox, the rest of the Indians placed him under the shade of a large tree, surrounded him by a fence of thorns, and leaving him some food and water, abandoned him to his fate, while they fled as far away as possible. On the path, they would halt at regular intervals and place thorny bushes so that the smallpox, in trying to overtake them, might pierce its "little sacks" and die in the attempt. When such an epidemic visited the missions it was with the greatest difficulty that the missionaries were able to keep the neophytes from running away. The indefatigable and devoted *Padres* would work night and day to prepare food for the sick and to give them such comfort as they could provide. The Indians who were not afflicted generally refused to take care of the sick, because they feared that they might contract the disease. At such times those who died were buried as soon as possible, and in cases where all the members of a family occupying one house succumbed, they were burned with all their belongings, for it was thought to be the surest means of preventing further infection.

The trying years of Governor Fernando Pérez de Almazán's administration were fruitful years. It was during this time that the real foundations for the civil administration of Texas were laid and that the missions became definitely organized. In spite of the unsympathetic and unfair report of Pedro de Rivera in 1727, and notwithstanding the reduction of all the garrisons, the work was to go on, because its roots had been planted deep in the soil. The untamed children of the plains had been brought in touch with a force hitherto unknown in their lives. The all-embracing love of the *Padres* had softened their hardened souls;

many of them had consented to live in the missions; many more had become friendly and in the course of time would join the ranks of the neophytes. The temporary structures and roughly surveyed fields of the early years had been replaced by more substantial buildings and better cultivated farms; the straggling droves of cattle, goats, sheep, mules, and horses, brought with so many hardships to the missions, had grown into respectable herds under the constant care of the missionaries. A real start had been made at the price of untold sacrifices.

CHAPTER VII

RIVERA'S INSPECTION AND THE REMOVAL OF THE QUERÉTARAN MISSIONS
TO SAN ANTONIO, 1723-1731

Abuses of the presidial system. Shortly after his arrival in New
Spain, Viceroy Casafuerte, one of the most able and energetic colonial
officials that ever came to Mexico, informed the king that in accordance
with his instructions, he had made a preliminary study of the excessive
drain on the royal treasury. This had convinced him that the root of
the evil was to be found in the rampant abuses that existed in the management of the frontier presidios, extending all the way from the Pacific
to far-away Texas. In the beginning, these posts had been established to
protect the young and exposed settlements on the outskirts of New Spain
against the frequent incursions of the fierce Indians who constantly
threatened them; to make the roads safer for the Spaniards who carried
on trade with those remote regions; and to enable prospectors to explore
the country for new mines. Some presidios, however, had had for their
main purpose to afford adequate protection to the new missions founded
in the unconquered wilderness by the zealous missionaries in their efforts to
civilize the natives and bring them into the fold of the Church, shielding
the neophytes from their more obstinate brethren and helping to keep
them from committing depredations and causing those already congregated to revolt and return to their former savagery. There were twenty
presidios in all, besides three unattached companies of soldiers stationed
at strategic points to give aid where it was most needed. Of the twenty
presidios, four had been recently established in Texas by his predecessor,
the Marquis of Valero, at a cost to the royal treasury of three hundred
and seventy thousand *pesos.*[1]

Every soldier on the frontier was paid on an average four hundred and
fifty *pesos* a year, but unfortunately about one-fourth of this amount never
reached them. Such salary as they received was paid in kind, the goods
and supplies being charged to them at exorbitant prices by the captains.
The soldiers had often complained against this evil, which the missionaries and settlers had confirmed by observations and testimony in their
numerous private and confidential reports. So lucrative was the trade in

---

[1]Casafuerte to the King, Mexico, May 25, 1723. *A. G. I., Audiencia de México,*
63-1-41 (Dunn Transcripts, 1723-1729).

supplies for the frontier outposts, however, that the wealthiest and most influential merchants in Mexico were often the agents of the captains, sharing in the unfair profits and encouraging the illegal transactions.

But even more serious in its effect on the efficiency of the garrisons was the frequent employment of the men in the private ranches and mines of the officers, who, in many instances, had acquired large holdings. It was the soldiers, according to the reports received by the viceroy, who acted as overseers of the mines and *haciendas* of the captains, who tended their cattle, and looked after their business. These occupations kept them away from the presidios which they were supposed to garrison and were the cause of serious consequences to frontier settlements and missions. As a result of such unpardonable abuses, the money of the royal treasury was being wasted in maintaining presidios which were such only in name, affording little or no protection and serving only to enrich unscrupulous captains.[2]

Furthermore, the viceroy judiciously pointed out, conditions had changed since the original establishment of many of the presidios. In some instances the country in their vicinity had become well populated and no longer required protection, while in others the Indians had either been reduced to mission life or had ceased their former hostilities, making the existence of a garrison unnecessary. In order to ascertain the true state of affairs and to determine with all fairness which presidios should be abolished, how much the soldiers should be paid, and how the other abuses should be corrected, it would be necessary to send an official to conduct a personal investigation in each and every one of the military posts. This measure, he knew, had been tried out before without success, but the failure could be attributed to the unwise choice of inspectors and the low pay allowed them for so important a mission.

Preparations for inspection. "This enterprise," the viceroy declared, "will require time and a person of character, intelligence, and unlimited devotion to Your Majesty, capable of carrying it out." To avoid the danger to which men are exposed in executing so delicate and responsible an undertaking, it would be well, he said, to allow whoever was chosen this time, a salary commensurate to its great responsibility and to give him and his assistants sufficient funds for their traveling expenses during the tour of inspection, otherwise the temptation to favor those who were

---

[2]*Ibid.* A comparison of the abuses described by Father González on conditions in Texas with those listed and so vividly depicted here shows clearly the extent of the influence it had on this official. See pp. 194-195.

defrauding the treasury, or to be lenient with them, might prove to be too great.

Pedro de Rivera chosen for inspection. Solicitous of the royal service, he had looked for and found the man to whom the undertaking could be entrusted with a fair expectation of success. This was Colonel Pedro de Rivera, commander *ad interim* of the Fortress of San Juan de Ulloa, who had served His Majesty with credit and honor in many posts, both military and civil, whose loyalty was beyond question, and who was energetic and capable. In order further to bind him to the faithful execution of the important mission which was to be committed to his care, he had promoted him to the rank of Brigadier General and allowed him the full pay of his new rank, by issuing to him one of the blank commissions given to the viceroys by the king to reward those who had served His Majesty well in America. As it was of the utmost importance to the interests of the royal service to take measures immediately to correct the abuses described, the viceroy had commissioned Brigadier General Rivera to undertake the inspection, subject to the final approval of the king.[3]

The abundant stream of revenue that flowed into the coffers of the kings of Spain during the first century of the conquest in America had noticeably dwindled and every possible economy was necessary to increase its volume at this time in order to maintain Spanish prestige in Europe. So flattering a proposal to bring about considerable savings to the royal treasury was naturally received with enthusiasm and approved without hesitation. On February 19, 1724, the king expressed his gratification with all that had been done and authorized the viceroy to proceed to the execution of the plan outlined "being as it is in full accord with the best interests of my royal service." He asked to be kept informed with all diligence of everything that was ordered and with the outcome of the inspection.[4]

Instructions given Rivera for inspection. By the time the royal *cédula* reached Mexico on July 28, Brigadier Don Pedro de Rivera was already discussing the details of his important mission with the viceroy. A very careful set of instructions was drawn for his guidance on September 15. His attention was first directed to what the viceroy considered "the root of all the evils." All, or almost all, the soldiers in the various presidios had

---

[3]Casafuerte to the King, May 25, 1723. *A. G. I., Audiencia de México,* 62-1-41.
[4]Real Cédula del Rey. Madrid, February 19, 1724. *A. G. I., Audiencia de México,* 62-1-41 (Dunn Transcripts, 1723-1729).

been and were being deprived of a part of their pay as a result of *quites,* or discounts. For example, a presidio with a garrison of fifty men, assigned four hundred and fifty *pesos* for each soldier and six hundred *pesos* for the captain, cost His Majesty twenty-three thousand one hundred *pesos* a year. But although this sum was paid in full by the royal treasury in Mexico City or its branches in the provinces, the following amounts were deducted by the captains as *quites* before it reached the soldiers: first, two thousand three hundred and ten *pesos,* then five hundred and eighty *pesos,* and lastly, one thousand more, making a total of three thousand eight hundred and ninety *pesos,* equivalent to a loss of seventy-eight *pesos* per soldier. As a result of this practice each man received only three hundred and seventy-two *pesos* a year. In some instances the amounts indicated were deducted as "expenses," but the rate of discounts was higher or lower in proportion to the number of men in the presidio. The inspector was to correct such abuses wherever found.

The provisions, personal equipment, arms, horses, and other supplies needed by the various garrisons were generally bought in Mexico City or other trading centers situated nearer to the different posts by agents or representatives of the captains to whom the consignment was sent. These goods were usually billed at as high a price as the greed or bad conscience of the agent dictated, to which the captain generally added a percentage for his own benefit before he sold them to the soldiers. Consequently the men received but a very small portion of goods or supplies for their salary. This was the reason why so many of them were poorly clad, poorly armed, and unfit to perform their duties as soldiers. Brigadier Rivera was to make a careful study of these conditions and to recommend means of putting a stop to such a deplorable practice.

It was customary, furthermore, for the captains to leave vacancies caused by desertions or death unfilled, continuing to report the men as present on their muster roll and collecting the full salary allowed. But more reprehensible than this, was the habitual employment of the soldiers paid by His Majesty to guard the presidios on the private *haciendas,* ranches, and mines of their officers. They not only lost all sense of discipline, but they were kept away from their posts, so that they were unable to oppose successfully the frequent raids of the Indians, who grew bolder in proportion as they found no resistance. The outcome of such neglect was a heavy loss of property and life in the unprotected settlements and missions that had been established in the vicinity of the poorly guarded presidios.

The inspector was further to determine with all care whether the original location of the various establishments was the most advantageous. Time could have altered conditions and made some of them unnecessary or required their removal now to other localities. The original number of soldiers assigned to each one might have become excessive with the growth of the civil population and the cessation of hostilities on the part of the natives. In such cases the reduction of the garrisons would save the treasury a superfluous expense. He was instructed to give his mature judgment to this important matter and to make such recommendations as he deemed prudent, keeping in mind that although it was the desire of the king to prevent the fruitless expenditure of royal funds, it was his purpose to afford adequate protection in all instances to the frontier settlements and missions, this having been the sole object for the original establishment and maintenance of the presidios.

In order that the inspector might be in position to proceed to the execution of the various objects of his mission with a full knowledge of the facts in each case, and to enable him to exercise better judgment, he was advised to communicate with the civil and ecclesiastical authorities in and about the various presidios before visiting them. He was to obtain from the officials, as well as the settlers, as many particulars as possible concerning the conditions that existed in the different localities and their opinion stating why the presidios should be continued in their present locations, or moved, or their garrisons reduced or increased. With this information he would be better able to conduct the personal investigation in each one of them and to make the most suitable recommendations in each case.

He was specifically requested to find out whether the guard of twelve soldiers kept at Saltillo to convoy trains of supplies and escort travelers to Texas was really needed. In the judgments of many this service was unnecessary. If in any of the presidios the soldiers lacked arms, equipment, or horses he was to see that they were fully supplied with everything they needed before leaving that post, in order that each garrison would be left in position to withstand all Indian hostilities.

He was to inquire into the character and habits of the various presidial captains, investigating whether they complied diligently with their duties, or whether they had any vices which were deemed incompatible with the military profession, or if their personal conduct gave cause for scandal, or whether they maltreated the soldiers, or defrauded them in any manner of their just dues. If he found them guilty of any irregularity he was authorized to suspend them and institute suit against them.

Desirous of determining what was a fair price for commodities supplied to the various presidios, Brigadier General Rivera was particularly instructed to ascertain the cost of transportation of these things to the different posts and compare the prices charged for similar products or goods in each one of them. With this information and such observations as the inspector might deem proper to make, a maximum price list for various commodities could be prepared for each presidio to prevent the captains from overcharging the soldiers as in the past.

In conclusion, Brigadier Rivera was to draw up a brief report after visiting each presidio, giving its location, the purposes for which it was originally founded, the character of the country where it was established, the names and extent of the different Indian tribes that lived in the vicinity, the nature of their hostilities, the distance to the nearest outpost and the means of communication between the two, and finally whether in case of distress it could give or receive aid. This information was to be used in compiling a descriptive map of all the frontier defenses of New Spain. In order to enable him to carry out his instructions, the viceroy conferred upon Rivera full power to act in his name in all cases and to put into effect any measures which in his judgment were necessary to correct the evils and irregularities found in the various presidios which were detrimental to the best interests of His Majesty.[5]

When the matter was referred to the *Fiscal* for his recommendations, he enthusiastically approved the plans and all the instructions. It was, he declared, time that the presidios should be made to fulfill the true object for which they were founded. Because of the greed and the unscrupulous character of many of their commanders, they had failed to promote the reduction of the Indians to mission life and to bring them by this means to a knowledge of God and the recognition of the authority of the king. Had this been done earlier, hostilities would have long since ceased and peace would have been established along the entire frontier, as had been done in other regions of New Spain, such as in San Miguel, Mesquitiqui, San Sebastián del Agua de Venado, Tierra Blanca, San Luis de la Paz, and Río Verde. Here seven presidios had been originally built, with ten companies of from twenty-five to thirty men each, at an annual cost of four hundred thousand *pesos* to the royal treasury. Not long after their establishment the garrisons were suppressed as a result of the interest which their captains took from the beginning in the conversion and paci-

---

[5]Instrucciones que se le dieron por S. E. á Dn. Pedro de Rivera, México, September 15, 1724. *A. G. I., Audiencia de México*, 62-1-41.

fication of the natives. The first year the Indians had been given clothes, tools, seed, grain, and cattle. In the course of a few years they became self-supporting and needed aid no longer. When compared with the success of the presidios on the northern and eastern frontier, it was shameful to observe how, after all this time, such little progress had been made. Not only had the Indians not been pacified, but their hostility and the extent of their depredations had increased. All this happened because the captains had been satisfied to wage an active campaign for only a few months each year, returning to their presidios without defeating the enemy or making the natives desire peace. He fully agreed that the inspector should be allowed the maximum expenses permitted by the laws of the Indies to insure the success of his mission, and recommended that he be allowed twelve *pesos* a day for traveling in addition to his regular salary as Brigadier General.[6]

The *Auditor* endorsed the recommendations of the *Fiscal* and advised that Brigadier General Rivera should set out as soon as possible, as the season was the most favorable to travel north now in the fall, when the torrential rains of early spring and summer had ceased. He called the attention of the viceroy to the fact that the *autos* concerning the death of Captain Ramón, the inefficiency of his son Diego, and the guard or escort of twelve men kept at Saltillo, were in the archives and suggested that copies of these should be given to Rivera for his information, as well as of others pertaining to various occurrences in the frontier presidios in recent years. The *Auditor,* who was Don Juan de Oliván Rebolledo, had held this position since 1715. He had a personal interest in Texas and the country of the Río Grande. He now took occasion to exhibit his intimate acquaintance with documents describing this region. With pardonable pride but evident lack of accurate information, however, he offered a number of facts about the Río Grande for the benefit of Rivera. The Río Bravo, generally called Río Grande del Norte, he declared, had its source in a lake about fifty leagues or more to the north of Santa Fe, the capital of New Mexico. Flowing in general from north to south, it emptied in the Gulf of Mexico. Its volume was increased by a number of rivers along its course, the point where the Sacramento (Concho) joined it being known as the Junta de los Rios. The presidio of El Paso del Río del Norte was located a short distance from the Junta. From this juncture to the Presidio of San Juan Bautista the river flowed from west

---

[6]Respuesta Fiscal, México, September 22, 1724. *A. G. I., Audiencia de México,* 62-1-41.

to east, resuming its southerly direction at this point and continuing through the provinces of Nuevo Reyno de León and Coahuila to a distance of about forty leagues from the sea, where it again turned east until it flowed into the Gulf. Close to its banks, he said, were situated the Presidios of Cadereita and Cerralvo de León, erring decidedly in the case of the first. Below San Juan Bautista, the river constituted a great natural moat or chasm which divided the barbarous nations that dwelt over this vast area as far as New Mexico and those that roamed the wilderness of Nueva Vizcaya and Coahuila, sometimes called Nueva Estremadura. The latter was separated from the former by a great chain of mountains that ran from north to south. He suggested that Brigadier Rivera should explore the river from the Presidio of El Paso to the mountain chain that divided Coahuila and Nueva Vizcaya (approximately present Langtry or Del Río) to determine if the land was fertile and suitable for settlement and the raising of cattle, in which case it might be advisable to move the Presidios of Cerro Gordo, El Gallo, and Mapimí or Pasage to this region. This would afford positive protection to the entire province of Nueva Vizcaya.[7]

The viceroy, who was a stickler for all legal formalities, called a general *Junta de Hacienda* to which he presented all the documents concerning the proposed *Visita* of the presidios and asked that it fix officially the amount to be paid Brigadier General Don Pedro de Rivera and the two assistants and a secretary who should accompany him for the more expeditious execution of this important mission. The *Junta* decided that in addition to his salary, he should be allowed, as recommended by the *Fiscal* and the *Auditor* the sum of twelve *pesos* a day for traveling expenses, and that his two assistants and secretary should be paid five *pesos* a day for the duration of the *Visita*. It further authorized the viceroy to advance the inspector such an amount as he deemed convenient to enable him to make the preparations for his immediate start.[8]

On October 10, the viceroy ordered the royal treasury to advance Rivera six thousand *pesos* for expenses and stipulated that contrary to the recommendations of the *Junta,* his two assistants would be allowed only two

---

[7]Opinión del Auditor, México, October 2, 1724. *A. G. I., Audiencia de México,* 62-1-41. Taking everything into consideration the description of this little known area, the information concerning it given here is remarkable. The idea advocated here by Rebolledo was to be urged by the Marquis of Rubí almost fifty years later in the reorganization of the frontier line of defense of the Interior Provinces.

[8]Opinión de la Junta de Hacienda, México, October 6, 1724, in *Ibid.*

pesos a day, which sum was considered sufficient. The pay of the inspector and his secretaries was to begin on the day they left Mexico City. The General of the Jesuits and all Commissaries General of the various religious orders, who had charge of missions in the territories to be visited were instructed to ask the reverend missionaries to lend all assistance possible to Rivera in the execution of his commission. Notice was sent to the Bishop of Durango, and the Governors of Parral, Nuevo Reyno de León, New Mexico, and Texas of the intended inspection, with a request that they give all assistance possible and hinder in no manner the accomplishment of the purposes desired in undertaking the *Visita*. Failure to coöperate with Rivera would be sufficient cause for their immediate suspension. The investigation was not to be limited to abuses committed during the years of the administration of Viceroy Casafuerte, but to include the last twenty years, and all officials were to be held responsible, whether dead or alive, for any irregularities during their terms of office. The order for payment was accordingly drawn up on October 14 and the dispatches to the various officials were sent out two days later.[9]

It is well to note that before Rivera set out on his long but transcendent tour of inspection, which was to affect the future course of events in Texas so vitally, he was given for his information copies of everything pertaining to conditions in that remote province found in the archives of the viceroy. After his departure he was kept informed of what transpired. Copies of the reports of Governor Pérez de Almazán, the missionaries, and the various captains of presidios were sent to him, so that when he finally arrived, he was fully informed of conditions.[10]

Rivera's inspection.   In spite of every effort to start with as little loss of time as possible, it was not until November 21, 1724, that Brigadier General Rivera finally left Mexico City for Zacatecas, armed with all the necessary credentials. It is not our purpose to follow him on his long journey over the entire frontier. After almost three years of constant traveling on horse and muleback, over roads little frequented and exposed to unexpected attacks by Indians, relentlessly ferreting out irregularities wherever he went, noting the advantages and disadvantages of each place, and making long and detailed reports on his observations, the tireless and ever watchful inspector arrived at last in Texas in the spring of

---

[9]Decreto del Virey Casafuerte, México, October 10, 1724, in *Ibid*.

[10]Razón [de documentos recibidos por Don Pedro de Rivera], México, October 30, 1724, in *Ibid*.

1727. From the distant fort at Conchos, he had first gone to Santa Fe, then retracing his steps, he had made a careful investigation of conditions at the Presidio of El Paso del Norte del Río Grande, before going to Sinaloa. It was from this remote outpost that he proceeded to Texas, stopping only for a few days at Janos, San Felipe el Real in Chihuahua, and continuing hence by way of Monclova, San Juan Bautista, San Antonio, and Los Tejas to the Presidio of Nuestra Señora del Pilár de los Adaes. "The distance from Sinaloa to this presidio, according to the itinerary followed, is nine hundred leagues," declared Rivera in his report.

Conditions found at Los Adaes. Here he found a garrison of one hundred men, including the officers, all under the command of the governor who resided at this post. The soldiers were employed in guarding the presidio, which although built of timber, was well protected by a stockade; in watching the horses; in the cultivation of a few fields where grain and vegetables for their maintenance were raised; in improving their quarters, and in helping the three missions founded in the vicinity by the Franciscan missionaries from the College of Zacatecas. Upon his arrival, a proclamation declaring his intention of conducting a formal inspection of the presidio was made. He asked the governor to present his book of accounts and his muster roll of enlistments and to retire with all subaltern officers to a safe distance, as required by law. These orders were placed in the guardroom for all to read. A questionnaire concerning the conduct of the governor and his officers was prepared and the various soldiers permitted to testify freely in the absence of their officers in order to determine if there were grounds for censuring them. When the investigation was concluded and the governor and subalterns had returned they were informed that no irregularities or serious offences had been discovered for which they could be held liable. An inspection held immediately thereafter disclosed that two of the men were unfit for military service and they were consequently replaced at once. A set of rules for the guidance of the officers in charge of the garrison was prepared and given to the governor, together with a list of the maximum prices that could be charged for the most commonly needed supplies, all of which had been sold heretofore at figures far above their actual value or cost. Agreeable to the authority granted to the inspector by the viceroy to fix salaries more equitably in accord with the conditions found, the rate of pay which had been four hundred and fifty *pesos* a year was reduced to four hundred and twenty.

Rivera listed eight tribes of Indians as living in the neighborhood: Adaes, Ays, Aynays (Hainais), Nazonis, Neches, Nacogdoches, Naconomes, and Navidachos. He declared that all these were extremely friendly and docile and lived in perfect peace with the Spaniards. But in spite of their apparent friendliness, very few Indians had come to stay in the three missions established for them by the zealous missionaries. Most of them still lived in their *rancherías,* located within a radius of ten or fifteen leagues where they were frequently visited by the diligent *Padres.*[11]

Conditions at Presidio de los Tejas. From Los Adaes, he went to the Presidio de Nuestra Señora de los Dolores de los Tejas, located in the vicinity of Mission Concepción, near the Angelina River. This was garrisoned by a captain, who received five hundred *pesos* a year, and twenty-four men, who were paid four hundred *pesos* each. The chief occupation of the soldiers was the cultivation of the presidial farm, the care of a small number of horses, and the assistance they were asked to give to the missionaries. As a result of their peaceful employment, the garrison had little notion of military discipline and was very deficient in the manual of arms and the duties of the military profession. The fort and houses of the soldiers were poorly constructed log huts with grass roofs. No guard duty was performed regularly and not even a sentinel kept watch. The Indians were peaceful, there being no record of their ever having caused the slightest trouble or given the least grounds for uneasiness. But as in the case of the missions in the neighborhood of Los Adaes, those founded here by the missionaries from the College of Querétaro had only a few neophytes living "bajo campana," or in the mission proper. Most of them dwelt from six to ten leagues away. They were friendly and seemed fond of the *Padres,* visiting them frequently and bringing them gifts.[12]

So disgusted was Rivera, however, with the lack of discipline of the garrison, that he dispensed with the military inspection and did not bother to draw up a set of regulations for their instruction. He contented

[11]Proyecto Mandado hacer por el Exmo. Sor. Marqués de Casafuerte Virrey Governador y Capitán General de esta Nueva Espana y Presidente de la Real Audiencia de ella, reducido a la Visita hecha por el Brigadier Dn. Pedro de Rivera, que contiene tres puntos: El Primero el Estado en que estaban los Presidios antes que se Visitasen; El Segundo El en que se pusieron después que se les hizo la Visita; El Tercero El en que por ultima disposición de su Exa. combendra se pongan. In *A. G. N., Provincias Internas,* Vol. 29. Copy also in *Archivo San Francisco el Grande,* Vol. 2.

[12]*Ibid.*

himself with giving the captain a list of the maximum prices he was to charge the soldiers for the most common supplies furnished to them and informed the officer he would hear from the viceroy as to the future course he was to follow. The salary paid the men and the captain he considered fair and consequently made no changes in this regard. Rivera evidently made up his mind at this time to urge the total abolition of this post upon his return to Mexico.

Conditions at Espíritu Santo. He now proceeded to the Presidio of Nuestra Señora de Loreto de la Bahía del Espíritu Santo, where Captain Bustillos y Cevallos had a garrison of ninety men. For some unexplained reason, this officer, he remarked, was called "governor." The order of the men and their military bearing offered a striking contrast to those at Los Tejas. This was more remarkable in view of the fact that it was the worst organized presidio in the province when the new captain had taken charge of it in 1725. "The garrison observed such good discipline, as a result of the care with which the commander performs his duty, that there was nothing to correct; rather I was particularly impressed to see the soldiers uniformly dressed and skilled in the manual of arms, executing the different drills with the proper words of command," declared the inspector. Although the provisions and supplies were furnished at excessive prices, the captain exercised such rigid economy, that all the men not only had everything they needed but had a balance in their favor in their respective salaries. The captain was instructed to charge all supplies hereafter in accord with a list of prices left for his guidance, in order that this abuse might be corrected. The rate of pay which had been four hundred *pesos* a year, was reduced to three hundred and eighty, an amount which, in view of the maximum price list left to be enforced, would better enable the soldiers to obtain all necessities than their former salary.[13]

Turning his attention to general conditions, he pointed out that in the immediate neighborhood were to be found the following tribes: Tacames, Aranames, Mayeyes, Pampopas, and Pastias, some of which had been congregated in the mission that had been established a short distance from the presidio. The Indians were in the habit, however, of going out frequently during the fishing season and when it was time to gather different wild fruits. Being nomads, they experienced great difficulty in remaining long confined to one place. They had none of the warlike

[13]*Ibid.*

characteristics of their kinsmen who lived to the north, were totally lacking in spirit, and were known for their cowardice. In addition to these
tribes, who were generally friendly and peaceful, there lived along the
coast the Cocos, Karankawas, Coapites, Cujanes, and Copanes. It was
these Indians who had rebelled against mission life and been the cause,
to a large extent, for the removal of the presidio to its present location
on the Guadalupe. But even the coastal Indians, according to Rivera, who
was decidedly misinformed or who purposely misrepresented the facts,
were not numerous and had little spirit. For this reason any attempt on
their part to destroy the post or the mission could be easily put down. It
is strange that he should have acquired so erroneous an idea of these
Indians, who were known to be the most dreaded cannibals. The Karankawas, who included the Cujanes, Coapites, Cocos, and Copanes, were
"fierce cannibals," according to Bolton, "and were regarded as particularly dangerous to mariners on the perilous coast."[14]

Conditions at San Antonio de Béjar.   From La Bahía, Rivera went on
to San Antonio de Béjar, where he found a company of fifty-four men,
including the captain and subaltern officers, all of whom were paid four
hundred *pesos* a year, without distinction of rank. Contrary to reports
made regarding the lack of discipline and the unfitness of many of the
soldiers for active duty, either because of their extreme youth or old age,
the formal inspection of the garrison disclosed they were all active and
fit, that the number on the muster roll was complete; and that they had
successfully opposed the frequent attacks of the Apaches, who lived in
Lomería Alta, inflicting upon them condign punishment for their daring
on various occasions. He correctly observed that these Indians were not
as numerous as had been heretofore supposed, admitting that the firmness
with which they had been repulsed by the garrison, had caused them
to respect the Spaniards. This fact had checked hostilities in recent
years to a certain extent, although being confirmed thieves, these Indians
still made attempts to steal the horses of the presidio from time to time,
whenever they suspected the vigilance had been relaxed, but they uniformly were made to pay dearly for their raids. After complimenting
the captain and soldiers for "their good quality," he gave the commander
a set of rules and regulations which were to be observed in the future
and a list of the maximum prices to be charged to the men for their

---

[14]Bolton, *Athanase de Mézières and the Louisiana Frontier,* 1, 19-20. Castañeda,
Morfi's History of Texas, Chapter II.

supplies. With regard to the salaries, he reduced the rate of pay of the soldiers to three hundred and eighty *pesos* and raised that of the captain to six hundred.[15]

The location of the Presidio of San Antonio de Béjar he deemed well chosen to withstand the attacks of the Apaches and to afford adequate protection both to the missions and such civil settlers as might decide to establish themselves in its vicinity. "It is situated in the best site I have been able to discover in all my travels," he declared. "At a distance of slightly more than half a league to the north, there is a hill, not very high, from whose sides gush forth two most abundant springs of water." These formed two streams, he said, that flowed past the presidio on either side, the one to the east, which would correspond to present San Antonio River, being larger, but both capable of supplying all the water necessary to cultivate the fertile and extensive fields in the neighborhood. The corn, wheat, and cotton now being raised in the small portions under cultivation gave evidence of the productivity of the soil when irrigated. Furthermore, a short distance away, about seven leagues from the presidio, where the Medina joined these streams, a large number of cattle grazed already, which feature promised to grow and would become sufficient in time to supply the largest settlement. The two missions that had been established in this locality had very many more Indians congregated under their care than those in East Texas. But in spite of their proximity to the garrison, soldiers were regularly assigned to them, who, because of their coöperation with the *Padres* in the management of the mission farms, were called *mayordomos,* or overseers.[16]

After almost three and a half years, Brigadier Rivera completed his tour of inspection, having traveled more than three thousand leagues, over mountains, through virgin forests, across deserts, fording numerous streams, traversing endless plains, patiently jogging along on horse or muleback over many a long and weary mile. "IIe has made himself worthy for the reward of Your Majesty," the viceroy said to the king, "because of the integrity and zeal with which he has executed so arduous an undertaking, as well as the constancy with which he has suffered the hardships and inconveniences of so long and painful a journey, undertaken at his advanced age."[17] But when he returned to Mexico in the

[15]Proyecto Mandado . . . *A. G. N., Provincias Internas,* Vol. 29.

[16]*Ibid.*

[17]Casafuerte to the King, México, March 2, 1730. *A. G. I., Audiencia de México,* 61-2-12 (Dunn Transcripts).

spring of 1728, he had not yet finished his work. Endless conferences with the viceroy, who consulted him on everything, followed. Each case was taken individually and every point carefully discussed before a decision was made. But in spite of the scrupulous care of the viceroy to avoid error and the upright and impartial spirit that animated the aging inspector, the final judgment in regard to the innovations and changes that were to be put into effect to improve conditions in Texas were destined to prove inadequate and ill-advised.

Rivera's recommendations. On March 23, 1728, Rivera prepared a long report for the viceroy in which he presented his recommendations with regard to Texas, based on his personal visit and a careful study of all the facts concerned. Taking Los Adaes first, he pointed out that its garrison should be reduced to sixty men. When the presidio was originally founded a force of one hundred men had been stationed there because of the danger of French attack and the hostility of the Indians. But since that time the natives had become friendly and were peaceful, even though few of them had been reduced to mission life. The French garrison at Natchitoches, located about seven leagues away, had a force of only twenty-five men, and there was little or no danger of attack from this quarter, now that peace between the two crowns had been established. Should hostilities break out, he said, even the one hundred men would be insufficient to check the advance of the French, who would bring large reënforcements of well trained and seasoned troops from Mobile and Canada, against which the garrison would prove a poor match. Furthermore, the French could penetrate the Province of Texas unopposed, if they so desired, by way of the country of the Cadodachos, located to the north, and by taking a position among the Navidachos, they could cut off all supplies to the Spanish garrison and cause its surrender without firing a shot. From the arguments presented up to this point, it seems that Rivera had a low opinion of the courage or ability of frontier officers and men. He added, however, that the sixty soldiers which he suggested should be left at Los Adaes, could be reënforced, whenever it became necessary, from La Bahía or San Antonio, forgetting the difficulties offered most of the year caused by the swollen rivers, the danger of Indian attacks, and the slow means of communication.[18]

With regard to the Presidio of Nuestra Señora de los Dolores de los Tejas, he recommended its total abolition. The Indians in its immediate

---

[18]Proyecto Mandado hacer . . . *A. G. N., Provincias Internas*, Vol. 29.

vicinity, he declared, were peaceful and friendly; the garrison had never been called upon, ever since its establishment, to take part in an active campaign; the only employment of the soldiers was to raise the crops necessary for their maintenance and to help the missionaries; while the captain had no other duty than to assign to each mission the soldiers requested. In view of these circumstances, the expense of supporting the presidio was entirely unjustified, as the only service it performed was to assist the missionaries. Although this assistance could be continued, yet since the greater part of the Indians still lived in their *rancherías,* this service rendered could be done by assigning two soldiers to each mission from Los Adaes to help the faithful Franciscans and to accompany them in their frequent visits to their wards.[19]

In the case of the Presidio of Nuestra Señora de Loreto at Bahía del Espíritu Santo he began by declaring that its force should never have been increased from forty men to ninety, affirming, with unpardonable ignorance, that he did not know what the occasion for the increase had been. He refers to the diary of the expedition of Aguayo as his source of information on this point, but evidently he did not read the document through, or he would have found out that Aguayo was ordered to leave fifty additional men by a direct order of the king, transmitted to him by the viceroy.[20] The presidio had been established originally to prevent any other nation from occupying the coast, as had happened in 1685, when the French erected a fort there. But time had shown that a landing by a group sufficient for settlement was next to impossible. The water over the bar was so low that it precluded the entrance of vessels of large draft, such as would be required, and the country was so swampy and unhealthful that the presidio established by the Spaniards had been moved by force of circumstances about ten leagues inland to the banks of the Guadalupe River. But Rivera misrepresented the facts in attributing the cause of the removal to the unhealthful character of the country. Although this was a factor, the real reason was the hostility of the Indians and their refusal to live in the mission after the indiscreet conduct of Domingo Ramón to punish them resulted in his own death. Regardless of the true facts, he recommended that the garrison be reduced to forty soldiers. This number, he argued, was sufficient to protect the mission, as the Indians of this region had little or no spirit and were known for their cowardice

---

[19]*Ibid.* The remainder of the recommendations given hereafter are found in the same document.

[20]Peña, *Derrotero.*

and the danger of an attempt by foreigners to effect a landing was too remote.

Unmindful of the apparent contradiction, he explained that before leaving Texas, he had instructed the captain of the presidio to explore the course of the Guadalupe to its mouth in the bay and make it navigable in order that communication with the Huasteca (Veracruz) might be established by water. A road overland was to be opened also to carry on trade with the Nuevo Reyno de León, which should be about a hundred leagues distant from this post. By building a dam, about six leagues from its mouth, the waters of this river could be used to irrigate the lands in the vicinity of the presidio, in spite of its high banks. In this way a number of settlements could be established along the river, which could be supplied with the products raised on the broad plains that bordered it and made prosperous by the trade established between this section and the commercial centers just mentioned. The garrison would be occupied in carrying out these projects, there being little else for them to do in the line of military duties in the absence of a foreign enemy and Indian hostilities.

Determined to cut down the number of soldiers in every presidio in Texas, he recommended that the garrison of San Antonio be Béjar be also reduced from fifty-four men to forty-four. Its admirable location, the excellent discipline of the soldiers, the efficiency of the captain, and the many victories over the troublesome Apaches, showed clearly that the same protection would be afforded to the missions founded here and the civil settlers who had established themselves in the neighborhood by the force he suggested. But to give to the reduced garrison added strength, he made his own suggestion which had been offered by the Marquis of Aguayo six years before. Describing enthusiastically the facilities afforded by this ideal location for a settlement, he urged the establishment of a group of families on this pleasant and fertile site. Unlike Aguayo, however, he thought that twenty-five families were sufficient for the purpose, assuring the viceroy that with this number, ample protection and security would be afforded the entire region. This successful colonization would induce similar groups to inhabit other suitable localities.

He then turned his attention to the guard of twelve men, including a captain, kept at Saltillo as an escort for trains of supplies for the missions and presidios in Texas and those entering the province. Each one received four hundred and fifty *pesos* a year. When he visited them he found they were all fully and adequately equipped with everything necessary for the performance of their duties. As the result of a memorial presented by Captain Matías de Aguirre, their commander, asking that the time for such be determined to make it less onerous, no regulations having ever been made since its creation, the matter had been referred to the viceroy. The practice heretofore had been for anyone going to Texas to demand an escort. It often happened that an escort had just set out when a new one was requested. This proved a great hardship on the small number of soldiers who constituted the guard and wore out their horses by keeping them constantly on the road to cover the one hundred and thirty leagues between Saltillo and the Presidio of San Juan Bautista on the Río Grande. The viceroy ordered that all information on the creation of the guard and its services should be gathered and turned over to the *Auditor* for his consideration, who on November 5, 1727, suggested that Rivera be consulted as to the best times during the year when the escort should be available and as to the advisability of making any changes in the present arrangement.

In view of the information on the subject, he declared that the guard had been created by the Marquis of Valero to insure the safe and prompt convoy of supplies to Texas which were threatened at the time of the Aguayo expedition by the rebellious Indians who had nearly annihilated the garrison of Coahuila (Monclova); that after the termination of the expedition its immediate purpose had ceased, as declared by Aguayo himself; but that the need for protecting the trains of provisions and supplies for the presidios and missions as far as the Río Grande and hence to Texas still existed because of the presence of hostile Indians. It was essential to the best interests of the king, therefore, that this service be continued. He suggested, however, that since the garrison of Coahuila (Monclova) had been increased by ten men in 1721 by order of the viceroy to strengthen it against attack by enemy Indians, following their revolt, which hostility had now practically disappeared, it would be advisable that the guard of twelve men kept at Saltillo be abolished and the service rendered by them in escorting travelers and trains conducting supplies to Texas be performed by the ten men who had been added to the garrison at Coahuila (Monclova).

This post was located between Saltillo and the Río Grande del Norte and could furnish the escort suggested both from Saltillo to Monclova and from Monclova to Texas by way of San Juan Bautista. To avoid the confusion and unnecessary hardships imposed upon the soldiers engaged in this service caused by the promiscuous demand for escorts at all times of the year, he recommended that only regularly scheduled trips be made at different seasons. The first was to be made in January, the second in April, the third in July, and the fourth in October. If this recommendation met with the approval of the viceroy he should order that an escort of ten men, including an officer to command it, set out from Coahuila (Monclova) to Saltillo four times a year, in time to be at the latter place on the first of each month indicated. The escort should be instructed to make the trip back to the Río Grande not by way of Boca de Leones, but by Monclova, first, because the road was less difficult to traverse, and second, because upon its arrival in Monclova the men who made the journey to and from Saltillo could remain at this post and be replaced by others from this garrison who would make the journey from there on to Texas. This would make the service less burdensome and save the hardships of the entire trip to both men and horses. In case that those who had become accustomed to demand an escort at all times of the year should complain of the inconvenience of such an arrangement, they were to be reminded that the convoys that entered New Mexico made only two trips a year from El Paso del Norte, the distance being almost the same as from Saltillo to the Río Grande. By timing their entrance to Texas, both persons and trains going to Texas would not have to wait long in Saltillo for the regularly scheduled escort which was to give them the necessary protection while *en route* to that province.[21]

In discussing conditions at San Juan Bautista, Rivera pointed out that, following an old established custom, each of the four missions in its vicinity kept two soldiers constantly, to act as managers and overseers of the mission farms. This service originated at the time of the establishment of the presidio by order of the viceroy in 1698, but since that time many Indians had become congregated and reduced to mission life, adopting the habits and customs of civilized men, which made the presence of the soldiers unnecessary, particularly in view of the proximity of the presidio to three of them. The services rendered by the two soldiers in each case could now be performed by the Indians themselves, choosing from among them those who had been in the missions the longest and who had become most trustworthy and capable. But if the missionaries believed this should be done by a Spaniard, they could secure the services of any one of a number of civil settlers who had established themselves in that vicinity, who would be glad to act as managers or overseers if

---

[21]Proyecto Mandado hacer. . . . *A. G. N., Provincias Internas,* Vol. 29.

the *Padres* gave them a small piece of land to cultivate for themselves and lodged and boarded them at the missions. In this manner the soldiers who were kept without doing military duty as long as one and two years at times, could be restored to their garrison and made to observe discipline, as the ordinance for the presidios provided. The conditions that existed at San Juan Bautista, he pointed out, were equally true of one hundred and fifty other missions established by Franciscan and Jesuit missionaries along the entire frontier.

Although the assignment of two soldiers to all of these missions had been justified in the beginning to afford the *Padres* protection and much needed help in reducing the newly congregated Indians, it was now no longer required in view of the progress made by these establishments. He recommended, therefore, that not only the two soldiers stationed at each of the four missions under the protection of the Presidio of San Juan Bautista, but those detailed for similar duty in San Antonio de Béjar, should be withdrawn and ordered back to their respective garrisons. Aware of the fact that he had advocated the continuance of a guard of two men for each of the missions of Los Adaes and Los Tejas, for which reason it might be said that he was not consistent in his recommendations, he explained that in the latter case it was justified because there were almost no Indians living regularly "bajo campana," and this made the need of the soldiers essential to assist the missionaries in their frequent trips to the *rancherías* and to keep them company in their solitude.[22]

Agreeable to the order of the viceroy of August 2, 1728, Rivera incorporated the voluminous papers and documents he had accumulated in his extensive *visita* in a general report arranged in three parts: the first, a description of the state in which he had found the presidios; second, the state in which he had left them after his *visita;* and, third, the changes recommended in each case. It took the industrious and painstaking inspector a little over four months of constant labor to make his final report, which he turned over to the viceroy on December 7, 1728. "This," he declared, "is all that my solicitude has been able to accomplish to satisfy, as far as my ability permitted . . . the orders of Your Excellency . . . I have been moved in this undertaking by no other motives, in expressing my opinion of each case, than the relief of the presidial soldiers, the service of the king, and the greater glory of God."

[22]*Ibid.*

If there were errors these were to be attributed to his short understanding rather than to partiality or design, he assured the viceroy.[23]

Approval of Rivera's report. The report with all its recommendations was, as usual, submitted to the *Auditor* and the *Fiscal* for their consideration. The first endorsed all the suggestions made by Rivera on March 21, 1729, and the second enthusiastically urged the immediate execution of all recommendations on March 29. The following day, the viceroy ordered that the corresponding dispatches be drawn to carry out all the changes and measures advocated by the inspector with the amendments offered by the *Auditor*. In the case of the Province of Texas, the final changes were even more radical than those recommended by Rivera. The garrison at Los Adaes was reduced from one hundred men to sixty; the Presidio de Nuestra Señora de los Dolores de los Tejas was abolished, the force at La Bahía del Espíritu Santo was reduced from ninety to twenty; the garrision at San Antonio de Béjar was cut from fifty-four soldiers to thirty-eight; the guard of twelve men kept at Saltillo as an escort was discontinued and the garrison at Monclova ordered to perform this service as recommended by Rivera; and the two soldiers assigned to each of the missions in the vicinity of the Presidios of San Antonio de Béjar and San Juan Bautista were ordered to discontinue this service.[24] As a result, the number of soldiers in the entire Province of Texas was reduced by one hundred fifty-one men, leaving a force of one hundred eighteen men, where there had been two hundred sixty-nine before. The royal treasury was saved over sixty thousand *pesos* a year by the reduction of the number of soldiers and the pay of those remaining. The savings effected in the rest of the frontier amounted to over one hundred thousand *pesos* a year.[25] There is no question that from the point of view of increasing the revenue of the king, the *visita* was a decided success. But although it improved the general condition of many of the garrisons, the effect in Texas was to retard the general progress of the province and cause so much dissatisfaction by the exposed condition in which the few settlers and the struggling missions were left, that the best interests of the king suffered to a greater extent than the money saved to the royal treasury. The reforms and changes were put into effect July

[23]Rivera to the Viceroy, December 7, 1728. *A. G. N., Provincias Internas,* Vol. 29.

[24]Proyecto Mandado hacer. . . . *A. G. N., Provincias Internas,* Vol. 29.

[25]Casafuerte to the King, México, March 2, 1730. *A. G. I., Audiencia de México,* 61-2-12 (Dunn Transcripts, 1730-1736).

1, 1729, together with a new ordinance and set of regulations for the administration of the presidios designed to correct all the abuses found by Rivera.[26]

Provisions of new ordinance for presidios. Before taking up the effects in detail of the recommendations of Rivera in Texas, it will be well to note some of the provisions and rules of the new ordinance. Nothing can afford a better picture of life on the frontier of New Spain, along its first line of defence against the unconquered hordes of wild Indians, who constantly preyed upon the outposts like a pack of hungry wolves, than the ordinance adopted at this time. Heretofore the presidio at Los Adaes had had a captain. The new regulations provided that the governor, who was to reside at this post, was to be the commander of the presidio without any other salary than that received as governor, performing all the duties of captain in addition to those of governor. By the time the regulations were finally adopted, on April 21, 1729, the number of soldiers at La Bahía was raised to forty, and that of San Antonio de Béjar to forty-four as originally recommended.[27]

Governors of provinces were not to appoint captains, lieutenants, or sergeants major in the various presidios under their jurisdiction, other than as *ad interim,* as all such appointments could be made only by the viceroy. In case of a vacancy caused by death or other reason, the captain was to be succeeded by the second officer in command, who was to perform all the duties of the commander until the viceroy either appointed some one else or confirmed him in his office. The governor might submit in such cases a list of three possible candidates for His Excellency to choose from. But even the appointments made by the viceroy were temporary, until confirmed by the king. All captains *ad interim* were to receive only two-thirds of the regular salary until so confirmed. Governors were not permitted to summon the captains or commanders of presidios to confer with them, unless it be to take part in an active campaign. All such officers were not to absent themselves from their respective posts except when required by the royal service. Neither the captains nor the governors were to use the soldiers to escort or tend their pirvate herds, or as private messengers, or special escorts for friends.

In regard to the policy to be observed with the natives, governors and

---

[26]*Ibid.*

[27]Reforma y ordenanzas de Presidios segn el Proiecto del Visitador, *A. G. I., Audiencia de México,* 62-1-41.

captains were not to make war on them under any circumstances, unless the Indians attacked them first. They were strictly enjoined to try to attract them by kindness and gifts and to give them no occasion for hostilities. No help or aid was to be given to one tribe of Indians against another, unless the natives against which the campaign was to be undertaken were the known enemies of the Spaniards, in which case the governors and presidial officers were in good faith bound to help the friendly tribe. These officers were to call upon the civil settlers in the vicinity of the different presidios whenever help was needed either to repel an attack or to conduct a campaign. Whenever two or more governors of the internal provinces combined their forces for a campaign, the governor of Nueva Vizcaya, if present, was to be considered the commander-in-chief, but in his absence, the governor with the highest military rank should assume command in order that there be no misunderstandings and jealousy as in the past. Each governor, furthermore, should reside in the capital of his province and should not absent himself except when he made the inspection of the presidios or had to attend to the royal service. It is of interest to note at this point, that Los Adaes is specifically designated as the capital of the Province of Texas at this time, where the governor was supposed to reside regularly.

The soldiers were required to provide themselves with a lance in addition to the broadsword. Each one must have in addition to these two, a rifle, six horses and a pack mule. The men were to be uniformly dressed as to color and style of clothing, but both were left to the judgment of the respective commanders. Their officers were to exercise strict vigilance to see that they were clean and that their clothes were not in rags. On feast days they were expected to hear Mass and they should be made to observe the Sacrament of Penance before setting out on any campaign so that with their consciences at ease they might put up a more determined fight.

The chaplains of the presidios, and in their absence the missionaries in their vicinity, were enjoined to say Mass regularly for the garrisons on feast days and to do this at the most convenient time, so that the largest possible number of soldiers and settlers could attend. Whenever an expedition was organized to pursue or chastise the Indians, a religious should always accompany the men in order to administer to them the spiritual comforts of religion while on the campaign. But the missionaries were requested not to interfere in any manner with the secular management of the presidios so as to avoid discord and serious difficulties. If they had anything to complain of, or which they thought should be done for the better service of God and the king, they were instructed to apply to the viceroy directly who would hear their complaints or suggestions with interest and try to remedy or improve the conditions described.

Special care in guarding the horses of the presidios should be exercised at all times. The soldiers assigned to this duty should make the rounds regularly and each man must guard a fixed distance, which he should pace at regular intervals, greeting the other sentinels at the extremities of his beat. In this way, if the Indians broke the fence at any point, it would be discovered before they could accomplish their evil designs. All soldiers should be fully armed and equipped when on this or any other duty and should never be permitted to leave their *cueras,* a rawhide shield used by frontier soldiers as a defence against Indian darts, arrows, and lances, even if they complained of fatigue. The officers themselves were not to mount their horses without their *cueras.* Whenever a group of soldiers changed mounts, to avoid surprise by the Indians, only half of the number should dismount for this purpose at a time. If this substitution became necessary with the enemy in view or close proximity, only a third of the soldiers should change their horses at a time.

Supplies and provisions intended for the Presidio of Los Adaes were to be escorted by a guard of ten men sent by the governor from that post to San Antonio and such additional men as the captain of this presidio deemed best to detail for this purpose. From Saltillo to San Juan Bautista, the escort was to be furnished by the garrison of Coahuila (Monclova) and from this place to San Antonio, by the Presidio of San Juan Bautista. Soldiers detailed to this duty were not to ask any aid in food or specie from the travelers attended or from the owners of the provisions, supplies, or herds being escorted. They were allowed to accept, however, whatever was given freely to them. Whenever traveling through the country of friendly Indians, the officer in charge of the troop was not to allow any of the soldiers to visit the *rancherías* or to trade with the natives, because misunderstandings might arise, which would endanger seriously the safety of the travelers or trains of supplies being escorted.

The Governor of the Province of Texas was to try by all means possible to maintain the peace that existed with all the Indians of that region and to avoid giving provocation for hostilities. Each year he was to send a troop of twenty-five men, composed of two detachments from both Presidios of Los Adaes and San Antonio under the command of a competent officer to explore the coast from the Presidio of Nuestra Señora del Espíritu Santo de la Bahía to the Sabinas River, in the vicinity of Los Adaes. The detachment from this last post should go to San Antonio, and setting out from there with the men furnished for the purpose by that presidio, proceed to the coast. From La Bahía, it should follow the seashore as closely as possible to the Sabinas River and hence to Los Adaes. Throughout the trip, all bays and sounds should be carefully examined to determine if any foreigners had established a settlement along the shore line. This portion had been explored by order of Rivera during his *visita*.

The Presidios of San Antonio and San Juan Bautista were advised to give each other mutual aid whenever it became necessary, by furnishing twelve men, including an officer, when forced to fight the various Indian enemies that infested this region.

In any campaign undertaken against hostile Indians, if men, women or children were taken prisoners, these could not be disposed of as slaves by the captain or any of the officers. On the contrary, whenever possible, the women and children should be released to their husbands or parents in order to incline them to peace and friendship through kindness and thus remove all cause for cruel reprisals on their part. A general policy of reconciliation was to be consistently observed. If after suffering a defeat, the hostile Indians expressed a desire to make peace, they were to be received with clemency and all prisoners taken should be returned to them as evidence of the good faith of the Spaniards, particularly in the case of women and children. Any Indian of an enemy tribe, if he peacefully presented himself at any presidio as a friend, ought to be welcomed in like manner.

But the most interesting part of the ordinance is a series of price lists determining the cost to soldiers for the most commonly used supplies. This, undoubtedly, was the first attempt at price fixing in Texas. The minute details which the officials employed to prepare the items, give the reader a splendid idea of the goods consumed at the frontier establishments by the soldiers, the Indians, and the few scattered settlers. In the case of Texas two different lists were prepared, including the same goods and items, but priced a little differently. One was designed for Los Adaes and the other for both San Antonio and La Bahía. Corn was to sell at Los Adaes for five *pesos* a bushel, flour for twenty-five *pesos* a hundredweight, cattle at sixteen *pesos* a head, chocolate already sweetened for a *peso* and a half, various grades of cloth ranged from one-half *peso* to four, brown domestic made in Puebla for six *reales,* ready-made skirts, of the best quality, either blue or red, for three *pesos,* a cheaper grade for twenty-two *reales,* fine cloth for shawls, in three *vara* lengths, twenty-two *reales,* powder puffs, of good grade for four *reales,* a cheaper grade at three *reales.* The first-class shawls of cotton and silk mixture were to sell for seventeen *pesos.* These were full size. Others of cheaper quality and not so large sold for twelve *pesos.* Hose for men and women cost five *reales.* Different grades of blankets ranged from slightly over three *pesos* to twelve *pesos* each, black hats, fully lined and of the best quality for four *pesos,* cheaper grade and only half lined for two *pesos,* a bundle of good, clean tobacco without grass for eleven *reales,* the ordinary grade for nine *reales.* All things considered, soap was cheap, ten cakes selling for one *peso,* and so were kid shoes, which could be purchased for twelve *reales,* the cheaper shoes for eight. Gourd cups were one *real* a piece. Horses were sixteen *pesos* each, a complete saddle with all the trimmings cost twenty-eight *pesos,* the saddles without leather-trimmed stirrups cost fifteen *pesos.* Mexican saddles fully equipped were twenty-five *pesos,* guns or rifles were thirty *pesos,* and the leather cases, lined with silk, ten *pesos.* A more ordinary gun case also of leather sold for six *pesos.* Gunstocks were three and a half *pesos,* short swords, fifteen *pesos,* scabbards made of leather and the corresponding belt and attachments six *reales,* hunting knives of good grade with leather cover three and a half *pesos,* a pair of iron stirrups eleven *pesos,* a pair of large spurs, good grade, six *pesos,* strong and best quality bridles four and a half *pesos,* ordinary quality three *pesos.* The *comales* on which the handmade corncakes were cooked and the copper kettles sold according to weight at the rate of ten *reales* a pound. A yard of satin ribbon sold for three *reales,* serge of all colors for one *peso,* silk in loose skeins for twelve *reales* an ounce in any color, men's heavy weave silk hose of all colors for six *pesos,* the same grade for women three and a half *pesos,* lace hose for women from Milan for six *pesos,* men's hose made of woolen yarn for fourteen *reales,* the same for women for ten *reales,* an ounce of cotton thread for five *reales,* paper pads for two and a half *reales.* Although this is not a complete list, sufficient items have been enumerated to give the reader a concrete idea of the extent and nature of the maximum price lists which were given to each presidio after a careful study of the actual cost of the goods and supplies and their transportation to the various posts.[28]

Abolition of Presidio de los Tejas. The viceroy lost no time in putting in force the recommendations of Rivera with regard to Texas. On April 26, 1729, he issued a decree ordering the official abolition of the Presidio of Nuestra Señora de los Dolores de los Tejas, originally established in 1716 by Ramón. The governor was instructed to notify the captain and the twenty-four soldiers of their discharge, which was to be effective immediately. The men were to be paid their salaries, however, to June 30, but they were not to be incorporated in any other garrison after that date or permitted to reënlist.[29] Although expected, the official notice, nevertheless, caused widespread consternation to the afflicted missionaries, who foresaw the ruin of their labors among these friendly Indians at a time when after so many hardships they were about to see the fruits of their efforts.

Protest of the Querétaran missionaries. On July 20, 1729, the *Padres* of the three missions in the vicinity of the presidio met at Mission Concepción and, after discussing the situation, decided to write a memorial to the viceroy in an attempt to persuade him in regard to the necessity of continuing the garrison. The soldiers should never have been withdrawn, they declared, considering that this presidio was sixty leagues from Los Adaes and one hundred and fifty from San Antonio de Valero. Its extinction left the missions without protection against the Indians, who, on seeing the soldiers removed and the *Padres* alone in their midst, would become insolent and would commit many petty thefts. It should be kept in mind, they pointed out, that all of the natives in this region possessed guns and rifles obtained from the French and had a ready supply of powder from the same source. The guard of two soldiers assigned to each one of the missions from the Presidio de los Adaes was totally inadequate, when the distance to the post from which reënforcements would have to be sent in case of hostilities, was considered. His Excellency could consult Don Fernando Pérez de Almazán, former governor of the province, in Mexico City, to find out whether it was practical for the garrisons at San Antonio or La Bahía to render assistance in case of danger to the missions of Los Tejas, as suggested by Rivera.

---

[28]*Ibid.*

[29]Decreto del Virey Casafuerte, México, April 26, 1729. In *San Francisco el Grande Archives,* Vol. 3, p. 4.

The reduction of the garrison of Los Adaes was as ill-advised as the abolition of the Presidio of Dolores. It left the former post at the mercy of the designs of the French, who, it was well known, had always looked with greed upon the Province of Texas. Numerous Indians were their friends and most of them had guns and used them with great skill. With the reduced force now left in the presidio and the extinction of Nuestra Señora de los Dolores de los Tejas, heretofore a rallying point for defence, the door had been left wide open for attack by the enemy.

Missionaries request permission to move from East Texas. In conclusion, they humbly begged the viceroy to reconsider the action taken and restore the presidio, issuing instructions to its commander to exert himself in the reduction of the Indians to mission life. If his Excellency did not think it advisable to grant the request, they asked that he permit them to move the missions to a more suitable location where their efforts would not be wasted. But if he could not accede to either one of the two requests, they implored him to issue the necessary orders to relieve the missionaries of their responsibility and to allow them to return to their College of the Holy Cross of Querétaro. The petition was signed by Fathers Fray Gabriel de Vergara, President, Fray Joseph Andres Rodríguez de Jesús María, Fray Juan Bautista García de Súarez, Fray Alonso Giraldo de Terreros, Fray Manuel de Ortuñón, and Fray Joseph de San Antonio y Estrada and sent to Mexico City by a special messenger.[30]

The missionaries were not alone in their protest. Governor Melchor de Mediavilla y Azcona, and Captain Becerra, formerly stationed at the presidio, bitterly complained of the action taken. The Guardian of the College of Querétaro stressed, vehemently, the dire effects to be expected from the extinction of the presidio. He predicted the ruin of the three Querétaran missions founded in its vicinity by the zealous missionaries and maintained for fourteen years at the cost of so many sufferings and so much money to the royal treasury and to the benefactors of the College of the Holy Cross, who had contributed so liberally for the propagation of the faith in far-away Texas.[31] All the opposing declarations

[30]Representación de los Religiosos exponiendo razones contra la extinción del Presidio de los Tejas. July 20, 1729. *San Francisco el Grande Archive*, Vol. 3, pp. 4-6.

[31]Fr. Miguel Sevillano de Paredes to the Viceroy, September 7, 1729; Mediavilla y Azcona to the Viceroy, July 30, 1729, in *Ibid.*; also Fr. Pedro Pérez de Mezquia to the Viceroy, November 12, 1729, *Archivo del Colegio de la Santa Cruz, 1716-1749* (Dunn Transcripts).

and memorials were referred to Brigadier Pedro de Rivera, who was now the private counselor of the viceroy in all matters pertaining to the frontier outposts.

Proposed location on the Colorado. On October 29, 1729, he wrote a long report answering the various objections raised by the petitioners against the extinction of the presidio and concluded by recommending that if the missionaries of Concepción, San Francisco, and San José felt they could not carry on their work any longer in East Texas unless the old garrison was restored, they should be permitted to move to a more suitable and congenial locality. He suggested that a convenient place might be found along the banks of the Colorado River, which he called the San Marcos;[32] that the river should be explored with this purpose in view; and that if a favorable location was discovered, the missionaries should be instructed to move to the new site. The Governor of Texas, Mediavilla y Azcona, should be ordered to assist the *Padres* in the removal, aiding them both in the exploration and the transportation of all the property of the missions and their persons. All this was to be done without cost to the royal treasury.[33]

The recommendations were approved by the viceroy and dispatches with the necessary instructions were sent to the Governor of Texas and to the missionaries. It seems that at this time it was also planned to move the Presidio of La Bahía to the Colorado River, to afford adequate protection to the missions which were going to be established there. In order to preserve the identity of the original presidio, this was to maintain its old name in its new location. Great hopes were entertained for success both by the officials and the undismayed Franciscans. The Indian nations along the Colorado were thought to be more peaceful and docile and the country better suited for the establishment of settlements and the raising of crops. On October 18, Father Miguel Sevillano de Paredes agreed to the proposed plan and assured the viceroy

---

[32]Hackett, *Pichardo's Treatise on the Limits of Louisiana and Texas*, I, 490-491. Quoting Buckley, the editor says "As Aguayo had not recognized the present San Marcos as such, he carried the name over to the next large river, and applied it to the Colorado. To Rivera this last named river was likewise the San Marcos (*Diario*, entry for August 23, 1727)."

[33]Rivera to the Viceroy, May 26, 1731, *A. G. N., Provincias Internas*, Vol. 236; Espinosa, *Chrónica*, I, 458-459.

that the removal could be carried out without additional cost to the king.[34]

With the aid of the governor, the country along the Colorado was explored and a site for the three missions selected. The details of the exploration and findings, as well as the moving, are indeed meager, but all evidence seems to indicate that by July 27, 1730, they were temporarily established on this river. At this time the governor reported to the viceroy he had complied with his orders and given all assistance in his power to the missionaries. But apparently either the location chosen was not entirely to the liking of the *Padres,* or perhaps the Indians were not as inclined to be congregated in the new missions as had been expected. The fact is that at the same time the governor made his report, Father Fray Miguel Sevillano sent a new petition to the viceroy for permission to move to the San Antonio River. He pointed out the disadvantages of the site recently chosen and now occupied and how much more advisable it would be to select the place best suited for missionary activity.

Removal of Querétaran missions to San Antonio. This, he again assured His Excellency, would not involve any additional expense and would result in the benefit of the king, by making these Christian labors for souls more fruitful.[35] The matter was once more referred to Rivera, who, on September 22, 1730, again recommended that the request be granted and that instructions be issued to the Governor of Texas to lend every assistance for the second removal, provided, however, that there be no cost to the royal treasury.[36]

Governor Mediavilla y Azcona gladly carried out the orders. "He executed them with such kindness," declares Espinosa, "that he personally inspected the banks of various rivers, explored the land, and did not omit any efforts to attain the purpose so ardently sought by the missionaries. After examining all the sites, together with Father President Fray Gabriel de Vergara, convenient locations, such as were desired, were discovered on the banks of the San Antonio River." By May 4, 1731, the three missions had been established on the spots chosen. Each had been placed along the river at easy distances from one another, all

[34]Memorial del Pe. Fray Miguel Sevillano de Paredes to the King, November 12, 1729, *Archivo del Colegio de la Santa Cruz de Querétaro, 1716-1749;* Rivera to the Viceroy, May 26, 1731, *A. G. N., Provincias Internas,* Vol. 236.

[35]*Ibid.;* Fr. Pérez de Mezquia to the Viceroy, August 8, 1731, in *Ibid.*

[36]*Ibid.;* Fr. Pérez de Mezquia to the Viceroy, August 8, 1731, in *Ibid.*

MISSION OF SAN JUAN CAPISTRANO LOCATED AT SAN ANTONIO IN 1731

in accord with the instructions given by the viceroy, in order to avoid unnecessary crowding and to be able to render each other mutual assistance in case of attack by enemy Indians. Temporary structures of rough timber, plastered with clay and roofed with grass, had been erected as chapels, quarters for the *Padres* had been built, and shelters made to store the provisions and supplies for the Indians. These had been induced to come to the new missions with much difficulty. Two trips to their distant lands had been made, one to persuade them of the advantages of mission life and the other to conduct them from their *rancherías* to the new establishments. Three nations were now congregated: the Pacaos, the Pajalat, and the Alobja or Pitalaques. The captain of the Presidio of San Antonio de Bejar, agreeable to the orders he had received from the viceroy, had officially placed them in possession of the sites selected, giving them sufficient lands and water for the raising of crops and the grazing of cattle. The governors and *alcaldes* for the Indian pueblos of the three missions had been elected and placed in office with great solemnity to impress the prospective neophytes. Espinosa estimated the number gathered in the new missions at one thousand, and Father Mezquia assured the viceroy that they were so numerous that some had to be asked to remain in their habitations until the missions had an adequate supply of provisions to feed them.[37]

It took a month and a day to move the missions to the new sites and to bring the Indians. Father President Gabriel de Vergara, Father Pedro Múñoz, and Father Juan de los Angeles, accompanied by seven soldiers and a corporal from the Presidio of San Antonio, and two Indian interpreters, went to bring the neophytes. In addition, a settler hired by the missionaries and paid a regular salary by them, assisted the party in conducting the Indians back to their new home. The tribes of East Texas had refused to go all the way to San Antonio. They had, moreover, strongly protested against the departure of the *Padres*. Unable to understand the reason for the abandonment of the old missions, they asked the governor what they had done to displease the missionaries or the Spaniards. During the fourteen years of their establishment, the Ais, the Nazonis, and the Neches had become deeply attached to the kind and gentle sons of St. Francis, who had lived among them all these years and had shared their hardships, sufferings, and privations. But if

---

[37]Father Pedro Pérez de Mezquia to the Viceroy, May 4, 1731; also Mezquia to the Viceroy, August 8, 1731, in *A. G. N., Provincias Internas,* Vol. 236; Espinosa, *op. cit.,* 459.

the Indians of this region had become fond of the *Padres,* the Franciscans also had developed a strong love for them. "God knows," declares Espinosa, writing sixteen years later, "that were my strength not yet all spent, I would consider it a particular joy to go and serve as a companion to the missionary in charge of that mission," referring to Nuestra Señora de Guadalupe de los Nacogdoches, which undertook to care for the former neophytes of the Querétarans.[38]

The new nations now congregated proved both willing and capable. When the bell rang out its call on the first day, they all came and listened attentively to the *doctrina.* After prayers, the missionaries started out to the fields, accompanied by a few Indians from their former missions, and the new converts followed and tried to plow and plant like the others, without having to be asked to work. They took to mission life with apparent joy, helping the *Padres* diligently in the building of the new quarters, in caring for the cattle and horses, and on the farm.[39]

The removals had been no small feat. Over a distance of about one hundred and fifty leagues, all the property of the missions had been transferred without mishap. Large rivers had been crossed with all the furnishings of the chapels, the herds of cattle, horses, mules, and burros. Two trips had been made to the Indian country to persuade the tribes to come, and a large group had been conducted satisfactorily to the new missions. No wonder Father Mezquia declared that the enterprise had been accomplished at the cost of "many hardships and the peril of life itself on more than one occasion." After the destination was reached new buildings had been erected, the fields had been plowed and made ready for planting, ditches had to be built for irrigation, and provisions had to be brought from the Río Grande to feed the large number of Indians that had been congregated. From San Juan Bautista eight hundred *fanegas* of corn were supplied which cost fourteen *reales* each, besides four and a half *pesos* for transportation. A herd of two hundred and fifty head of cattle was also purchased at the Río Grande for six *pesos* and two *reales* a head, without including the cost of transportation to San Antonio. In view of the many difficulties, and more particularly, of the material expense involved, Father Mezquia asked the viceroy to grant the recently established missions such financial aid as he might deem proper. The request was, of course, referred to Rivera,

---

[38]Espinosa, *Chrónica,* I, 460; Father Pérez de Mezquia to the Viceroy, May 4, 1731, *A. G. N., Provincias Internas,* Vol. 236.

[39]Mezquia to the Viceroy, May 4, 1731, in *Ibid.*

who, on May 26, 1731, advised the viceroy that Father Sevillano had repeatedly assured His Excellency that the removal would cause no expense to the royal treasury. He thought, therefore, that there was no moral obligation to grant financial aid as requested. He recommended, however, that the viceroy might use his own judgment in the matter. Casafuerte, who seems to have been more and more influenced by Rivera as time went on, appears to have done nothing to relieve the need of the missionaries after the heavy expenses they incurred in removing the missions to the San Antonio.[40]

The immediate effect of the extinction of the Presidio of Nuestra Señora de los Dolores de los Tejas had resulted in the abandonment of the East Texas field by the missionaries of the College of Querétaro; the undoing of all that had been accomplished in fourteen years of patient toil and constant endeavor, the weakening of the defence of the province against possible French incursions, and the loss of influence with the natives. On the other hand, it had enlarged the missionary activity in the neighborhood of San Antonio, where the Apaches offered the greatest menace to the development of Spanish settlement in Texas.

Mission guards restored. The suppression of the mission guards formerly furnished to the missions under the protection of the Presidios of San Juan Bautista and San Antonio de Béjar by the new ordinance had also caused deep concern to the missionaries. No sooner were the new regulations promulgated than protests poured into the office of the viceroy. But as these were referred to Rivera, with whom the idea had originated, the petitions for relief went unheeded. Convinced of the futility of their efforts, Father Miguel Sevillano addressed a long petition to the king. He argued that the regulations were adopted without consideration of all the essential facts. The Indians along the Río Grande and in Texas were very different in nature from those of the interior of Mexico. They were much wilder and more inclined to murder and theft. The two soldiers assigned to the missions in this region had often saved life and property and prevented serious damages. At the Mission of La Punta de Lampasos, situated fifty leagues from San Juan Bautista, a party of Tobosos, surprised two missionaries, who were bringing supplies and took everything away. In the night, thanks to

---

[40]Mezquia to the Viceroy, May 4, 1731; Rivera to the Viceroy, May 26, 1731; Mezquia to the Viceroy, August 8, 1721, in *A. G. N., Provincias Internas,* Vol. 236.

the mission guards, they had succeeded in saving the lives of the missionaries but not the property.

The hostilities of the Apaches in San Antonio, he declared, were well known. In 1726, in plain view of the garrison, they captured an Indian shepherd from one of the missions, who was rescued by the soldiers. When he was brought back it was discovered he had been seriously wounded with a lance. In 1727, just a short distance from the mission, the Apaches cut a neophyte to pieces. In 1728, they had attacked Mission San Juan Bautista on the Río Grande and done much damage before aid was sent from the presidio. Had it not been for the two guards, who kept them at bay with their firearms, the Apaches would have destroyed the mission. The two soldiers were necessary, he said, because they not only afforded protection to the Indians congregated, but enabled the missions to hold out against surprise attacks until aid arrived. Without them, by the time help was sent from the neighboring presidios, many lives had been lost and much damage done. Contrary to the insinuation that the insistence for guards was due to fear, he emphatically declared the missionaries did not fear for their lives, knowing as they did, that they might be called to make this sacrifice at any time in the fulfillment of their daily labors. The reasons that moved them to request the presence of two soldiers in each mission was the salvation of souls and the propagation of the faith. The success in the attainment of these objects was seriously jeopardized, if the mission guards were removed.[41]

Before the king had time to act, it seems the viceroy changed his mind on the subject. Early in 1730, Rivera wrote a long report, answering the arguments advanced by the missionaries against the withdrawal of the two soldiers furnished to the missions in the vicinity of San Juan Bautista and San Antonio de Valero. Although insisting that they were unnecessary as protectors, citing numerous instances in New Mexico and other provinces visited, where the missions were making satisfactory progress without mission guards, he recommended in the end, that if the viceroy wished, he could order the captain of the Presidio of San Antonio de Bejar to furnish each mission in its vicinity one soldier. He was not to reside at the mission, however, but he was to go from the presidio to the mission each morning, returning to his garrison in the afternoon. With characteristic irony he declared that with this aid for

---

[41]Memorial of Fray Miguel Sevillano to the King, November 12, 1729. *Archivo del Colegio de la Santa Cruz, 1716-1749.*

the temporal welfare of the mission all cause for complaint would be removed.[42]

Regulations concerning escort for travelers and train supplies. The new regulations adopted with regard to the escort for travelers and supply trains, providing for four periodic journeys at specified times of the year, had likewise proved a great handicap to the missionaries. With the changed conditions brought about by the removal of the three Querétaran missions to the San Antonio River, the *Padres* had been obliged to make frequent trips to the Río Grande. On January 9, 1731, two missionaries, with a special but insufficient escort of five men, furnished by the Presidio of San Antonio, were attacked by a party of Apaches on the Medina River, while on the way to San Juan Bautista. At the time of the assault, one of the soldiers was away, and, of the remaining four, one fled as soon as he saw the Indians. In the skirmish that followed, a woman was killed and a young child was taken captive, but the *Padres* managed to escape with their lives, losing, however, all their baggage and belongings. For some unexplainable reason, the captain at San Antonio, who was notified of the outrage, had made no efforts to pursue or chastise the Indians. Since that time, the Apaches had, on one occasion, caused the neophytes recently congregated in one of the new missions to run away while the missionary had gone to San Antonio de Valero. A few days before April 17, a party of eighty hostile Indians surprised a group of soldiers conducting a drove of horses to the Río Grande, at the same place where the missionaries had been previously attacked. The soldiers escaped but they lost all the horses.[43]

As no reprisals from the garrison at San Antonio followed, the Apaches seemed to have become bolder. Shortly afterwards, they entered the Mission of San Antonio de Valero, the nearest to the presidio, and carried away a drove of fifty burros, which belonged to the neophytes and were used on the farm to haul provisions to the Indian pueblo. On June 25, Father Fray Benito de Santa Anna and Brother Esteban Zaes set out from San Antonio de Valero for the Río Grande, but before they traveled very far, they were attacked by a band of Apaches, who, in spite of the five soldiers that were escorting the missionaries, took away

---

[42]Decreto del Virey, February 23, 1730. *Archivo del Colegio de la Santa Cruz,* 1716-1749.

[43]Father Pérez de Mezquia to the Viceroy, May 4, 1731. *A. G. N., Provincias Internas,* Vol. 236.

all the horses they were driving and their personal baggage. Two of the men were wounded, and had it not been for the *cuera* (rawhide shield) carried by the Brother, he also might have been hurt, an arrow having spent itself on the *cuera*. The baggage, however, Father Mezquia says, was not particularly valuable.[44]

He declared that it was because of the dangers to which the missionaries were exposed on such occasions when it became necessary to journey to and from the Río Grande to bring supplies for the newly established missions, that an adequate guard should be provided. He assured the viceroy that these trips were not undertaken except when it was absolutely imperative. He suggested that a competent escort of eight men and a corporal should be furnished them when they had to go after provisions and supplies, both to safeguard their persons and the goods convoyed for the benefit of the neophytes. Father Mezquia pointed out that he had written concerning this urgent need on several occasions without receiving an answer. "In order that my words may not be doubted," he said, "I assure Your Excellency *in verbo sacerdotis* all these things are true . . . but I say them with considerable hesitation, having grounds to suspect that full credit is not given to what missionaries, who serve only God and the king, have declared, although it is evident and palpable that they desire nothing but the conversion of souls. Malice, moved by interest and selfish gain, has tried to discredit so clear and manifest a truth." [45]

Before the urgent request just cited reached the viceroy, the matter had already been referred to Rivera for his consideration and opinion. In a long report, written on May 26, 1731, he explained that the various hostilities engaged in by the Apaches near the Medina River and their depredations in the vicinity of the new missions on the San Antonio described by the *Padres,* were true, but he pointed out, with his accustomed meticulous mania for details, the circumstances were not given with accuracy. In order to prove his statement, he recounted the first attack suffered by the missionaries while on the way to the Río Grande, saying that the escort furnished at that time had not been larger because the *Padres* themselves had agreed that it was sufficient for their safeguard. This could be proved by the statement made by Miguel Núñez Morillo, one of the soldiers of the escort. He failed to say, however, that he had been the one who ran away. Taking up the complaint that the captain

---

[44]Father Mezquia to the Viceroy, August 8, 1731, in *Ibid.*
[45]*Ibid.*

of the presidio had done nothing to pursue or punish the Indians, he stated that Juan Antonio Pérez de Almazán (perhaps a brother of the former governor), who was captain, had since that time asked His Excellency for permission to wage a campaign against the Apaches in order to inflict upon them the punishment they deserved and to check their boldness. According to the new regulations, he could not start a campaign against them without the consent of the viceroy. Rivera now said that it was highly advisable for the safety of the missions, that, in view of the facts presented with regard to the frequent hostilities of these Indians, His Excellency should authorize the Captain of San Antonio de Béjar to lead an expedition to chastise these savages for their insolence and to fight them in self-defence, as the natural law of peoples dictated. Concerning the escort of eight men and a corporal to be furnished to the missionaries, when it was imperative for them to go to the Río Grande for provisions, he recommended that the request be granted and the captain at San Antonio de Béjar, as well as that at San Juan Bautista, be instructed in this regard. The recommendations in both instances were approved by the viceroy and the corresponding orders to carry them into effect were issued on August 8, 1731, the very day on which Father Mezquia had pleaded that a remedy should be provided.[46]

Use of soldiers to bring back runaway Indians. It has already been pointed out that the Indians congregated in the various missions were in the habit of running away at different seasons, whenever they felt a strong urge to return to their former roaming irresponsible ways. It had been customary for the missionaries to go to the distant *rancherías* to persuade them to come back. As these journeys often took them over long distances into the territory frequented by hostile Indians, two or more soldiers had generally accompanied them in their peaceful quest for the neophytes. But on August 6, 1729, at the suggestion of Rivera, the viceroy had ordered the captains of the Presidios of San Antonio de Béjar and San Juan Bautista not to furnish soldiers for this purpose any longer. In the future the missionaries were either to allow those who ran away to remain in the woods and *rancherías,* or go after them alone. It was not advisable, the former Inspector General thought, for soldiers to recover the Indians who ran away, because their presence might arouse the hostility of those among whom the apostates had taken refuge. When

---

[46]Rivera to the Viceroy, May 26, 1731; Approval of the Viceroy, July 30, 1731; Orders by the Viceroy, August 8, 1731. *A. G. N., Provincias Internas,* Vol. 236.

Padres had to instruct them in the use of the tools used by masons and carpenters, how to build their living quarters, and how to help erect the new chapels and the houses for the missionaries.

Experience, he said, had demonstrated that unless the missionary was constantly with the neophytes everything was neglected, and they soon became so discouraged that they abandoned the mission, returning to the woods. Every captain of a presidio or soldier on the frontier could testify to the truth of this fact. If the provisions stored in the common barn and kept by the *Padre* were not rationed to them daily, they would consume the whole stock in two days. They had no conception of regular habits. Used to a hand-to-mouth existence, they had difficulty in becoming used to setting aside a sufficient amount of food from one day to another. Game had always been plentiful during certain seasons of the year, and at such times they had gorged themselves. When winter came, they had subsisted on wild roots and insects.

When the provisions in the missions were plentiful, the neophytes were always happy, but when there was a scarcity of food it was extremely difficult to keep them from running away. Even those who were Christians and had lived in the missions for several years became restless and sullen under these circumstances. They all disliked work. It took much urging and tact to make them become accustomed to labor day after day in the fields or in the mission pueblo. Regularity and routine was distasteful to their wayward natures and it took all the patience of the *Padres,* Father Sevillano assured the king, to instruct them in the numerous duties of mission life and in the *doctrina.* It was in the instruction of manual labors that the soldiers assigned to the missions in the past had been so helpful to the missionaries. It was impossible for the religious in charge to be out in the fields and in the mission, and in the Indian pueblo supervising the work at all times. The soldiers generally had looked after the work outdoors, such as the planting and tending of the cattle; while the missionary looked after the construction of new quarters, or the improvement of the old, or the completion of the mission chapel, or the construction of rough furniture for the needs of the *Padres* and neophytes, or the weaving of rough cloth. All this was done by the neophytes under the direction of the two soldiers and the missionary. But in addition to these duties, the religious in charge of a mission had to give instruction in the *doctrina,* celebrate Holy Mass every day, baptize the Indians when they were ready to receive this sacrament, marry the neophytes, administer the sacraments, hear confessions, bury the dead, and look after the spiritual welfare not only of the Indians, but of those in the nearby presidio.

At this time, Father Sevillano stated that the missions were far from a flourishing condition. The chief article of food for the Indians and the missionaries was corn, and this had to be carefully rationed. Meat was served only every fifteen days, in order to conserve the mission herd. Every two weeks a cow was killed and everybody was given his share, but as the number of neophytes was large, this supply was not very large. Out of the meager allowance made by His Majesty for the subsistence of the missionaries were bought all the necessary tools, the things needed for the church and divine service, and at times, even clothing and food for the Indians. It was customary for the college to send each religious a supply of food, clothing, and other articles for his own personal use, purchased with the money given annually by the royal treasury for that purpose. It was not uncommon for most of these goods to go to the neophytes. "With the exception of a little chocolate, some soap, salt, enough cloth for one habit, and sandals . . . all the rest is used for the Indians," said Father Sevillano. From the slender means at their disposal they had to buy rosaries, hats, cheap cloth and tobacco to give to the natives as presents. Nothing was a more powerful incentive to the good will of the Indians than tobacco. This was the chief means of keeping them pacified and of attracting new converts. He asserted that it was his belief that without it, most of the Indians would leave their missions.

When the crops were abundant and there was a surplus of corn the Indians of the missions on the San Antonio traded these to the soldiers and settlers, through the missionary, for cloth with which to dress themselves. But as there had been several bad years, there was a scarcity of wearing apparel at this time. With the arrival of new Indians who applied frequently, the supply of clothing had been exhausted. It was not rare to see many of the neophytes poorly clothed now, and in some instances naked. On two occasions, Father Sevillano had been obliged to take off his cloak and divide it so as to permit some Indian women to cover themselves, and more than once his extra tunic and that of his companions had been used to make clothing for their almost naked wards. The tribes congregated were not like those of Mexico. They were of a different character and much less inclined to work.

But no hardships, no privations, no sufferings, no sacrifices seemed to dismay the ever-enthusiastic sons of Saint Francis, whose hearts bled with almost divine sorrow when they beheld the unfortunate and helpless

Indians of Texas left without the comforts of religion. In their appeal to the king, they confidently declare that if His Majesty will but restore the mission guards, order that proper escorts be furnished them to protect the trains of provisions and supplies, and command that soldiers be permitted to accompany them when obliged to go to the woods to bring back the neophytes who ran away, the missions would grow and develop until, in a future not too far removed, the Indians would become civilized and be able to govern themselves and look after their own interests, saving all further expense to the king.[50]

Request for new missionaries. In May, 1729, Father Fray Matías Sáenz de San Antonio, son and ex-Guardian of the College of Nuestra Señora de Guadalupe of Zacatecas, appeared before the Council of the Indies in the name of the College of the Holy Cross of Querétaro to petition the king to grant permission for twelve new missionaries to be sent to Mexico to help maintain the missions established in Texas. Father Sáenz de San Antonio had waited almost six years in Spain for the hearing, where he had been since 1724, having been sent originally to make a private report on the conditions of the missions in the province. Prior to his going to Spain, he had been in Texas for four years, in charge of Mission Guadalupe. In the petition he asked that twelve missionaries be sent at the expense of the king to replace many of those who had died, offering to conduct them to the College of Querétaro. In support of his petition he presented statements made with regard to the need for new missionaries by the Right Reverend Bishop of Puebla de los Angeles, Viceroy Casafuerte, the Bishop of Guadalajara, the *Cabildo* of Mexico, and the Guardian of the College of Querétaro.[51]

The Council of the Indies referred the petition to the *Fiscal* of His Majesty on May 28, 1729. Two weeks later, on June 1, he made his report. He stated that he had previously been given the various recommendations from the officials of New Spain, both civil and ecclesiastical, all of whom agreed on the urgent need of missionaries which was being experienced by the College of the Holy Cross of Querétaro as a result of the death of so many of those who had gone to America in 1715. In that year the king had authorized a group of seventeen to proceed to the College for the purpose of founding new missions among the unsubdued tribes of the

---

[50]Memorial of Father Miguel Sevillano de Paredes to the King, November 12, 1729. *Archivo de la Santa Cruz, 1716-1749.*

[51]Petition of Father Fray Mathías Sáenz de San Antonio, (May) 1729. *Audiencia de México,* 62-2-29 (Dunn Transcripts, 1723-29).

frontier of New Spain. Many of these had died during the thirteen years that had elapsed, either while actively engaged in the new establishments, or while exercising their holy zeal for the conversion and salvation of souls. He recommended, therefore, that the king should accede to a petition which was so in accord with the Catholic zeal and pious desires of His Majesty.[52]

At this time, according to the petition, there were only fourteen missionaries in the College capable of carrying on the work of the Indian missions and of preaching among the Spaniards. This small number was obliged to preach in the various Spanish towns, cities, and villages in the rest of New Spain as their ministry required, and to instruct the young seminarians who were preparing themselves for the priesthood. Shortly after the arrival of the seventeen *Padres* in 1715, the College had undertaken the establishment of four missions in Texas, which had been maintained at great cost and many hardships throughout these years. In that time Fathers Fray Diego de Salazar, Fray Manuel Castellanos, Fray Juan Suárez, Fray Francisco Ruiz, Fray Francisco Hidalgo, and Fray Lorenzo García, had died while in the missions of Texas or those in the vicinity of the Presidio of San Juan Bautista on the Río Grande. Brother Joseph Pita suffered death at the hands of the Apaches, while on the way to East Texas, during the Aguayo expedition, and Father Joseph González perished on the road from Texas to the Río Grande. After laboring incessantly either attempting to convert the barbarous Indians or preaching the Gospel to the Spaniards, the following missionaries had passed away in the College of Querétaro: Fathers Fray Francisco Esteves, Fray Joseph Diez, Fray Antonio de Olivares, Fray Angel García Duque, Fray Francisco Xavier Molina, Fray Juan Orma, Fray Joseph Granizo, Fray Bartholome de Torres, and Fray Francisco Cumbreras. In addition to these, Fathers Fray Andres Martínez and Fray Gaspar de Vargas had expired while preaching missions among the Spaniards.

In 1728, Father Sevillano de Paredes declared that the following sons of the College of Querétaro were stationed in the missions of Texas: Fathers Fray Gabriel de Vergara, President, Fray Joseph Rodríguez, Fray Juan Bautista García, Fray Alonso Giraldo de Terreros, Fray Manuel de Ortuñón, and Fray Joseph de San Antonio y Estrada. At this time Father Fray Joseph Gonzáles (evidently a younger missionary than the one recently deceased, who had the same name) was President

---

[52]Opinión del Fiscal, June 15, 1729. *A. G. I., Audiencia de México,* 62-2-29 (Dunn Transcripts).

of the Missions at San Juan Bautista. With him there were five others: Fathers Fray Francisco Vergara, Fray Joseph Hurtado, Fray Benito Sánchez de Santa Anna, Fray Salvador de Anaya, Fray Luis de la Cruz, and Fray Antonio de San Juan. In addition to those here mentioned, two lay brothers were assigned to take the supplies sent to the missions with the aid received from the royal treasury for that purpose. These were Fray Francisco Bustamente and Fray Juan de los Angeles. Out of the fifteen religious enumerated, only twelve received an allowance from the king for their maintenance as missionaries.[53]

Fourteen other *Padres* lived at the College as already stated, but some of these were too old now for active service, and others were too young. Many of the latter were studying to become missionaries. The Guardian went on to explain that, according to the rules of the College of the Holy Cross of Querétaro of *Propaganda Fide,* no religious could be forced to take charge of Indian missions. They could, furthermore, leave the College under the conditions and stipulations of the Apostolic Brief of Pope Innocent XI, which begins with the words *Ecclesiae Catholicae,* given in Rome, on October 16, 1686. But such religious as were sent expressly for missionary work by the king, those requested now by him, had to serve in the frontier establishments for ten years before they could ask to be transferred from the College, unless they were excused by His Majesty. Being independent of the Provinces, the Colleges of Querétaro and Zacatecas could not get *Padres* in New Spain to replace those that died and had to depend entirely upon those sent by the king and those who joined the Colleges and made their vows.[54]

"In virtue of these [circumstances]," the Guardian pleaded, "and because the need of evangelical workers is evident, certain, and clear, I beg Your Majesty with all humility, submission, and reverence, in the name of this holy community, to grant a mission of twelve religious, who are able to preach and hear confessions and are inclined to so sacred and praiseworthy an undertaking for the salvation of souls." To reënforce his petition, he explained that missionaries had labored with exemplary zeal for thirteen years in Texas, where many of them had died, but that in spite of every effort the Indians had not as yet been congregated or induced to live in pueblos near the missions. This was not the fault

---

[53]Representation of Father Fray Miguel Sevillano de Paredes, Guardian of the College of Querétaro, August 28, 1728. *A. G. I., Audiencia de México,* 62-2-29 (Dunn Transcripts).

[54]*Ibid.*

of the sons of Saint Francis. The civil officials should be instructed to coöperate with the *Padres* in reducing the natives to mission life, in order that their work might not be wasted.[55]

The just request was granted by the king in June, 1729, and the corresponding instructions issued to the treasury to defray the expenses of the twelve missionaries which were to be taken by Father Fray Matías Sáenz de San Antonio to the College of the Holy Cross of Querétaro, for the purpose of helping to take care of the missions maintained by that College on the Río Grande and in Texas. The officials of the treasury were requested to make an estimate of the cost of equipping them, paying their expenses to the port of embarkation, during their stay there, and on the trip to Mexico. They reported that for the twelve *Padres*, Father Matías Sáenz de San Antonio, and a lay brother who made up the party, it would take two hundred sixty-four thousand five hundred twenty-six *maravedis* to furnish them supplies, clothing, and other necessities for the journey. This may sound like a fabulous sum, but a *maravedi* is equivalent to one-sixth of a cent, so that the estimated cost was only slightly over four hundred dollars. In addition to this sum, the officials declared that it was customary to allow ten *pesos* to each religious who went to America by order of the king. To this must be added the expenses incurred by each missionary in going from his respective monastery to either Sevilla or Cádiz, for which they were generally given seven *reales* a day, provided they traveled eight leagues. After they arrived at the port of embarkation, they received two *reales* for each day they waited for the ship that was taking them to New Spain. The officials of the royal treasury explained that they were not able to estimate the cost of transportation, as that would depend on the special arrangement that was made with the shipmaster in whose ship they sailed.[56]

The details of the journey are not known, nor has a list been found of the names of the brave Franciscans who came so willingly to carry on the work in far-away Texas and on the Río Grande. But in a letter of Father Mezquia, the new Guardian of the College of the Holy Cross of Querétaro to the viceroy, written in August, 1731, he said that the new missionaries had arrived in the fleet that had come from Spain in November of the previous year. The cost of transportation for the Franciscan

---

[55]*Ibid.*

[56]Informe de la Contaduría de Junio de 1729. *A. G. I., Audiencia de México,* 62-2-29 (Dunn Transcripts).

friars from Sevilla to Querétaro was four thousand and eighty *pesos,* which was paid by the royal treasury in Mexico City.[57]

But the year 1731 seems to have been an unfortunate one for the missionaries. This amount was paid to Captain Gazpar García del Rivero, *Sindico,* or legal representative, of the College, who died shortly after. When the College executives tried to collect this sum and five thousand four hundred *pesos* more, which had likewise been paid to him as the allowance for the missionaries already in charge of missions that year, they found out that the property left by the former trustee and custodian of funds was not sufficient to cover his personal debts.[58] As related in the course of this chapter, large sums had also been spent by the missionaries in moving from East Texas to the San Antonio. In the letter to the viceroy, the Guardian explained that these and many other unexpected expenses had been borne by the College during the last three years with the aid of the alms given to it by His Majesty and its many benefactors. But in spite of all that the pious friends had done, and were doing, debts had been incurred which now had to be paid. The death of the *Sindico* and the loss by him of all recently acquired Franciscan funds, through no fault of the *Padres,* whose rule prohibited them from handling their own finance, made it imperative for the head of the College to appeal to the generosity of His Excellency.[59]

The petition was, as usual, referred by the viceroy to Rivera, who reported a few days later that His Excellency should do in the matter whatever his judgment dictated. He declared that the College was entitled to receive help and that the request for the grant of a special aid in view of the circumstances described seemed justified. As to the amount, it was a matter for the viceroy to decide.

Conditions in La Bahía and Los Adaes. It will be well to turn now to conditions in La Bahía and Los Adaes. From the report of Rivera, the progress made at La Bahía up to 1727 has been seen. The garrison had been so improved since the removal of Diego Ramón, that it forced the inspector to admit that it was the best in Texas. On December 28, 1728, Captain Bustillo y Ceballos wrote a letter to the viceroy to inform him that salines had been discovered by a scouting party about fifty leagues to the south of the presidio. The salt they yielded was so abundant

---

[57]Father Pedro de Mezquia to the Viceroy, August 8, 1731. *A. G. N., Provincias Internas,* Vol. 236.

[58]*Ibid.*

[59]*Ibid.*

CHAPEL TOWER AND RUINS OF THE PRESIDIO OF NUESTRA SEÑORA DE LORETO DE LA BAHÍA DEL
ESPÍRITU SANTO LOCATED AT GOLIAD IN 1749

that in a few days more than fifty *cargas* had been brought back. It was necessary to send an escort of forty men, with two one-pound fieldpieces, to protect the convoy against the numerous hostile tribes that infested the country in that region. He expressed the opinion that the salines should be worked regularly for the benefit of the king and asked permission to extract the salt as had been done after its discovery. When the matter was referred to Rivera for his opinion, he declared that he believed it would be best to abandon the idea of working the product as suggested by Captain Bustillo y Ceballos. The presence of such a large number of soldiers as he had used to convoy the salt acquired in the territory of the Indians, who were already inclined to be hostile, might arouse their animosity and cause serious consequences.[60] The viceroy approved the suggestion and ordered that the plan proposed be abandoned.

Some time in the fall of 1730, Don Gabriel Costales became captain of the Presidio of La Bahía. His appointment was made by Viceroy Casafuerte to serve *ad interim,* subject to the approval of the king, as provided in the new regulations for the frontier presidios. The action taken was immediately reported to His Majesty by the viceroy, who explained that Captain Costales had entered the Province of Texas with the Marquis of Aguayo in 1721-1722; had previously served the king for thirteen years as soldier, sergeant, and *alférez* of infantry in Cataluña, having been promoted to the rank of captain in the said expedition organized by Aguayo, and that he had held other posts of honor and responsibility, in all of which he had served with loyalty. As a vacancy had been created by the promotion of Captain Bustillo y Ceballos to the governorship of the Province of Texas, Costales had been commissioned captain of La Bahía.

On September 16, 1731, the king approved the appointment made by the viceroy and issued him a patent. He was to enjoy all the honors and privileges of his rank and was to be obeyed by the soldiers and all subalterns, as well as the Indians congregated in the missions established in the vicinity of the presidio. He was requested to exercise the greatest care in coöperating with the missionaries for the propagation of the faith through the instruction of the neophytes and their reduction to mission life, refraining from the use of harsh measures or the infliction of severe punishment upon them for trivial offences. He should encourage them to persevere by the exercise of kindness, and to act with prudence in all

---

[60]Opinión del Brigadier Rivera, July 19, 1731. *A. G. N., Provincias Internas,* Vol. 236.

matters for the attainment of the object desired, which was the conversion and civilization of the Indians. In accord with the newly adopted
ordinance for presidios, he received six hundred *pesos* a year, payable
from the day he took charge of his office with the temporary appointment of the viceroy, and was excused from payment of any dues or fees
as required by the provisions of the *Media Anata*. This was a law which
provided that those appointed to fill vacancies must deduct a percentage
of their salary for the time during which the office had been unoccupied.
All military officers appointed to active duty in America had been excused
from the payment of this fee by a special *cédula* issued by the king on
September 23, 1727.[61]

On January 7, 1731, Captain Costales informed the viceroy that according to the orders of October 2, the previous year, recently received, he
had detailed nine soldiers from his garrison to guard the three new missions that were being established by the Querétaran Fathers on the San
Antonio River. He expressed great fear that these men would lose all
idea of discipline, if allowed to reside fifty leagues from their official
quarters. Soldiers assigned for such duty generally indulged in gambling with the mission Indians and often lost even their horses and military equipment. From this it followed that they became dissatisfied with
the service and deserted. He pointed out that it was very difficult to
replace such men because no one wished to enlist. Furthermore, the allot-
ment of nine men to guard the new missions left him without a sufficient
number of men to take care of the presidio and to attend to the various
duties that must be performed, particularly in case the Indians renewed
hostilities. According to his present organization, ten men were required
to escort the provision trains that came from the Río Grande, seven were
on duty at the presidio, seven guarded the horses, and two acted as mission guards in Nuestra Señora del Espíritu Santo. These left only three
soldiers and two officers for special duty in case of an emergency.[62]

On the other hand, general peace prevailed at this time, he declared.
The three coastal tribes with whom a treaty was concluded shortly before,
had maintained their friendly attitude and came in large numbers to the
presidio and mission, there being about sixty or seventy warriors now

---

[61]Titulo de Capitán del Presidio del Espíritu Santo, en la Provincia de los Tejas
de la Na. España con el sueldo de 600 pesos al año. *A. G. I., Audiencia de Guadalajara,* 104-6-8 (Dunn Transcripts, 1710-1738).

[62]Captain Costales to the Viceroy, January 7, 1731. *A. G. N., Provincias Internas,*
Vol. 236.

congregated in the mission pueblo. But the two nations that had not made peace were even more numerous. They had assumed a policy of neutrality and he hoped that they would soon become friends. He expected that at least two hundred more would be added to the mission when this happened. But he assured the viceroy that the Indians were so fickle that they were more to be feared when they pretended to be at peace because of their treachery than when openly hostile.[63]

Upon being consulted concerning the letter of Captain Costales, Rivera declared that when the order was given for the presidio of La Bahía to furnish a guard of nine soldiers for the newly established missions on the San Antonio, the evil consequences that would follow as a result of the lack of military training and discipline were known; that Costales should not feel uneasy about this matter, as he would not be held responsible for the effect of this duty on the soldiers so detailed. He pointed out that it had been a well established custom generally observed and there was no reason to discontinue it. Considering the distance, however, and the other circumstances described by Captain Costales, it might be advisable to relieve four of the men assigned to the new missions and permit them to return to their official quarters, replacing them with four from the Presidio of San Antonio. At the time of the original order, which was given on October 2, 1730, the Canary Island families had not been settled in San Antonio, but with their establishment, which had now been decreed and was being put into execution, the Presidio de Béjar would be fully protected and could well afford to spare the men suggested. He said that the fears entertained by Costales with regard to the treacherous designs of the Indians in time of peace were unfounded because they were not likely to renew hostilities, unless the garrison or its commander provoked the savages, as was the case when Captain Domingo Ramón was killed. He pointed out, also, that the ten men employed to convoy supply trains to and from the presidio, were not, nor could they be, required to perform this duty continuously, since such trips were undertaken only twice a year, according to the schedule adopted for this service in the new regulations. Consequently it was only during the time they were so engaged that the garrison was handicapped by the small number of men who remained at La Bahía. He advised, however, that the captain be instructed not to relax his usual vigilance at any time,

---

[63]*Ibid.*

so that he might prevent the possibility of a surprise.[64] The viceroy adopted the various suggestions made by Rivera and ordered that they be put into effect. On July 30, the orders for the purpose were issued and on August 8 they were sent to the captains of the Presidios of San Antonio and La Bahía for their execution.

Before these instructions were received, Captain Costales again wrote to the viceroy to inform him that he was doing everything in his power to maintain the peace with the Indians and to conclude a treaty with the two nations that had as yet not come to an agreement. These had promised to assemble with their chiefs, but up to the time of his letter, written on June 1, 1731, they had failed to fulfill their promise, although they had engaged in no hostilities during all the year. He promised to observe most faithfully the regulations with regard to trade with foreigners, particularly in dry goods. He called the attention of His Excellency, however, to the extreme need of salt which this post was experiencing and asked for permission to go in person or send a detachment of soldiers to secure a supply from the salines discovered by his predecessor in order to stock the presidio for a year or two. He assured the viceroy that he was not moved by any selfish motives in making this request and that he had in view only the welfare of the garrison and mission.[65]

As usual, the letter was immediately referred to Rivera, who in his reply explained that the proposal to extract salt from the salines discovered about fifty leagues to the south of La Bahía had been previously made and rejected as inadvisable. He affirmed that he was still of the same opinion for the reasons he had previously stated. If it had been deemed inexpedient for this enterprise to be undertaken in the time of Captain Bustillo y Ceballos, when the presidio had a few more men at its disposal than it had now, it was still more so in the present instance, as the force that could be detailed for this purpose would be smaller and the garrison left to guard La Bahía would be inadequate. This division would expose both the escort and the presidio to destruction by the Indians if they became aroused as a result of this activity. The lack of salt could be remedied by securing it from the same source that the other supplies for the post and the mission were obtained. Thus there would be much less risk of giving occasion for dissatisfaction among the

---

[64]Opinión del Brigadier Rivera, April 16, 1731. *A. G. N., Provincias Internas,* Vol. 236.

[65]Captain Gabriel Costales to the Viceroy, June 1, 1731. *A. G. N., Provincias Internas,* Vol. 236.

natives, who might renew hostilities at a time when peace reigned in the region.[66]

The viceroy was content to adopt the opinion expressed by Rivera in the case, and issued instructions that the captain of La Bahía should be informed accordingly, sending him a copy of the recommendations made by the former inspector of presidios for his information. This was done on August 8, and the attempt to secure salt from the salines discovered by Bustillo y Ceballos was abandoned.

At the close of 1731 the Mission of Nuestra Señora del Espíritu Santo and the Presidio de la Bahía seemed to have attained a degree of prosperity and peace. The Indians continued to be friendly and many came to live in the mission. The missionary in charge was able, for a while, to devote his time to the systematic instruction of the neophytes not only in the *doctrina,* but in the various duties of mission life. Harmony and understanding between the new commander and the mission prevailed and everything seemed promising.

The former governor of the province, Don Fernando Pérez de Almazán, had been forced to resign his office on account of sickness. In his letters to the viceroy, in 1726 and 1727, he repeatedly referred to his failing health. Shortly afterwards, he declared that he had appointed, subject to the approval of the viceroy, Mediavilla y Azcona, Captain of Los Adaes, naming him also his lieutenant governor, much as Aguayo had done in 1722 in his case. By 1729, Pérez de Almazán was in Mexico City, as indicated by the representation against the extinction of the Presidio de los Tejas, which the missionaries made in July of that year.[67] It is safe to conclude, therefore, that he left Texas either in the fall of 1728, or in the spring of 1729, shortly after the termination of the Rivera inspection. As the appointment of Mediavilla y Azcona as lieutenant governor had been provisional and it was never sanctioned by the viceroy, upon the formal resignation of Governor Almazán, it seems it was decided to name Captain Juan Antonio Bustillo y Ceballos, who had rendered such efficient service at La Bahía and to whom Rivera took a decided liking, as shown by his report on that presidio, governor of the province. The official appointment or its confirmation have not been found, but from the commission issued to Captain Costales, in which it is

---

[66]Opinión del Brigadier Rivera, July 19, 1731. *A. G. N., Provincias Internas,* Vol. 236.

[67]Representación de los Misioneros, July 20, 1729. *San Francisco el Grande Archives,* Vol. 3, p. 6.

declared that a vacancy was created at La Bahía in 1730, as a result of the promotion of its former commander, it must have been at that time that the viceroy appointed him to the governorship.[68] It was at the suggestion of Rivera, declares Father Morfi in his *History of Texas,* that he received this appointment.[69]

It was on April 28, 1731, that the new governor finally arrived in Los Adaes, his official residence, and took possession of his office. He had set out from La Bahía on March 8, with a large train of over ninety *cargas* of flour, arms, clothes, and other supplies, a drove of two hundred horses, a herd of two hundred and fifty head of cattle, and five hundred sheep, all of which had retarded his progress while on the march. The winter had been unusually severe and the snow had prevented him from starting until the spring with the large train of provisions and supplies which he had gathered in the fall on the Río Grande. This was generally the best season to travel and he had decided to wait and to go later with the convoy so as to make certain it was not unduly delayed. Well aware of the extremes to which Los Adaes was frequently reduced by such a contingency, he had chosen to escort the train himself.[70]

Upon his arrival in Los Adaes, Captain Melchor Mediavilla y Azcona made formal delivery of the garrison and all its belongings to the new governor and commander. There were at that time sixty men, including a lieutenant, an ensign, and a sergeant, according to the official list drawn up on April 30, when Bustillo y Ceballos reviewed the troops. He reported that all the soldiers were not fully provided with the necessary arms and equipment and that most of them did not have the lances, nor the *cueras,* prescribed by the new *Ordinance of Presidios.* Several of the men entirely lacked horses or did not have the number they should. From a preliminary exploration of the vicinity, he had been impressed with the want of suitable watering places for the stock. In the report on the age and character of each man, he declared with regard to himself, that he was forty years old and had seen eight years of service in the province, being an *Hidalgo* of a well known family in the mountains of Burgos in Spain. After the name of each person he listed whether he was Spanish, mestizo, mulatto, Indian, or a mixture of any of these types. An analysis shows that there

---

[68]Título de Capitán del Presidio del Espíritu Santo . . . *A. G. I., Audiencia de Guadalajara,* 104-6-8 (Dunn Transcripts, 1710-1738).

[69]Castañeda, *Morfi's History of Texas,* Chapter VII.

[70]Bustillo y Ceballos to the Viceroy, May 24, 1731. *A. G. N., Provincias Internas,* Vol. 236.

were twenty-nine Spaniards, fourteen *mestizos* of mixed blood, and one Indian. This is typical of the composition of the frontier garrisons. The inventory of the property belonging to the presidio which was turned over to him by the former commander consisted of one large spoon, a cannon ramrod, six field brass cannons, two of them out of order, nine pounds of cord, sixty-six lead balls of the size used in the cannon, other odds and ends, such as twelve lances, sixty-seven scythes, and three iron shovels.[71] There was no powder for the brass cannons in the presidio at the time he took possession of it.

The new governor informed the viceroy that he had published all the instructions received and the news of the friendly relations that now existed between the Crown of Spain and that of France. As a result, a number of Frenchmen were now in the habit of coming from Natchitoches to the presidio to dispose of vegetables and other products raised by them. They generally traded these to the soldiers for chocolate, sugar and soap. He said the foreigners were closely watched to prevent their introducing other merchandise than the things they raised. Their goods were inspected by the sentinel before they were allowed to enter the presidio. One of the Frenchmen had asked the governor for permission to enter the province beyond the presidio to trade with the Indians, but he had been emphatically informed this was impossible. Bustillo y Ceballos declares that as a matter of fact considerable trade had been and was being carried on between the French at Natchitoches and the Indians, but that the latter went to that post to obtain the things they desire. It was well known, he said, that from San Pedro de los Navidachos to Los Adaes, a distance of about fifty or sixty leagues, the Indians were bountifully supplied with guns, powder, lead, French cloth, and shirts, where these objects could be seen everywhere and nothing else was talked of by the natives than the French.[72]

The relations with the eight tribes of East Texas continued peaceful, he assured the viceroy, but the Navidachos, the Neches, and the Hainais had cooled considerably and showed signs of being very much dissatisfied with the removal of the missions of San José, Concepción, and San Francisco to the San Antonio River. The chiefs of these nations appeared

[71]Lista y relación jurada, April 30 and May 4, 1731. *A. G. N., Provincias Internas,* Vol. 236.

[72]Bustillo y Ceballos to the Viceroy, May 24, 1731. *A. G. N., Provincias Internas,* Vol. 236. The remainder of the details concerning Los Adaes in 1731 are based on this interesting and valuable letter.

before the governor shortly after his arrival and expressed their regret and sorrow because they were deprived of the service of the *Padres*. The *Capitán Grande* of the Tejas had ignored the messages of the governor to come and see him three times, until at last, Bustillo y Ceballos sent him his horse, fully saddled. When he saw the governor he expressed the same opinion as the other chiefs and asked what he or his people had done to make the Spaniards angry and what had caused the *Padres* to abandon their country. The governor explained to him as best he could that the orders had come for the removal from his *Capitán Grande* and explained to them that the other three missions near the presidio would welcome them and that the missionaries would continue to look after them. He tried to console them, he said, and to make his words more effective, gave them presents of cloth, beads, knives, and tobacco, assuring them that the Spaniards were their friends and that the missionaries would continue to care for them. All this explanation was made through a good interpreter. On his way to Los Adaes, he had visited each one of the tribes of the territory through which he had passed, and he had spent a day with each. He promised the viceroy to do everything he could to maintain the peace and persuade the Indians to congregate in the missions as he was instructed.

In accord with the new ordinance, he had requested the captains at La Bahía and San Antonio de Béjar to make detailed reports to him of the soldiers, their arms and equipment, the number of horses, the racial descent and breeding of each man, and the property of these presidios. As soon as these items were received he assured the viceroy that he would forward them without delay. The lieutenant and the *alférez* of Los Adaes having become chronically ill, as happened so often in this unhealthy climate, the governor appointed Don José Cayetano de Vergara and Don Joseph González to fill the vacancies, respectively. It is a strange coincidence, however, that the only two men in the garrison who had to be replaced on account of continued illness were the two principal subaltern officers. The appointments, of course, were temporary and subject to the approval of His Excellency.[73]

The detailed account of conditions at Los Adaes and the Province of Texas in general was turned over to Rivera for his consideration and recommendations with regard to the various points raised by the new governor. After studying the document with care, he reported on July 21,

---

[73] *Ibid.*

1731. The most important matter was the maintenance of peace, he declared. Captain Bustillo y Ceballos had had considerable experience in dealing with the natives in the past and had demonstrated his tact and good judgment during the time he was at La Bahía. When he went there the Indians were openly hostile and had no love for the Spaniards, but before he left that post, peace had been concluded with three tribes that had revolted, and general contentment prevailed. Nevertheless, in view of the circumstances described by the governor in his letter as existing among some of the nations of East Texas, it would be well to remind him to act with all prudence so as not to give occasion or provoke the natives to become hostile.

If the soldiers were not fully equipped, he pointed out, it was because of the neglect of the former captain. It would be a question of a short time for Bustillo to remedy this situation, his activity and diligence in such matters being well known. The lances and the horses he could provide. Although the type of the soldiers, according to the list reported, was not as high as it should be, it would be too expensive to enlist enough Spaniards to replace the various breeds enumerated. These made just as good soldiers for frontier service. In regard to the lack of powder, His Excellency should order that a box should be sent to Los Adaes immediately, in order that the ammunition might be used in case of need to repel an attack or to fire salutes as occasion demanded.

The question of trade with the French had always been a very delicate matter. It is surprising, therefore, to find Rivera take the news of the exchange of goods and supplies between the soldiers of the Presidio of los Adaes and the French from Natchitoches so calmly. The new commander of the post, he said, was capable of enforcing the regulations concerning illicit trade with foreigners and would know how far the innocent exchange of products raised by the French at Natchitoches should go, without putting in jeopardy the peace now existing between the two crowns. The extensive trade now carried on between the Indians of the Province of Texas and the French could not be stopped by the presidio, he explained, because of its location and the intimate relations that existed between the natives and the foreign traders at Natchitoches. To attempt it at this time might not only antagonize the Indians but would displease the French with whom Spain was at peace. The extent of the trade, he commented, was not of sufficient importance to endanger the tranquility that now prevailed, so no attempt should be made to stop the barter. The exchange of vegetables between the soldiers of the two frontier outposts was being carried on even at the time of the *visita* as he himself had noticed, and was not prohibited by the instructions concerning the introduction of foreign goods in the dominions of the king in America.

Regarding the appointment of a lieutenant and an *alférez* by the new governor, subject to the approval of the viceroy, he believed that since the places had become vacant as the result of the poor health of the former incumbents, His Excellency should officially approve them. Unless the viceroy had others in mind for these appointments, the men named by the governor could be given their official commissions.[74]

The viceroy took nine days to weigh the various recommendations made by Rivera in this case, which he must have considered important. On July 30, he ordered that the corresponding instructions be drawn up for the information of the new Governor of Texas in the various matters he had reported to the viceroy. In these, the recommendations of Rivera were to be followed as outlined in his communication on the subject and the commissions for the lieutenant and *alférez* of Los Adaes were likewise to be drawn up and sent to the interested officials as soon as possible. The two men temporarily selected by the Governor were thus issued their appointments on August 17, 1731.[75]

There was one other officer of importance replaced at this time. It will be remembered that Captain Nicolás Flores was reinstated as commander of the Presidio de San Antonio de Béjar in 1728, by order of the viceroy. He continued in this post until his death which seems to have occurred either in the fall of 1729 or the spring of 1730. When the vacancy was reported to the viceroy, he filled it temporarily by assigning Don Juan Antonio Pérez de Almazán, probably related to Don Fernando of the same name who had been governor, subject to the approval of the king. In informing the king of the choice, he said that the captain *ad interim* had seen service in Texas before and had taken part in different campaigns against the Indians. The king approved the recommendations of the viceroy on June 6, 1731, and issued him a royal commission as captain of the Presidio of San Antonio with a salary of six hundred *pesos* a year as fixed by the new *Ordinance*.[76]

---

[74]Opinión del Brigadier Rivera, July 21, 1731. *A. G. N., Provincias Internas,* Vol. 236.

[75]*Ibid.*

[76]Don Juan Antonio Pérez de Almazán—Patente de Capn. Comandante del Presidio y Compa. de Sn. Antto. de Véjar, uno de los de tierra adentro en la Na. España. June 6, 1731. *A. G. I., Audiencia de Guadalajara,* 104-6-8 (Dunn Transcripts, 1710-1738).

In the course of the events described in this chapter the presidios of Texas were reorganized as a result of the Rivera inspection. The oldest presidio, that of Nuestra Señora de los Dolores de los Tejas was abolished, and the garrisons of the remaining three were reduced far more than the missionaries and Texas officials frankly believed was advisable. Three of the missions founded originally by the missionaries from the College of Querétaro in East Texas were removed to the banks of the San Antonio. The general condition of the military outposts was on the whole improved and the new missions gave promise of rapid progress.

There is one other major event which took place at this time and which was decidedly to affect the future development not only of the missions but of the entire province. This was the establishment of the first official civil settlement near the Presidio of San Antonio de Béjar. Ever since the time of Alarcón the idea of establishing one or more civil settlements with Spanish families, either from New Spain, or from Spain, or the Canary Islands had been consistently advocated by various officials, chief among them the Marquis of Aguayo. The plan was finally put into execution in 1731. But this event, which is of such great importance, because of its effect on the future history of the province, has never been accurately and fully recorded. It is a debt to the first civil settlers of Texas and their descendants which should long since have been paid. This stirring episode in the history of the State requires a separate chapter and is not out of place in the history of the mission era, because it was the greatest incentive and the most important single aid for the propagation of the faith through the extension of missionary efforts.

CHAPTER VIII

ESTABLISHMENT OF SAN FERNANDO DE BÉJAR, FIRST CIVIL SETTLEMENT
IN TEXAS, 1723-1731

Origin of plans for civil settlement of Texas. Over two hundred
years have elapsed since the establishment of the first civil settlement
on the present site of San Antonio. The connected story, however, of the
forces that brought about this most significant event, the details of the
tiresome sea voyage from the Canary Islands to Veracruz, the long and
painful journey from Veracruz to Mexico City and hence to distant Texas,
and the untold hardships endured by the first settlers, in spite of the
solicitude of colonial officials, remains to be told.[1] The need of a civil
settlement was first realized by the missionaries, who urged such action
shortly after the Ramón Expedition in 1716. Contrary to the general
belief, it was the Council of the Indies and not the Marquis of Aguayo
who first recommended that families from the Canary Islands or Galicia
be sent for that purpose. Heretofore it had been suggested, chiefly by
the missionaries, that families from New Spain should be induced to
settle in the vicinity of the missions founded in Texas. "It is advisable,"
declared the Council on March 27, 1719, "that Your Majesty issue orders
to the officials of the Canary Islands and the kingdom of Galicia for two
thousand families to be transported by way of the city of Veracruz."[2]
The immediate occasion for this recommendation was the proposed occupation of the Bay of Espíritu Santo, designated at that time as San
Bernardo Bay, and the establishment of a permanent settlement at this
point to prevent the possible incursion of the French. But the king did
not receive the suggestion favorably. In his instructions to the viceroy
he asked that suitable sites for settlements in this region be chosen and
that these be supplied with families from New Spain, who could be transported with much less expense to the royal treasury and with much greater
ease than from the Canary Islands or Spain.[3]

---

[1]The only attempts at a critical presentation of the facts are Bancroft, *North
Mexican States and Texas,* Vol. I, I. J. Cox, "The Founding of the First Texas
Municipality," *Texas Historical Quarterly,* II, 217-226; Mattie Alice Austin, "The
Municipal Government of San Fernando de Béxar," *Quarterly,* VIII, 277-353.

[2]Satisfacción á la orden de V. M. con que se sirvio Remitir tres cartas . . .
March 27, 1719. *A. G. I., México,* 61-6-35 (Dunn Transcripts, University of Texas).

[3]Royal *Cédula,* April 22, 1719, *Historia,* Vol. 298.

The general impression has been that the petition for the location of families in Texas was directed from the beginning to the establishment of a civil settlement on the site of the present city of San Antonio. The documents show, however, that the final placement of the Canary Islanders on the San Antonio River was accidental; that the original plan was to found a series of such colonial groups, beginning at Espíritu Santo Bay; and that the factor that first determined the king to adopt this measure in 1723 was the apparent necessity of occupying this coast permanently as a protection and a prevention against repeated French encroachments. It was La Salle's settlement in its vicinity that precipitated the actual occupation of the province; it was the suspected plans of the French for the reoccupation of this area in 1719 and 1720 that occasioned the emphatic instructions to Aguayo to establish a fort at the Bay of Espíritu Santo, and it was the belief that this measure was not sufficient that finally prompted the king to adopt the suggestions made by Aguayo upon his return from Texas. This outlook was far more extensive than the establishment of a single civil settlement on the San Antonio. It will be seen, in the course of this chapter, that Aguayo's plan called first for the location of families on Espíritu Santo Bay, the establishment of similar settlements in the vicinity of the presidios already founded with a view of obviating the necessity of maintaining these military establishments, and the founding of a halfway station between San Antonio de Béxar and the Presidio of los Adaes.

Immediately upon the return of Aguayo from his expedition, Viceroy Valero urged the king, on July 9, 1722, to send two hundred families, either from Galicia or the Canary Islands, to be settled in Texas in order to make the reoccupation just effected by the Marquis more permanent and lasting. In letters to the viceroy and the king, Aguayo had suggested this measure as essential to safeguard the new province and to save unnecessary expense to the king in maintaining so many presidios and soldiers. He said that civil settlements should be founded on San Bernardo Bay, Los Adaes, the Presidio of San Antonio de Béjar, and at some point between the two places last mentioned, because the distance between the existing posts was about one hundred and seventy-two leagues. The establishment of a halfway station would be of inestimable value to both. He explained that La Anguila or San José de Buenavista were two sites that could be chosen for that purpose. In addition to the two hundred families from Spain, he thought that a similar number of Tlaxcaltecan Indians should be settled in the mission already established to help instruct the neophytes and to serve as an example to the natives. Both the Spanish families and the Indians could be taken from Veracruz to the Bay of Espíritu Santo by water without much cost to the king.[4]

First order for settlement of Canary Islanders in Texas.   After reading the long communication of the viceroy and the suggestions made by Aguayo, it seems the king changed his mind and decided to order the transportation of two hundred families from the Canary Islands to be settled in the vicinity of the Bay of Espíritu Santo. The corresponding orders were therefore issued on March 18, 1723, to Juan Montero, Intendant of the Islands. He was to publish a proclamation to the inhabitants of all the islands and call for volunteers who wished to go to America to settle on San Bernardo Bay. These persons should be sent in small groups on board the ships that sailed regularly to Campeche, in Yucatan, from where they could be taken in the same manner to Veracruz and sent from there to their final destination. The Intendant was warned that all those sent agreeable to the royal order were to go voluntarily and in no other way. He was instructed to give timely notice to the Governor of Yucatan and to the viceroy each time a group of the families embarked in order that these officials might prepare for the reception and make all the necessary arrangements to supply them with whatever they needed.[5] A similar communication was sent on May 10 of the same year to the Governor of Yucatan, ordering him to supply all families sent in accordance with the king's instructions with everything they needed and to provide houses and food for them while they were in port waiting to be sent on to Veracruz. He should see that they were taken on board the first ships sailing from Campeche to that port and to give them anything they might need for their journey. He should notify the viceroy of their arrival and departure in order that he might make arrangements for their reception at Veracruz.[6]

The Intendant of the Canary Islands reported on July 24, 1723, that

---

[4]Satisfacción á una Rl. ordén del Rey nro. Sor. *A. G. I., Audiencia de Guadalajara,* 67-1-37 (Dunn Transcripts, 1710-1738).

[5]Cédula Real sobre la remisión de 200 familias de Canarias a nueba Espa. para poblar la Bahía de Sn. Bernardo. *A. G. I., Audiencia de Guadalajara,* 67-1-37 (Dunn Transcripts, 1710-1738).

[6]Al Gobernador y ofiziales de Yucatan sobre las familias de Canarias que han de ir á Campeche para pasar despues á la Veracruz y de allí á la Bahía de Sn. Bernardo. *A. G. I., Audiencia de Guadalajara,* 67-1-37 (Dunn Transcripts, 1710-1738).

in accordance with the royal order of March 18, he had published a proclamation to the inhabitants of the islands informing them of his royal
will and calling for volunteers. He assured the king that all those who
volunteered would be registered in a special book and that they would be
sent as fast as opportunity offered. He expressed serious doubts, however,
concerning his ability to execute the royal order promptly, due to the
fact that the products of export raised by the islanders were few,
and hence there were not many ships sailing to Yucatan during the
year. The largest vessel in port had sailed on July 5 for Porto Rico
with twenty-five families who were migrating to that island. He must
now wait until another craft was ready to take the first consignment of
volunteers for Texas to Campeche. He suggested that it would be well
for His Majesty to permit some of the families destined for the proposed settlement to go by way of Havana, from where they could proceed to Veracruz just as easily as from Yucatan.[7]

This letter is significant because it explains why the settlers were
chosen from the Canary Islands. The king in the original order expressed
the opinion that the inhabitants of the islands had proved good settlers.
Evidently the fact that these regions were closer to America than Spain
was also a factor, but the chief reason was, perhaps, that the productivity
of the islands was so poor that its people were glad that an opportunity
presented itself to find new homes in more fertile lands. A call for settlers, therefore, always met with an enthusiastic and prompt response.
This conclusion is borne out by a letter of the Intendant written on September 19, 1723, less than two months after his acknowledgment of the
receipt of the king's order. He now declared that in reply to his proclamation, the two hundred families desired had already registered voluntarily and were ready to be sent to Texas. But there were no ships sailing
for Campeche and it might be a long time before even a portion of the
settlers could be sent. Solicitous of the royal service, however, the *Cabildo*
of the islands had proposed to him to outfit two vessels at its own expense
to transport the families directly to Veracruz in order that they might
reach their final destination with as little delay as possible. The *Cabildo*
offered to pay all the expenses involved until they were turned over to the
viceregal officials in Veracruz on condition that it be allowed to send two
cargoes of products raised in the islands and to exchange them at that
port. The Intendant explained that he was fully aware that such a pro-

---

[7]Juan Montero, Intendant, to Marquis of Grimaldo, July 24, 1723. *A. G. I.,
Audiencia de Guadalajara*, 67-1-37 (Dunn Transcripts, 1710-1738).

cedure was opposed to the general practice observed in colonial trade and that it was detrimental to the interests of the Spanish trade fleet. He so told the *Cabildo*, but he was submitting their proposal, nevertheless, for consideration by the crown.[8]

Although everything seemed to promise an early execution of the king's orders with regard to the transportation of the Canary Islanders and the establishment of the intended settlement on the Bay of Espíritu Santo, the ardor of the Intendant, or of the settlers, or of the king, seems to have suddenly cooled for some unexplainable reason, and time slipped by without further action for almost three years. The proposal of the Intendant naturally affected the interests of the great merchant princes of Cádiz and Seville and this might be the cause for the unexpected lull in the execution of the plan. To the residents of the Canary Islands the concession meant a great deal and consequently it is only natural to conclude that the officials of the islands decided to wait and see that the offer was finally accepted, before taking any definite action to send any families on the ships making the regular trip to Yucatan.

It is of interest to note that in the meantime the plan presented by Aguayo was discussed at great length in the Council of the Indies more than a year after the king had actually acted upon it and had issued his order for the transportation of two hundred families as suggested by the viceroy. At a meeting held on July 28, 1724, the various reports made by the Marquis of Aguayo concerning the advisability of establishing civil settlements in Texas and the means of carrying out such a project were carefully examined and considered. The Council finally reached the conclusion that four hundred families should be sent from the Canary Islands for the purpose of founding civil settlements in Texas. It recommended to the king on that date that these could be transported, as the Intendant of the islands had suggested either by way of Yucatan or Havana, from either of which points they could continue their journey to Veracruz and hence to the Bay of Espíritu Santo. In spite of the care with which the Council considered the whole proposition, it is interesting to note how that body committed a serious error as to the number of families originally requested, that the whole four hundred, instead of two hundred, be sent from Spain. This recommendation accounts for the change in the number designated in the royal order issued two years

---

[8]Juan Montero to Marqués de Grimaldo, September 19, 1723. *A. G. I., Audiencia de Guadalajara,* 67-1-37 (Dunn Transcripts, 1710-1738).

before in 1723.[9] When the report was submitted to the king, he accepted the alterations made and wrote a note that Viceroy Casafuerte be informed before the final orders to carry out the suggestions were issued.

Renewed interest in settlement of Canary Islanders.   Three years passed before the matter was again presented to the Council for consideration. On July 3, 1727, Joseph Patiño, the private secretary of His Majesty, transmitted to that body an order of the king instructing it to issue the corresponding orders to put into effect the recommendations made on July 2, 1724. He called attention to the fact that the king wished the counsellors to remember that the two hundred families ordered sent on March 18, 1723, must be included in the four hundred now stipulated and that under no circumstances should the number be increased. At this time the secretary also transmitted two letters dated July 24, and September 29, 1723, written by Juan Montero, Intendant of the Canary Islands, stating the measures taken by him in fulfillment of the royal orders and the proposal made by the *Cabildo* of the Islands for the immediate transportation of the families at its own expense.[10]

The Council, after studying the matter, declared that it was proper that the two hundred families ordered sent prior to its recommendations should be included in the number and advised that the necessary orders be issued by the king for the transportation of the additional two hundred designated. With regard to the two letters of Montero, the officials said that they agreed with the *Fiscal* who declared it was never the intention of the Council that the two hundred families should be sent at one time. He had ably pointed out that two hundred families meant about one thousand persons, allowing an average of five members to each family; that the arrival of such a large group either at Campeche or Veracruz would embarrass the officials who would be unable to gather the necessary supplies to feed them, minister to their wants, and to furnish transportation to their final destination. The Council recommended, therefore, that the plan suggested by them be followed, and that the families should be sent in groups of ten or twelve at a time. If the king agreed, some of them could be sent by way of Havana, as suggested by the Intendant of the Canary Islands, but in that case the Governor of Havana should be informed of the king's pleasure so that

---

[9]Satisfacción á un Rl. orden del Rey nro. Sor. July 28, 1724. *A. G. I., Audiencia de Guadalajara,* 67-1-37 (Dunn Transcripts, 1710-1738).

[10]Joseph Patiño to Duque de Arión, July 3, 1727. *A. G. I., Audiencia de Guadalajara,* 67-1-37 (Dunn Transcripts, 1710-1738).

he might make the necessary arrangements for the reception of the families and the continuation of their voyage. It would also be necessary for the king to decide whether the families should be sent from Havana to Veracruz or directly to the Bay of Espíritu Santo,[11] in accord with the orders given by the viceroy. Both of the recommendations were finally adopted.

Nothing further was done, however, for two years. It was not until February 14, 1729, that the king again turned his attention to the matter. On that date he issued a long *cédula* which was immediately transmitted to the viceroy of New Spain. After reviewing in detail the services rendered by the Marquis of Aguayo during the expedition in Texas, his plan for the establishment of civil settlements with families from Spain or the Canary Islands and Tlaxcala was carefully summarized. The king then went on to state that in view of the facts presented, he had ordered four hundred families to be sent from the Canary Islands for the purpose indicated; that in this number were included the two hundred previously ordered on March 18, 1723; and that they were to be taken from the Islands to Havana in groups of ten or twelve at a time. Upon their arrival at Havana, the governor was to inform the viceroy, who was to make all arrangements for their reception at Veracruz. He was requested to treat the new settlers with all consideration and provide them with everything they needed for their maintenance, the continuation of their journey to Texas, and the raising of their first crops, all of which was to be at the expense of the king. The families being sent should be established in the vicinity of La Bahía del Espíritu Santo, the Presidio of San Antonio de Béjar and Los Adaes. A new settlement should also be founded at a convenient location between the two posts last mentioned. After the settlers reached their final destination, they should be supplied with all they needed both for their maintenance and the sowing of the first crop for an entire year.[12]

Upon receipt of the *cédula,* on November 27, 1729, the viceroy ordered that a copy be made and turned over to Brigadier Rivera, who was still in Mexico and was constantly consulted by the Marquis of Casafuerte on all matters pertaining to the interior provinces. He was asked to report whether the number of families indicated in the royal order was needed

---

[11]Recommendations of the Council of the Indies, and the Royal *Fiscal,* July 15 and August 8, 1727. *A. G. I., Audiencia de Guadalajara,* 67-1-37 (Dunn Transcripts, 1710-1738).

[12]Royal *Cédula,* February 14, 1729. *A. G. N., História,* Vols. 298-299.

in Texas, and what was the most convenient way in which such families as might arrive, pursuant to the king's pleasure, might be sent to their destination in the remote province. He was requested to make such suggestions as he deemed best both as to the manner of traveling and the route that should be followed. His report must be referred to the *Fiscal* for his opinion and approval.[13]

Rivera's criticism of Aguayo's plan. Rivera seems to have welcomed this opportunity to point out the weaknesses of all the proposals of the Marquis of Aguayo, at whose instigation the plan outlined in the royal *cédula* had been adopted. In a long report drawn up on January 16, 1730, he attempted to show how impractical was the project here presented. He first described the province from his personal observation in order to lay the premises for his conclusions. He declared that it began fourteen leagues to the south of the Presidio of San Antonio de Béjar on the Medina River, which formed its boundary, and extended from this stream to the Cadadachos River, where the French settlements began. In the vast expanse of territory between the two rivers, which extends for a distance of two hundred and fifty leagues there were twenty-seven streams, large and small, most of which were unsuited to irrigation because of their high banks. But the land was so fertile and the rain so abundant throughout most of the province, that without the aid of irrigation almost any part could be made productive under proper cultivation.

Granting that Aguayo's plan for settling part of the province with families brought from the Canary Islands was the result of his intense desire to serve the best interests of the king, Rivera, nevertheless, called the attention of the viceroy to the fact that the Marquis had overlooked the great obstacles that must be surmounted in carrying out his proposals. The transportation from the Canary Islands to Veracruz and hence to the Bay of Espíritu Santo involved considerable expense and no small hardships. But if the natural difficulties of the long journey could be overcome successfully, the families would find, upon reaching their destination, that the sites proposed by the Marquis for a new colony were unfit for settlement. He pointed out that San José de Buenavista, one of the places suggested, was about one hundred leagues from the bay (to the northeast) and lacked the necessary water. The little spring found at this spot was scarcely sufficient to meet the needs of

---

[13]Order of the viceroy, November 27, 1729. *A. G. I., Audiencia de Guadalajara,* 67-4-38 (Dunn Transcripts, 1710-1738).

more than one or two families, except in the rainy season. La Anguila, the other site, although closer to the bay, had likewise not much water and the fields in the neighborhood were covered with rocks. Rivera expressed surprise that Aguayo should have suggested either of these two places for the establishment of a new settlement. He concluded this part of his report by declaring that if all the difficulties of the long distance and the unfavorable conditions of the sites selected were overcome, the settlements proposed would still be doomed to failure, because the settlers would be unable to dispose of their products with advantage and profit.

In his opinion the settlement of Texas should be undertaken from Coahuila as a base, and the fringe of outposts gradually extended without losing communication with the portions already occupied. This was the only wise and sound policy. The Indians of the new province, Rivera declared, were extremely jealous of their liberty. The establishment of isolated settlements, far from the frontiers of New Spain, would only arouse their suspicions and result in hostilities. This condition would necessitate the establishment of garrisons to protect the new settlements and instead of saving expense to the royal treasury the foundations would involve additional expenditures.

Rivera's plan. Having shown how impractical and unsound was the project presented by Aguayo for the establishment of civil settlements in Texas, he now offered a substitute plan of his own. He said that the Sabinas River, which was only two days' journey from Los Adaes, formed a comfortable bay at its mouth, capable of accommodating vessels of medium draft. Upon the arrival in Havana of the families intended for settlement in Texas they could be sent directly to this bay and established in the vicinity of the eastern group of missions. The country was occupied by the Tejas Indians, who were the most friendly, and the lands were by far the most fertile in the entire province. A settlement founded at or near this point could be given all the necessary protection by the garrison stationed at Los Adaes without additional expense to the royal treasury.

But he added that he fully realized considerable time would be required before his suggestions could be carried out, as it was necessary to submit them to the king for his approval. In view of this fact, which precluded the possibility of settling the first families in the vicinity of Los Adaes, where they were most needed to prevent the further advance of the French, the next best place would be near the Presidio of San Antonio de Béjar. He recalled the recommendations he had made shortly after his inspection of that Presidio in 1728 and again urged that twenty-five families of those designed for settlement in Texas be established there. He considered this number would be sufficient to strengthen the presidio and to form a nucleus for a civil settlement. By reënforcing this locality, if Los Adaes were surprised by hostile forces as in the past, the garrison at San Antonio could hold out until reënforcements were sent to drive out the invaders.

Other equally suitable locations for additional settlements could be found on the San Marcos River (Colorado), which was about thirty leagues from the Presidio of San Antonio de Béjar. Rivera remarked that His Excellency had already given instructions for the tentative establishment of the Presidio of La Bahía del Espíritu Santo at this site as a protection for the missions that were going to be moved from East Texas by the Querétaran missionaries. Along its banks, he declared, there were some excellent locations where settlements could be established. No increase in families from Spain would be needed for this purpose because many persons living in Coahuila and Nuevo Reino de León would be glad to avail themselves of the opportunity to fill the quotas, because all colonists were offered, as inducements, the cost of transportation, all the tools, cultivators, seed and food necessary for maintenance of the group for an entire year. The establishment of one or two successful settlements on this river would encourage others, and in a short time, the civil population of the new province would be sufficient to withstand the hostilities of the Indians.

He concluded his long report by suggesting that such settlements as were founded, should be established at convenient distances so that they could render mutual aid to each other in case of danger. But for this object the emigrants from New Spain would serve the purpose much better than those from Spain or the Canary Islands, he thought, because the former were more used to the conditions they would encounter in the new province. Until the whole matter was reconsidered by the king, Rivera thought it would be well for the viceroy to instruct the governor of Havana that if any families arrived there in the interim, pursuant to the order of the king of February 14, 1729, he should keep them there until further notice. Should it be decided that they be sent on to the Province of Texas, these colonists might be sent to the mouth of the Sabinas River for a settlement at that point as suggested.[14]

Arrival of Canary Islanders in Veracruz. In the meantime the first ten families sent from the Canary Islands by way of Havana for the settlement in Texas, in accord with the orders of the King of February 14, 1729, arrived in Veracruz on June 19, 1730.[15] After seven years, the plan of the colonization in the province became a reality. But at the time of their arrival, the viceroy was still undecided where they were to be established or how they were to be transferred, whether by water or overland. From the documents cited, it is evident that the idea of establishing a settlement in the vicinity of the Presidio of San Antonio had not as yet been definitely adopted, having been urged only by Rivera. The apparent purpose of sending the Canary Islanders to Texas was primarily to furnish settlers for the coastal region near the Bay of Espíritu Santo which in the meantime had been abandoned both as a mission and as a military post. Consequently, it was impossible to follow the instructions of the king as to this location.

Immediately upon the arrival of the Canary Islanders in Havana, the officials there had sent them to Veracruz, transmitting to the royal officers of the post a certified list of the families and the number of persons in each. Upon their landing in Veracruz, the lists were sent on to the viceroy, and the settlers were housed, clothed, and fed by officials in that city. They were asked to remain there until instructions for the continuation of their journey were received. Casafuerte was now confronted with a real and not an imaginary problem. He hastily consulted both Rivera and Aguayo as to what should now be done to transport the families just arrived and where they should be settled.

Destination and route to be followed. On July 13, 1730, Rivera made a long report in which he argued that to send the ten families so recently arrived by water from Veracruz to the Bay of Espíritu Santo would expose them to the known hostility of the Indians in the vicinity and the proximate dangers of shipwreck along the coast. If they were to be settled near the Presidio of San Antonio, as he had already suggested, it would be much better to send them to Mexico City under

[14]Recomendaciones del Brigadier Don Pedro de Rivera. *A. G. I., Audiencia de Guadalajara,* 67-4-38 (Dunn Transcripts, 1710-1738).

[15]Viceroy to the King, August 1, 1730. *A. G. I., Audiencia de México,* 67-3-23 (Dunn Transcripts, 1730-1736).

an adequate guard and under the care of an able guide or conductor and to allow them to rest from their long trip here, while the Governor of Texas and the Captain of the Presidio of San Antonio could make the arrangements for their reception. The necessary supplies, horses, mules, tools, clothes, tents, and other things necessary for the journey must be gathered and made ready in the meantime. He inclosed a detailed itinerary that should be followed in conducting them from Veracruz to Cuatitlán, one of the outskirts of Mexico City, and he suggested that Francisco Duval, a resident of Mexico, be appointed as guide.[16]

The recommendations of Rivera were immediately referred to Oliván Rebolledo, the *Auditor de Guerra,* who, on July 17, informed the viceroy that he agreed with all the suggestions made by Brigadier Rivera as to the arrangements for the removal of the settlers to Cuatitlán and hence to Texas. He approved the selection of Francisco Duval as conductor and said that the overland route was preferable to the sea voyage. He fully endorsed the idea of establishing the families in the vicinity of the Presidio of San Antonio de Béjar. Thus the final destination of the Canary Islanders was definitely determined in this report. With his accustomed care, the *Auditor* pointed out that the daily journeys suggested in the itinerary prepared by Rivera were too long for women with young children and advised that the guide or conductor be allowed to use discretion. He concluded by declaring that the group of ten families was the minimum number required by the Laws of the Indies for the establishment of a town. This entitled the settlers to organize their own civil government, to receive lands for the construction of their homes and the sowing and raising of crops, to have a church and town hall, and to build a town with a public square and regularly planned streets.[17] It will be remembered that up to this time no word had been said in the royal orders concerning the establishment of an independent municipality by the Canary Islanders, although this purpose has been properly inferred. It was Oliván Rebolledo, however, who called the attention of the viceroy to the advisability of permitting them to found a separate town and the granting to them of all the rights and

[16]Report of Rivera, summarized in the *Opinión del Auditor,* July 17, 1730. *A. G. I., Audiencia de Guadalajara,* 67-4-48 (Dunn Transcripts, 1710-1738).

[17]Opinión del Auditor de Guerra, July 17, 1730. *A. G. I., Audiencia de Guadalajara,* 67-4-38 (Dunn Transcripts).

privileges, as well as the title of *Hijo Dalgo,* prescribed by the Laws of the Indies to first settlers.

March to Mexico. Satisfied with the opinion of the *Auditor* and the recommendations of Rivera, the viceroy lost no time in ordering that the necessary instructions be issued to the officials at Veracruz to turn over the families to Francisco Duval, who was to conduct them to Cuatitlán, under a competent guard for their protection. The settlers were to be supplied with everything they needed for the trip at the king's expense, and they should start as soon as possible. At the same time he issued instructions to the *Alcalde Mayor* of Cuatitlán to secure houses where the families could stay, to purchase the necessary supplies, to give a daily allowance to each person, to furnish them medical assistance if it became necessary, to give them medicines, to bury the dead, and to take care of the horses and beasts of burden from the day of their arrival until their departure.[18]

After a much needed period of rest in Veracruz the ten families set out early in August for Cuatitlán, where they arrived on August 27, 1730, under the able leadership of Francisco Duval, who looked after all their needs and had helped them on the march. A corporal and a squad of soldiers accompanied the wearied travelers on their journey and were paid by the *Alcalde Mayor* of Cuatitlán forty *pesos* for their services. The necessary houses had been prepared in advance and everything made ready for their reception. Here they were to stay until November 15, 1730, when they started for their final destination in San Antonio.[19]

Choosing the site for the settlement. While the Canary Islanders, tired after their long march, rested at Cuatitlán, the viceroy was busy making final plans for their actual settlement in Texas. The question that was uppermost in his mind now was the exact location in the vicinity of the Presidio of San Antonio de Béjar where the settlement should be established. He naturally consulted the Marquis of Aguayo and Brigadier Rivera on this question. Aguayo was the first to report. With many details, he explained the manner in which the families should be conducted from Cuatitlán to San Antonio; he listed the supplies they would need for the trip, the tools, the seed, the equipment,

---

[18]Quenta y Relación Jurada que presenta Dn. Franco. Domingo de Laba, Alcalde Mayor de Cuatitlán. *A. G. N., Provincias Internas,* Vol. 32.

[19]Viceroy Casafuerte to Francisco Domingo de Laba, August 28, 1730. *Provincias Internas,* Vol. 32.

and the tents; and estimated the horses and mules required for the transportation of the travelers. To make himself very clear as to the exact
location, where the families should be settled, he drew up a map of the
presidio and the surrounding country, which he sent to the viceroy with
his report.

Immediately upon receipt of this information, the Marquis of Casafuerte sent it on to Rivera, who finally expressed his views on the whole
matter on September 30. Prior to this date, he had made a report similar
to that of Aguayo as to the best manner of conducting the families to
Texas. He now remarked that he had nothing further to add as to their
conveyance and the necessary arrangements for the entire trip. He
thought that His Excellency could determine for himself which of the
two plans outlined for this portion of the enterprise should be followed.
But with regard to the map presented and the site suggested for the
actual establishment of the proposed town he pointed out a number of
errors in the directions and corrected other significant details.

To the north of the Presidio of San Antonio de Béjar, he declared,
there was a low hill not far away, from which two springs flowed to
form the San Antonio River, which passed to the east of the presidio
and the San Pedro which passed to the west. Both followed a southerly
course and joined a short distance below, before they entered the Medina
as one stream, about eight or nine leagues beyond. The presidio had been
constructed, therefore, between the two rivers. The Mission of San Antonio
de Valero was on the east bank of the San Antonio River, to the east
of the presidio, while the Mission of San José y San Miguel de Aguayo
was to the west of the river, on the same side as the presidio. This obvi-
ated the need of crossing the river in going from this mission to the
fort. But according to the map drawn by Aguayo, the two missions had
been erroneously placed on the east side of the river, or more correctly,
on the bank of the river opposite the presidio, which, according to the
compass rose drawn on the map, would be the north side.[20] This was an
evident mistake, perhaps due to carelessness or an oversight of the
draftsman. Furthermore, the map showed a bridge over the San Antonio
River. There had never been a bridge over this stream, Rivera affirmed
in his report. Ordinarily the women waded across it when they went to
Mass from the Presidio to the Mission of San Antonio de Valero. Only
when the rain caused the river to rise was the usual passageway obstructed.

---

[20]Aguayo's map, correctly criticized here by Rivera, was published for the first
time in Bolton, *Texas in the Middle Eighteenth Century.*

At such times, the trunks of trees were generally laid across its banks to permit the families of the soldiers to walk over, but this was a temporary makeshift. In view of these facts, it would be inadvisable to permit the Canary Islanders to establish a town across the river from the presidio, where they would be cut off from the garrison in times of floods and too far removed to be given adequate protection by the soldiers of the presidio.[21]

Having shown how inaccurate the map was, and consequently how unreliable the information on which Aguayo based his judgment in recommending that the settlement be established on what was in reality the east side of the San Antonio River, the Brigadier proceeded to make his own recommendations as to the best site for the proposed town. To the west, about a musket shot from the presidio, was a low, flat hill which formed a plateau upon which the town could be located. He had personally explored the land at the time of his visit and had remarked in his report how appropriate it was for a settlement of twenty-five families. The lands to the north and south of the presidio were ample for the farms which should be granted to the settlers for cultivation. They would have, furthermore, the presidial chapel within easy distance to comply with their Christian duties until a church was built for them.[22]

Proposed distribution of settlers among missions. But while plans for the actual settlement of the newly-arrived Canary Islanders were being seriously discussed by the viceroy with his advisers, Father Sevillano, of the College of Querétaro, presented a plan of his own for the disposition of the settlers. He proposed to the viceroy that the ten families should be distributed among the three missions which were now being removed from East Texas to the San Antonio River. He argued that they would serve as a nucleus for the refounded missions and would be of great help in instructing the Indians in the various duties of mission life. This proposal was referred to Rivera, as usual. In reply he declared that it would be very unwise to permit the settlers to establish themselves in the missions as suggested by Father Sevillano, because, as the number of neophytes grew, innumerable difficulties would arise from the intimate relations of the Canary Islanders and the natives. It

---

[21]Rivera to the Viceroy, September 30, 1730. *A. G. N., Provincias Internas,* Vol. 236, Pt. 1.

[22]*Ibid.*

would be better to establish a separate and independent municipality than to allow the settlers to be distributed among the missions.[23]

Reason why no more settlers were sent.   The influence which Rivera's usually sound judgement and powerful intellect exercised upon the viceroy is evident from the course followed throughout the matter. He not only accepted his recommendations as to the guide who was to conduct the families from Veracruz to Cuatitlán, but he adopted every measure he advocated with regard to the conveyance of the settlers from Mexico to Texas. The site he suggested for the establishment of the new muncipality became the final destination of the settlers, and his conclusion as to the futility of any more settlers for Texas from the Canary Islands was responsible for the discontinuance of every effort to settle the new province with Spaniards. In a letter to the king, written on August 1, 1730, the viceroy incorporated all the arguments presented by Rivera against the sending of more families from the Canary Islands or Spain for the purpose of settling the Province of Texas. He assured the king that if it became necessary to introduce settlers, these could be recruited and sent from New Spain much more easily and without so much expense. He declared that in view of the circumstances described, he had instructed the Governor of Havana, subject to the king's approval, not to send any more families to Veracruz should they arrive in the meantime, but to keep them there until further notice. He informed His Majesty that the ten families who had arrived in Veracruz on June 19, had been provided with all they needed and would be sent as soon as possible to establish a settlement in the vicinity of the Presidio of San Antonio, agreeable to the orders received. In closing, he begged the king to reconsider the whole matter in the light of the facts presented.[24]

The request of the viceroy that no more families be sent was received in Spain and referred to the Council of the Indies on March 22, 1732. It is here that the explanation for the abandonment of the policy to colonize Texas with Spanish families is found. It accounts, in no small degree, for the slow development of the province in subsequent years. Rivera, like the Marquis of Aguayo, was sincere in his recommendations, but he failed to see the far-reaching implications of his shortsighted policy, dictated by his mania for economy and to some extent

---

[23]*Ibid.*

[24]Viceroy Casafuerte to the King, August 1, 1730. *A. G. I., Audiencia de México*, 67-3-23 (Dunn Transcripts, 1730-1736).

by his personal aversions to the views of the Marquis of Aguayo. If the order of the king for the establishment of a number of civil settlements in Texas had been carried out and four hundred Canary Island families had been introduced, there would have been about two thousand full-blooded Spaniards established in the province. The significance of the placement of this group of industrious and skillful Spanish farmers in Texas cannot be overestimated. Let us return to the action taken by the Council. The *Consejo* took the recommendations of the viceroy under consideration, together with a letter from the Governor of Havana of July 14, 1730. In this communication, the governor informed the king that on June 1, two more ships had arrived from the Canary Islands with fifteen additional families destined for the colonization of Texas, but that agreeable to the instructions received from the viceroy, they had been detained in Havana to await new orders. In the meantime, he had decided to permit them to settle in the Hacienda of Sacalaondo, subject to the final approval of the king. In view of the sound and convincing reasons of the viceroy, all the antecedents of the question, and the letter to the Governor of Havana, the Council came to the conclusion that it would be useless to send any more colonists.[25] It is to be regretted that the plan to establish civil settlements in Texas should have been abandoned just as it was being put into execution.

Canary Islanders in Cuatitlán. It is necessary at this point to direct the attention of the reader to the Canary Islanders still resting and waiting at Cuatitlán. The long and tiresome trip in the old-fashioned ships and the unhealthy climate of Veracruz caused the death of three members of the party before they reached Mexico City. Two of them died shortly after their arrival in port, while making preparations to proceed inland to their temporary homes. These were Juan Rodríguez Granadillo, who was survived by a widow and five children, and Lucas Delgado, who left a widow and four children to go on to Texas. While on the road, Juan Cabrera died in the little town of Apa. His widow and three children continued the march with the rest. Upon their arrival in Cuatitlán, they were all placed in three dwelling houses which had been previously rented in accord with the instructions given to the *Alcalde Mayor* by the viceroy. He had urged him as early as August 1,

---

[25]En vista de lo que informa el Virrey de Nueva España . . . sobre que no se envien familias a la Provincia de los Tejas, representa á V. M. lo que se le ofrece. *A. G. I., Audiencia de México*, 67-3-23 (Dunn Transcripts, 1730-1736).

to procure ample and comfortable lodgings for the weary travelers.[26] The three buildings belonged to Nicolás Carranza, Francisco Carranza, and Antonio Dávalos, who each received fifteen, ten, and four *pesos* respectively as rent.[27]

There is considerable confusion as to the number of persons that made up the original ten families who arrived in Veracruz. How many actually set out from the Canary Islands cannot be determined from the documents available, but there is no question that at the time of their arrival, there were fifty-nine persons recorded, including men, women, and children. The names of the respective families and their members deserve to be preserved for posterity. They were listed as follows:

1. Juan Leal Goraz...Age 54 years
2. Luisa Hernández (wife)................................. " 46 "
3. José Leal (son)... " 22 "
4. Vicente Leal (son)... " 18 "
5. Bernardo Leal (son)...................................... " 13 "
6. Catarina Leal (daughter)............................. " 16 "
7. Juan Curbelo .... " 50 "
8. Gracia Perdomo y Umpierres (wife)........... " 46 "
9. José Curbelo (son).. " 20 "
10. Juan Francisco Curbelo (son)....................... " 9 "
11. María Ana Curbelo (daughter)..................... " 18 "
12. Juana Curbelo (daughter)............................. " 14 "
13. María Curbelo (daughter)............................. " 13 "
14. Juan Leal, Jr.. " 30 "
15. Gracia Acosta (wife)..................................... " 30 "
16. Manuel Leal (son).. " 12 "
17. Miguel Leal (son).. " 10 "
18. Domingo Leal (son)....................................... " 7 "
19. María Leal (daughter).................................... " 6 "
20. Pedro Leal (son)... " 3 months
21. José Leal (son, died in Cuatitlán)................
22. Antonio Santos .... " 50 years
23. Isabel Rodríguez (wife)................................. " 34 "
24. Miguel Santos (son)....................................... " 17 "
25. Ana Santos (daughter)................................... " 15 "

---

[26]The Viceroy to the *Alcalde Mayor* of Cuatitlán, August 1, 1730. *A. G. N., Provincias Internas*, Vol. 32.

[27]Alquiler de las Casas 29 p. *A. G. N., Provincias Internas*, Vol. 32.

26. Catarina Santos (daughter).. " 12 "
27. María Santos (daughter)... " 7 "
28. Josefa Santos (daughter).. " 2 "
29. José Padrón .... " 22 "
30. María Francisca Sanaria or Zanabria (wife).............. " 20 "
31. Manuel de Nis.. " 50 "
32. Sebastiana de la Peña (wife)................................... " 44 "
33. Josefa de Nis (daughter).. " 19 "
34. Salvador Rodríguez .... " 42 "
35. María Pérez Cabrera (wife)..................................... " 42 "
36. Patricio Rodríguez (son).. " 15 "
37. Juan Cabrera (died at Apa, on way to Cuatitlán)........
38. María Rodríguez (widow).............................Age 40 years
39. José Cabrera (son).. " 15 "
40. Marcos Cabrera (son).. " 6 "
41. Ana Cabrera (daughter).. " 13 "
42. Juan Rodríguez Granadillo (died in Veracruz)............
43. María Rodríguez Rovaina (widow)............................. " 27 "
44. Pedro Rodríguez Granadillo (son)............................. " 13 "
45. Manuel Francisco Rodríguez Granadillo (son)............ " 3 "
46. Paula Rodríguez Granadillo (daughter)...................... " 8 "
47. María Rodríguez Granadillo (daughter)...................... " 5 "
48. Josefa Rodríguez Granadillo (daughter)..................... " 10 "
49. Lucas Delgado (died in Veracruz).............................
50. María Melean (widow).. " 30 "
51. Juan Delgado (son)... " 19 "
52. Francisco Delgado (son).. " 16 "
53. Domingo Delgado (son)... " 2 "
54. Leonor Delgado (daughter)...................................... " 4 "
55. Antonio Rodríguez (bachelor)................................... " 18 "
56. Phelipe Pérez (bachelor)... " 20 "
57. José Pérez (brother of Phelipe)................................
58. Martín Lorenzo de Armas (bachelor).......................... " 20 "
59. Ignacio Lorenzo de Armas (brother of Martín).......... " 24 " [28]

As shown by the list, there were originally ten families and five unattached bachelors, with a total of fifty-nine persons. This number had been reduced to fifty-six by the time the brave little band of set-

[28]This list was compiled from the official roll made on September 9, 1730, at Cuatitlán by order of the viceroy. *A. G. N., História*, Vol. 84.

tlers arrived in Cuatitlán. Here they were to remain for two and a half months before they started on the last part of their journey to Texas on November 15, 1730. The hardships of the trip from the Canary Islands to Mexico City, however, did not stamp out the spirit of romance in the little group. Shortly after they were comfortably established at Cuatitlán, two young men, Francisco Arocha and Vicente Alvarez Travieso, who had come independently from the Islands some time before, on hearing that a group of their countrymen was waiting to continue on its way to Texas, appeared before the *Alcalde Mayor* and asked permission to join the settlers and to marry Juana and María Curbelo, respectively, the two maiden daughters of Juan Curbelo. It seems the two young men knew the girls back in the Islands and had gone to America in search of fortune in order to return to their sweethearts. When they learned they were in Mexico and were about to set out with their family to settle in Texas, the young men lost no time in asking for permission to marry them at once and proceed with them to the new colony. In a letter to the viceroy, written on September 16, the *Alcalde Mayor* informed him of the desire of the two young men. He declared they wished to appear before His Excellency to solicit his permission to marry the girls and to join the party of settlers. He also asked for the consent of the viceroy for the marriage of Antonio Rodríguez, one of the bachelors who had come from the Canary Islands, and had contracted to marry Josefa de Nis before they set out on the long trip.[29] The viceroy graciously acceded to the request on September 18 and instructed the *Alcalde Mayor* to inform the petitioners of his consent to their marriage. He explained that it would not be necessary for them to appear in person before him to solicit his approval. The two young men, Francisco Arocha and Vicente de Alvarez Travieso, were to be enrolled in the list of first settlers, to be given the same allowance as the others, and to be supplied with all they needed for the journey to Texas and their establishment in the new settlement.[30] Thus three new families were added to the original ten, and the little group of Canary Islanders gained two new recruits.

But before they started for Texas, two other marriages took place. It is not clear from the records whether these were the culmination of old

---

[29]Francisco Domingo de Laba to the Viceroy, September 16, 1730. *A. G. N., Provincias Internas,* Vol. 32.

[30]The Viceroy to the *Alcalde Mayor,* September 18, 1730. *A. G. N., Provincias Internas,* Vol. 32.

romances, as in the case of the three already listed, or whether they developed during the long journey. José Leal, son of Juan Leal Goraz, married Ana Santos, daughter of Antonio Santos; and Juan Delgado, son of Lucas Delgado, married Catarina Leal, the young daughter of Juan Leal Goraz.[31]

Contrary to the general belief, the list of settlers does not include all those that actually arrived in Veracruz. It seems that some of them made their escape shortly after they disembarked. The long and tiresome trip, the inexcusable delays, and the prospects of many more long marches to distant Texas discouraged a few of the colonists, who decided to run away from the little band in Veracruz. In a letter of the viceroy to the *Alcalde Mayor,* dated August 28, 1730, he enjoins the official to do everything he can to make the stay of the Canary Islanders as pleasant and comfortable as possible. He should spare no pains in supplying all their needs and in giving them an opportunity to recuperate from the hardships of their long journey. He was told to exercise special vigilance, however, to prevent any of them from escaping as they had done in Veracruz. In addition to supplying them with everything they might need, he was ordered to give them a daily allowance of three *reales.*[32] On August 30, the *Alcalde Mayor* informed the viceroy that everything had been done in accord with his instructions to make the settlers as comfortable as possible, but that Juan Leal Goraz, the oldest member of the group who acted as their leader, and Juan Curbelo, had asked him for permission to appear before His Excellency to explain to him personally the wants of the little band. The viceroy readily acceded to the request on August 31, and instructed the *Alcalde Mayor* to permit the two gentlemen to come and see him.[33]

As a result of the interview and the reports of the *Alcalde Mayor,* the daily allowance of three *reales* a day was increased to four on September 6.[34] Sickness broke out among the little group. They were worn out by the fatigue of the long journey, their health had been seriously impaired by the poor and irregular rations they had received during the apparently endless trip. On September 13, it became necessary to call a

---

[31]See list of settlers made at Cuatitlán on September 9, and November 14, 1730. *A. G. N., Provincias Internas,* Vol. 32; *História,* Vol. 84.

[32]The Viceroy to the *Alcalde Mayor,* August 28, 1730. *A. G. N., Provincias Internas,* Vol. 32.

[33]The Viceroy to the *Alcalde Mayor,* August 31, 1730. *A. G. N., Provincias Internas,* Vol. 32.

[34]The Viceroy to the *Alcalde Mayor,* September 6, 1730. In *Ibid.*

physician to look after the indisposed. The members of the party were suffering from different ailments at this time. Fray Bernabe de Santa Cruz, a lay religious of the Order of Saint Augustine, a Master in surgery and anatomy, graduate of the National University of Mexico, was chosen as the official physician to look after the Canary Islanders during their stay at Cuatitlán. Fray Bernabe asked six *pesos* a day for his services. When the viceroy was informed of the situation, he recommended that the physician be employed as long as it was necessary, that the medicines that might be required for the treatment of the patients be purchased from an authorized pharmacist, and that a detailed account of all expenditures be kept in order that these might be paid by the royal treasury. He asked the *Alcalde Mayor* to try to make an arrangement with Fray Bernabe which would be less expensive to the king, explaining to him that his services were for the public good.[35]

In view of the circumstances, Fray Bernabe agreed to charge only five *pesos* a day. He accordingly began to minister to the sick on September 13. Three days later, the *Alcalde Mayor* reported that the ten patients whom the physician was treating were all improving, with the exception of a woman who was suffering from dropsy. For forty days, Fray Bernabe continued to look after the patients and was successful in nursing most of them back to health. During this time he attended nineteen cases, of which only three died. These were Juan José Leal, an infant who died soon after he was born; Luisa Hernández, the wife of Juan Leal Goraz; and María Rodríguez Granadillo, the daughter of Juan Rodríguez, who had died shortly after his arrival in Veracruz. Although Fray Bernabe ministered to the sick for forty days, he only charged the king for twenty-three and was consequently paid one hundred and fifteen *pesos* for his services. The apothecary, Francisco Moroso, Master in pharmacy, graduate of the University, presented a bill for forty-eight *pesos* and six *reales* for the medicines he supplied to the sick and was paid in full by the *Alcalde Mayor*.[36]

It is of interest to note the cost of the shrouds purchased for the burial of the deceased. The one for little María Rodríguez cost four

---

[35]The Viceroy to the *Alcalde Mayor*, September 12, 15, October 1, 1730: The *Alcalde Mayor* to the Viceroy, September 14, 15, 1730. *A. G. N., Provincias Internas*, Vol. **32**.

[36]The *Alcalde Mayor* to the Viceroy, September 16, 1730; Recibo del Médico, October 28, 1730; Recibo del Boticario, no date; List of persons with births and deaths. *A. G. N., Provincias Internas*, Vol. **32**.

pesos, the one of Luisa Hernández cost twelve *pesos* and four *reales,* and the one for the little child cost four *pesos.*[37]

The solicitude of government officials extended to the horses of the Canary Islanders as well as to the settlers. On September 12, the *Alcalde Mayor* of Cuatitlán received one hundred and forty-six horses by order of the viceroy, which were to be used in transportation of the families to Texas. Until the date of their departure, which was finally set for November 15, he was instructed to employ as many men as might be necessary to take care of these horses and to pay each one of the herders four *reales* a day. Ignacio de Tapia, Pedro de Tapia, Juan de la Vega, and Manuel Vázquez, all residents of Cuatitlán, were accordingly employed to look after the stock and were paid one hundred and twenty-eight *pesos* for services rendered during sixty-four days. This assistance was provided to give a period of complete rest to the worn-out colonists before they started on their march to distant Texas.[38]

It cost the king two thousand four hundred eighty-nine *pesos* and five *reales* to pay for all the expenses of the prospective settlers during their stay at Cuatitlán. This amount included the rent for the three houses, the daily allowance given to each member of the party, medical attention furnished to the sick, medicines, shrouds for the dead, the payment of caretakers for the horses, and the fee paid to the guard that escorted them from Veracruz to Mexico City. The accounts presented by the *Alcalde Mayor* were finally approved by the viceroy on December 20, 1730, and the reimbursement made to him on April 16, 1731.[39]

Route followed from Cuatitlán to Saltillo. While the Canary Islanders were resting in Cuatitlán, the viceroy was busy making the final arrangements for their transportation to the Presidio of San Antonio de Béjar, where they were to establish an independent municipality, as advised by Brigadier Don Pedro de Rivera and endorsed by the *Auditor* Oliván Rebolledo. At the request of Casafuerte, Rivera had presented an itinerary that might be followed from Cuatitlán to Saltillo, where the families were to rest once more while the escort that was to conduct them to the San Antonio River arrived from the Presidio of Coahuila at Monclova. This matter was referred to Oliván Rebolledo, who, on October 31, 1730, gave his opinion.

---

[37]Recibos de gastos. *A. G. N., Provincias Internas,* Vol. 32.

[38]Recibo de los cuatro hombres que cuidaron los Cabos. 128 pp. *A. G. N., Provincias Internas,* Vol. 32.

[39]Informe del Factor de esta. R. Caja. *A. G. N., Provincias Internas,* Vol. 32.

According to the recommendations of Rivera, the ten families from the Canary Islands, which were by this time fifteen, because of the marriages that had taken place, were to be conducted to Saltillo by Francisco Duval. He had executed a similar commission most successfully in taking them from Veracruz to Mexico. It was planned that he should set out from Cuatitlán on November 15 and proceed to Tepejé del Río, which was to be his first stop. From here he was to continue to San Francisco, and from there he was to make daily marches to the following stations: Ruano, San Juan del Río, Los Colotillos Chicos, Amascala, Puerto Pinto, Las Carboneras, San Luis de la Paz, Sauceda de los Mulatos, Valle de San Francisco, San Luis Potosí, Las Bocas, La Hedionda, El Venado, Laguna Seca, Arroyo Seco, Mateguala, Cedral, Pozo Nuevo, Agua Dulce, Cieneguilla, La Encarnación, Agua Nueva, and Saltillo. This provided for twenty-five marches, covering a distance of about one hundred and sixty leagues. The little troupe was to be allowed four extra days to provide for unforeseen circumstances which might delay their progress.

The *Auditor* declared the distance indicated could be easily traveled as outlined. He pointed out that it would be well to allow each person four *reales* a day for traveling expenses, which would amount to eight hundred and twelve *pesos* for the twenty-nine days required to make the trip. This amount should be paid to the Conductor, Francisco Duval, that he might secure the necessary supply of meat, flour, and other necessities for the entire group while on the road. Duval should be paid at the rate of five *pesos* a day for his services and the amount of pay which corresponded to the twenty-nine days should be likewise paid to him in advance.

The *Alcalde Mayor* of Cuatitlán should be instructed to make formal delivery to the conductor of the families placed under his care, using the list made on September 9, for that purpose, and taking care to note those who died since their arrival at Cuatitlán and those who had been born. He should also turn over all the horses and beasts of burden, the tents, tools, and all other equipment bought for the use of the new settlers. Complete list of these items should be drawn up before a notary public.

It would be well, furthermore, to notify the *Alcalde Mayores* of Guicapa, Querétaro, San Luis de la Paz, San Luis Potosí, El Venado, Charcas and Saltillo, through whose jurisdictions the party was to travel, so that each and every one of them might render to Francisco Duval such assistance as he might need in the fulfillment of his commission. These officials should be instructed to assist the conductor and the families in every way possible and to see that such supplies as they might require along the road, were furnished at the most convenient price.

The conductor should be given full power to use discretion as to the distance to be traveled each day and to lengthen the stops in accordance with the circumstances. Should a rest of more than a day be required, he should use his judgment. Although the daily journeys outlined were not long for ordinary travel, the fact that many women and children were among the group, might make it necessary to take more than a day to cover some of the distances suggested. Furthermore, sickness and other unforeseen accidents, common to families when on a long march, might necessitate a change in the itinerary.[40]

Instructions for the conveyance of the settlers. The viceroy was satisfied with the recommendations made by Rivera and the suggestions of the *Auditor*. On November 8, he ordered the *Alcalde Mayor* of Cuatitlán to turn over the families placed under his care, designed to settle in Texas, to Francisco Duval, making a careful list of every person. At the same time Duval was informed that he must make all the arrangements necessary to start on November 15 from Cuatitlán and that he should follow the itinerary as outlined by Rivera and the *Auditor,* exercising his judgment while on the road as to the length of each day's journey. He was instructed to conduct not only the settlers, but all their baggage, equipment, tools, and other belongings. The list of the persons in the party and an inventory of all goods in transit should be furnished by him to Captain Mathías de Aguirre in Saltillo, who was ordered to take charge of them at that place.[41]

On the same day he notified the *Alcalde Mayores* and the *Justicias* of the various jurisdictions along the route to be followed by the Canary Islanders of the orders issued for their conveyance to Texas. Each one of them was enjoined to furnish Francisco Duval all supplies which he might need and to help him to house the travelers properly at each stop within their jurisdictions. He informed them that although the itinerary called for only twenty-five days in which to make the trip, he had

[40]Parecer del Auditor, October 31, 1730. *A. G. N., História,* Vol. 84.
[41]Acuerdo del Virrey, November 8, 1730. *A. G. N., História,* Vol. 84.

decided to allow him as many as thirty-three, permitting him to use his discretion in making longer or shorter stops than those indicated.[42]

As ordered by the viceroy, the ten original families and the five recently married couples, making a total of fifteen, with fifty-six persons, started out from Cuatitlán on November 15, 1730, under the care of Francisco Duval, who took charge of all the arrangements for the journey to Saltillo. The five new families were Francisco Arocha and his wife, Juana Curbelo; Vicente Alvarez Travieso and his wife, María Curbelo; Antonio Rodríguez and his wife, Josefa de Nis; José Leal and his wife, Ana Santos; and Juan Delgado and his wife, Catarina Leal.[43] The rest of the settlers have already been listed.

While the brave little band traveled to Saltillo, the viceroy gave instructions as to their reception, the continuation of their journey to the San Antonio, and their final settlement. On November 28, he issued detailed instructions to Captain Mathías Aguirre, at Saltillo, stating what he should do in preparation for the arrival of the fifteen families. He informed him that it had been decided that as soon as ten soldiers from the Presidio of Coahuila at Monclova arrived in Saltillo as ordered, to escort the settlers, they should be ready to start for the Presidio of San Antonio de Béxar. Still under the guidance of Francisco Duval, the official conductor, they should proceed, as soon as practicable, to their final destination along the following route: from Saltillo they were directed to go to the Hacienda de Santa María and to continue from there, traveling from day to day to Hacienda de las Mesillas, el Despoblado de Anelo, Espinazo de Ambrosio, La Hoya, Charco Redondo, Castaño, Presidio de Coahuila (Monclova). Here they should rest for three days. Resuming their march, they should continue to Las Adjuntas, Alamo Viejo, Río de Salinas, Arroyo de Calzones, Ojo de San Diego, and the Presidio de San Juan Bautista. The Captain of this presidio would be responsible for the escort that was ordered to accompany the travelers to San Antonio de Béjar. After two days' rest at this post, they should be escorted by the captain in person as far as the Río Grande. He should also see that they encountered no difficulty in crossing the stream. It would be better for the party to pitch its camp across the

[42]Para que las Justicias de los Partidos por donde ha de Transitar Francisco Duval, con las diez familias (15), que van á Poblar á los Texas, de el auxilio que se le pidiere para su comodo transporte. *A. G. N., História,* Vol. 84.

[43]List of settlers made on November 14, 1730, at Cuatitlán, on the eve of their departure. *A. G. N., Provincias Internas,* Vol. 32.

river. On the following day, the travelers should continue to Rosas de San Juan, Caramanchelito, Charcos de la Tortuga, Río Frío, Arroyo Hondo, Charco de la Pita, Arroyo de los Payayas, and Presidio de San Antonio de Béjar, their ultimate destination. The conductor was to be allowed discretion in following the itinerary outlined.

Captain Aguirre was notified that the fifteen families, consisting of fifty-six persons, had set out from Cuatitlán on November 15, and that they were now on the way. He was, therefore, told to make haste in preparing for their reception. He was instructed to secure a supply of meat and flour sufficient for their needs in traveling from Saltillo to San Antonio de Béjar, in accord with the itinerary outlined. He was authorized to get, also, fifteen *metates* with the corresponding pestles, to grind corn, and thirty trained oxen from his *hacienda,* in order that each family might have a yoke with which to cultivate their farms. The oxen were to be sent to San Antonio with the first herd of cattle that might enter the province.

He was ordered further to provide for everything the party might need during their stay in Saltillo, while waiting for the arrival of the military escort from Monclova, which was to accompany them on their way to San Antonio. He was told to practice the strictest economy, however, in making all the necessary arrangements, keeping in mind that each member of the party had been assigned an allowance of four *reales* a day for their maintenance. He was to be responsible for supplies needed by the colonists while in Saltillo and all that was necessary for the continuation of their trip to their final destination. According to the itinerary, it would take them twenty-three days for the journey, but ten extra days were to be allowed in making the calculations for the supplies they would require and to take care of their unforeseen or unavoidable delays. He was authorized to furnish Francisco Duval nine hundred twenty-four *pesos* worth of supplies or specie, which was the equivalent of the allowance made to the families for the thirty-three days, at the rate of four *reales* each per day. In addition to this amount he was ordered to give the conductor one hundred sixty-five *pesos,* which was equivalent to his allowance for the same length of time at the rate of five *pesos* a day. The families and the conductor should determine how much should be supplied in commodities and how much in specie.

Captain Aguirre was also to see that the settlers had with them all the things that had been given them before they left Cuatitlán, checking every item with the official list sent to him. He was required to make a copy of this list, and after having checked it with all care, he was to send it on to the Governor of Texas, together with such things as he furnished to the colonists at Saltillo in order that the governor might be able to do the same upon their arrival in San Antonio de Béjar. The conductor was to deliver the families, their baggage, tools, tents, horses, and other belongings to the Governor of Texas, or in his absence to the Captain of the Presidio of San Antonio de Béjar, and demand a certified receipt as proof of the fulfillment of his commission.[44]

On the same day, the viceroy issued instructions to the Governors of Nuevo Reyno de León and Coahuila, and all the *Justícias* through whose jurisdictions the Canary Islanders would pass on their route to Texas from Saltillo, to give all aid and assistance to the conductor and the party, "desirous that they should have all the comfort and facilities possible in the course of their journey."[45] He reminded them that whatever they did in the matter was for the best interests of the royal service.

Instructions to the Governor of Texas for the care of the settlers. Orders were sent to Juan Antonio de Bustillo, Governor of the Province of Texas, which, in his absence, must be executed by the Captain of the Presidio of San Antonio de Béjar, for him to provide for all the wants of the fifteen families, immediately upon their arrival at their final destination. He was instructed that an allowance of four *reales* a day had been granted to each person for a year, until they were able to cultivate the land, plant, and harvest their first crop. He should supply them with flour, meat, corn, and any other thing they might need for their daily maintenance, but the cost of these provisions were not to exceed four *reales* a day. The time during which they were to receive this aid was to be reckoned from the day they arrived in the presidio. All supplies furnished them were to be charged at the prices fixed by the regulations for the internal presidios, the same as if the goods were intended for the soldiers.

In addition to the daily allowances, he was told to give the settlers, when it was time to plant, the seed necessary for sowing their fields.

---

[44]Para q el Capitán Dn. Mathías de Aguirre Vezino del Saltillo tenga prevenido todo lo q necesitaren las quinze familias quando lleguen allí, y van a poblar a los Texas . . . November 28, 1730. *A. G. N., História,* Vol. 84.

[45]Para que los Governadores del nuevo Reyno de León y Coaguyla, y demas Justícias de los parages por donde Transitare Francisco Dubal, conductor de las quince famílias que van a los Texas, le den el auxílio que les pidiere. *A. G. N., História,* Vol. 84.

It was suggested that he give them wheat, corn, beans, chick peas, peas, pumpkin, chile, pimento, and such other grain and vegetables as it was necessary to plant in the region. These should be furnished to each head of a family, who was to cultivate his farm with the aid of the yoke of oxen sent by Captain Aguirre from Saltillo for that purpose. All seeds for planting were to be charged to the families at the cheapest price possible and an accurate account of everything kept, in order that this might be presented to the royal treasury for payment. The captain of the presidio should see that when the season for planting came, the families cultivated the land and practiced all diligence in raising their first crop, in order that by the second year, they might be able to make their own living without the need of royal aid. He was urged to assign persons who were skilled in the cultivation of the land in this region and who knew the best seasons for planting the different crops to instruct the new settlers and acquaint them with the best methods of agriculture. He was asked to make a full and complete report of everything he did in the execution of the orders received in this regard.[46]

In a separate decree of the same date, the viceroy instructed the Governor, and in his absence the Captain of the Presidio, to make a new list of each member of the party, immediately upon their arrival, noting those who had died on the way or who had been born. A list of those who set out from Cuatitlán was sent to him for this purpose. It was his duty to record the full name of each settler, his parents, the place where he was born, his age, and whether the person was single or married. Similar details were demanded from the parents regarding their children. He was then, by virtue of the viceroy's decree and the provisions of the Laws of the Indies, authorized to declare every one of them *Hijo Dalgo*. Each of the new settlers was entitled to a copy of the decree as proof patent of his title of nobility.

From the heads of the families, the governor or the captain of the presidio, was ordered to select six councilmen *(regidores)*, a sheriff *(alguacil mayor)*, and an official secretary *(escribano de consejo y público)*. He was furthermore to appoint a *mayordomo* or administrator of the public or common lands. These officers were to have the right to

---

[46]Para que el Governador de la Provincia de Texas y en su ausencia el Capitán del Presidio de San Antonio, acuda alas quinze familias, que van á poblar con los bastimentos q hubieren menester á Razón de quatro Reales al dia que goza cada persona, por tiempo de un año, como lo demás que contiene. November 28, 1730. *A. G. N., História,* Vol. 84, Pt. 1.

elect two ordinary *alcaldes* to administer justice. In the selection and appointment of these officers the governor was told to exercise his serious judgment and try to choose those who were best fitted for the purpose, as their appointment and election was for life. He should attend their first meeting in person in order to install them officially in their offices and to take their oath. He was instructed to send a certified copy of the appointments and election to the viceroy for their confirmation and approval. The governor was directed to preside at the election of the *alcaldes* in order to teach them how an election should be conducted.[47]

Since the municipality to be established by the Canary Islanders was to be the first civil settlement in the province of Texas, the viceroy declared it was his wish and desire that it should be designated a *ciudad* (city) and become the capital of the province. At this time, however, he was undetermined as to what should be its name and left the space blank where this information should be inserted. The act of foundation should be sent to him in order that this might be forwarded to the king for his confirmation and the assignment of a coat of arms.[48]

Further instructions were sent to the governor, ordering him to lodge the fifteen families in the houses of the presidio, immediately upon their arrival, where they were to remain until they were able to build their own homes. He was told to place their horses, oxen, and other stock in the pasture lands used by the animals that belonged to the soldiers, but they were not to be mixed indiscriminately either with those of the garrison or of other persons living in the vicinity of the presidio. He should see that experienced herders went out with the new settlers to show them where the best pasture lands were and how far from the post they could graze their stock without exposing it to the ravages of the Indians. In this manner the Canary Islanders could learn to take care of their horses and cattle without the need of aid. Both the settlers and all their stock were to be treated with every consideration and given an opportunity to recuperate from the hardships of the long trip. The governor could determine the approximate time of their arrival by keeping in mind that they had set out from Cuatitlán on November 15, and that it would take them about thirty days to reach Saltillo and as many to arrive in San

---

[47]Para que el Govr. de Texas, y en su falta el Capitán del Presidio de Sn. Antonio, haga nueva Reseña delas quince familias, que van a poblar; elección delos sugetos, que han de exercer oficios consejiles, y las demás providencias, que se le previenen en este despacho. November 28, 1730. *A. G. N., Historia*, Vol. 84.

[48]*Ibid.*

Antonio. He should, therefore, prepare the houses where they should be lodged and every provision necessary to supply their immediate wants should be made according to the very definite instructions given by the viceroy.[49]

Instructions for survey of town site. In a long and detailed dispatch, the viceroy gave minute details for the survey of the location where the settlement was to be established and the procedure which was to be followed in distributing the lands assigned to the city. As soon as possible, after the arrival of the Canary Islanders, the governor was directed to examine the land which was immediately to the west of the presidio, about a musket shot's distance. Here, he declared, there should be a low hill which formed a plateau upon which a beautiful city could be laid out. He pointed out that the settlers could go from this location either to the presidial chapel or to the Mission of San José y San Miguel de Aguayo without having to cross the river, in order to comply with their religious duties until they could build a church of their own. Detailed instructions were given for the survey of the central square, on one side of which the church was to be built and on the opposite the *Casas Reales,* with other public buildings, as indicated in the attached plan of the city. From the main entrance of the church as a center, the remainder of the town proper was to be laid in accordance with the prearranged design. Beyond the city, to the north and south of the presidio, the farm lands must be surveyed into plats of approximately equal size in order that these might be distributed among the fifteen families. Still farther away lands suitable for grazing would be located where the colonists could keep their horses and cattle.

The lots in the immediate vicinity of the main square were to be given to the more prominent families. Each of these groups should be placed in possession of its lot and urged to start building a home at as early a date as possible. In the interim, each family could pitch, in the center of the field, its tent with which the head had been supplied. Sufficient areas of land should be laid out not only for the new settlers but for such families as might want to join them. The buildings were required to have symmetry of design and each house should have interior *patios.* Nearby should be placed *corrales* where the horses and other animals might be kept. The homes should be close enough to each other so that in

---

[49]Para que el Governador dela Província delos Texas, y por su ausencia . . . el Capitán del Presidio . . . Reciban las quinze familias . . . les tenga prevenido lo necessario para su substento . . . November 28, 1730. *A. G. N., Historia,* Vol. 84.

case of attack, the dwellers might protect each other; but plenty of room for ventilation should be allowed, so that air currents might enter the different houses from the four cardinal points of the compass. This would make the residences more sanitary.

Each family should be provided with ten ewes and a ram, ten goat does and a buck, five sows and a boar, five mares and a stallion, and five cows and a bull. The governor was authorized to purchase all these animals at the most reasonable price and to include them in the list of supplies furnished to the colonists by order of the king. He was asked to make a complete report of the survey of the lands, their distribution, and all the measures taken in carrying out the orders of the viceroy for his information and approval.[50]

Arrival of Canary Islanders in San Antonio. Notwithstanding the careful calculations of the viceroy and his able advisers, it took the little group of undaunted Canary Islanders from November 15, 1730, to March 9, 1731, finally to reach their destination. On that day, at about eleven o'clock in the morning, the worn-out travelers filed slowly before the Captain of the Presidio of San Antonio de Béjar, after their long and fatiguing march from Mexico City to Texas. Agreeable to the express orders of the viceroy, Captain Juan Antonio de Almazán, received them in person. The conductor, Francisco Duval, presented him with the list of the families and of all the supplies and equipment that they had been given when they set out from Cuatitlán and what they had received from Captain Aguirre at Saltillo. It seems that they did not leave this latter city until January 28, and that it took them forty days to make the trip to San Antonio.

Hardships of the march. Nothing gives a better idea of the hardships of the journey than the report of the number of exhausted or jaded horses left by each family on the roadside. Juan Leal Goraz declared that he had everything which he had received as equipment, except the horses that had been given to him. He had left all of them, worn-out at various places along the way. Juan Curbelo lost ten horses in the same manner. Juan Leal, Jr., stated he was forced to abandon thirteen horses for the same reason. Antonio Santos lost a bridle and a quilt, which

---

[50]Para que el Governador de Texas; y en su ausencia el Capitán del Presidio de Sn. Antonio, Reconosca el Parage donde ha de fundarse la Poblazón a que han ido las quince familias, lo mida, deslinde, y Reparta . . . November 28, 1730. *A. G. N., História,* Vol. 84.

were stolen and he had to leave thirteen horses on the road because they were too tired to continue the march. José Padrón lost three horses; Manuel de Nis, five; Vicente Alvarez Travieso, six; Salvador Rodríguez, seven; Francisco Arocha, seven; Antonio Rodríguez, five; José Leal, four; Juan Delgado, who married after leaving Mexico, two; José Cabrera, who married on the road, six; María Rodríguez, widow, thirteen; Mariana Melean, widow, eight; and the four bachelors, eleven. The little band lost one hundred and twenty-five horses in all as the result of the fatigue of the trip. They declared that they had received at Cuatitlán two axes, two roasting irons, two cutlasses, two crowbars, ten hack saws, carpenter's adzes, ten chisels, ten harrows tipped with steel, ten *comales,* and twelve tents with all the necessary poles and attachments. Before leaving the Canary Islands they had been given eleven crowbars, twenty-four cutlasses, twelve roasting irons, eighteen axes, and twelve harrows. These comprised all the tools that were furnished them. All of these things were checked and distributed again to the families.[51]

On the following day, Captain Almazán officially reported that pursuant to the orders of His Excellency, he had lodged the fifteen families in the best houses of the soldiers. He remarked, however, that this arrangement had placed the garrison at great inconvenience, but that since the measure was temporary, the men were glad to comply with the instructions. With regard to the horses, he informed the viceroy that he had been obliged to corral them with those of the presidio because the new settlers were so physically weak at the time that they could not help take care of them in separate droves. To divide the guard of fifteen soldiers assigned to watch the presidial horses, in order to keep those of the settlers distinct, would be to expose both to the wiles of the Indians. The cows, oxen, and other stock they brought were permitted to graze in the best lands in the neighborhood of the presidio, but they could not be taken too far away because of the great danger of theft by the Indians, who still committed many depredations at and near San Antonio. He assured the viceroy that he had taken steps to supply the new settlers with everything they needed for their maintenance as instructed,

---

[51]Testimonio de Autos y diligencias executadas en Virtud de Despacho del Exmo Señor Virrey de esta nueva España . . . March 9, 1731. *A. G. N., Provincias Internas,* Vol. 32, Pt. 2.

and that he would carry out all the other orders as soon as it was practicable.[52]

Of the fifty-six persons that set out, only one died en route at San Juan Bautista. This was María Rodríguez Granadillo, a little girl five years old. The rest of the party arrived in good health in spite of the long and toilsome march. Agreeable to the orders of the viceroy, a careful list of each one of them, with their full name, the names of their parents, the place where they were born, and all the other information requested, was made on July 18, 1731. On the following day Captain Almazán summoned all the new settlers before him and read to them the decree of the viceroy of November 28, 1730, by virtue of which he now declared them *Hijos Dalgo,* persons of noble lineage, entitled to all the honors and preëminences granted by His Majesty to those who founded new settlements and to their descendants and heirs *in perpetuum.* To the grant of these honors and distinctions all of them replied by giving thanks to the king with all humility for the singular favors bestowed upon them through the viceroy. Thus by this ceremony the fifty-five original settlers of the new *villa,* which was officially called San Fernando de Béxar, were made *Hijos Dalgo,* knights of nobility, entitled to all the privileges, dignity, and prerogatives granted the Hidalgos of Castile.[53]

Agreeable to the detailed instructions of the viceroy for the actual survey and distribution of the lands for the establishment of the new civil settlement in the Province of Texas, the governor declared, on the same day that the Canary Islanders arrived, that he was ready to carry out the commands. He consequently read the decree and ordered that it be put into execution at the earliest possible moment. But he pointed out immediately afterwards, that it was not possible to proceed at this time to the exploration, survey, and distribution of the lands designated and chosen for the purpose for several reasons. He stated that the site to the west of the presidio lacked an irrigation ditch to supply the families and the proposed town with the necessary water, and although it was not impossible to build the *acequia,* this would require time and labor. It was far more important to prepare the farm lands for cultivation, this being the best season for the planting of corn, than to attempt to sur-

[52]Auto en q se da razón de haver ospedado alos Ysleños y otras providencias. March 10, 1731. *A. G. N., Provincias Internas*, Vol. 32, Pt. 2.

[53]Diligencias y Declaración de su nobleza y Ydalguia. July 18 and 19, 1731. *A. G. N., Provincias Internas,* Vol. 32, Pt. 2.

vey the new town site. The raising of a crop was essential to the maintenance of the new settlers. In the meantime, he had ordered the families to be lodged in the houses of the soldiers where they were fairly
comfortable.[54]

On March 12, 1731, Captain Juan Antonio de Almazán summoned
all the heads of families to appear before him. In their company and in
that of others who were already established in the vicinity of the presidio, he proceeded to investigate personally the spring which formed
the stream generally called the Arroyo (San Pedro Creek). He examined
all the land that lies between the San Antonio River and the San Pedro.
The families agreed to divide all the lands roughly among them, without the formality of being officially given possession individually, leaving this act for a time when they might be able to survey the land with
more care. Three days later, in accord with the agreement made on the
12th, the Captain went out with all the heads of families to the lands
north and south of the presidio and distributed among them all the
arable portions which already had been cleared by those who first established themselves near the presidio. They immediately set about to plow
the fields and to clear more land, being urged and encouraged in their
labors by the governor.[55]

The fields having been made ready to plant corn and other grains
and cereals, the governor urged the settlers to plant as much as they
could on June 30. They willingly responded to the call and each one
exerted himself so that about twenty-two bushels of corn were sown, as
well as some beans, oats, cotton, melons, chile, watermelons, pumpkins,
and other vegetables. Not only had they planted all these various seeds,
but they had been successful in transplanting a number of fruit trees
which they had brought from the Province of Coahuila. Notwithstanding the scarcity of rain, all the fields of corn and other grains looked
well, and there was promise of a plentiful crop.

The official establishment of San Fernando. By July 2, the new
settlers had gathered their fruitful harvests from the fertile fields they
had worked so well and faithfully in the spring. They could now give
their time and attention to the actual establishment of the villa ordered

---

[54]Acta de Fundación de la Villa San Fernando. This interesting and singular
document is in Guadalajara, in the State Public Library, where the writer made a
photostat copy of it in 1931. Most of the remainder of the reference will be to
this document which will be closely followed.

[55]*Ibid.*

by the viceroy. The captain of the presidio ordered each family to prepare ten stakes and to haul two cartloads of large rocks collectively to
the site designated for the founding of the new Villa of San Fernando.
When this had been done, he went, with the colonists, to the table-land
chosen by the viceroy for the establishment of the proposed town, which
was found to be about the distance of a musket shot from the presidio
to the west. Once on the ground, a site was chosen for the church and
the public square, and with the aid of a sun dial and a fifty-*vara* chain,
a line running from southwest to northeast was determined. Using this
as a base, the survey was begun. Taking the center of the main entrance
to the church as a starting point, a line was run in a northeasterly direction for a distance of two hundred *varas,* or six hundred feet, as ordered
by the viceroy and as indicated by the map. At the end of the line a
marker was placed where the *Casa Real* was to be erected directly opposite to the church across the square. Another line was run at right angles
from the center of the church for one hundred and thirty-three *varas*
and two equal squares were marked off with heavy rocks and stakes. The
center of the plaza was indicated by a large rock, as were also the four
corners; while the streets, which were forty feet wide, were set off by
stakes. The perimeter of the plaza was delineated with the aid of a
plow and it measured two hundred *varas* in length and one hundred and
thirty-three and a third *varas* in width, including the width of the streets.
The laying out and surveying the plaza and the squares on which the
church and the *Casa Real* were to be placed, consumed all the day.[56]

The following day, July 3, Captain Almazán, accompanied by the
principal families, went out to continue the survey of the previous
evening. Beginning on the northwest side of the plaza, two lots were
surveyed, one for the customshouse and another for one of the most
prominent families. Two similar lots were then marked off on the opposite side; that is, the southeast; each of them two hundred and forty
feet, or eighty *varas* square, designed for homes of the settlers. The
intervening streets were marked by heavy stakes, allowing thirteen and
a third *varas* or forty feet for each, and placing large rocks on the corners and centers of the lots. This consumed the entire day and the operations were suspended until the following morning.

On July 4, Captain Almazán and the heads of the principal families

[56]Acta de Fundación de la Villa de San Fernando. Photostat copy in the possession
of the writer. All the remainder of the descriptions concerning the survey and distribution of the lands are based on this document.

repaired to the location of the new town which was being surveyed. There he continued the laying out of lots and marked off thirteen additional home sites. Each one was eighty *varas* square, or two hundred and forty feet, with a street forty feet wide between them. The lots immediately adjoining the church and the *Casa Real* on opposite sides of the square were three hundred and twenty feet square. The corners and centers of each lot were further delineated by making a deep furrow with a plow along its boundaries as suggested in the order of the viceroy.

The following day the survey was resumed. This time, taking a cord fifty *varas* long, a line was drawn from the center of the main entrance of the proposed church, due northeast, for a distance of one thousand and ninety-three *varas*. Here a hole was dug and a large boulder placed to indicate the terminal. Returning to the starting point, a similar line of equal length was run due southwest and its end was marked in the same manner. Returning to the center of the door of the church, another line was run at right angles to the northwest, for one thousand and ninety-three *varas,* where another boulder was placed to show the spot. This line was extended from center in the opposite direction; that is to the southeast, for a similar distance and another stone placed where the line ended. Thus a large cross was formed with the main entrance of the church as the radiating point. By completing each of the four squares of the four sides of the cross a perfect larger square two thousand one hundred eighty-six *varas* on each side was delineated, the corners of which were identified by four long rocks as markers. A deep furrow was then plowed along its perimeter from corner to corner to indicate the exact boundary of the town site surveyed in accord with the instructions of the viceroy.

Going then to the northeast extremity of the original cross formed by the two center lines of the town site, this was prolonged for a distance of one thousand nine hundred twelve and three-fourths *varas*. At this point a hole was dug in the ground and a large stone placed there to mark the spot. This was destined to be the boundary of the *ejido* or town common. Captain Almazán, accompanied by the settlers, now went to the northwest extremity of the cross and from the stone placed at that point, extended the line for a distance of one thousand six hundred thirty-nine and one-half *varas* and marked the end in the same manner as before. He then went to the third extremity of the cross on the southwest and extended this line in the same direction for one thousand nine hundred twelve and three-fourths *varas,* marking the spot as before. In surveying the town common, he was unable to follow the exact instructions given by the viceroy, as he had done in the case of the town site because there was no room to extend the line on the southeast side. The one thousand ninety-three *varas* of the city had carried the boundary to the San Antonio River in this direction, and since this stream formed the boundary between the mission lands of San Antonio de Valero, located on the east side of the river, it was impossible to lay out in this direction the corresponding part of the *ejido* or town common. Because of this fact Captain Almazán increased the length of the lines on the other three sides, to allow for the additional land designated in the original order.

On July 6, Captain Almazán and the Canary Islanders undertook to continue the survey and to mark off the pasture lands for the cattle, horses, and other stock, in accord with the instruction of the viceroy. But as in the case of the *ejido,* it was impossible to carry out the survey as indicated because there was no room for further extension to the southeast. Consequently, it became necessary to add a corresponding amount of land on the three remaining sides to make up the area designated. Beginning at the farthest extremity of the central cross on the northeast side, a line was run in the same general direction with a fifty-*vara* chain, for three thousand eight hundred twenty-five and one-half *varas*. Having placed a large stone at this point as a permanent marker, the line was extended from its farthest extremity in the opposite direction for an equal distance to the southwest, where a large stone was buried in the ground to indicate the exact spot of limit. This was directly opposite to the crossing of the San Pedro at the place known as El Paso de los Nogalitos. From here they went to the third extremity of the central cross on the northwest, from where the line was extended for three thousand three hundred sixty-eight *varas* and an adequate marker placed. In this manner the area intended for pasture lands was properly surveyed. They were roughly bounded as follows: on the northeast, they extended from the head of the main spring of the San Antonio River, along a straight line to the Arroyo del Novillo, hence to the west to the Real of Nicolás Hernández, which lies slightly to the northwest, hence to the south along the Llano del León and the Real de la Escaramuza to the place known as Los Jacalitos, hence to the east northeast to the Paso de los Nogalitos, where the survey closes. To the east are the farm lands which extend as far as the San Antonio River, which runs from north to south.

Having completed the survey as ordered by the viceroy, Captain Almazán publicly declared one-fifth of all the pasture lands belonged to the Villa de San Fernando *in perpetuum*. The revenue or rent derived from the lands thus set aside was to be used to pay the cost of the administration of the city and of all public festivals and functions undertaken or ordered by the city council. He then declared the boundaries of the public lands of the villa to be as follows: on the south side of the city they began on the end of the *ejido* lands and extended as far as the Paso de los Nogalitos, hence to the west southwest to La Lagunilla where a corner or angle is formed, hence north across the Llano del León and La Escaramuza to the Real de Nicolás Hernández, where another corner is located, and hence to the east to the end of the survey. The fifth part of the farm and irrigable lands would later be set aside in a similar manner and for the same purpose.

In sumarizing the limits of the new city of San Fernando, with its *ejido,* farm lands, pastures, and public lands, Captain Almazán declared that on the east side it was bounded by the San Antonio River, on the west Arroyo de León, on the south by the lands of the Mission of San José and Paso de los Nogalitos, and on the north by Arroyo Salado.[57]

Provisions made for a parish priest. It would have been strange indeed if, after having made such careful provision for the physical welfare of the colonists, and the survey and distribution of the lands of the new municipality, the viceroy should have failed to provide for the spiritual welfare of the Canary Islanders. At the same time that the minute details for their transportation to distant Texas were prepared, and the precise orders for their reception and establishment were issued, the Marquis of Casafuerte wrote a letter to the Bishop of Guadalajara, in whose ecclesiastical jurisdiction the new settlement was being founded, to request that he send a priest to look after their religious faith and practices. After stating that it was most important for their consolation that they should have some one to administer to them the Holy Sacraments, he begged the Right Reverend Doctor Nicolás Carlos Gómez de Cervantes, Bishop of Guadalajara and member of the Council of His Majesty, to appoint a parish priest from the Oratory of the Oblate Clerics of San Carlos, well

---

[57]The facts summarized in the foregoing paragraphs constitute the original survey of the present city of San Antonio and could serve in identifying the original boundaries of the Villa de San Fernando. They have been carefully outlined from the *Acta de Fundación* previously cited, a photostat copy of which is in the possession of the writer.

known for their virtues, their piety, their wisdom, and their zeal in the service of God and the salvation of souls, to proceed to the Presidio of San Antonio de Béjar, where a new colony was about to be established by fifty-six settlers who had come from the Canary Islands for that purpose. It should be his duty to administer all the sacred rites of the Church to them. He should be appointed parish priest *(cura)* of the new villa which was being founded there and should be designated vicar and ecclesiastical judge. He begged the bishop to grant the appointee as his delegate full power of dispensation in all cases which could not be submitted to his episcopal decisions, because of the long distance to the remote settlement.

The parish priest selected in accord with the request of the viceroy, was to be assigned four hundred *pesos* a year, out of the royal treasury, for his maintenance. This amount was equivalent to the salary allowed the *alférez* or ensign of the presidio, and would be granted to him from the day he set out for Texas until the parish revenue was sufficient for his livelihood. He should be instructed to submit certified proof of the date of his departure so that his allowance might be paid by the officers of the royal treasury from that time on. Furthermore, he should be given authority to minister not only to the Canary Islanders but to all such as might come to settle in the new municipality or who now reside in the vicinity. The bishop was asked to notify the viceroy of the appointment in order that he might issue the corresponding instructions to the governor of the province who should arrange for the priest's reception and give him such aid as he might need.[58]

Establishment of the first civil government.   There now remains to be treated only the establishment of the official government of the new municipality on the banks of the San Antonio River. After the survey of the lands was completed, and the new settlers had been put in possession of their lands and declared *Hijos Dalgo,* Captain Almazán proceeded to carry out the instructions of the viceroy concerning the selection and appointment of the members of the city council and the other officers. On July 20, 1731, he officially appointed Juan Leal Goraz, the oldest of the settlers and the one who had acted as their leader and spokesman ever since they left their island homes, first *regidor,* or councilman. The captain

---

[58]De ruego y encargo para que el Ylustressimo Señor Obispo de Guadalaxara, elija Vn Clérigo de aquella Ciudad, que pase a la nueva Poblazón, que ha de fundarse en el Presidio de San Antonio de Vejar, y administre los Santos Sacramentos, con las demás facultades que se previenen. November 28, 1730. *A. G. N., História,* Vol. 84.

declared that the appointee was fully qualified, because of his experience and knowledge, to fill this important position, and ordered all the settlers to respect and honor him as such. Subject to the final approval of the viceroy, he was to enjoy all the honors and prerogatives of his office for life. In the same manner and by virtue of the authority conferred upon him by the viceroy, Almazán appointed Juan Curbelo, second councilman; Antonio Santos, third; Salvador Rodríguez, fourth; Manuel de Nis, fifth, and Juan Leal, Jr., sixth. To each of these, he extended an official appointment and sent a copy of all the proceedings to the viceroy for his approval.[59]

On the same day, he appointed Vicente Alvarez Travieso, who seems to have shown evidence of leadership from the day he joined the little band of settlers at Cuatitlán, as sheriff *(alguacil mayor)*, declaring that he possessed the requisites required for the position. He was to receive such remuneration for the execution of the various duties of his office as the justices or *alcaldes* might assign him. The *regidores* were merely honorary positions with no salaries attached; but that of *alguacil mayor* usually carried the benefit of fees. A copy of the appointment was to be sent to the viceroy for his confirmation.[60]

The friend of Travieso was appointed to the most important office of secretary and notary public. Captain Almazán declared that Francisco de Arocha, being one of the most prominent settlers and having the qualifications required for this delicate office, had been chosen to fill the position. All documents drawn up by him were to be given full credit, as prescribed by the Laws of the Indies, and he should be compensated for his work in accord with the established tariff for legal documents.[61]

The appointment of *Mayordomo de los Propios* (administrator of the public lands) fell to Antonio Rodríguez. He was told to keep a separate book in which he was required to set down the amount or amounts received as rent or the sale of products raised in the public lands set aside for the benefit of the government of the Villa de San Fernando. He should have no authority, however, to spend or distribute any of the money thus received, either in part or as a whole, without the consent of the *Cabildo* (city council), to which body he was responsible and must make an annual report of all moneys received and spent, for its approval.[62]

---

[59]Titulos de Regidores, July 20, 1731. *A. G. N., Provincias Internas,* Vol. 32, Pt. a.

[60]Titulo de Alguacil Mayor. In *Ibid.*

[61]Titulo de Escribano de Consejo y ppco. In *Ibid.*

[62]Titulo de Mayordomo de los proprios. In *Ibid.*

First election in Texas. But the crowning event of the settlement of the new municipality of San Fernando was the first election held in Texas to designate the first two *alcaldes ordinarios* (justices of the peace). On August 1, 1731, agreeable to the orders of the viceroy, Captain Juan Antonio Pérez de Almazán summoned the six *regidores,* the *alguacil mayor,* the *escribano de consejo,* and the *mayordomo de propios* recently appointed, to appear before him for the first meeting of the *cabildo* of the Villa de San Fernando. Having all gathered in the home of Captain Almazán, for there was as yet no *cabildo* building erected, the said officer explained to them that the purpose of the meeting was to elect two *alcaldes,* as ordered by the viceroy. But this act must be preceded by each one taking the oath of office. Beginning with the first councilman, every member stood up in turn, and made the sign of the cross with the right hand. They all solemnly swore to fulfill the duties of their respective positions faithfully and loyally, without using their authority for selfish aims, and to act always in harmony. After this ceremony, they all sat down and proceeded to the election of the two *alcaldes.* It was declared that there were no possible candidates for the two offices, outside of those in the *Cabildo,* but each one of the members expressed his unwillingness to nominate or vote for himself. After some discussion, it was greed, however, to present the names of Juan Leal Goraz and Juan Curbelo for the first *alcalde,* and Salvador Rodríguez and Manuel de Nis for the second. Having named the candidates, they proceeded to ballot for the first *alcalde* and when the votes were counted, Juan Leal Goraz was declared elected first *alcalde* by a majority of the *Cabildo.* In the second balloting, Salvador Rodríguez received a majority of the votes for second *alcalde* and was declared elected. Captain Almazán, who presided at the election, proclaimed the two successful candidates legally elected, and approved the proceedings as having been conducted properly. He thereupon delivered to each of the newly-chosen officers the insignia of their office and authorized them to proceed to the execution of the duties as the *alcaldes* of the new Villa of San Fernando de Béxar. A copy of the minutes of the meeting, of the official appointments of all the members of the *cabildo,* and of the returns of the elections of the two *alcaldes* was ordered sent to the viceroy for his final approval and confirmation and the first meeting of the new municipality adjourned.[63]

The viceroy approved the appointments and the elections and on October 24, 1731, ordered ten patents for each and every one of the new officers,

---

[63]Auto de Elecciónes. In *Ibid.*

to be drawn and sent to them in the name of himself and the king. Thus the first civil settlement in the Province of Texas was at last established and the officers of the first municipality legally and officially recognized by the highest authority in New Spain. What the course of events might have been if the remainder of the two hundred Canary Island families had been permitted to come to settle in the Province of Texas, in groups or ten or twelve at a time, will ever remain a conjecture. There is no question, however, that the abandonment of the plan so soon after it had been put into execution stunted the growth of the little colony established on the banks of the San Antonio, and doomed the unfortunate settlers to many hardships and privations which would have been avoided in part, had the civilian population been reënforced periodically until its number had reached approximately a thousand, as was intended in the original order of the king of February 14, 1729.

CHAPTER IX

EARLY EXPLORATION OF THE BIG BEND COUNTRY FROM EL PASO TO SAN JUAN BAUTISTA, 1683-1731

Most historians of Texas have consistently ignored the vast area that lies between the old Presidio of San Juan Bautista on the Río Grande, in the neighborhood of present day Eagle Pass, and the Presidio del Paso del Norte, better known today as Juarez. More than five hundred miles of almost impassable hills and mountains separated the two outposts on the Río Grande, one on the road that connected the new Province of Texas to the settled regions of New Spain, and the other on the highway to the Province of New Mexico. About half way between the two presidios, at La Junta de los Rios, where the Conchos joins the Río Grande, a series of six missions was established mainly on the west or south side of the river about the close of the seventeenth century. Before the end of the first quarter of the eighteenth century, however, strenuous efforts were being made to find a route that would connect both San Juan Bautista and El Paso del Norte with the new establishments at La Junta de los Rios. The chief interest of Spanish officials in this vast region was not gold, or treasures, or mythical kingdoms, but the more practical purpose of putting a stop to the frequent incursions of the numerous savage tribes that lived in this area, who preyed habitually upon the frontier settlements of Coahuila, Nuevo Reyno de León, and Chihuahua. It will be seen in the course of this chapter, that the officials of New Spain fully realized the strategic importance of extending their influence over this region, while the missionaries saw, in the numerous tribes that lived here, a chosen field for their zealous Christian endeavors.

It is true that the area between the Junta de los Rios and the Presidio del Paso del Norte has not generally been considered by historians of the Spanish Southwest to be a part of Texas. This accounts for their neglect of its history. But since it is a part of the State today, it is unfair to continue to ignore it. Generally associated with the Province of New Mexico, it has received little or no attention up to the present, although the curtain of history rises in this region long before it does in the lower Río Grande in the vicinity of San Juan Bautista. As early as 1683, a formal attempt to explore a portion of this country was undertaken as the result of the request of the Jumano and Tejas Indians for missionaries to instruct them in the faith.

Request of Jumano Indians for missionaries.   In that year a certain Juan Sabeata, an Indian chief of the Jumano nation, who had journeyed on several occasions from far-away Santa Fe and Chihuahua to the remote province of the Tejas, petitioned the Governor of New Mexico, Captain Domingo Jironza Petris de Cruzate, and the Reverend Father Fray Nicolás López, *Custodio* and Ecclesiastical Judge of New Mexico, to send missionaries to his people. He was joined in his petition by a number of other chiefs of his nation and of the Tejas, all of whom had come expressly for the purpose.[1]

The Mendoza-López Expedition.   Several expeditions had been sent in search of the Jumanos and the Tejas during the preceding fifty years, as well as the mythical kingdom of La Gran Quivira and the Seven Cities of Cíbola. Interest in the fabulous wealth of these kingdoms had not entirely died out, while the missionary desire to bring into the fold of the Church the thousands of misguided souls that roamed the vast unknown regions beyond the Río Grande had been quickened anew by the request of Juan Sabeata and his companions. It was not strange, therefore, that the Governor and the zealous *Custodio* of the Franciscans in New Mexico should have readily acceded to the request. Active preparations for an expedition were begun in the fall and by December 15, 1683, everything was in readiness for the start. The Presidio of El Paso del Norte was wisely chosen as the starting point rather than Santa Fe. The old presidio was on the west or south side of the Río Grande, more or less on the site of the present city of Juarez. About twelve leagues to the south, on the same side of the river was the Mission of San Lorenzo of Manso Indians. It was from here that Juan Domínguez de Mendoza set out with the little band of soldiers and Indian allies to visit the Jumanos and the kingdom of the Tejas. On December 1, fourteen days before, Fathers Nicolás López, Custodio and Vicar General of the Inquisition, and Fray Antonio Acevedo had set out for the Junta de los Rios in advance of the main expedition.

---

[1]Diario y derrotero del mtre. de Campo Juan Domínguez de Mendosa Cavo y Caudillo . . . *A. G. N., Provincias Internas,* Vol. 37, Pt. 2. The diary of this expedition has been translated and published with excellent notes in Bolton, *Spanish Exploration of the Southwest,* 311-343. References to this expedition are also found in the scholarly edition of Benavides *Memorial* of F. W. Hodge, and Hackett, *Pichardo: Limits of Louisiana and Texas.* There is a copy of this diary also in *A. G. N., História,* Vol. 298, where many other related documents are found.

It was not until December 29 that Mendoza overtook them, after he crossed the Río Grande near the *rancherías* of the Julimes.[2]

The entire diary of this expedition is available in English.[3] It is one of the most interesting documents of its kind because few diaries give more vivid or minute details as to the topography of the country, the flora, the fauna, the various tribes encountered, their customs and habits, and the distances traveled each day. But unfortunately, the direction of each day's march is omitted in most of the entries, with only a stray reference here and there. This has given rise to considerable confusion as to the place where the expedition crossed the Río Grande into Texas, what was the course followed from this point until the goal was reached, and what was the route taken on the return march to the Río Grande. The only explanation for the failure to give the general direction in which the expedition traveled day by day may lie in the fact that the country they traversed is so filled with hills and mountains that there are but few courses that can be followed even today, other than those of the water-sheds. It is the opinion of the writer that the course pursued differs greatly from that surmised by those who have attempted to locate it up to the present. The conclusions and deductions offered in the present chapter are based on a personal investigation of the route, in which more than a thousand miles were traveled and many streams and mountains visited and explored.

It is time to return, then, to Mendoza and his men at San Lorenzo, from where they set out on December 15, 1683, and marched five leagues, or approximately fifteen miles, to San Bartolomé. Here they camped in the old adobe ruins of the former home of the Maestre de Campo, Thome Domínguez de Mendoza. The following day they took up the march and traveled seven leagues, or approximately twenty-one miles, to the first *ranchería* of the Zuma nation, on the west or south bank of the river. The Zumas were a numerous tribe of Indians who had a number of *rancherías* along the river and who were soon to be congregated in the new missions established in the vicinity of the Junta de los Rios. They

---

[2]Diario y derrotero . . . Juan Domínguez de Mendoza . . . *A. G. N., Provincias Internas,* Vol. 37, Pt. 2. Entry for December 29, 1683.

[3]Bolton, *Exploration of the Spanish Southwest,* 311-343. The copy used in this case was that found in Vol. 37 of *Provincias Internas* but for some reason the translator and editor did not include the *certificaciones* appended to the diary after the entry for May 25, 1684, which are followed by the itinerary to El Paso on the return march and are a part of the diary.

were quickly to tire of mission control and to rebel against the monotony of ordered life.[4]

On December 17, the expedition continued to the south along the river, passing through several *rancherías* of the Zuma Indians. They were all poor people, who lived chiefly on baked palms, called *mescal,* declared Mendoza. The chiefs of the various villages along the way welcomed the Spaniards kindly and assured them they were anxious to become Christians and be reduced to pueblos. They declared their people were constantly being attacked by the Apaches and they pleaded with the Spaniards to protect them against this fierce enemy. Mendoza promised the chiefs that he would help them and would try to secure a mission for them when he returned from his expedition. They camped for the night at one of the largest villages of the Zumas, which they called Nuestra Señora del Pilár de Zaragoza. In the course of the day, the little band had traveled eight leagues, or approximately twenty-four miles, along the west side of the Río Grande.[5]

On December 18, they came upon a deep creek which emptied into the Río Grande, about twenty-four miles from the large pueblo of the Zumas. This creek or stream can easily be identified from the description given by Mendoza. He declared that it was a deep *arroyo* which formed a fan-like delta of rocks and stones where it entered the river and that there was a pleasant valley with abundant grass and wood. Taking into consideration the winding road he had to follow and the fact that he had covered about seventy-four miles from San Lorenzo to this spot, it seems that he was at this time opposite present day McNary or its immediate vicinity.[6] He called the place Nuestra Señora de la Límpida Concepción.

From here the expedition continued its march the following day and traveled about eight leagues, or approximately twenty-four miles, in a general southwestern direction, camping for the night at a place which they called Nuestra Señora de la Soledad, about nine miles from the river and opposite a large mountain from which a stream of water flowed toward the river. They were now in the vicinity of the only high peak of the Mexican sierra, almost due west of Fort Hancock and McNary, slightly south of the last mentioned place. The country here is rough and the

---

[4]Diario y derrotero . . . de Mendoza, in *Ibid.;* Testimonio de los Auttos fhos sobre la sublebación, y Alzamiento de los Yndos, Sumas; de las Misiones de Sn. Tiago de la Zienega de el Coyame, y Junta de el Río de el Norte. *A. G. I., Audiencia de Guadalajara,* 67-3-12 (Dunn Transcripts, 1710-1738).

[5]Diario y derrotero . . . Entry for December 17. In *Ibid.*

[6]*Ibid.* Entry for December 18.

valley of the Río Grande is narrowed, as it approaches Sierra Blanca on the east side. The expedition could have crossed the river at this point and followed the present highway from McNary to Finlay and on down to Van Horn, but having passed this point it became impossible for them to cross for a distance of almost a hundred miles, as the mountains hug the Río Grande on the east side closely, as far as the vicinity of present day Presidio.

On December 20, they turned southeast in order to approach the Río Grande and, after traveling twenty-four miles, more or less, camped at a place they called Nuestra Señora del Tránsito. Mendoza remarks that the country was rougher than before and that they passed many high hills. About halfway they came upon a hot spring. From this spring to the river the country was rolling and almost impassable, he declared. In these almost inaccessible regions they found a number of *rancherías,* which were deserted at this time. Perhaps this is the reason why Mendoza failed to point out the tribe that lived here. There were abundant grass and wood and a fairly spacious clearing surrounded by hills, where the camp was pitched for the night.

The next day the course was first to the west and then to the east again. The canyon through which the river passed at this point had to be abandoned in order to go around a very high hill. The advance was slow and difficult and the expedition halted after traveling four leagues or about twelve miles on the river. It is evident that the distance southward covered on this day was very short. They passed through three *rancherías* of Zuma Indians and they called the place where they camped, Nuestra Señora del Buen Suceso.

On December 22, they continued the march and experienced extreme difficulty over the mountainous route followed. They were now opposite Eagle Mountains, which attain an elevation of about seven thousand five hundred feet on the Texas side of the river. The Río Grande flows down a canyon along this region and Mendoza and his men were forced to find their way without getting too far from the stream. After traveling the usual twenty-four miles, more or less, they again camped on the Río Grande, at a place they called Nuestra Señora del Rosario, where they found a number of *rancherías* of Zuma Indians, good pasture, abundant wood, and water.

Mendoza crosses into Texas.   Continuing as close to the river as possible, the expedition reached a place which they called Nuestra Señora de Belén on December 24, after marching about forty-eight miles from

Nuestra Señora del Rosario. It was a short distance from here that the expedition finally crossed the Río Grande and entered Texas. It had traveled eighty-four leagues, or approximately two hundred and fifty-two miles since it left San Lorenzo. When they set out from Nuestra Señora de Belén, they went over a mountain pass on the summit of a range, about half a league beyond the camp. The pass, Mendoza declared, resembled a window and opened upon a beautiful valley which had the shape of an O, surrounded by hills and a heavy grove of trees, evidently along the river.[7]

It is not only important, but essential to try to determine in a definite manner the exact spot where the expedition crossed the Río Grande in order to determine from this point the course followed by the expedition on the way to the Río de las Perlas or San Pedro, as Mendoza called it, where he turned back. Taking into consideration the circuitous route that had to be followed to this point, and allowing for the fact that a league is slightly less than three miles, it is safe to assume that the expedition had traveled in a straight southeasterly course approximately three-fourths or two-thirds of the distance indicated. This is equivalent to about one hundred and eighty miles, more or less. If we take a modern map we will find that Mendoza and his men had reached a point on the Río Grande somewhere in the vicinity of present day Ruidosa, perhaps opposite the Chinati Mountains, which rise to a height of about seven thousand seven hundred feet. There is a pass in this vicinity, on the west side of the river, which may be made to fit the description given by Mendoza. It is approximately forty miles from Ruidosa to modern Presidio, which is opposite Ojinaga. It is at this point that the Conchos enters the Río Grande and it was here that Mendoza and his men recrossed the river on the return march at a point lower down than where they had passed before.[8] It is safe to assume, then, that it was somewhere in the vicinity of Ruidosa and the Chinati Mountains that Mendoza and his men crossed the Río Grande into present day Texas, about twenty or thirty miles to the northeast of Presidio.

Route followed after crossing the Río Grande. On Christmas day, the expedition continued its march east-southeast, keeping in sight of the

---

[7]Diario y derrotero . . . de Mendoza. A. G. N., *Provincias Internas,* Vol. 37, Pt. 2. In the preceding pages, this diary has been followed closely and will be continued in all references to this expedition. According to Bolton, the expedition was still on the south side of the river. Bolton, *op. cit.,* 324. Hackett in *Pichardo: Limits of Louisiana and Texas* places the party on the north side.

[8]Diario y derrotero . . . de Mendoza. Entry for May 22, 1684. In *Ibid.*

river and camped at a place which they called Nuestra Señora de Atoche. The country, declared Mendoza, opened to the south. This is correct, because being just south of Chinati Mountains, the country opens towards Presidio which lies to the southwest. They traveled about twenty-four miles on this day. On the following day the going was difficult and only three leagues were covered. It was observed at this time that the mountains were now to the west and the country opened towards the south and east. On December 27, they noticed a high mountain to the north of their line of march and observed that the Río Grande flowed due east along a fairly wide valley.

On December 28, they were at a place they called Nuestra Señora de Guadalupe. The camp was located between two ranges of mountains, one to the north, about three leagues distant, and one to the south about a quarter of a league. This last one was on the opposite side of the Río Grande, which seemed to flow east. There were heavy woods of sycamores in the surrounding country. On December 29, they reached a place which they called La Navidad de las Cruces. Here they found a large number of *rancherías* of the Julime nation, settled on both sides of the Río Grande, whose course, it seems, they were still following. These Indians knew the Mexican language well and were all industrious in the cultivation of the soil. They planted and harvested both corn and wheat. It was here that the main body of the expedition overtook the Reverend Fathers Fray Nicolás López, *Custodio* of New Mexico, Fray Juan de Zavaleta, Commissary of the Inquisition, and Fray Antonio de Acevedo. Many of the Indians requested the waters of Baptism and over one hundred of them were baptized with much rejoicing by the zealous missionaries. The land in the vicinity was extremely fertile and the weather favorable to its cultivation. There were abundant grass and firewood. The expedition remained here until December 31, while the missionaries ministered to the Indians and the horses rested from the journey.[9]

From the point where they crossed the Río Grande between Belén and Nuestra Señora del Populo, to Navidad de las Cruces, the expedition traveled twenty-four leagues, or approximately seventy-two miles. But in following the tortuous course of the river, which in this area is extremely difficult, they hardly went half of that distance in a straight line. Consequently the settlement or *pueblos* of the Julimes on the Río Grande must have been slightly above present day Presidio and Ojinaga. There

---

[9]*Ibid.* Entry for December 29.

is little doubt that by now they had reached this vicinity and were
not very far from the Junta de los Ríos. The nature of the country here
determined their future course. There is no possible way in which they
could have continued either along the course of the Río Grande or east.
The general arrangement of the hills and mountains in this area makes
it imperative to follow an almost due north course from here, along the
small valley of the only large stream in this region, which is Alamito
Creek. It seems from the description of the following three days' journey,
that this is exactly what Mendoza did.

On January 1, 1684, they were at a place which they called Apostol
Santiago (St. James the Apostle), seven leagues from La Navidad de
las Cruces, where Father Antonio Acevedo had stayed to minister to the
Indians and to try to establish a mission. Here Mass was said by the
two religious who accompanied the expedition from this time. In describing
the country over which they had traveled Mendoza declared that it was
rough and rocky, but passable. At Apostol Santiago there was a large
creek which flowed from north to south and carried an abundance of good
water. There was much grass along its banks, some of which was half
dry and some green.[10] There is no stream in this region which would fit
the description other than Alamito Creek. On January 2 they reached a
high hill from whose side flowed a hot spring. This country became less
mountainous, and although there was plenty of grass, the trees became
scarce. They traveled seven leagues on this day, but there is nothing to
indicate the direction in which they went. The following day, it is
expressly stated that the general direction they were now following was
north. They pitched camp at a place they called San Nicolás, after traveling seven leagues. During the day they had marched over a plateau,
which extended to the north. At the end of the plateau they came upon a
natural reservoir of rain water, with solid rock walls on either side. To
the west there was a large plain. Near the water was a number of trees,
mainly willows. Mass was said by one of the *Padres* before setting out
again.

By January 7 they had reached a place where a large group of Jumano
Indians requested them to halt. From Apostol Santiago to this site, the
expedition traveled about forty leagues, or approximately one hundred
and twenty miles in a general northeastern direction. If we assume that
Santiago was somewhere in the vicinity of present day Presidio, the

---

[10]Entry for January 1, 1684. *Ibid.*

expedition must have now reached a place somewhere in the neighborhood of present day Sanderson or Fort Stockton. The description of the country fits either place. Since it is essential to try to find accurately the location of this site it will be well to quote the exact description given in the diary by Mendoza.

"On the seventh day of said month and year (January 7, 1684) we halted at this place which we called San Pedro de Alcántara. It is six leagues, more or less, from the camping place of Los Reyes. We stayed here at the request of the Indians of the Jumano nation and others who came with them, constrained to do so by the absolute lack of supplies with which to feed [the men]. It was decided to hunt deer and such other game as abounds in this region to replenish our exhausted supply of food. The said site had a beautiful plain which extends to the west. To the north there are some mountains without trees. From the side of one of these, a beautiful spring flows, in the vicinity of which there are excellent black lands. There are no trees."[11]

If Mendoza followed a more easterly course, he must have been at this time in the vicinity of present day Sanderson, but if he inclined more to the north in his march from the Río Grande he must have been near present day Fort Stockton.

Continuing his march, evidently almost due east from this point, he traveled twelve leagues during the next two days without finding water or wood. It was not until January 10 that they came upon a spring which flowed from a round hill to the north of the spot selected for a camp. It was here that they discovered the first tracks of buffalo. There were mesquite trees and fairly good pasturage. Anxious to kill a buffalo, Mendoza dispatched a number of hunters to follow the tracks, but they returned without meat. The next day they reached a beautiful plain where they camped for the night. There were four mesas, or plateaus, around it. From the lowest of the four, which was to the north, flowed a spring, with five others a short distance from the first. The water from these springs joined to form a beautiful stream of clear water less than half a league from the springs, but without trees along its banks. The water was slightly alkali, but drinkable, and there was an abundance of fish. It was here that the expedition killed its first three buffaloes, which helped greatly to replenish their almost exhausted supply of meat.

---

[11]*Ibid*. Entry for January 7, 1684.

Mendoza reaches the Pecos. On January 12 they continued their march without finding other water than a small spring which flowed from north to east, where there was a chain of low mesas. It seems that on this day they followed a northeastern direction, because Mendoza declares they inclined to the right, which if facing north, would be to the east. It was on the following day, January 13, that the expedition reached a large river which carried as much water as the Río Grande and which they called Río Salado (Salty River), because the water was brackish. Mendoza declares that this river has its source in New Mexico.

There is no question that this was the Pecos. From their camp at Apostol Santiago, in the vicinity of Fort Stockton, to the Pecos, the expedition had traveled about twenty-seven leagues, or approximately seventy miles. Allowing for the shifting course followed, it is safe to assume that Mendoza and his men had traveled about fifty miles in a straight line to the banks of the Pecos River. If we take a compass and set one end either at Fort Stockton or Sanderson and find a place where the other end intersects the Pecos River on a modern map, it will be seen that the expedition struck the Pecos either in the vicinity of Sheffield, if it passed by Sanderson, or somewhere to the south of McCamey, if it passed near Fort Stockton. There were no trees, the chronicler noted, other than mesquite, and the waters of the river were muddy, and somewhat alkali.[12]

The following day they continued the march along the river for a distance of six leagues and halted at a place they called San Cristóbal. The Pecos flows almost due east for a distance in the vicinity of either Sheffield or McCamey, although it is slightly more southeast at Sheffield. We may assume, therefore, that on January 14, the expedition followed an almost due east course. From the camp, a chain of low lying mesas was visible, one of which was directly opposite the line of march and seemed to be separated from the others. The expedition spent all day here hunting buffalo, which had now become plentiful. The travelers succeeded in killing six bulls. While hunting, they discovered a saline with no water but considerable salt. It was on the north or east side of the river, about a league beyond, between a high hill and a flat mesa, or plateau.[13]

---

[12]Bolton places the expedition slightly above Horsehead Crossing on the Pecos, decidedly northwest of the places suggested here. Bolton, *op. cit.,* 329, note 1.

[13]*Ibid.* Entry for January 15, 1684. The saline has been located in the vicinity of Horsehead Crossing on the Pecos: Bolton, *op. cit.,* 330.

Greeted by Sabeata and friends.   Resuming their march on January 15, they followed the Pecos River downstream for a distance of about nine leagues during the next two days. On January 17, they came upon the Jediondo (ill-smelling) Indians. "Their chiefs and the rest of the people came out to welcome us with much joy," declares Mendoza. "Most of them came on foot, others on horseback. They brought a very well made cross, which seemed to measure about two and a half *varas*. It had been fashioned out of heavy timber, was painted red and yellow, and it had a large nail [to hold the two arms]. It was evident that they had made the cross some time before. They also brought a white taffeta flag, a little less than a *vara* in length. In the center of the flag, there were two crosses of blue taffeta, very well made. As they met us, Juan Sabeata fired several salutes with the barrel of an arquebus without locks, which he set off with a fuse. On our part we replied with two volleys. I ordered the men to assemble and gave instructions that no one dismount. The only ones who dismounted were the Reverend Fathers Fray Nicolás López, the *Custodio*, and Fray Juan de Zavaleta, Commissary of the Inquisition. With great devotion, they knelt and kissed the cross. I, as well as the rest of the soldiers, did the same, without dismounting from our horses. The Indians kissed the habits of the missionaries, and together we proceeded to the *ranchería*. On the way we crossed the said Río Salado (Pecos River). When we arrived and all the women and children saw us, they shouted with joy at the sight and all kissed the habits of the *Padres*."[14] The Indians were expecting the Spaniards, for they had prepared huts made out of rushes in the *ranchería* for their lodging. But suspicious or cautious, Mendoza thanked the chiefs and the Indians for their thoughtfulness and, without giving offence to them, explained that he would rather establish his camp for the night on a hill, which was a short distance from the village, and which protected the *ranchería* from the attacks of the Apaches.

Find a French flag.   Significant as the cross borne by the Indians was, the possession of a French flag, for it was no other, was even more so. It is incontrovertible proof that French traders had been as far as the Pecos by 1684, or that the Indians of this region traded with the French to the east either directly or through other tribes. This fact has not been fully appreciated by the early historians of Texas. La Salle's ill-starred settlement on Matagorda Bay was not, then, the first formal incursion into Texas by the French. A year before La Salle landed on the coast, the

---

[14]*Ibid.* Entry for January 17, 1684.

Jediondo Indians on the Pecos had a white taffeta flag which could have come from no other source than French traders or explorers.

Mendoza and his men stayed in the village of the Jediondos for seven days, at the request of the Jumanos and other chiefs, who on January 19, held a council and asked Mendoza for a formal interview. Mendoza ordered all his officers to assemble and notified Juan Sabeata and the Indian chiefs he was ready to receive them. After they had all come before him, he asked them what they wanted, and they all declared that the Apaches were their mortal enemies and the enemies of the Spaniards. They begged Mendoza, therefore, in God's name, to wage war against this nation. The Spanish commander assured them that he would help them in their war against the Apaches and all the chiefs were glad to hear the good news. The next day, Juan Sabeata brought seventeen tanned deerskins for the soldiers and promised to bring more as soon as they were ready. These were distributed to Miguel Luján, Melchor de Arsuleta, Felipe Montoya, Felipe Romero, Ignacio Vaca, Antonio Solís, Baltazar Domínguez, Juan Domínguez, Jr., and Antonio Gómez. While in camp Mass was said every day. On Saturday, a High Mass was celebrated in honor of the Holy Virgin, in addition to the ordinary low Mass. On Sunday two Masses were also said. The hunters of the expedition killed twenty-seven buffaloes during their stay here and a good supply of meat was prepared for the remainder of the journey.

Route from the Pecos to the Conchos River. From January 24 to February 2, the expedition traveled about thirty leagues, or approximately ninety miles, in a general northeastern direction and were joined while on the way by a tribe of Indians called Arcos Fuertes (Strong Bows).[15] They now reached the source of a river which they called the Nueces. Mendoza declared there were several springs at this place which joined to form the river, where there were many fish. He remarked that it was a beautiful spot with many trees and that the river flowed almost due east. If from the point where the expedition crossed the Pecos in the neighborhood of either Sheffield or McCamey, we measure the distance traveled to the headwaters of the river, which Mendoza believed was the Nueces, it will be seen that they were now in the vicinity of the headwaters of the present day middle Conchos. In order to reach this spot, already sug-

[15]In the Bolton translation *Fuertes* has been read as *Tuertos*. This is a pardonable error as in the manuscript used for the translation it is difficult to distinguish between a capital *T* and a capital *F*. Bolton, *op. cit.*, 333.

gested by Bolton,[16] the expedition must have traveled almost due north from the Pecos, otherwise it would have struck the source of the Devil's River in the vicinity of Barnhart.[17] Mendoza and his men stayed here for three days before continuing their journey.

On February 5, after traveling three leagues, they came upon a very large river that seemed to gush forth from a group of rocks, which was called "The Place of the Dogs." The name was very appropriate, declared Mendoza, because there were many dogs in this stream, who lived in the water, but were the same as other dogs. He remarked that it was said that these dogs were very fierce and killed the buffalo when they came to drink water. This stream, like the previous one, flowed east. It was here that Mendoza noted the first pecan trees. As the expedition had been reduced to meat only for many days, the men were glad to vary their diet with the pecans. The oak trees were so large that heavy carts could easily be built out of them, Mendoza pointed out. There were many wild hens in the region, which made a lot of noise at dawn. The river had some clam shells, as the Río de Las Perlas, which it joined lower down. The buffaloes were numerous all along the river.

The expedition followed the course of this stream to the east until they reached a river which they called San Pedro, which was evidently the main stream of the Concho. It took them nineteen days to travel eighteen leagues. They halted frequently along the river to allow the horses to feed and rest in order to hunt buffalo, which were very numerous. After the expedition reached this region, it seems that Juan Sabeata did not wish Mendoza to go farther. He began to make false reports of the presence of Apaches, until Mendoza became disgusted and ordered him out of the camp on February 19, together with several Jumano scouts that had been accompanying the expedition. Two Piro Indians left camp with them.[18]

Mendoza had been on the Conchos before.   Mendoza identified this river, which he called San Pedro, and which doubtless was the main stream of the Conchos, as that visited by Diego de Guadalajara thirty years before. He was in a position to know, because he had been a member of the former expedition.[19] The instructions given to Mendoza by Governor

---

[16]Bolton, *op. cit.*, 334, note 3.

[17]*Ibid.* Entry for February 2, 1684.

[18]Diario y derrotero . . . de Mendoza. Entry for February 19, 1684.

[19]Bolton, "The Spanish Occupation of Texas, 1519-1690," *Southwestern Historical Quarterly*, XVI.

Cruzate were to explore the country as far as the Río de Las Perlas. He, therefore, declared he had fulfilled his orders. He described the spot reached as being eight leagues down the stream from the point where Guadalajara had been. He declared it was bordered by fertile fields, many trees, mostly pecans, and that it carried much more water at this place, which he called San Pedro, than above, because it was joined by other tributaries.[20]

Temporary mission at San Clemente.   Although he had reached his goal, Mendoza went still farther east along the main Concho to its juncture with the Colorado, which he called San Clemente. He arrived on March 15 and seems to have stayed for a while on the Colorado, somewhere in the neighborhood of present Leaday. He finally decided to return to New Mexico to report to the governor. On May 1, he held a council of war on the San Clemente (Colorado) to determine his course of action. It seems that the Apaches had swept down from the north and attacked Mendoza and his Indian allies three times both by day and night. In the last of the three attacks, which was at night, the enemy had wounded a soldier with three arrows. He had also been attacked at night three times by the Salinero Indians from Nueva Vizcaya, who had killed two Indian hunters while they were out getting game. The two Indians were of the Jediondo nation and seem to have been surprised by the enemy while asleep. In view of these facts, the Reverend Fathers Fray Nicolás López, *Custodio* of New Mexico, and Fray Juan de Zavaleta, Commissary of the Inquisition, Sergeant Major Diego Lucero de Godoy, Captain Hernán Martín Serrano, interpreter of the Jumano language, Alférez Diego de Luna, and Alférez Diego Varela, were all of the opinion that it would be best to return to New Mexico. They declared the number of men was inadequate and that their ammunition was almost spent. It was decided to return and make a report to Governor Domingo Jironza Petris de Cruzate in order that he might decide what was best for the service of both Majesties.[21]

It will be well to describe in detail the site where Mendoza and his men camped for almost a month and a half. At the place where he struck the Colorado, the river flowed to the east. There were no clam shells at this point, but he was told by the Indians that six days' journey down the stream there were numerous large shells, many of which had pearls. The

[20]*Ibid.* Entry for February 24, 1684.
[21]*Ibid.* Entry for May 1, 1684.

country along the river was very fertile and there were many pecan and mulberry trees. He also noted some wild plum trees. The woods were filled with game, he declared, and there were many wild chickens, deer, and other animals. The buffalo were so numerous that it was impossible to count them. He explained that the reason for their long stay at this place was that he was waiting for the envoys of forty-eight nations. Chiefs and warriors of sixteen different tribes had joined his expedition and were in camp with him from March 16 to May 1, when he decided to return to New Mexico. During this time Mass was celebrated regularly every day. A rough two-story structure was built for this purpose. In the lower story or ground floor services were held all during Holy Week. Many Christian Indians attended these special ceremonies with great devotion and many of those who had joined the expedition asked to be baptized. The upper story was used by the *Padres* and a lookout was kept there to prevent a surprise by the enemy.

While in camp one of the soldiers, a certain Diego Varela, was bitten by a poisonous water snake on the little finger. By the time four creeds could be said, the poison coursed through his body so quickly that he suffered intense pain and he began to vomit. Everybody thought that he would die. But the Reverend Father *Custodio* had with him a herb which was an antitoxin for the poison. He washed the wound with the essence and gave him a potion of the same medicine to drink; he got well in a few days.

The buffaloes were so plentiful that the soldiers and their Indian allies killed four thousand and thirty during the time that they were in camp. This number did not include those left in the field wounded, or the young calves that were brought in for daily consumption. The skins of these animals were cured and packed.[22]

The friendly nations that were in camp were the Jumanos, the Horrorosos (the horrible ones), the Beitonijures, the Acubares, the Cujados, the Toremas, the Jediondos, (the ill-smelling ones), the Caulas, the Hineis, the Ytomes, and the Hanacines. Those for whom they were waiting were the Tejas, who had sent word that they would come, the Huicasiques, the Aielis, the Aguilas (the Eagles), the Flechas Chiquitas (Small arrows), the Echancotes, the Anchimos, the Bobidas, the Injames, the Dijus, the Colabrotes (Budding Tails), the Unofitas, the Juamas, the Yoyehis, the Acanis, the Humez, the Bibis, the Conchumuchas (Many shells), the

---

[22]*Ibid.* Entry for May 1, 1684.

Teancas, the Hinsas, the Pojues, the Quisabas, the Paiabunos, the Papanes, the Puchas, the Paguachianis, the Iscanis, the Tojumas, the Pagaiames, the Sabas, the Bajuneros, the Novraches, the Pulchas, the Tobites, the Puehames, and the Oranchos.[23]

Return march to the Río Grande. In view of the reasons given in the council held on May 1, it was decided not to wait any longer for the envoys of these nations. To those who were in camp, Mendoza and Father López faithfully promised they would return and establish missions for them. Some of the chiefs left with their followers for their pueblos and others remained with the expedition, which started on its return march the following day. Instead of following the same route over which they had come, they now took a general southwestern direction and tried to reach the Junta de los Ríos by the shortest route possible. Juan Sabeata and some of his followers stayed behind. Mendoza declared that Sabeata had not been dependable and that he had been afraid to return with the Spaniards.

By May 23, the expedition had again reached the Pecos River which they consistently called Río Salado. On the return trip they crossed this river twice and came upon their former camp which they had called San Juan del Río. From this point, it was decided to follow the former trail back to the Junta de los Ríos, where the expedition arrived some time before June 12.

Establishment of missions at La Junta de los Ríos. Having crossed the Río Grande, Mendoza declared in an official report drawn up for the Governor of New Mexico on June 12, 1684, that on this day the Indian governors and chiefs of seven nations, who lived in the neighborhood of the Junta de los Ríos del Norte and Conchos had appeared before the Reverend Father Fray Nicolás López, *Custodio* of New Mexico, and with five hundred of their people had solicited six missionaries to instruct them in the holy faith and minister to them. They had explained that the two missionaries promised them were not sufficient, because their different *pueblos,* or villages, were far apart and the number of Indians very large. They stated that they had already built six temporary chapels or churches of timber, thatched with straw, and that when the missionaries came they would rebuild them of adobe.

---

[23]*Ibid.* Compare this list with that given in Hackett, *Picardo: Limits of Louisiana and Texas,* II, 338; also Bolton, *Spanish Exploration of the Southwest,* 339-340.

The following day, Mendoza called the governors and chiefs together and all their followers. When they had assembled, he asked them if they knew or had heard of any other Spanish soldiers or officers who had visited them before, who had taken formal possession of the land in the name of the king and had asked them to swear allegiance to His Majesty. To this they all replied that they knew of no one who had come to their country before and had taken formal possession of the land. They explained, however, that they had been visited by two missionaries on two different occasions. They said that the first one who came to see them was the Reverend Father Fray García de San Francisco, who had said Mass for them and had left them after a short while with the promise that he would return soon. After a time, they declared, another missionary, named Fray Juan de Sumesta, another Franciscan, had come to the first of their pueblos, but went away after his arrival without visiting the other villages. Since then, they had seen no other Spaniards or missionaries than those who were with Mendoza. In view of the circumstances the leader of the expedition felt it his duty to take formal possession of this area in the name of the king as a part of the Province of New Mexico, which he did with all formality.[24] At the request of the Indians congregated at the time, he appointed four *Capitanes,* or native governors, for the missions which were to be established and gave them the insignia of their office, which was a short cane.

Return march to El Paso. On June 14, Mendoza and his men started back to Presidio del Paso del Norte. Although it had been their intention to follow the eastern side of the Río Grande on the return march, it was decided, after a consultation was held, to follow the Conchos to the Sacramento, and proceed thence to El Paso del Norte. It had been pointed out in the council that it was approximately one hundred leagues from the Junta de los Ríos to Presidio del Norte, along the Río Grande, but that the river had to be crossed four times. This was dangerous at this season of the year because of the frequent floods. The route lay along country which was difficult to traverse because of the steep mountains and the rough and narrow canyons that had to be followed. Furthermore, news had been received that most of the Indian nations that inhabited this region were in rebellion, particularly the Zumas. It was believed that these Indians and their allies were actually waiting in ambush for the

---

[24]Certificaciones del Capitán Juan Domínguez de Mendoza. Junta de los Ríos, June 12-13, 1684. *A. G. N., Provincias Internas,* Vol. 37, Pt. 2.

Spaniards. With the reduced number of soldiers, the exhausted condition of the horses after their long journey, and the small supply of ammunition, it was not safe to attempt to march back by way of the Río Grande. The expedition, therefore, followed the Conchos for several days and finally turned due north. On July 18, 1684, after stopping on several occasions for two, three, and even six days to rest the horses, they finally arrived at San Lorenza and went from there to the Presidio del Paso del Norte.

Mendoza and his men, accompanied by three Franciscans, had traveled over six hundred leagues during this important expedition. They had explored the west side of the Río Grande from El Paso del Norte to within eighty or ninety miles of present day Ojinaga, had crossed the river somewhere in the vicinity of present Ruidosa, and following the river for fifty or sixty miles to the neighborhood of Presidio, had turned northeast and traveled across the great plains as far as the juncture of the Concho and the Colorado, well beyond San Angelo. They had explored about eighteen hundred miles of new territory, eight hundred of which were in West Texas. They had come into contact with over sixty different nations, and they had succeeded in returning without the loss of a single man and carrying a load of over four thousand skins of buffalo. Such was the accomplishment of Captain Juan Domínguez de Mendoza and Fathers Fray Nicolás López, *Custodio* of New Mexico, Fray Juan de Zavaleta, Commissary of the Inquisition, and Fray Antonio Acevedo.

The expedition of Mendoza was followed by the establishment of six missions among the various tribes of Indians that inhabited the region in the vicinity of the Junta de los Ríos, but since most of these were on the west side of the Río Grande, they form no part of our history.

Interest in the Big Bend Country. Viceregal officials, however, were seriously interested in the entire area watered by the Río Grande from El Paso del Norte to San Juan Bautista. When arrangements for the inspection of all the frontier establishments were being made and the instructions for Don Pedro de Rivera had been prepared, these were referred to *Auditor* Oliván Rebolledo. Among other things, he suggested that special orders be given to the inspector to make a careful exploration of the Río Grande. Rebolledo declared that as far as known, this river formed a great chasm from El Paso del Norte to San Juan Bautista, which divided the unconquered Indians of the Province of New Mexico from those of Nueva Vizcaya and Coahuila. He pointed out that the last named province was divided from Nueva Vizcaya by a great mountain range which ran from north to south. It would be highly advisable, he said, for Rivera was to make a careful exploration of this area, noting if the land was fertile, if there were woods, if the country was suitable for grazing, and if it was appropriate for settlement. If so, the Presidios of Cerro Gordo, Gallo, Mapimí, and Pasaje could be moved and placed at convenient distances from each other along the Río Grande to protect such settlements as were founded there. Spanish families and friendly Indians could be induced to move to this region if it were suitable for settlement. This would afford effective protection to the entire northeastern frontier of Nueva Vizcaya, because the river would protect the new settlements and the presidios from the enemies that lived beyond it to the north and east.[25]

Such a task, however, could not be undertaken by a man who had so many other things to do while on his inspection of the presidios. The idea did not go unheeded. After Rivera's return to Mexico, in view of his own experience, he advised that a special expedition be sent to explore the Río Grande from San Juan Bautista to the Junta de los Ríos, and another from El Paso del Norte to the same point. But before we take up the results of his recommendations and the actual accomplishments of the expedition that set out from San Juan Bautista, let us see what the condition of the Presidio of El Paso was at the time of the inspection.

Rivera's report on El Paso.   In 1726, Rivera passed through the presidio, on his way from the Conchos to Santa Fe, where he had a special investigation to carry out in regard to the conduct of the former governor of that province in an expedition ordered in 1720 to the river of Jesús María.[26] He did not stop at El Paso on the way up, but on his return he reported that there were forty-nine soldiers in the presidio and that each one received four hundred and fifty *pesos* a year. The captain had a salary of six hundred. He found no irregularities in the management of the military affairs of this outpost. He commended the captain for his zeal in the royal service and the general peace maintained with the Indians in the vicinity. He declared that the captain had founded a *pueblo* of

---

[25]Parecer del Auditor Oliván Rebolledo. October 2, 1724. *A. G. N., História,* Vol. 52.

[26]This river has been identified with the Platte, but it is more likely the Arkansas or the Red River. Thomas, "The Massacre of the Villasur Expedition at the Forks of the Platte River," in *Nebraska History and Record of Pioneer Days,* Vol. VIII, No. 3.

Zuma Indians at the Real de San Lorenzo at his own expense. An inspection of the garrison disclosed that the men were all fit, that they were properly equipped with all the necessary arms, and that they were well drilled.[27]

It had been proposed by the viceroy that the garrison of the Presidio del Paso del Norte be reduced to thirty men and that the nineteen left over, together with other detachments from the presidios in this region, be used to establish a new outpost at the Junta de los Ríos. After having visited the Presidios of Janos, Fronteras, Mapimí, and El Gallo, and having seen the actual conditions that confronted the garrison of El Paso del Norte, Rivera emphatically declared that this presidio needed the entire force which it now had. It was the target, he said, for about fifteen hundred Apache Indians who lived in the Gila Mountains. There were six tribes in this nation: the Mescaleros, Caninos, Gilas, and others. In all they numbered approximately five thousand, who had their strongholds in the Gila Mountains. This range was about one hundred leagues long and ran from northwest to southeast. The southeastern extremity was about sixty leagues from El Paso, and the same distance from Janos and Fronteras, so that these Indians could attack any one of the three presidios when they pleased. He recommended, therefore, that the forty-nine men now at El Paso del Norte be left there and that their pay be reduced from four hundred and fifty *pesos* to four hundred, because, with the maximum price list for commodities placed in effect after the inspection, the soldiers could secure all the supplies and equipment they needed for much less than before. The salary of the captain was to continue at six hundred *pesos* a year.[28] As usual, the viceroy approved the recommendations of Rivera and the idea of reducing the garrison was abandoned.

Governor Valverde's Expedition to the Panana Indians. When in 1719, the French surprised the Presidio of Nuestra Señora de los Dolores and the missionaries in East Texas, causing them to abandon the missions and to retreat to San Antonio, Captain Diego Ramón, it appears, wrote a letter to the Governor of New Mexico, Captain Antonio Valverde Cossío, warning him of the designs of the French upon that province. Ramón informed Governor Valverde that the French were on the way to Santa Fe with the intention of taking possession of the rich mines of that province.[29]

---

[27]Proyecto y vissita de Presidios . . . *A. G. N., Provincias Internas,* Vol. 29.

[28]*Ibid. A. G. N., Provincias Internas,* 29.

[29]Confesión del Governador y Capitán General de la Provincia de la Nuevo Mexico, July 5, 1726. *A. G. N., Provincias Internas,* Vol. 37, Pt. 2.

The governor immediately transmitted this information to the viceroy, adding that while engaged in a campaign against the Comanches in the northern part of New Mexico, he had learned, while at Napestle River, from a wounded Apache, that the French were living among the Panana (Pawnee?) Indians, on the Jesús María River.

He explained that when the Comanches had started hostilities, he had held a council of war in Santa Fe. It was decided at this time that it would be best for him to go in person and chastise these Indians. He accordingly had set out immediately. On the way to the northeast, he had been joined by one hundred Apaches from La Jicarilla, who promised to lead him to the country of the Comanches. The expedition traveled about two hundred leagues in a general northeastern direction, but when they arrived in the land of the Comanches they found no trace of them. This was in the vicinity of a river which they called Casse. He was advised by the Apaches that the Comanches had either fled or were in hiding, and that it would be better to return to Santa Fe before winter set in. Snow had already begun to fall, although it was only the month of September. Moved by the logic of the advice of the Apaches, Governor Valverde turned back to Santa Fe to save the men from unnecessary hardships and to avoid the loss of the horses through the rigors of the winter.

On the return march, the expedition followed a different course and came to a river called Napestle.[30] This was a large stream which flowed near the *pueblo* known as El Cuartelejo, where many Apaches lived. Two of the Indians from the *ranchería* came out to the river and begged Governor Valverde to stay in their *pueblo* two days to rest and to give their people a chance to see him. While at Cuartelejo, he noticed one of the Apache chiefs had been wounded with a firearm. When he inquired how he had been wounded, the Indian explained he had been shot in a fight his warriors had sustained against the Panana Indians, in which they had been aided by the French.

The Governor became curious and asked for more information concerning the Panana Indians, their country, and the French who lived among them. He was told that the Panana nation lived on the banks of a large river which was called Jesús María, that their country was to

---

[30]This river has been identified as the Arkansas River. Hackett, *Pichardo: Limits of Louisiana and Texas,* I, 35, 192, 234, 201-206.

the east,[31] and that the French lived among them. The Indians described the forts built by the French by saying that they had large houses with only one door and with guns on the roofs. They said the men dressed generally in red and that their women wore white. Valverde asked them if they had observed these things with their own eyes. To this the Indians replied that they had not seen them, but that their squaws, who had been prisoners of the Pananas, had beheld them and had told them.[32]

Immediately upon his return, early in 1720, Governor Valverde had communicated the additional information he had obtained to the viceroy and offered to lead an expedition to the land of the Pananas, if His Excellency desired it. As a result of the information given to the viceroy, he ordered the governor to set out with a competent number of men and to go to the Jesús María River to find out the truth of the stories told by the Indians.

By the time this order came, it seemed that hostilities among the Comanches had again broken out. Instead of proceeding to the execution of the instructions for a visit to the Pananas, in person, as he had promised, the governor ordered his lieutenant, Captain Pedro de Villasur, to take charge of the expedition. Unfortunately, this officer was surprised by the Pananas and he suffered a severe defeat for which the governor was held responsible.

When Rivera made his inspection of the presidios in 1726, he was ordered to hold an investigation into the whole matter to determine the guilt of Governor Valverde, who was now Captain of the Presidio of Nuestra Señora del Pilár y Señor San José del Paso del Norte. Although this incident may be considered at first as unrelated to the history of Texas, its significance lies in the fact that the expedition to the Pananas, undertaken in 1720, passed through a portion of North Texas, at least, being one of the first to traverse the region of the Panhandle in the vicinity of Amarillo. But more significant than this fact is the possibility that Jesús María may be either the present day Red River or the Arkansas.[33] It is for this reason that the details of this incident are given in this chapter.

---

[31]It is of interest to note the Apaches said Pananas lived to the east. If so they were not on the Platte River.

[32]Confesión del Governador y Capitán General de la Provincia de la Nuevo Mexico, July 5, 1726. *A. G. N., Provincias Internas,* Vol. 37, Pt. 2.

[33]The Pananas ranged the country between the Red River and the Platte. They are mentioned as one of the tribes that lived in this region. Hackett, *Pichardo: Limits of Louisiana and Texas,* I, 72.

On his way to Santa Fe, Rivera stopped at Presidio del Paso del Norte, long enough to serve notice on Captain Antonio Valverde Cossío to appear in Santa Fe within a month to answer charges against him for the failure of the expedition to the country of the Pananas in 1720.[34] Captain Valverde replied immediately with a long letter in which he pleaded not guilty. He declared that the orders of the viceroy clearly stated that the expedition was to be under his charge or that of his lieutenant governor. He explained that he had other more pressing matters to attend to at the time and that in placing the expedition in charge of his lieutenant, Captain Pedro de Villasur, he had done so fully aware of the ability, courage, and prudence of this officer. Villasur had been *Alférez* of Presidio del Paso del Norte, having been promoted later to captain of this post, that he had been *Alcalde Mayor* and *Capitán á Guerra* of the Province of Santa Barbara, in Nueva Vizcaya, Inspector at Rosario, and *Alcalde Mayor* and *Capitán á Guerra* of the Real de Minas of Chihuahua. His courage, ability, and zeal were well known and he had every reason to place full confidence in him.

Villasur's Expedition. When the investigation was held in June, 1726, at Santa Fe, several witnesses who had been on the expedition were called to give testimony as to the entire expedition. Among these were Ildefonso Real de Aguilar and Phelipe Tamarís, both Spanish soldiers. From their declarations it appears that the expedition was undertaken as Valverde averred, at his instigation, and as a result of the information he had obtained from an Apache chief at the Napestle River. The force consisted of fifty men from the Presidio and Villa of Santa Fe, under the command of Captain Pedro de Villasur. They started from Santa Fe on June 14 and traveled approximately for sixty-three days, according to one of the witnesses, before they reached the river of Jesús María. According to the other witness they arrived at their destination on August 10. The general direction of the march had been east, with some deviations to the north.[35]

If, as the witness stated, they had traveled from June 14 to August 10 from Santa Fe, in a general eastern direction, they must have covered

---

[34]Notificazión, May 13, 1726. *A. G. N., Provincias Internas,* Vol. 37, Pt. 2.

[35]Declaraciones de testigos. July 1 and 2, 1726. *A. G. N., Provincias Internas,* Vol. 37, Pt. 2. A good account of the entire incident, based on the documentary sources is found in Hackett, *op. cit.,* I, 191-213. See also Thomas, "The Massacre of the Villasur Expedition at the Forks of the Platte River, August 12, 1720," in *Nebraska History and Record of Pioneer Days,* Vol. VIII, No. 3.

approximately two hundred leagues, or between five and six hundred miles. Such a course would take them across the Panhandle in the vicinity of Amarillo and through a good part of Oklahoma before they reached the large stream which they called the Jesús María. In order to have gone to the Platte River, as suggested by some, he would have had to go in an almost due north direction. Furthermore, it is to be remembered that one of the causes for this expedition had been the incursion of the French in East Texas, consequently the goal would have been to the east. If, therefore, they turned slightly to the south, they very likely followed a course parallel to the Red River along the northern boundary of the State, between this stream and the Arkansas.

But be that as it may, when they came to the *rancherías* of the Pananas, which were on the opposite side of the river called Jesús María, Captain Villasur decided to send an Indian of that nation, who was in the expedition, across the river with presents and with a message to inform them that the Spaniards were their friends, who had come to obtain information about the whites who had introduced themselves among the Indians. The native scout took some bundles of tobacco, knives, and other things to present to the Pananas. The messenger did not return that day. But a number of chiefs or warriors came to the Spanish camp. Unfortunately there was no one who could understand their language and the Spaniards could learn nothing from them. The visitors showed great reserve during the stay and appeared to be suspicious of the designs of the Spaniards. The next day the messenger was seen on the opposite bank of the river. He informed the Spaniards through signs that he could not come over because he was being kept a prisoner by the Pananas. When asked if there were white men among the Indians, he replied that he did not know.

Captain Villasur wanted to cross the river immediately to find out for himself the true state of affairs, but a council was held and it was decided to find a good passageway first. While the deliberations were going on some of the friendly Indians who had accompanied the Spaniards went into the river for a swim. The Pananas attacked them and succeeded in capturing one of them. Because of this hostile act, the council of officers decided it would be wise for the exploring party to retire. The leader of the expedition agreed to abide by the decision and ordered a retreat on the following day, August 12. The men marched so fast that in one day they retreated the distance they had advanced in two days. They came upon a river, which they called San Lorenzo, and passed over it, pitching camp just beyond. Shortly after dark a dog was heard to bark and the noise of men crossing the river was reported. Captain Villasur sent word to the soldiers who were guarding the horses to redouble their watchfulness, and he dispatched some friendly Indians to scout the river. The natives returned after a while and said they had neither seen nor heard anything unusual. Early next morning, at dawn, Captain Villasur ordered horses brought in and the guard was told to change mounts. Contrary to the general instructions which provided that all the soldiers should never change mounts at one time, they unsaddled and were about to prepare fresh mounts when, with a loud yell, about five hundred Indians swept down upon the little band, firing both arrows and muskets. Taken unawares the Spaniards tried to rally three times, after which, those who had not been killed, fled. A few of the soldiers had saddled their horses and these tried to charge the enemy, but being so greatly outnumbered, they had to flee reluctantly. One of the witnesses declared he had received nine wounds and had been rescued by one of the mounted soldiers. The Indians had already begun to scalp him, but succeeded in taking off only half of his scalp. He said *"una trenza,"* one braid of hair, but evidently he meant half of the scalp as the soldiers sometime wore their hair braided in two short braids, one on each side of the head.[36]

Of the fifty men that set out with Captain Villasur, only twelve escaped. This was one of the worst defeats ever suffered by a Spanish expedition in this region. All their baggage and supplies were left in possession of the enemy, and most of the horses and mules stayed behind also. The Indian allies remained true and put up a brave fight, which permitted the Spaniards who survived the first of the three onslaughts to escape. Ex-Governor Valverde was exonerated of any blame in the disaster, however, since this engagement had been under the command of Villasur.

Exploration of the Big Bend Country. Upon the recommendation of Rivera, after his return to Mexico, Viceroy Casafuerte decided to order an expedition to explore the region of the Río Grande between the Presidio of San Juan Bautista and the Junta de los Ríos. From El Paso del Norte to the Junta, the area had been well explored by the Mendoza expedition, which had been followed by the establishment of a group of missions at La Junta and to the north, along the western bank of the Río Grande, but the territory to the south, which is what is known today as the Big Bend Country, still remained unsettled. On October 29, 1728, the viceroy ordered Governor Ignacio Francisco de Barrutia, of the Province

---

[36]Declaraciones de testigos. *A. G. N., Provincias Internas,* Vol 37, Pt. 2.

of Nueva Vizcaya, to organize an expedition with soldiers from the Presidios of Conchos, Mapimí, Coahuila (Monclova), and San Juan Bautista, and placing it under the command of Captain José de Berroterán, of the Presidio of Conchos, to let it explore the territory from San Juan Bautista to the Junta de los Ríos, Conchos and Río Grande. The expedition was to start its exploration from San Juan Bautista and follow the river to the north until it came to its juncture with the Conchos. It was to note the character of the country and to find out all information possible concerning the various nations who lived in this unexplored region. It was pointed out that this area had been and was the refuge of hostile Indians, who preyed upon the frontier settlements of Nueva Vizcaya and Coahuila.[37]

Berroterán's Expedition.   The orders were accordingly transmitted to Captain José Berroterán, at Presidio de Conchos. Agreeable to the instructions, Berroterán started from Conchos on January 13, 1729, arriving at Santiago de Mapimí, on January 24, where he was to be joined by twelve additional men. Upon his arrival he found the soldiers from Mapimí were not ready to start. The rest of the men, who numbered fifty-eight, were fairly well equipped with arms, supplies, and horses. Each man had a minimum of six horses and two mules. He consequently notified the governor that he was leaving for Nazas River with the fifty-eight men and six Indian guides, having left instructions for the other twelve to follow as soon as possible.[38]

On January 26, Berroterán marched out of Mapimí in the afternoon and traveled for a distance of three leagues due east. He camped in the vicinity of some rain pools, from where he started early next morning, following a course to the southeast. After traveling about eight leagues he decided to halt, although there was no water, to allow the horses to graze, but that night, at about eight o'clock, they stampeded. The twenty-seven mounted guards on watch were unable to check the rush and as many as three hundred and fifty horses and mules ran away. Next morning, he left the baggage and supplies in camp with an adequate guard and went after the runaway animals with the rest of the men. At a distance of about ten leagues, he came upon the horses and mules and suc-

[37]Expedientes relativos á reconocimientos hechos en Ríos del Norte, Conchos, etc. *A. G. N., Historia,* No. 52; Copia del Diario de la Campaña executada de orden del Exmo. Señor Marqués de Casafuerte, por Dn Joseph Berroterán Capitán del Presidio del Conchos . . . *A. G. I., Audiencia de Guadalajara,* 104-6-15 (Dunn Transcripts, 1710-1738).

[38]Diario de la Campaña executada . . . por Dn. José Berroterán. *A. G. I., Audiencia de Guadalajara,* 104-6-15.

ceeded in rounding up about one hundred and eighty. From here he dispatched instructions to the camp for them to follow with the baggage and supplies to Las Cruces, where he would join them.

From January 29 until February 4, Berroterán kept on the track of the runaway horses and mules and succeeded in rounding them all except twenty-two. He joined the main expedition at Las Cruces on this day, after receiving a letter from the Governor of Nueva Vizcaya, informing him that orders had been issued to the commander at Mapimí to hasten the departure of the detachment which he was to supply for the expedition. He waited at Las Cruces, on the Nazas River, until February 8, but seeing that the reënforcement and supplies that should come from Mapimí did not arrive, he resumed his march on this day, traveling as far as San Pedro, eight leagues hence.

On February 9, he marched twelve leagues, but finding no water, he ordered the expedition to halt to allow the horses to rest. About midnight he started again and traveled as far as Laguna de Parras before sunrise, where he stayed until February 14. While here he sent out Indian scouts to locate a watering place for the next march. Upon their return, he decided to go to Aguachile. On the following day, therefore, he set out early in the morning, traveling to the northeast, until he reached Aguachile Pass, ten leagues beyond his camp. Although there was no water here, he decided to stop and allow the horses to graze a while before proceeding. Early in the morning on February 16, he resumed the march and after traveling about eleven or twelve leagues to the north, he arrived at Aguachile. Here he found plenty of water and good pasturage for the horses. It was decided to stay in camp while scouts were sent to ascertain whether there was sufficient water at Cuatro Ciénegas. The scouts returned on February 19 and reported water at San Marcos. They said they had found traces of hostile Indians who were conducting a drove of horses.

The route they followed now lay to the northeast. The expedition went fifteen or sixteen leagues, but found no water. It was decided to halt and allow the horses to rest. Early next morning they continued the march and traveled about sixteen leagues, before they arrived at San Marcos, about eight o'clock in the evening. Here they found good water and plenty of good grass. An investigation of the Indian tracks disclosed that the savages were going in a direction opposite to that of the expedition and it was decided not to give them chase, as they had too much of a start and it would only tire the horses. Berroterán now made his way to Boca de Nadadores, where he arrived on February 22, in the afternoon, after traveling ten leagues. The following day he went to Santa Rosa de Nadadores. Here Father Fray Martín Silva, the missionary of the *pueblo,* informed him that there was little water and grass in the vicinity of Coahuila (Monclova). Berroterán decided to halt at this place and rest the men and horses before proceeding to Coahuila.

On February 24, leaving the main body of the expedition in camp, he set out with twenty soldiers for the Presidio of Coahuila (Monclova), which was six leagues from the camp at Santa Rosa. Here he was met by Don Manuel de Sandoval, Governor of Coahuila, to whom he gave the orders he had received from the viceroy with regard to the contingent which this officer was to give him for the expedition. The governor declared he was ready to comply, but asked for time to get the men together and equip them with arms and supplies. Berroterán returned, therefore, to his camp at Santa Rosa de Nadadores.

On February 27, he requested the governor to give him four good Indian scouts, which he did promptly. Berroterán gave them provisions for six days and sent them, with two others from Santa Rosa, to find out where the Indian tracks in the neighborhood of Cuatro Ciénegas led to. They returned on March 6 and reported that the hostile Indians had gone towards Tenaute, which was more than forty leagues from Santa Rosa. Berroterán gave up all idea of following them in view of the distance.

On March 7, the expedition moved from Santa Rosa to within one league of Coahuila (Monclova) and camped at the Hacienda del Cura. The next day the commander was assured by the governor that the men from the Presidio of Coahuila would be ready shortly and would follow Berroterán as soon as they could. He, therefore, started for San Juan Bautista and traveled seven leagues on March 8, to Las Adjuntas. The following day the expedition covered ten leagues and halted at Alamo Seco. Here they stayed a day to take care of a servant who had suffered severe injuries as a result of a fall from his horse. Continuing by moderate stages, he arrived at San Juan Bautista on the Río Grande on March 15, after traveling thirty-four leagues from Alamo Seco.

Captain Berroterán stayed at San Juan Bautista for several days, waiting for the detachments that were to join him and for the necessary supplies before he started on his mission of exploring the unknown regions of the Río Grande from this presidio to the Junta de los Ríos. On March 20, Alférez Diego Jiménez, from the Presidio of Coahuila, brought fourteen men and a train of supplies from that post. On March 26, Berrotéran asked Captain José Antonio de Eca y Músquiz to hold a council of the most experienced officers and men to try to determine the best route he should follow. The council was held, but all of those who attended, among whom were Diego Ramón, José Hernández, Santiago Jiménez, and Andrés Ramón, knew nothing of the country that was to be explored. They all declared that the Indian nations that lived in this territory were hostile, that the land was rough and lacked water, and that no one had ever penetrated this area.[39]

Undaunted by the information given him by the council, Captain Berroterán held a review of his forces on March 28, in preparation for his departure to the unknown land of the Río Grande. He found he had fifty-eight soldiers from Nueva Vizcaya, fifteen from Coahuila (Monclova), and fifteen from San Juan Bautista, making a total of eighty-eight. There were also forty friendly Indians from the Province of Coahuila, and six he had brought from the Presidio de Conchos. The men were well equipped with the necessary arms and ammunition, and sufficient supplies for the expedition that had been gathered. Immediately upon the completion of the review, he set out for the Río Grande and proceeded along its western bank for a distance of seven leagues, to a place which he called Santo Domingo. From here he dispatched eight Indian scouts to explore the country and to locate the San Antonio and San Rodrigo Rivers. They were instructed to watch for any sign of enemies in the neighborhood. Without waiting for their return, he continued the march the following day and reached San Antonio River (on the west side of the Río Grande, about twenty-five miles from modern Eagle Pass). Here he waited for information from his scouts until April 1.

On this day he resumed the march and reached San Rodrigo River, without finding a trace of the enemy or learning anything of its whereabouts. The next day he dispatched ten Indians to reconnoitre the banks of the San Diego and explore its source, as well as Las Vacas, another stream beyond the San Diego.[40] It was at the headwaters of the San Diego and on Las Vacas that the hostile Indians generally had their headquarters, according to the opinion of the council held at San Juan Bautista. For this reason Berroterán was proceeding with great caution during this

---

[39]Expedientes relativos á reconocimiento . . . *A. G. N., História,* Vol. 52.

[40]The San Diego River is about twenty miles to the south of present Villa Acuña which until very recently was called Las Vacas, because it is located at the mouth of the stream that bears this name, which flows into the Río Grande at this point.

stage of his march. The scouts sent out were instructed to report without delay the discovery of the enemy, and to try to locate it without being noticed.

While at San Rodrigo River, Berroterán received a letter from the commander of the Presidio of San Juan Bautista and another from the Governor of Coahuila, on April 3. These officers informed him that a band of hostile Indians had struck Parras and Saltillo, had stolen a good drove of horses, and had killed several persons. In view of this circumstance, he was asked to divide his party into three detachments, one to return to Presidio de Coahuila (Monclova), one to go to Santa Rosa de Nadadores, and the third to march to the pass that led into Cuatro Ciénegas. Upon receipt of this information and request, he called a council of his officers and most experienced soldiers. They were all of the opinion that it was seventy leagues to Coahuila and ninety to Cuatro Ciénegas, in an opposite direction from that in which the expedition was supposed to travel. If the party was divided as suggested the success of the entire expedition and the safety of the men were seriously jeopardized. There was little hope that by the time the detachments arrived in the field of activity of the marauding band they would be able to chastise the enemy, who would be gone. It was decided, therefore, it would be best to continue on the journey along the route mapped out.

On April 4, two Indian scouts reported the presence of a band of Indians hunting buffalo, about ten leagues from San Rodrigo. The following day four other scouts returned and confirmed the statement. Leaving a competent guard of thirty men in camp to protect the baggage and supplies, Berroterán set out in search of these bands with the rest of the expedition, allowing the Indians to guide him. They traveled about ten leagues to the San Diego River but could discover no trace of the hostile Indians, said to be Apaches. From here seven more Indians were sent out in search of the enemy. On April 8 they returned and reported that they had followed the tracks and had come upon some Pascuache Indians who were hunting buffalo. They explained that these Indians were friendly to the Spaniards and that when asked if they knew of any other natives in the vicinity, they had all said that there were none.

Still fearful of the presence of hostile Indians, Berroterán dispatched six Indian runners, on April 9, from San Diego River to reconnoitre and observe both banks upstream as far as its source and all water holes in its vicinity. Six others were sent at the same time to do likewise with regard to Las Vacas and its vicinity, with strict instructions to report the presence of Apaches or any other enemies discovered in either place. He sent word to Diego Jiménez, who had stayed behind with thirty men and the baggage at San Rodrigo River, to join him at his new camp on the San Diego.

On April 10, Berroterán decided to call a council of his officers and most experienced men to consult with them about the policy he should follow. The Indian scouts did not seem reliable and it looked as if they were purposely delaying the advance in order to consume all the provisions and cause the expedition to return to San Juan Bautista or desist, at any rate, from going farther. When the officers had been assembled, they all declared they knew nothing about the country they were to explore. Upon questioning the oldest and most experienced soldiers, no additional information could be gained. He was forced, therefore, to depend upon such information as the scouts could give him from day to day.

On April 11, the expedition resumed its march to Las Vacas, but halted after traveling about six leagues. The following day they arrived at Las Vacas River, a small stream in the present site of Villa Acuña, opposite Del Río. From there he followed the west bank of the Río Grande, and, after traveling seven leagues, or approximately twenty miles, he came to the crossing known as Las Cíbolas, on April 13. This must have been in the neighborhood of present day Comstock. Opposite this little town there are some springs on the east bank of the Río Grande. But as the river runs through a fairly deep canyon along this area, Berroterán did not discover the spring. Unable to continue along the river, he sent scouts to discover a possible route and an appropriate place to water the horses and stock. On April 15, he obtained news that there was a place where the horses and stock could be watered on the river above the camp. In order to reach it, however, the expedition would have to make a long detour to the west. The following day they started and traveled eight leagues before they came to a place to camp, which they called Virgen del Socorro. From here the march was resumed on April 17, in search of some water holes said to be to the northwest, about fourteen leagues beyond. By traveling since before dawn on April 18 they managed to reach the watering place they were looking for, after marching about fourteen leagues. All the Indian scouts who had been sent out returned to the camp and informed Berroterán that the river was about six leagues distant and that the road crossed to the east or north side.

On April 19, early in the morning, the expedition again set out and reached the Río Grande at noon, crossed it, and traveled about two leagues, along its bank upstream before camping. From the time they left Las Vacas, present Villa Acuña, the expedition had traveled along the west bank of the river about forty leagues, but they had been obliged to make long detours to the west, so that in a straight line they must have gone about twenty leagues, or approximately fifty or sixty miles, to the point where they crossed the river. This would put them in the neighborhood of present day Langtry. It was here that Berroterán crossed the Río Grande into Texas, somewhere in the neighborhood of Langtry, Osman, or Shumla. The description of the place where they camped is meager. All that is recorded is that there was grass for the horses and that the stock could be watered in the river. The country was not so rough as that already traversed.

Here they stayed for a day, while scouts were sent ahead to explore the land and find suitable places to water the horses. On April 20, one of the Indians returned and reported a good camp site on the river about four leagues up the stream. The expedition moved that day to the new place. The following day they traveled up the river about six leagues and pitched camp at a place where there was plenty of grass. On April 22 they again advanced three leagues farther up stream. Here they were informed by the Indian scouts that it was impossible to proceed farther. They had traveled about thirteen leagues, almost due west, along the river. They must have been at this time about thirty or forty miles from the point where they crossed the river. If such was the case they were in the neighborhood of present day Dryden, to the south, along the river, just where the Río Grande makes a big bend to the southwest. The Indians declared that from here on the river ran through a deep canyon and that the mountains on either side were practically impassable. Late that evening, however, one of the scouts reported a watering place about five leagues above, adding that it would be necessary to travel ten to reach it. On April 23, Berroterán and his men set out for the new site and arrived on the river again. He was informed there that a smoke had been seen in what was believed to be Las Animas Mountains and that from here on the country was extremely difficult for travel. Upon examining the river and noting the deep canyon through which it flowed, Berroterán decided to cross to the south side for fear of a flood which might keep him on the north side longer than his supplies held out. He accordingly established his camp on the south side of the river. He had thus explored only a short distance of about eighty or one hundred miles of the Río Grande from the neighborhood of Shumla to a point south of Dryden before returning to the Mexican side.

He remained in camp until April 28, waiting for news from various Indians he had sent to explore the country and to find a route which could be followed by the expedition. On this day the scouts returned and reported that they had explored Las Animas Mountains, which were about forty leagues beyond. In all that distance they said there were no suitable watering places; the mountains were very rough; and although they had examined the country to the north and south of the river, they had not been able to find a way by which the expedition could continue. Three of the Indians had been left, too tired to travel, near the Río Grande, in the mountains. Berroterán called a council of his officers, and, after discussing the difficulty of continuing the march to La Junta de los Ríos along the Río Grande, it was unanimously decided it was impossible to do so with the reduced supplies at hand. He consequently ordered the detachments from Coahuila to return to their presidios by way of Santa Rosa de Nadadores and to explore the mountains in that neighborhood. He asked them to report to him whatever they found, by way of Saltillo, in order that he might inform the viceroy.

Return march of Berroterán.   On April 29, the detachments from the Province of Coahuila started back home as ordered. The remainder of the expedition, which was composed of soldiers from Nueva Vizcaya set out across the country to their respective presidios, traveling that day about eighteen leagues. They halted and camped without water, continuing early the next day until they came upon what they thought was the Río Grande, where they found the three Indian scouts who had stayed behind, worn out with fatigue. After many similar forced marches, Berroterán succeeded in arriving at the Presidio de Conchos in Nueva Vizcaya on May 16. He immediately notified the governor of his return and was ordered to send the various detachments to their respective presidios and to make a personal report of the expedition to the governor that he might transmit the same to the viceroy. Accordingly, on May 22, 1729, Berroterán made his report and sent a detailed diary of the expedition placed under his charge to explore the country from the Presidio of San Juan Bautista to La Junta de los Ríos.[41]

---

[41]The details summarized in the preceding pages concerning the expedition to explore the Río Grande are taken in their entirety from the official Diario de la Campaña executada de orden del Exmo Señor Marqués de Casafuerte, por Dn. Joseph Berroterán, Capitán del Presidio de Conchos, para el reconocimiento de las

Rivera's opinion of the exploration and his conclusions. The report and diaries of the expedition were immediately transmitted to the viceroy who, on July 28, 1729, referred them to Brigadier Rivera for his inspection and opinion. With characteristic promptness, the old inspector replied on September 9.[42] It was evident, he declared, that Captain Berroterán had not exerted himself as became an officer of the king to carry out the implicit orders and instructions of His Excellency in the conduct of the expedition, which had failed miserably in attaining the end desired. Proof of the reluctance with which this officer had proceeded in the entire expedition was the fact that he made up his mind before he started that the undertaking was impracticable and impossible. In this state of mind, it was only natural that he should be inclined to prove by the actual failure of the expedition the futility of the project. He had gone from Mapimí to the Presidio of Coahuila, over an uninhabited region, much against his will. To have called a council at this presidio to determine the route and policy to be followed in exploring an unknown area, showed lack of judgment, or an evident unwillingness to follow the simple instructions given him for the expedition. Rivera very logically stated that an expedition undertaken to explore an undiscovered territory must follow a route which is unknown. If the way was known it would obviate the necessity of finding a route. In the case of the expedition entrusted to Berroterán, all he had to do was to follow the river. He needed no other direction or guide.

Having had considerable experience in traveling long distances over the dry and arid regions of the frontiers of New Spain during his inspection of the presidios, Rivera pointed out that the difficulties which such arid country offered and which were considered unsurmountable by Berroterán, were easily overcome by traveling early in the morning until noon, resting during the hot part of the day, and resuming the march in the cool of the evening. He declared that he had covered many leagues of arid territory without water during his inspection of the presidios of Nueva Vizcaya and New Mexico. The council which Berroterán called on April 28, on the Río Grande, was equally useless he said. There was then, as in the beginning, only one thing for him to have done, to follow

---

Margenes del Río del Norte, en el año de 1729, *A. G. I., Audiencia de Guadalajara,* 104-6-15, and from the documents concerning this expedition found in *A. G. N., História,* Vol. 52.

[42]The Viceroy to Rivera, July 28, 1729. *A. G. I., Audiencia de Guadalajara,* 104-6-15; also Rivera to the Viceroy in *Ibid.*

the river as instructed. He placed entirely too much reliance on his Indian scouts and did not explore the country for himself. He should have exercised more judgment and initiative in an unexplored country.

Rivera pointed out that to depend entirely on the information which friendly Indians were able to give in traveling over an unexplored region was foolish. The general method used by all those who had led such expeditions was to follow a given direction, the leader finding the way for himself, while his Indian scouts investigated the country to either side, keeping in contact with him by following his trail. In this manner, with the aid of the additional information, the leader could modify his route according to circumstances.

He called the attention of the viceroy to the fact that much more difficult explorations had been accomplished in the past without the help of guides and without any specific instructions, such as that of Juan de Oñate, from Santa Fe to the Gulf of California, Alonso de León to the country of Navedachos, and Francisco Alvarez Barreyro, who had explored the coast of Texas from the Bay of Espíritu Santo to the Neches River in the vicinity of Los Adaes, crossing many rivers and marshes. The difficulties encountered by Berroterán were not so great as he made them out to be in his report. The best index to the actual hardships of any expedition, he declared, was the number of horses and beasts of burden that were lost. In the entire expedition, Berroterán lost only twenty-five horses and three mules, which were left on the road worn out or tired. Compare this to the five hundred horses lost by Domingo Terán de los Rios in his expedition to East Texas, or the losses sustained by Alonso de León, who, on his return, had less than half of those with which he started, or the eight hundred which Aguayo lost in his expedition in 1722, Rivera declared.

The main object of the expedition had been to explore the country between San Juan Bautista on the Río Grande and the point where the Conchos joins this river, generally known as La Junta de los Ríos. This land had never been entered by Spaniards and was the known refuge of all the marauding Indians that preyed on the exposed settlements of Nueva Vizcaya, Coahuila, and Nuevo Reyno de León. In this attempt the expedition had been an utter failure, as it had explored this country for only a short distance beyond the Presidio of San Juan Bautista. But on the other hand, the march from Mapimí to San Juan Bautista by way of the Presidio of Coahuila was the first of its kind. It opened a new route which connected Nueva Vizcaya with the Presidio of San Juan

Bautista on the Río Grande heretofore ignored and thought impossible. Likewise the route back from San Juan Bautista, by way of the Río Grande to the Presidio de Conchos had opened a large area heretofore unexplored and had shown a new route of communication. The greatest advantage enjoyed by the hostile Indians that inhabited these regions was their intimate knowledge of the country through which they made their escape. The ignorance on the part of the presidial soldiers accounted for their inability to check the depredations of the Indians in this vast frontier. But with a growing knowledge of the lands where the Indians took refuge, the time would come, Rivera said, when such depredations would cease entirely. In closing his *parecer,* Rivera emphatically declared that the country left unexplored along the Río Grande from San Juan Bautista to the Junta de los Ríos should be explored and that His Excellency should issue the necessary orders for a new expedition as soon as possible.[43]

Opinion of the Auditor. The diary and report of Berroterán, together with the opinion of Rivera were referred to the *Auditor* Oliván Rebolledo, who, after a careful study of all the related documents of this expedition, wrote an opinion on May 12, 1730. He pointed out that the undertaking entrusted to Berroterán had had two purposes in view: to explore the country along the Río Grande from San Juan Bautista to the Junta de los Ríos, and to open a new means of communication between Nueva Vizcaya and Coahuila, in order that the presidios in these two provinces might be better able to render each other mutual aid. The accomplishment of these two objectives would have naturally resulted in forcing the Indians who inhabited these regions to make peace. The additional knowledge gained by the expedition, had it succeeded in its two purposes, would have permitted the location of the Presidio of Sacramento, now in Nueva Vizcaya, somewhere along the Río Grande, where it could render more effective service in checking the depredations of the Indians from the north.

But it was evident that the first object of the expedition had not been attained and that the failure to do so was due to the reasons so ably presented by Rivera. The second object, however, had been accomplished and a new route opened for communication and transit between the presidios of Nueva Vizcaya and those of Coahuila. It would be highly advisable,

[43]Parecer del Brigadier D. Pedro de Rivera. September 9, 1729. *A. G. I., Audiencia de Guadalajara,* 104-6-15.

nevertheless, Rebolledo concluded, that a new expedition be ordered before the end of the year, to be undertaken during the rainy season, possibly the fall, in order to traverse under more favorable circumstances the arid regions feared by Berroterán.[44]

The viceroy, in view of the opinions of Rivera and Oliván Rebolledo, ordered on June 17, 1730, that the Governor of Parral be informed of the laxity with which Captain Berroterán conducted the expedition entrusted to him; and that this was not as impossible or difficult as he had reported, as evidenced by the opinions of the two counselors. Since it was not only important, but essential, to explore the land from San Juan Bautista to the Junta de los Ríos, the Governor of Nueva Vizcaya was requested to make arrangements for a new expedition, which was to be undertaken as soon as possible, at a season of the year when the water was more abundant in the arid regions that were to be explored. The expedition, in addition to examining the land and noting its characteristics and the Indians that lived there, was to keep in mind the selection of a suitable place for the location of the Presidio of Sacramento on the Río Grande.[45]

It is evident that viceregal officials fully realized the importance of exploring this undiscovered area, which was justly considered to be the refuge of the hostile Indians of the Great Plains that constantly menaced and harassed the frontier settlements of New Spain along the north and east.

---

[44]Parecer del Auditor Oliván Rebolledo. *A. G. I., Audiencia de Guadalajara,* 104-6-15.

[45]Acuerdo del Virrey, June 17, 1730. *A. G. I., Audiencia de Guadalajara,* 104-6-15.

BIBLIOGRAPHY

PRINTED WORKS

Arricivita, Juan Domingo
    Crónica Seráfica y Apostólica del Colegio de Propaganda Fide de la Santa Cruz de Querétaro en la Nueva España, Dedicada al Santísimo Patriarca el Señor San Joseph. Segunda Parte. Mexico, 1792.

Bancroft, Hubert Howe
    . . . *History of the North Mexican States and Texas.* . . . San Francisco, 1884-1889, 2 Vols. (The Works of Hubert Howe Bancroft, Vols. XV-XVI.)

Benavides, Alonso de
    The Memorial of Fray Alonso de Benavides, 1630; Translated by Mrs. Edward E. Ayer, Annotated by Frederick Webb Hodge and Charles Fletcher Lummis. Chicago, 1916.

Bolton, Herbert Eugene
    Athanase de Mézières and the Louisiana-Texas Frontier, 1768-1780. Cleveland, 1911. 2 Vols.
——"The Native Tribes about the East Texas Missions," in Texas State Historical Association, *The Quarterly,* Vol. XI, No. 4, April, 1908, pp. 249-276.
——*Spanish Exploration in the Southwest, 1542-1706.* New York, 1916.
——"Spanish Mission Records at San Antonio," in Texas State Historical Association, *The Quarterly,* Vol. X, No. 4, April, 1907, pp. 297-308.
——*Texas in the Middle Eighteenth Century; Studies in Spanish Colonial History and Administration.* Berkeley, 1915. (University of California Publications in History . . . Vol. III.)

Buckley, Eleanor Claire
    "The Aguayo Expedition into Texas and Louisiana, 1719-1722," in Texas State Historical Association, *The Quarterly,* Vol. XV, No. 1, July, 1911, pp. 1-65.

Castañeda, Carlos Eduardo
    "The First American Play" in *The Catholic World,* January, 1932.
    Morfi's History of Texas, 1673-1779. See Morfi, Fray Juan Agustín.

Clark, Robert Carlton
    . . . *The Beginnings of Texas,* 1684-1718. [Austin, Texas, 1907.] (University of Texas Bulletin No. 98, Humanistic Series No. 6, December 1, 1907.)

Cox, Isaac Joslin
    "The Founding of the First Texas Municipality," in Texas State Historical Association, *The Quarterly,* Vol. II, No. 3, January, 1899, pp. 217-226.

Dunn, William Edward
    "Apache Relations in Texas, 1718-1750," in Texas State Historical Association, *The Quarterly,* Vol. XIV, No. 3, January, 1911, pp. 198-274.
——*Spanish and French Rivalry in the Gulf Region of the United States, 1678-1702; the Beginnings of Texas and Pensacola.* Austin, Texas [1917.] University of Texas Bulletin No. 1705: January 20, 1917.)

Espinosa, Isidro Félix
  *Chrónica Apostólica, y Seráphica de Todos los Colegios de Propaganda Fide de
    Esta Nueva-España* . . . Madrid, 1746.
——. . . . *The Espinosa-Olivares-Aguirre Expedition of 1709* [translated] by Rev.
    Gabriel Tous. [Austin, Texas, 1930.] Texas Catholic Historical Society
    Preliminary Studies, Vol I, No. 3, March, 1930.
——. . . . *Ramón Expedition: Espinosa's Diary of 1716* [translated] by Rev. Gabriel
    Tous. Austin, Texas. 1930. Texas Catholic Historical Society, *Preliminary
    Studies,* Vol. I, No. 4, April, 1930.

Foik, Paul J., tr. See Ramón, Domingo

Forrestal, Peter P., tr.
  . . . *Peña's Diary of the Aguayo Expedition.* See Peña, Juan Antonio.

Fortier, Alcée
  A History of Louisiana. New York, 1904. 4 Vols.

French, Benjamin Franklin, ed.
  Historical Collections of Louisiana . . . New York, 1846-1853. 5 Vols.

Hackett, Charles Wilson, tr. and ed.
  Pichardo's Treatise on the Limits of Louisiana and Texas. See Pichardo, José
    Antonio.

Hassall, Arthur
  The Balance of Power, 1715-1789. New York, London, 1900.

Hatcher, Mrs. Mattie Austin
  "The Municipal Government of San Fernando de Béxar, 1730-1800," in Texas
    State Historical Association, *The Quarterly,* Vol. VIII, No. 4, April, 1905,
    pp. 277-353.

Heinrich, Pierre
  La Louisiane sous la Compagnie des Indies, 1717-1737. Paris [n. d.]

Hodge, Frederick Webb, ed.
  Handbook of American Indians North of Mexico. Washington, 1907-1910. 2
    Vols. (Smithsonian Institution. Bureau of American Ethnology. Bulletin
    No. 30.)

Le Page du Pratz
  *Histoire de la Louisiane, Contenant la Découverte de ce vaste pays: sa Descrip-
    tion géographique; un Voyage dans les Terres; l'Histoire Naturelle, les
    Moeurs, Coûtumes et Religion des Naturels, avec leurs Origines; deux Voy-
    ages dans le Nord de nouveau Mexique, dont un jusqu' à la Mer du Sud* . . .
    Paris, 1758. 3 Vols.

Margry, Pierre
  *Découvertes et Etablissements des Français dans l'ouest et dans de Sud de
    l'Amérique Septentrionale (1614-1754)* . . . Paris, 1879-1888. 6 Vols.

Morfi, Fray Juan Agustín
  History of Texas, 1673-1779 . . . Translated with biographical introduction and
    annotations by Carlos Eduardo Castañeda, Quivira Society, 1935.

Ogg, Frederick Austin
  The Opening of the Mississippi; a Struggle for Supremacy in the American Interior. New York, London, 1904.

Peña, Juan Antonio de la
  Derrotero de la Expedición en la Provincia de los Texas, Nuevo Reyno de Philipinas, que de orden del Excmo. Señor Marqués de Valero, Vi-Rey, y Capitán General de esta Nueva-España passa á executar el Muy Illustre Señor D. Joseph de Azlor . . . que escribe el Br. Juan Antonio de la Peña. Mexico, Juan Francisco de Ortega Bonilla, 1722. (Photostat copy in possession of the author. A translation has been made by Peter P. Forrestal in Texas Catholic Historical Society, *Preliminary Studies,* Vol. II, No. 7, January, 1935.
——*Peña's Diary of the Aguayo Expedition; Translated by Rev. Peter P. Forrestal.* [Austin, Texas, 1935.] Texas Catholic Historical Society, *Preliminary Studies,* Vol. II, No. 7, January, 1935.

Pichardo, José Antonio
  Pichardo's Treatise on the Limits of Louisiana and Texas . . . Translated into English by Charles Wilson Hackett . . . Austin, Texas, 1931-1934. 2 Vols.

Ramón, Domingo
  . . . Captain Don Domingo Ramón's Diary of His Expedition Into Texas in 1716 [*translated*] by Rev. Paul J. Foik. Austin, Texas, 1933. Texas Catholic Historical Society, *Preliminary Studies,* Vol. II, No. 5, April, 1933.

St. Denis, Louis Juchereau
  . . . "St. Denis's Declaration Concerning Texas in 1717" [translated and edited by] Charmion Claire Shelby, in Southwestern Historical Association, *The Quarterly,* XXVI, No. 3, January, 1923. (Spanish text in *A. G. I., Audiencia de México,* 61-6-35. Dunn, Gulf Region, 1713-1721, pp. 34-50.)

Shelby, Charmion Claire, tr. See St. Denis

Thomas, Alfred
  "The Massacre of the Villasur Expedition at the Forks of the Red River," in *Nebraska History and Records of Pioneer Days,* Vol. VIII, No. 3.

Tous, Gabriel, tr.
  "The Espinosa-Olivares-Aguirre Expedition of 1709." See Espinosa, Isidro Félix.

List of Manuscripts Cited

In listing the manuscript materials used in the preparation of this volume, they have been placed in strict alphabetical order. This arrangement will make it easier for the reader to find the references given throughout the text. As few abbreviations as possible have been used. In the citations A. G. I. means Archivo General de Indias, Sevilla, and A. G. M. means Archivo General y Público, Mexico. In addition to the numerous transcripts from these two invaluable depositories of sources for the period covered, much pertinent information heretofore unknown has been found in the Archivo de San Francisco el Grande, the archive of the mother house of the Franciscans in Mexico, only recently made available to the public in the Biblioteca Nacional de México. All the documents concerning Texas in this rich archive were listed, calendared, and copied with a photostat machine by the author. Approximately ten thousand pages, covering the period from 1673 to 1800, were reproduced and bound in thirty-six volumes. The Saltillo Archives consist of approximately thirteen thousand pages of documents pertaining to the history of Texas, from 1688 to 1800, which were calendared and copied by the author from the State Archives of Coahuila, in the Biblioteca del Estado, at Saltillo. They have been bound in fifty volumes. Copies of these two collections are now in the University of Texas Library. Practically every manuscript cited is found in the University of Texas Library or the Catholic Archives of Texas, St. Edward's University, Austin. Those not in either of these two depositories are in the author's possession.

Acta de Fundación de la Villa de San Fernando. 1731. (Photostat copy of the Ms. from the Guadalajara Archives in possession of the author.)

Aguayo, San Miguel de
   . . . Diferentes Autos y otras prouidencias dictadas por el Govor. Marqués de S. Migl. de Aguayo. Año 1720. (Saltillo Archives, I, 179-192.)
——[Decree for the establishment of San José], January 22, 1720. (A. G. I. Audiencia de Guadalajara, 67-3-11, Dunn Transcripts, 1710-1738.)
——[Public proclamation of Aguayo concerning deserters], August 2, 1720. (Saltillo Archives, I, 187-189.)
——Letter to Valero. [August 19, 1721.] (A. G. I. Audiencia de México, 61-2-2. Dunn, Gulf Region, 1713-1721, pp. 251-262.)
——Letter to the viceroy, November 7, 1721. (A. G. I. Audiencia de México, 61-2-2. Dunn Transcripts, 1713-1722.)
——[Appointment of Nicolás Flores y Valdez as Captain of San Antonio de Béjar], April 30, 1722. (A. G. M. Provincias Internas, Vol. 32, pt. 2.)
——[Certificatión de servicios del Capitán Nicolás Flores.] May 3, 1722. (A. G. M. Provincias Internas, Vol. 32, pt. 2.)
——[Testimonio á favor de Nicolás Flores.] May 3, 1722. (A. G. M. Provincias Internas, Vol. 32, pt. 2.)
——Letter to the King, June 13, 1722. (A. G. I. Audiencia de Guadalajara, 67-3-11. Dunn Transcripts, 1710-1738.)
——Letter to the Viceroy, November 21, 1723. (A. G. M. Provincias Internas, Vol. 181, pt. 1, pp. 279-286.)
——Letter to Margil, July 4, 1724. (Archivo del Colegio de la Santa Cruz de Querétaro. Dunn Transcripts, 1716-1749.)
——Letter to the Viceroy, February 26, 1725. (A. G. M. Provincias Internas, Vol. 32, pt. 2.)
——Memoria de lo que dá el Marqs. de Sn. Migl. de Aguaio pa formal la Mision de Sn. Franco. Jauier Junto al Presidio de Sn. Antonio de la Prouincia de Tejas . . . [July? 1725]. (Archivo del Colegio de la Santa Cruz de Querétaro. Dunn Transcripts, 1716-1749, pp. 6-7.)
——Letter to Espinosa, July 3, 1725. (Archivo del Colegio de la Santa Cruz de Querétaro. Dunn Transcripts, 1716-1749, pp. 8-9.)

Alarcón, Martín de
   Letter to the Viceroy [December, 1716]. (A. G. I. Audiencia de México, 61-6-35. Dunn, Gulf Region, 1713-1721, pp. 207-209.)
——Letter to the Viceroy, asking that salary be paid in advance. [December 10, 1716]. (A. G. I. Audiencia de México, 61-6-35. Dunn, Gulf Region, 1713-1721, pp. 227-229.)
——Letter to the Viceroy, December 11, 1716. (A. G. M. Provincias Internas, Vol. 181, pt. 1, p. 204.)

Alarcón, Martín de
 Letter to the Viceroy, December 14, 1716. (A. G. M. Provincias Internas, Vol. 181, pt. 1, pp. 206-208.)
——Letter to the Viceroy, June 27, 1717. (A. G. I. Audiencia de México, 61-6-35. Dunn, Gulf Region, 1713-1721, pp. 22-23.)
——Letter to the Viceroy, September 28, 1718. (Archivo San Francisco el Grande, 1722-1728, II, 2.)
——Letter to the King, November 3, 1721. (Archivo San Francisco el Grande, IX, 21-25.)

Almazán, Fernando Pérez de. See Pérez de Almazán, Fernando.

Almazán, Juan Antonio. See Pérez de Almazán, Juan Antonio.

Alonso González, Fernando
 [Orden que salga inmediatamente sacerdote de San Antonio de Valero para la Bahía], December 9, 1726. (A. G. M. Provincias Internas, Vol. 236, pt. 1, p. 65.)

[Approval of the] Junta de Hacienda, October 6, 1724. (A. G. I. Audiencia de México, 62-1-41. Dunn Transcripts, 1723-1729.)

Arriola, Andrés de
 Letter to the Viceroy, June 4, 1700. (A. G. I. Audiencia de México, 61-6-22. Dunn Transcripts, 1700-1702, pp. 170-171. Cited in a letter of Francisco Martínez to the king, April 14, 1702.)

Autto de Elecciónes. August 1, 1731. (A. G. M. Provincias Internas, Vol. 32, pt. 2.)

[Auto de Fundación de la Misión de Nuestra Señora de la Concepción de los Aynais.] August 8, 1721. (A. G. I. Audiencia de México, 61-2-2. Dunn Transcripts, 1713-1722.)

[Auto de Fundación de la Misión de Nuestra Señora de Guadalupe de los Nacogdoches.] August 18, 1721. (A. G. I. Audiencia de México, 61-2-2. Dunn Transcripts, 1713-1722.)

[Auto de Fundación de la Misión de Nuestra Señora de los Dolores.] August 23, 1721. (A. G. I. Audiencia de México, 61-2-2. Dunn Transcripts, 1713-1722.)

[Auto de Fundación de la Misión de San Miguel de los Adaes.] September 29, 1721. (A. G. I. Audiencia de México, 61-2-2. Dunn Transcripts, 1713-1722.)

[Auto de Fundación de la Misión de San Francisco de los Neches.] August 5, 1721. (A. G. I. Audiencia de México, 61-2-2. Dunn Transcripts, 1713-1722.)

[Auto de Fundación de la Misión de San José de los Nazonis.] August 13, 1721. (A. G. I. Audiencia de México, 61-2-2. Dunn Transcripts, 1713-1722.)

[Auto de Fundación del Presidio de Nuestra Señora del Pilár de los Adaes. November 4, 1721. (A. G. I. Audiencia de México, 61-2-2. Dunn Transcripts, 1713-1722.)

[Auto de] Fundación del Pueblo y Misión de san franzco. solano en el nuebo Valle de la zircunzición de Yndios Gentiles de las Naciones Sarames; Papanac: Payaguan: y siguam. 1700. (A. G. M. Provincias Internas, Vol. 28, pp. 70-77.)

[Auto de posesión de la Misión de Nuestra Señora de Loreto.] April 10, 1722. (A. G. I. Audiencia de Guadalajara, 67-3-11. Dunn Transcripts, 1710-1738.)

Auto de Posesión [de la Misión de San Francisco Xavier.] March 12, 1722. (A. G. I. Audiencia de Guadalajara, 67-3-11. Dunn Transcripts, 1710-1738.)

Auto en q se da razón de hauer ospedado a los Ysleños y otras probidencias. March 10, 1731. (A. G. M. Provincias Internas, Vol. 32, pt. 2. (Bolton Transcripts, 1725-1730.)

Autos fechos en la Bahia de el Espíritu Santo Sobre dos muertos que ejecutaron los Yndios en los Soldados que guardauan la Cauallada de dho Presidio el dia, 13 de Eno. de este Año de 1724, por Dn. ferndo. Perez de Almasán Gouor. y. Capn. Genl. de esta Proua. de Tejas Nuebas Philipinas. (A. G. M. Provincias Internas, Vol. 181, pt. 1, pp. 292-330.)

Autos sobre el descubrimiento de la Gran Quivira segun lo consultado por el Marqués de San Miguel de Aguayo, Superior Govierno, año de 1715. Cited by Buckley, "Aguayo Expedition Into Texas and Louisiana, 1719-1722," in Texas State Historical Association, *The Quarterly,* Vol. XV, No. 1, July, 1911, p. 21. Copies of these documents are also found in the Archivo San Francisco el Grande, VIII.

Autos sobre diferentes noticias que se han Participando a su Exa. de las entradas que en estos Dominios hazen los franseses por la paz de Coahuila y Prouidencias dadas para evitarselas y fundación de la Mición en la Prouincia de los Tejas. 1715. (A. G. M. Provincias Internas, Vol. 181, pt. 1.)

Balverde y Cosío, Francisco
    Confesión [del Gobernador y Capitán General de la Provincia de Nueva México.] July 5, 1726. (A. G. M. Provincias Internas, Vol. 37, pt. 2.)

Berroterán, Joseph
    Copia del Diario de la Campaña executada de orden del Exmo. Señor Marqués de Casafuerte, por Dn. Joseph Berroterán Capitán del Presidio de Conchos, para el reconocimiento de las Margenes del Río del Norte, en el año de 1729. (A. G. I. Audiencia de Guadalajara, 104-6-15. Dunn Transcripts, 1710-1738.)

Bustillo y Ceballos, Juan Antonio de
    Letter to the Viceroy, June 18, 1726. (A. G. M. Provincias Internas, Vol. 236, pt. 1, pp. 61-63.)
——Letter to the Viceroy, May 24, 1731. (A. G. M. Provincias Internas, Vol. 236, pt. 1, pp. 16-22.)
——[Listas y relaciones juradas de soldados y pertenencias de los Adaes.] April 30, May 24, May 27, 1731. (A. G. M. Provincias Internas, Vol. 236, pt. 1, pp. 29, 32, 35.)

Casafuerte, Juan de Acuña, Marqués de
    Letter to the King, May 25, 1723. (A. G. I. Audiencia de México, 62-1-41. Dunn Transcripts, 1723-1729.)
——Decreto del Virey Casafuerte, October 10, 1724. (A. G. I. Audiencia de México, 62-1-41. Dunn Transcripts, 1723-1729.)

Casafuerte, Juan de Acuña, Marqués de

·[Decreto] para q se dediquen los Rs. Ps. Misioneros a la redución y enseñanza de los Yndios y lengua Castellana. November 15, 1724. (A. G. M. Misiones, Vol. 21, pt. 1, pp. 170-171.)

——[Order of Viceroy for establishment of San Francisco Xavier.] July 2, 1725. (Archivo de la Santa Cruz de Querétaro. Dunn Transcripts, 1716-1749.)

——[Aprobación del parecer del auditor.] August 26, 1726. (A. G. M. Provincias Internas, Vol. 236, pt. 1, p. 64.)

——Despacho del Señor Virrey [aboliendo el presidio de los Tejas.] April 26, 1729. (Archivo San Francisco el Grande, III, 4.)

——Letter to Rivera, July 28, 1729. (A. G. I. Audiencia de Guadalajara, 104-6-15. Dunn Transcripts, 1710-1738.)

——[Order of the Viceroy.] November 27, 1729. (A. G. I. Audiencia de Guadalajara, 67-4-38. Dunn Transcripts, 1710-1738.)

——Transumpto de vn Despacho del Exmo. Señor Virrey Marqs. de Casafuerte dado en 23 de febrero de 1730 á Mandando á los Cappnes. del Río grande, y Sn. Antonio, den un soldado para cada Misión de su distrito pertenecientes a este Collo. de la SSma. Cruz (Archivo del Colegio de Santa Cruz de Querétaro. Dunn Transcripts, 1716-1749.)

——Letter to the King, March 2, 1730. (A. G. I. Audiencia de México. 61-2-12. Dunn Transcripts, 1730-1736.)

——[Provisions for new expedition to explore the Río Grande from San Juan Bautista to El Paso.] A. G. M. Historia, Vol. 52, p. 64.)

——[Acuerdo del Virrey.] June 17, 1730. (A. G. I. Audiencia de Guadalajara, 104-6-15. Dunn Transcripts, 1710-1738.)

——Letter to the King, August 1, 1730. (A. G. I. Audiencia de México, 67-3-23. Dunn Transcripts, 1730-1736.)

——Letter to Laba, August 1, 1730. (A. G. M. Provincias Internas. Vol. 32, pt. 1.)

——Letter to Laba, August 28, 1730. (A. G. M. Provincias Internas, Vol. 32, pt. 1.)

——Letter to Laba, August 31, 1730. (A. G. M. Provincias Internas, Vol. 32, pt. 1.)

——Letter to Laba, September 6, 1730. (A. G. M. Provincias Internas, Vol. 32, pt. 1.)

——Letter to Laba, September 12, 1730. (A. G. M. Provincias Internas, Vol. 32, pt. 1.)

——Letter to Laba, September 18, 1730. (A. G. M. Provincias Internas, Vol. 32, pt. 1.)

——[Approval of the Viceroy.] July 30, 1731. (A. G. M. Provincias Internas, Vol. 236, pt. 1, p. 7.)

——[Orders by the Viceroy.] August 8, 1731. (A. G. M. Provincias Internas, Vol. 236, pt. 1, p. 15.)

Castañeda, Carlos Eduardo, tr. and ed.

Morfi's History of Texas. See Morfi, Juan Agustín, Historia.

Céliz, Francisco

Comienza el diario derrotero de la entrada que hizo a la Bahía del Espíritu Santo y Provincia de los Tejas el General Don Martín de Alarcón Cavallero del Orden de Santiago, Governador y Theniente de Capitán General de las provincias de Cohaguila, Nuevo Reyno de Philipinas Provincia de los Tejas. April 9, 1718-February 10, 1719.

This diary was discovered in the Archivo General de la Nación, Mexico, in 1932. It was first published in Spanish by Ing. Vito Alessio Robles in *Universidad de México,* Tomo V, No. 25-26, 27-28, 1932-1933. It has since been translated and edited by Leo Fritz Hoffman and published by the Quivira Society as Volume V of its *Publications.* The copy used by the author was a typewritten copy presented by Señor Alessio Robles to the University of Texas Library.

[Certificación del Cabildo Justicia y Regimiento de la Villa de Santiago de la Monclova.] August 6, 1717. (A. G. M. Provincias Internas, Vol. 181, pt. 1, page 221.)

[Certificaciónes del Capitán Juan Domínguez de Mendoza] Junta de los Ríos, June 12-13 [1684.] (A. G. M. Provincias Internas, Vol. 37, pt. 2.)

Certificason. dada por el cavo. y Justia. de la Villa de Sanctio. de qe. para la entrada en la Prova. de texas está preparando su Govor. la avilitason. de ganads. y demas necesario y alistando los soldados pa. la compa. que se debe lebantar Sepe. 18 de 1717. (Archivo San Francisco el Grande, VIII, pp. 192-193.)

[Consulta al Consejo de Indias.] April 26, 1712. (A. G. I. Indiferente General. University of Texas transcripts, 1608-1717.)

[Consulta] de Junta de Guerra, June 6, 1701. (A. G. I. Audiencia de México, 61-6-35. Dunn Transcripts, 1700-1702, pp. 96-102.)

[Consulta] de Junta de Guerra de Indias, June 21, 1701. (A. G. I. Audiencia de México, 61-6-35. Dunn Transcripts, 1700-1702, pp. 78-95.)

[Consulta de] Junta de Grra de Yndas. a lo. de Agosto 1702. (A. G. I. Audiencia de México, 61-6-35. Dunn Transcripts, 1700-1702, pp. 74-76.)

Consta. y aprovon. pa. la visita de Presidios. May, 1723-July, 1737. (A. G. I. Audiencia de México, 62-1-41. Dunn Transcripts, 1723-1729.)

Costales, Gabriel
Letter to the Viceroy, January 7, 1731. (A. G. M. Provincias Internas, Vol. 236, pt. 1, pp. 8-10.)
——Letter to the Viceroy, June 1, 1731. (A. G. M. Provincias Internas, Vol. 236, pt. 1, pp. 3-5.)

Council of the Indies
[Recommendations of the Council of the Indies and the Royal Fiscal.] July 15 and August 8, 1727. (A. G. I. Audiencia de Guadalajara, 67-1-37. Dunn Transcripts, 1710-1738.)

De Ruego y encargo para que el Ylustressimo Señor Obispo de Guadalaxara, elija Vn Clérigo de aquella Cuidad, que pase a la nueva Poblazón, que ha de fundarse en el Presidio de San Antonio de Véjar, y administra los Santos Sacramentos, con las demas facultades que se previenen. [November 28, 1730.] A. G. M. Historia, Vol. 84, pt. 1, p. 41.)

Depositions of Yldefonso Real de Aguilar and Phelipe Tamaris, June [i. e. July] 1 and July 2, 1726. (A. G. M. Provincias Internas, Vol. 37, pt. 2.)

Díez, Joseph
> Letter to the Viceroy notifying him of the departure of Olivares. February 10, 1717. (A. G. I. Audiencia de México, 61-6-35. Dunn, Gulf Region, 1713-1721, pp. 218-219.

Diligenca y Dedan. de su nobleza y Ydalguia. July 19, 1731. (A. G. M. Provincias Internas, Vol. 32, pt. 2.)

Dilixencias Executadas Se. el restablesimto. de Misiones perthenesientes a la Proua. de los Texas Nueuas Philipinas y Consulta echa á su Ex. por Marqués de S. Migl de Aguayo con lo demas que dentro se persiue. 1721. (A. G. I. Audiencia de México, 61-2-2. Dunn Transcripts, 1713-1722.)

Directorio que ha de observar, y ordenes que ha de practicar el Sargento maior dn. Martín de Alarcón . . . (Archivo San Francisco el Grande, VIII, 217-225. A copy is also in Provincias Internas, Vol. 183. The copy in Historia, Vol. XXVII, is defective and unreliable.)

Domínguez de Mendoza, Juan
> [Diario y derrotero del Mtre. de Campo Juan Domínguez de Mendoza Cavo y Caudillo que va caminando al descubrimiento del oriente y reino de los Texas á pedimento de Don Juan Sabeata] December 15, 1683-July 18, 1684. (A. G. M. Provincias Internas, Vol. 37, pt. 2. A copy is also in Historia, Vol. 298. The diary of this expedition has been translated and published with the excellent notes in Bolton, Spanish Exploration of the Southwest, 311-343.)

En vista de lo que informa el Virrey de Nueva España . . . sobre que no se embien familias á la Provincia de los Tejas, representa a V. M. lo que se le ofrece. (A. G. I. Audiencia de México, 67-3-23. Dunn Transcripts, 1730-1736.)

Espinosa, Isidro Félix
> Diario derrotero de la nueva entrada á Prova. de los Tejas. Año de 1716. (A. G. M. Provincias Internas, Vol. 181, pt. 1, pp. 95-121. Translation by the Rev. Gabriel Tous appears in *Preliminary Studies* of the Texas Catholic Historical Society, Vol. I, No. 4, April, 1930.)
> ——Letter to the Viceroy, July 22, 1716. (A. G. M. Provincias Internas, Vol. 181, pt. 1, pp. 122-174.)
> ——Letter to the Viceroy, July 26, 1716. (A. G. I. Audiencia de México, 61-6-35. Dunn, Gulf Region, 1713-1721, pp. 167-168.)
> ——Letter to the Viceroy, February 28, 1718. (A. G. M. Provincias Internas, Vol. 181, pt. 1, p. 225.)
> ——Letter to the Viceroy, February 28, 1718. (A. G. M. Provincias Internas, Vol. 181, pt. 1, pp. 228-230.)
> ——Letter of Espinosa and Margil to the Viceroy, July 2, 1719, summarized in Espinosa *Chronica Apostólica*, 453-455. Quoted also in Buckley, "The Aguayo Expedition Into Texas and Louisiana, 1719-1722," in Texas State Historical Association, *The Quarterly*, XV, No. 1, July, 1911.

Espinosa Ocampo y Cornejo, Joseph Antonio de
> Dictamen Fiscal México Agto. 15/715, de que resulbe en todos puntos qe. expone se de quena a S. M. (Archivo San Francisco el Grande, VIII, 32-37.)
> ——[Recommendations to the Viceroy.] August 15, 1715. (A. G. M. Provincias Internas, Vol. 181, pt. 1, p. 11.)

Espinosa Ocampo y Cornejo, Joseph Antonio de
    Dictamen Fiscal Méxo. Octe. 29/715, de que se remitan por Factoria y se tome
        la provida. mandando como se pide. (Archivo San Francisco el Grande, VIII,
        56-57.)
——Opinion to the Viceroy. (A. G. M. Provincias Internas, Vol. 181, pt. 1, pp.
        134-138.)
——Respta fiscal [concerniente la Misión de San Antonio de Valero.] (A. G. I.
        Audiencia de México, 61-6-35. Dunn, Gulf Region, 1713-1721, pp. 177-182.)
——[Expedientes relativos á reconocimientos hechos en Ríos del Norte, Conchos,
        Colorado, y Gila.] (A. G. M. Historia, Vol. 52, pp. 1-78.)

Flores y Valdés, Nicolás
    Letter to San Miguel de Aguayo, October 21, 1723. A. G. M. Provincias
        Internas, Vol. 181, pt. 1, pp. 258-261.)
——Letter to Aguayo, November 2, 1723. (A. G. M. Provincias Internas, Vol. 181,
        pt. 1, 263-265.)

Franck, Jayme
    Letter to the King, June 4, 1700. (A. G. I. Audiencia de México, 61-6-22.
        Dunn Transcripts, 1700-1702, pp. 6-11.)

González, Joseph
    Certificason dada por el Je. Gonzáles de lo ocurrido en la Misión de Sn. Anto.
        Valero fha en 10 de heno de 1724. (Archivo San Francisco el Grande, X.)

Hoffman, Leo Fritz (see Céliz, Francisco)

Junta General [de Guerra y Hacienda sobre establecimiento de una misión en el Río
        San Antonio.] December 2, 1716. (A. G. I. Audiencia de México, 61-6-35.
        Dunn, Gulf Region, 1713-1721, pp. 182-202.)

Laba, Francisco Domingo
    Letter to Casafuerte, September 16, 1730. (A. G. M. Provincias Internas, Vol.
        32, pt. 1.)
——Quenta y Relación Jurada que presenta Dn. franco Domingo de Laba alcalde
        mayor de Quautillán á el Exmo Sor. Marqués de Casafuerte virrey de este Rno
        de lo que gasto en el prediario, Medico botica, Mortaxas, cuidado de los
        Cavallos alquiler de casas, y lo dado á el cavo de Dragones de la Veracruz,
        todo en Virtud de ordenes de S. E. interin se Mantubieron en dho Pueblo
        las familias que Vinieron de Canarias para pasar á poblar á la prova. de
        Texas, con todas los instrumentos de su comprobación—2489, p. 5 [1730-
        1731.] (A. G. M. Provincias Internas, Vol. 32, pt. 2.)

Libro en que se assientan los Bautismos de los Indios de Esta Missión de S. Anto.
        de Valero, II. Mission Records, San Fernando Cathedral, San Antonio, Texas.

Linares, Fernando de Alencastre, Noroña y Silva, Duque de
    Decreto de su Exa. México y Septe. 30/715, sobre el nombramto. de cabos
        asignación de sueldos de los soldados. (Archivo San Francisco el Grande,
        VIII, 53-54.)

Lists of Canary Islanders made at Cuatitlán on September 9 and November 14, 1730.
        (A. G. M. Provincias Internas, Vol. 32, pt. 2; also in Historia, Vol. 84,
        pt. 1, 9-17.)

Margil de Jesús, Antonio de

Letter to Duque de Linares, February 23, 1716. (A. G. I. Audiencia de México, 61-6-35. Dunn, Gulf Region, 1713-1721, pp. 150-152.)

——Letter to the Viceroy, February 26, 1716. (A. G. M. Provincias Internas, Vol. 181, pt. 1, pp. 46-49.)

——Letter to Valero, February 13, 1718. (A. G. M. Provincias Internas, Vol. 181, pt. 1, pp. 238-240.)

——Letter to Aguayo, December 26, 1719, in Testimo. de la posson. y. Missón. de Sn. Joseph. (A. G. I. Audiencia de Guadalajara, 67-3-11. Dunn Transcripts, 1710-1738.)

——Letter to the Viceroy, July 20, 1724. (A. G. M. Provincias Internas, Vol. 32, pt. 2.)

Martínez, Francisco

Letter to Governor Diego de Córdova Lazo de la Vega, February 21, 1699. (A. G. I. Audiencia de México, 61-6-22. Dunn Transcripts, 1698-1699.)

——Letter to Viceroy Conde de Moctesuma, May 4, 1699. (A. G. I. Audiencia de México, 61-6-22. Dunn Transcripts, 1698-1699.)

Massanet, Damian

Letter to the Viceroy, June 14, 1693. (A. G. I. Audiencia de Guadalajara, 67-4-11. University of Texas Transcripts, 1694, pp. 61-64. Also summarized in Provincias Internas, Vol. 181, pt. 1, pp. 151-152.)

Mediavilla y Azcona, Melchor

Letter to the Viceroy, July 31, 1729. (Archivo San Francisco el Grande, III, 6-7.)

——Memoria de los Jeneros que son necesarios Para el avio de los 25 ombres que Pasan a la probincia de las Texas. (A. G. M. Provincias Internas, Vol. 181, pp. 25-30. A copy also found in Archivo San Francisco el Grande, VIII, 45-48.)

Memoria delo que presisamte. nesesitan los Religiosos que han de entrar a la Prova. de los Texas, pa. fundar quatro Missiones. (A. G. M. Provincias Internas, Vol. 181, pt. 1, pp. 42-43.)

Miranda, Ignacio Joseph

Factura de los generos para la Misión México. y Sepe. 9/715, remitidos por dn Ygno. Jph Miranda. (Archivo San Francisco el Grande, VIII, 48-52.)

Missn. de sn. Anto. Oposición a la fundn. de la Missn. de Sn. Joseph del río de Sn. Anto. año de 1720. (Archivo del Colegio de la Santa Cruz de Querétaro. Dunn Transcripts, 1716-1749.)

Moctezuma y de Tula, José Sarmiento Valladares

El Virrey de Na. España Da quenta a V. M. con Autos de las prouidencias que aplicó pa. que los Nauios del gl. Don Mrn. de Zauala pasassen al exterminio de escozesses, por las noticias repetidas que tubo de haverse empezado á poblar y fortificar en la Ysla del Oro en el Darien. July 14, 1699. (A. G. I. Audiencia de México, 61-6-33. Dunn Transcripts, 1698-1699.)

Montero, Juan
    Letter to the Marquis of Grimaldo, July 24, 1723. (A. G. I. Audiencia de Guadalajara, 61-1-37. Dunn Transcripts, 1710-1738.)
——Letter to the Marquis of Grimaldo, September 19, 1723. (A. G. I. Audiencia de Guadalajara, 67-1-37. Dunn Transcripts, 1710-1738.)

Morfi, Juan Agustín
    . . . Historia de la Provincia de Texas por el Padre Juan Agustin Morfi años de 1673-1779. 244 numbered leaves. (Archivo San Francisco el Grande [V. 34.] (A photostat of the original manuscript in Biblioteca National de México. The manuscript has been translated by C. E. Castañeda as a Doctor's dissertation, University of Texas, 1932.)
——[Memorias para la Historia de la Provincia de Texas.] (Photostat copy of an original manuscript in the Library of Congress. It is in Morfi's handwriting, without title-page and incomplete. The Memorias were notes for his Historia.)
——Morfi's History of Texas; a Critical, Chronological Account of the Early Exploration, Attempts at Colonization, and the Final Occupation of Texas by the Spaniards, by Fr. Juan Agustín Morfi, O. F. M., Missionary, Teacher and Historian of his Order, 1673-1779 . . . Translated into English . . . with a Biographical Introduction and Annotations . . . by Carlos Eduardo Castañeda. (Doctor's Dissertation, University of Texas, 1932.)

Núñez de Haro, Miguel
    Testimony given at San Antonio de Valero, June 14, 1724. (A. G. M. Provincias Internas, Vol. 32, pt. 2.)

Oliván Rebolledo, Juan
    Opinion to the Viceroy, January 27, 1724. (A. G. M. Provincias Internas, Vol. 181, pt. 1, pp. 279-291. A copy also in Archivo San Francisco el Grande, X, 179-183.)
——Opinion to the Viceroy, September 4, 1724. (A. G. M. Provincias Internas, Vol. 181, pt. 1, pp. 328-330.)
——Parezer de el Sor. Auditor, October 2, 1724. (A. G. I. Audiencia de México, 62-1-41. Dunn Transcripts, 1723-1729.)
——[Opinion to the Viceroy.] May 31, 1725. (A. G. M. Provincias Internas, Vol. 32, pt. 2.)
——[Parecer del Auditor sobre mutación del Presidio de la Bahía.] August 19, 1726. (A. G. M. Provincias Internas, Vol. 236, pt. 1, pp. 63-64.)
——[Parecer del Auditor Oliván Rebolledo.] May 12, 1730. (A. G. I. Audiencia de Guadalajara, 104-6-15. Dunn Transcripts, 1710-1738.)
——Paracer del Sr. Auditor de la Guerra, July 16, 1730. (A. G. I. Audiencia de Guadalajara, 67-4-38. Dunn Transcripts, 1710-1738.)
——Paracer del Sor. Auditor, October 31, 1730. (A. G. M. Historia, Vol. 84, pt. 1, pp. 17-21.)

Olivares, Antonio San Buenaventura
    Petition to the Viceroy. [n. d.] (A. G. M. Provincias Internas, Vol. 181, pt. 1, p. 214.)
——Carta del Pe. Fr. Anto. Olibares, en qe. Noticia á su Exa. de las qualidades así de las naciones como de lo particular que hay en las tierras en la Prova. de texas. [n. d.] (Archivo San Francisco el Grande, VIII.)

Olivares, Antonio San Buenaventura

[Memorandum of things necessary for establishment of Mission on San Antonio River, November, 1716.] (A. G. I. Audiencia de México, 61-6-35. Dunn, Gulf Region, 1713-1721, pp. 174-177.)

——[Report on Conditions in Texas, November, 1716.] (A. G. I. Audiencia de México, 61-6-35. Dunn, Gulf Region, 1713-1721, pp. 169-174.)

——Letter to the Viceroy [November 20, 1716?] (A. G. M. Provincias Internas, Vol. 181, pt. 1, pp. 131-134.)

——Memoria y razón de lo que se necesita para poblarse la Misión de Río de Sn Antonio de Padua . . . [December? 1716.] (A. G. I. Audiencia de México, 61-6-35. Dunn, Gulf Region, 1713-1721, pp. 210-214.)

——Letter to the Viceroy. [December, 1716.] (A. G. I. Audiencia de México, 61-6-35. Dunn, Gulf Region, 1713-1721, p. 214.)

——Letter to Francisco Antonio Solorzano, June 5, 1717. (A. G. I. Audiencia de México, 61-6-35. Dunn, Gulf Region, 1713-1721, pp. 18-19.)

——Letter to Alarcón, June 5, 1717. (A. G. I. Audiencia de México, 61-6-35. Dunn, Gulf Region, 1713-1721, pp. 19-22.)

——Letter to the Viceroy, June 22, 1718. (Archivo San Francisco el Grande, VIII, 205-212.)

Palacios, Prudenzio

Respta. fiscl. Sept. 22, 1724. (A. G. I. Audiencia de México, 62-1-41. Dunn Transcripts, 1723-1729.)

Para despachar dos cartas de Dn Andres de Arriola. Sobre Vahía de Pansacola y Población de franceses en aquella Costa. escritas desde la misma Vahía y las que después se han recibido y van puestas. (A. G. I. Audiencia de México, 61-6-35. Dunn Transcripts, 1700-1702, pp. 103-108.)

Para q el Capitán Dn. Mathías de Aguirre Vezino del Saltillo tenga provenido todo lo q necesitaren las quinze familias quando lleguen allí, y van á poblar a los Texas y execute las demás providencias, q se le previenen. [November 28, 1730.] (A. G. M. Historia. Vol. 84, pt. 1, p. 30.)

Para que el Govr. de Texas, y en su falta el Capitán del Presidio de Sn. Antonio, haga nueva Reseña de las quinze familias que van a poblar; elección de los Sugetos, que han de exercer ofizios Consejiles, y las demás providencias, que se le previenen en este despacho. [November 28, 1730.] A. G. M. Historia, Vol. 84, pt. 1, p. 26.)

Para que el Governador de la Provincia de Texas y en su aucencia [sic] el Capitán del Presidio de San Antonio, acuda a las quinze familias, que van a poblar con los bastimentos q huvieren menester a Razon de quatro Reales al dia que goza cada Persona, por tiempo de vn año, con lo demás que contiene. [November 28, 1730.] (A. G. M. Historia, Vol. 84, pt. 1, p. 24.)

Para que las Justicias de los Partidos por donde ha de Transitar franco. Dubal, con las diez familias, que ban a Poblar a los Texas, den el auxilio, que se pidiere, para su mas commodo transporte. [November 8, 1730.] (A. G. M. Historia, Vol. 84, pt. 1, p. 7.)

Para que los Governadores del nuevo Reyno de León y Coaguyla, y demas Justizias de los Parages por donde Transitare Francisco Dubal, Conductor de las quinze familias, que van a los Texas, le den el auxilio que les pidiere. [November 28, 1730.] (A. G. M. Historia, Vol. 84, pt. 1, p. 24.)

Paredes, Miguel. See Sevillano de Paredes, Miguel

Patiño, Joseph
    Letter to Duque de Arión, July 3, 1727. (A. G. I. Audiencia de Guadalajara, 67-1-37. Dunn Transcripts, 1710-1738.)

Patrón y Guzmán, Agustín
    Letter to Aguayo, April 8, 1722. (A. G. I. Audiencia de Guadalajara, 67-3-11. Dunn Transcripts, 1710-1738.)

Peredo, Diego de
    Letter to Enrique Enríquez de Guzmán, March 14, 1698. (A. G. I. Audiencia de México, 61-6-21, cited in Dunn, *Spanish and French Rivalry in Gulf Region,* 173 (note)).

Pérez, Mateo
    Letter to the Viceroy, June 6, 1724. (A. G. M. Provincias Internas, Vol. 32, pt. 2.)
——Testimonial of Mateo Pérez, June 17, 1724. (A. G. M. Provincias Internas, Vol. 32, pt. 2.)

Pérez de Almazán, Fernando
    Letter to Casafuerte, March 24, 1724. (Archivo San Francisco el Grande, X, 110-115.)
——Letter to Casafuerte, March 14, 1724. (Archivo San Francisco el Grande, X, 107-109.)
——Letter to Casafuerte, May 1, 1724. (A. G. M. Provincias Internas, Vol. 181, pt. 1, pp. 322-327.)
——Letter to Casafuerte, October 24, 1724. (Archivo San Francisco el Grande, X, 137-144.)
——Letter to the Viceroy, October 25, 1724. (Archivo San Francisco el Grande, X, 130-133.)
——Letter to the Viceroy, July 4, 1726. (A. G. M. Provincias Internas, Vol. 236, pt. 1, pp. 58-60.)

Pérez de Almazán, Juan Antonio
    Patente De Capn. Comandante del Presidio ,y Compa. de Sn. Antto. de Véjar uno de los de tierra adentro en la Na. España. June 6, 1731. (A. G. I. Audiencia de Guadalajara, 104-6-8. Dunn Transcripts, 1710-1738.)

Pérez de Mezquia, Pedro
    Letter to the Viceroy, June 2, 1725. (A. G. M. Provincias Internas, Vol. 32, pt. 2.)
——Letter to the Viceroy, June 22, 1725. (Archivo del Colegio de la Santa Cruz de Querétaro. Dunn Transcripts, 1716-1749.)
——Letter to the Viceroy, May 4, 1731. (A. G. M. Provincias Internas, Vol. 236, pt. 1, pp. 37-40.)
——Letter to the Viceroy, August 8, 1731. (A. G. M. Provincias Internas, Vol. 236, pt. 1, pp. 48-53.)

Pontchartrain, Louis
    Letter to the Duke of Harcourt, March 23, 1701. Spanish translation in A. G. I. Audiencia de México, 61-6-22. Cited in Dunn, *Spanish and French Rivalry in the Gulf Region of the United States, 1678-1702*, 200 (note).

Ramón, Diego
    Letter to the Viceroy, May 2, 1717. (A. G. I. Audiencia de México, 61-6-35. Dunn, Gulf Region, 1713-1721, pp. 2-4.)
    ——Letter to the Viceroy, May 30, 1718. (A. G. M. Provincias Internas, Vol. 181, pt. 1, p. 236.)
    ——Letter to the Viceroy, March 24, 1724. (Archivo San Francisco el Grande, X, 109-110.)

Ramón, Domingo
    Derrotero pa. las misies. de los Presidos. internos su fha. febro. 17 de 1716. (Archivo San Francisco el Grande, VIII, 63-88. Translated by Rev. Paul J. Foik in *Preliminary Studies* of the Texas Catholic Historical Society, Vol. II, No. 5, April, 1933.)
    ——Letter to the Viceroy, March 17, 1716. (A. G. I. Audiencia de México, 61-6-35. Dunn, Gulf Region, 1713-1721, pp. 154-156.)
    ——Letter to the Viceroy, July 22, 1716. (A. G. I. Audiencia de México, 61-6-35. Dunn, Gulf Region, 1713-1721, pp. 160-163.)
    ——Letter to the Viceroy, July 26, 1716. (A. G. M. Provincias Internas, Vol. 181, pt. 1, pp. 52-53. A copy also in Archivo San Francisco el Grande, VIII, 62-63.)
    ——Letter to Martín de Alarcón, May 21, 1717. (A. G. I. Audiencia de México, 61-6-35. Dunn, Gulf Region, pp. 81-84.)
    ——Letter to the Viceroy, February 28, 1718. (A. G. M. Provincias Internas, Vol. 181, pt. 1, p. 225.)
    ——Letter to the Viceroy, February 29, 1718. (A. G. M. Provincias Internas, Vol. 181, pt. 1, pp. 226-227.)

Razón [de documentos recibidos por Don Pedro de Rivera.] October 30, 1724. A. G. I. Audiencia de México, 62-1-41. Dunn Transcripts, 1723-1729.)

Reforma y ordenas de Presidios segn el Proiecto del Visitaor, April 20, 1729. (A. G. I. Audiencia de México, 62-1-41. Dunn Transcripts, 1723-1729.)

Relación de los empleos, meritos y servicios del Sargto. Mor. dn Martín de Alarcón cavo. del orden de Sanctiago México y Hen 18 de 1721. (Archivo San Francisco el Grande, IX, 8-21.)

Representación de los Religiosos [exponiendo razones contra la extinción del Presidio de los Tejas.] July 20, 1729. Signed by Gabriel de Vergara, Joseph Andrés Rodríguez de Jesús María, Juan Bauta. Garzía de Suárez, Alonso Giraldo de Terreros, Manuel de Ortuña, Joseph de Sn Antonio y Estrada. (Archivo San Francisco el Grande, III, 4-6.)

Representason. hecha á Su Exa. por los pes. misions. dando noticia de su fundason. su fha Julo. 22 de 1716. (Archivo San Francisco el Grande, VIII, 114-116.)

Resumen generl. sacado de los autos formados en este supor. Govno de todas las noticias qe. del año de 688 hta. el prnte se han tenido de las naciones de los

Asinais, texas y demás de aquellas remotas Provas. decripson. de la Vahía del Esptu. Sto. lo util qe es en q se pueble por los Españoles, embarasando á los franceses, distancia que hay de texas a la Movila, lo qe. amenasa sino se estorba la conquista a las Francess. providens, dadas á este fín y pa. la conbernn de dhos Ynds. sobre otros puntos en qe pa. la segurd. de este reyno expone largamente el Sor Fisl. sobre las providencias q. pa. su buen exito juzga ser combenientes México y Nove. 30 de 1716. (Archivo San Francisco el Grande, VIII, 126. A copy is also found in Provincias Internas, Vol. 181, pt. i, pp. 139-180.)

Rivera, Pedro de
    [Notice of investigation of conduct of Antonio Balverde de Cossio.] May 13, 1726. (A. G. M. Provincias Internas, Vol. 37, pt. 2.)
——. . . Proyecto mandado hacer por el Exmo. Sor. Marqués de Casafuerte Virrey Governador y Capitán General de esta Nueba España y Presidente de la Real Audiencia de ella, reducido de la Visita hecha por el Brigadier Dn. Pedro de Rivera, que contiene tres puntos. El Primero. El Estado en que estaban los Presidios antes que se Visitasen. El Segundo. El en que se pusieron después que se les hizo la Visita. El Tercero. El en que por ultima disposición de su Exa. combendrá se pongan. Y por fín de todo Un Mapa que pone presente quanto el Citado Proyecto yncluye, con mas algunas adbertencias necessarias. (A. G. M. Provincias Internas, Vol. 29. A copy also in the Archivo San Francisco el Grande, II, 11-253.)
——Letter to the Viceroy, December 7, 1728. (A. G. M. Provincias Internas, Vol. 29, pp. 133-134.)
——[Parecer del] Brigadier D. Pedro de Rivera. September 9, 1729. (A. G. I. Audiencia de Guadalajara, 104-6-15. Dunn Transcripts, 1710-1738.)
——Informe [sobre recomendaciones del Marqués de Aguayo relativas a poblar la Provincia de Texas.] June 19, 1730. (A. G. I. Audiencia de Guadalajara, 67-4-38. Dunn Transcripts, 1710-1738.)
——Letter to the Viceroy, September 30, 1730. (A. G. M. Provincias Internas, Vol. 236, pt. i, pp. 54-57.)
——Opinión del Brigadier Rivera, April 16, 1731. (A. G. M. Provincias Internas, Vol. 236, pt. i, pp. 11-15.)
——Opinión del Brigadier Rivera, July 19, 1731. (A. G. M. Provincias Internas, Vol. 236, pt. i, pp. 5-7.)
——Letter to the Viceroy, May 26, 1731. (A. G. M. Provincias Internas, Vol. 236, pt. i, pp. 42-47.)
——Opinión del Brigadier Rivera, July 21, 1731. (A. G. M. Provincias Internas, Vol. 236, pt. i, pp. 23-28.)

Royal approval of the appointment of Martín de Alarcón as Governor and Captain General of Texas. (A. G. I. Audiencia de México, 61-6-35. Dunn, Gulf Region, 1713-1721, pp. 223-226.)

Royal *cédula*, April 19, 1698. (A. G. I. Audiencia de México, 61-6-22. Dunn Transcripts, 1699, pp. 2-7.)

Royal *cédula*, June 11, 1718. (A. G. M. Historia, Vols. 298-299, pp. 308-313.)

Royal *cédula*, January 30, 1719. (A. G. M. Historia, Vols. 298-299, pp. 314-316.)

Royal *cédula*, April 22, 1719. (A. G. M. Historia, Vols. 298-299, pp. 319-329.)

Royal *cédula*, November 1, 1719. (A. G. M. Historia, Vols. 298-299, pp. 322-325.)

Royal *cédula*, March 16, 1721. (A. G. M. Historia, Vols. 298-299, pp. 351-352.)

Royal *cédula*, May 26, 1721. (A. G. M. Historia, Vols. 298-299, pp. 352-355.)

Royal *cédula*, October 27, 1722. (A. G. M. Historia, Vols. 298-299, pp. 364-365.)

Royal *cédula*, March 18, 1723. (A. G. I. Audiencia de Gualalajara, 67-1-37. Dunn Transcripts, 1710-1738.)

Royal *cédula* al Gobernador y ofiziales de Yucatan sobre las familias Canarias que han de ir a Campeche para pasar después a la Veracruz y de allí á la Bahía de Sn. Bernardo. May 10, 1723. (A. G. I. Audiencia de Guadalajara, 61-1-37. Dunn Transcripts, 1710-1738.)

Royal *cédula*, February 19, 1724. (A. G. I. Audiencia de México, 62-1-41. Dunn Transcripts, 1723-1729.)

Royal *cédula*, February 14, 1729. (A. G. M. Historia, Vols. 298-299, pp. 411-414.)

Sáenz de San Antonio, Mathías
Petition to the King [May], 1729. (A. G. I. Audiencia de México, 62-2-29. Dunn Transcripts, 1723-1729.)

St. Denis, Luis Juchereau
Declarasón dada por dn Luis de San Dionis y dn Medar Jalot de Francia que se contiene á la causa qe. tubieron de entrarse en este reino, derrotos. fue hicieron y lo particular qe. observarón hta. el Presio. del Capn. Ramón. sin fha. (Archivo San Francisco el Grande, VIII, 27-32.)
——Declarasón de sn. Dionis. September 1-18, 1717. (A. G. I. Audiencia de México, 61-6-35. Dunn, Gulf Region, 1713-1721, pp. 34-50. Translated by Charmion Claire Shelby in The Southwestern Historical *Quarterly*, Vol. XXVI, No. 3, January, 1923.)

Salinas Varona, Gregorio
Letter to the King, January 20, 1717. (A. G. I. Audiencia de México, 61-4-26. Dunn, Gulf Region, 1713-1721, pp. 233-239.)
——Letter to the Viceroy, February 15, 1717. (A. G. I. Audiencia de México, 61-6-35. Dunn Transcripts, 1713-1721, pp. 9-15.)

Santiago de la Cruz, Juan de
Depositión of Juan de Santiago de la Cruz, July 12, 1724. (A. G. M. Provincias Internas, Vol. 32, pt. 2.)

Satisfaciendo a la orden de V. M. con q se sirvio Remitir tres Cartas y vn testo. del Virrey de Na. Espa. y Corregor. de la Veracruz que tratan de los designios de la Compaña de francia en querer ocupar la Abadía de Sn Berndo. do q se le ofreze. (A. G. I. Audiencia de México, 61-6-35. Dunn, Gulf Region, 1713-1721, pp. 241-251.)

Satisfaciendo a vn Rl. orden del Rey nro. Sor. Pe.; con que se sirvio remitir dos memoriales; y diferentes cartas del Marqs. de Sn. Miguel de Aguayo, en que

solicita se le confiera el grado de Thente. Genl . . . (A. G. I. Audiencia de
    Guadalajara, 67-1-37. Dunn Transcripts, 1710-1738.)

Sevillano de Paredes, Miguel
    Representación que haze Fray Miguel Sevillano de Paredes Prer Appco y
        Presidente de las Misss. del Río Grande del Norte; al Muy Reuo. Padre
        Fray Pedro Pérez de Mezquia Guardian del Collegio de la SSma. Cruz de
        la ciudad de Querétaro, y al Reuo. y Venerable Discretorio, Acerca de
        algunos puntos que se ofrezen sobre la Consistencia y adelantamiento de la
        Conuersión de los infieles de estas Misss. [January, 1726.] (Archivo de la
        Santa Cruz de Querétaro. Dunn Transcripts, 1716-1749.)
——Representation to the King, August 25, 1728. (A. G. I. Audiencia de México,
        62-2-29. Dunn Transcripts, 1723-1729.)
——Letter to the Viceroy, September 7, 1729. (Archivo San Francisco el Grande,
        III, 4-6.)
——Transsumpto de vn Memorial que por parte de este Collegio se remitio al Rey
        en el Consejo Real de Indias estaño de 1729 en 12 de Nobe. November 12,
        1729. (Archivo del Colegio de Santa Cruz de Querétaro. Dunn Transcripts,
        1716-1749.)

Testimonio de Autos ejecutados en Virtud de Rl Cédula de Su Magd. Sobre la
    fortificazón y Poblazón de la Bahía de Sta Ma de Galue y Panzacola, y
    representasiones hechas pr Dn Martn. de aranguren zabala q con horden
    de Su Magd Vino a la misma preocupazón. 1699. (A. G. I. Audiencia de
    México, 61-6-22. Dunn Transcripts, 1699, pp. 1-343.)

Testimonio de Auttos sobre las Prouidencias Dadas Por el Exmo. Señor Conde de
    Galue Virrey de esta nueva España pra los Socorros y Permanencia de los
    Religiosos Misioneros en la Proua. de los Texas hasta su retirada y razones
    Porque se executto. 1694. (A. G. I. Audiencia de Guadalajara, 67-4-11,
    pp. 1-86.)

Testimonio de Autos y diligenzias executadas en Virtud de Despacho del Exmo.
    Señor Birrey de esta nueva España sobre el ospedaje Relista y demás que
    se contiene; con las familias de las yslas de Canarias Executadas por el
    Capitán Dn. Juan Antonio Pérez de Almazán. [March 9, 1731.] A. G. M.
    Provincias Internas, Vol. 32, pt. 2.)

Testimonio de Diligencias hechas por El sor Oydor Dn Juan de Oliván Contra las
    Personas de Nación fransesas sobre la Yntrodución de Mercansias que de
    la Mouila y Masacra han hecho a la Prouia. de Quahuila. 1717. (A. G. I.
    Audiencia de México, 61-6-35. Dunn, Gulf Region, 1713-1721, pp. 1-143.)

Testimo. de la Missón. de Sn. Franco. Xauier. (A. G. I. Audencia de Guadalajara,
    67-3-11. Dunn Transcripts, 1710-1738.)

Testimo. de la possón y Missón de Sn Joseph. (A. G. I. Audiencia de Guadalajara,
    67-3-11. Dunn Transcripts, 1710-1738.)

Testimo. de la Missón. de na. sra. de Loreto. (A. G. I. Audiencia de Guadalajara,
    67-3-11. Dunn Transcripts, 1710-1738.)

Testimo. de los autos fhos sobre dar su ssa; prouidensia de Bastimentos Para la
    Nueba Población de Sancta María de Galue allias Pansacola Junta de Ofizes;

Rs y otras diligencias condusentes al transporte de dha Prouidencia. 1699. (A. G. I. Audiencia de México, 61-6-22. Dunn Transcripts, 1698-1699.)

Testimonio de los Auttos fhos sobre la sublebación, y Alzamiento de los Yndios, Sumas; de las Misiones de Sn. Tiago de la Zienega de el Cayome, y Juntta de el Río de el Nortte. 1726-1728. A. G. I. Audiencia de Guadalajara, 67-3-12. Dunn Transcripts, 1710-1738.)

Testimo de los Autos hechos sre las voces desparramadas por los franzeses de la Mouila de q han de procurar Apoderarse de Una de las dos Bahías de Panzacola y Prouidencias dadas a este fin por su Exa. 1718. (A. G. I. Audiencia de México, 61-6-35. Dunn Transcripts, 1700-1702, pp. 31-110.)

Testimo de los autos que se han formado sobre la expedicion de la Prouincia de los Tejas en que se yncluyen la pruidencias que se han dado por este Supeor Gouierno, 1717. (A. G. I. Audiencia de México, 61-6-35. Dunn, Gulf Region, 1713-1721, pp. 149-220.)

Testimonio del Segundo Quaderno De Autos fhos En Virtud de Rl. Cedula de Su Magd. Sobe. la Población y fortificazión de la Bahía de Santa Ma. de Galue y de las Prouidencias dadas pa. este fin. 1699. (A. G. I. Audiencia de México, 61-6-22. Dunn Transcripts, 1698-1699.)

Titulo de Alguacil Mayor, July 20, 1731. (A. G. M. Provincias Internas, Vol. 32, pt. 2.)

Titulo De Capitán del Presidio del Espíritu Santo, en la Provincia de los Tejas de la Na. España con el sueldo de 600 pesos al año. September 16, 1731. (A. G. I. Audiencia de Guadalajara, 104-6-8. Dunn Transcripts, 1710-1738.)

Titulo de Esno de Conzejo y ppco, July 20, 1731. (A. G. M. Provincias Internas, Vol. 32, p. 2.)

Titulo de Mayordomo de los propios, July 20, 1731. (A. G. M. Provincias Internas, Vol. 32, pt. 2.)

[Titulos de Regidores], July 20, 1731. (A. G. M. Provincias Internas, Vol. 32, pt. 2.)

Torres de Ayala, Laureano
   Letter to the King, September 16, 1699. (A. G. I. Audiencia de México, 61-6-22. Dunn Transcripts, 1698-1699.)

Tous, Gabriel, tr.
   Ramón Expedition; Espinosa's Diary of 1716 (see Espinosa, Isidro Félix.)

Tovar, Baltasar
   Respta fiscal in Testimonio del Segundo Quaderno de Autos . . . (A. G. I. Audiencia de México, 61-6-22. Dunn Transcripts, 1698-1699.)

Valero, Baltasar de Zúñiga, Marqués de
   Decreto [nombrando a Don Martín de Alarcón Gobernador y Capitán de la nueva expedición a Texas] December 7, 1716. (A. G. I. Audiencia de México, 61-6-35. Dunn, Gulf Region, 1713-1721, pp. 202-203.)

Valero, Baltasar de Zúñiga, Marqués de

Despacho del Sor. Marques de Valero, para q los Caps. den los auxilios necesarios, qdo. yba a fundar la Missn de Sn. Anto. el P. Olivares. December 28, 1716. (Archivo del Colegio de la Santa Cruz de Querétaro. Dunn Transcripts, 1716-1749.)

——Letter to Alarcón, November 7, 1718. (Archivo San Francisco el Grande, IX, 1.)

——Letter to the King regarding Aguayo in Texas, November 11, 1721. (A. G. I. Audiencia de México, 61-2-2. Dunn, Gulf Region, 1713-1721, pp. 252-254.)

Ynformasón. dada por los Soldados Sobe. no haber conseguido el tratado de paces con los Apaches fha. en Sn. Anto. Valero a 6 he heno. de 1724. (Archivo San Francisco el Grande, X, 115.)

Ynstrucción y orden que á de observar el Mre. de Campo Dn Andrés de Arriola como Gouernador y Cavo Superior de las fregatas y gente que lleba á su cargo . . . (A. G. I. Audiencia de México, 61-6-22. Dunn Transcripts, 1699, pp. 166-177.)

INDEX

Acevedo, Father Fray Antonio, set out with Father López in advance of the main Mendoza expedition, 312-313.

Acuña, Juan de, see Casafuerte.

Aguado, Father Juan López, Guardian of the College of Santa Cruz of Querétaro, visited the viceroy in Mexico City, 40; listed supplies necessary for Texas missions, 40-41.

Aguayo, Marqués de, see Azlor.

Aguirre, Captain Mathías, took charge of Canary Islanders in Saltillo, 292; instructed by the viceroy to make preparation for the arrival of settlers, 294-295.

Aguirre, Captain Pedro de, one of the leaders of the Spanish expedition of 1709 into Texas, 22.

Alarcón, Martín de, appointed Captain General of the expedition of 1718 and Governor of Texas and Coahuila; previous services rendered, 78; asked to provide military escort for Father Olivares; instructed to make monthly visits to Espíritu Santo, 79; made preparations for the expedition, 81-82; ordered to take immediate possession of his new post, 82; investigated trade activities of St. Denis, the Ramóns and others, 82-83; criticized severely by Father Olivares, 83; took official control of Coahuila as governor, 83-84; continued preparations for expedition to Texas but postponed departure, 84-85; 86-88; received instructions from the viceroy; began journey to Texas, but changed the route as previously planned, 88-92; arrived at San Antonio River, selected sites for Mission San Antonio de Valero and Presidio de Béjar, 92-93; treated Indians harshly, 94-95; began work of organization and settlement, 95-96; gave tardy relief to East Texas missions, 96-100; explored Espíritu

Santo Bay, 100-102; departed for inspection of East Texas missions, 102-106; completed visit to all the missions; returned to San Antonio; resigned his governorship, 107-108; his failure as governor, 110.

Albadadejo, Father Fray Joseph, appointed as resident missionary at Nuestra Señora de los Dolores Mission, 157-158.

Almazán, Don Fernando Pérez de, sent by Aguayo with a detachment of soldiers to aid post at San Antonio, 136; set out with Captain Costales to inspect French outpost at Natchitoches, 143-144; recommended as the successor of Aguayo as Governor of Texas because of his qualifications, 172; appointed governor, 173; sought supplies for East Texas in San Antonio; took up his residence at Los Adaes, 173; gave a vivid account of conditions in Texas to the viceroy, 175; received instructions from the viceroy prohibiting trade and communication with the French; his reply to these orders, 178-179; pointed out the inadvisability of moving San Antonio de Béjar close to the mission, 202-203; sent supplies to La Bahía, 203; his administration summarized, 203-204; resigned because of illness; appointed Mediavilla y Azcona as governor *ad interim;* that appointment not approved by the viceroy, 261.

Almazán, Juan Antonio de, Captain of the Presidio of San Antonio de Béjar; received in person the Canary Islanders at the post; fulfilled the instructions of the viceroy regarding settlers, 299-301; summoned them and read the decree making them *Hidalgos,* 301; made a temporary distribution of land to settlers, 302; surveyed with their aid

and their appeal to the viceroy for funds, 255-256; three friars joined Mendoza expedition, 312-328.

French, temporarily lost interest in Texas; reasons, 1; interest revived, 2-3; search for the Mississippi, 3; Texas and Louisiana, 3; successful settlement on the Mississippi, 3; colonial expansion planned, 3-4; expedition under the direction of d'Iberville, 3-4; found Pensacola occupied by Spaniards, 5-6; went to Mobile Bay, finally reached the Mississippi, established Fort Maurepas, 7; established settlement at Biloxi, 7; approached by Englishmen, who were forced to leave the settlements by Bienville, 8-9; erected a third fort on the river, 8; actually occupied Louisiana, 9; removal demanded by the Spanish, but no heed paid to these orders and protests, 10-11; requested free title to the region occupied, 12; presented reason for occupation of Louisiana—protection of the Spanish domain against English aggression, 12; sent dispatches, memorials and maps explaining situation in Louisiana, 12-13; occupied Mobile Bay, 15; continued to establish themselves and expanded their dominions, 16; concerned about extension of trade with the Indians and the discovery of mines, 19-20; explored the Red River country under St. Denis and Bienville, 20; commissioned St. Denis to search for Spanish settlements in Texas, but without results, 20-21; made trading expeditions to the Río Grande, 20-21; warned about these intrusions, 21-22; again sent an expedition to the Río Grande under St. Denis, who was arrested, sent to Mexico City and there questioned regarding illicit trade with the northern provinces of New Spain, 26-27; active in trade relations with various Indian tribes in Texas area, 70; designs and ambitions for commercial advantages and supremacy caused the *Fiscal* to recommend the occupation

of Espíritu Santo Bay as a prevention, 74; need of more adequate protection against French encroachments, 77; continued freely their traffic with frontier provinces of New Spain, 83; French aggression prompted action by Spanish officials, 87-88; controlled Indians by gifts and flattery, 107-108; made a surprise attack at Los Adaes, 108-109; plans for expansion; occupation of Espíritu Santo Bay; designs on the possession of Pensacola; declaration of war with Spain; invasion of Texas, 111-115; informed about the retreat of the soldiers and missionaries and the abandonment of missions and presidios in East Texas, 117-118; fugitives seek passports through Texas to Espíritu Santo Bay; thought by Aguayo to be spies, 176-177; trade and communication prohibited by instructions of the viceroy to the governor, 178; flag with emblems found among the Jediondo Indians during the Mendoza expedition, significance of the discovery, 321-322; among the Panana Indians, 331-332.

García de San Francisco, Father Fray, first missionary for the region of Junta de los Rios, 327.

Gómez de Cervantes, Rt. Reverend Doctor Nicolás Carlos, Bishop of Guadalajara, appointed a priest to look after the spiritual welfare of Islanders and others in the vicinity of San Fernando de Béjar, 306-307.

González, Father Fray Joseph, missionary, at San Antonio de Valero Mission witnessed the establishment of Mission of San Francisco Xavier de Nájera and promised service of a *Padre ad interim,* 161-162; lost interest in the new mission, 162-163; attempted peace negotiations with the Apaches, but failed; blamed Captain Flores for failure, 191-194; reported bad conditions at the Presidio of San Antonio de Béjar; suggested the removal of Captain Flores and the appointment of Mateo Pérez to the viceroy as a substitute, 194-196; made further recommendations for the entire Province of Texas, 195-197; bearer of commission for Pérez as Captain of San Antonio de Béjar, 198; regarded unfavorably by Aguayo and by the testimony given by Fathers Espinosa, Margil and Núñez de Haro, 199; 200; attacked the reputation of Aguayo who resented the injury to his good name; the missionary's removal suggested in the report of the *Auditor* to the viceroy, 200-201; influenced Rivera by his many recommendations for economy and stricter regulation of the frontier posts, 221.

Guerra, Father Fray Joseph, missionary, awaited arrival of Aguayo in San Antonio, 136; sent to rebuild the temporary church and dwelling place for the *Padres* at San Francisco de los Neches; appointed resident missionary there, 149-151.

Harcourt, Duke of, French Ambassador to Spain, received instructions from Pontchartrain on position of France in Louisiana, 12; presented dispatches, memorials, and maps to Philip V, 12.

Hidalgo, Father Fray Francisco, eager to return to Texas, 27; sent letter to Cadillac, Governor of Louisiana, seeking coöperation for the spiritual and temporal welfare of the Tejas Indians, 27-28; sent with the Ramón expedition of 1716 to Texas, 44; 45; sought by St. Denis, 33; named by the *Fiscal* as missionary for East Texas in advice to the viceroy, 35; 36; joined the main body of the Ramón expedition at the Río Grande, when the party entered Texas, 45; appointed by Father Espinosa minister of the first reëstablished Mission of Nuestro Padre San Francisco de los Tejas; his co-worker, Father Manuel Castellanos (q. v.), 58-59; his influence among the Tejas Indians reported by St. Denis in a message to the Spanish officials, 62; taken ill

with malaria for several months after his arrival in East Texas, 68; 96-97; found the work of congregating the Indians at the mission very difficult, 97; welcomed Alarcón on his tour of inspection to the missions of East Texas, 102-103.

Iberville, see Le Moyne d'Iberville, Pierre.

Jalot, Mendar, accompanied St. Denis to Río Grande; questioned in Mexico City about trade relations of the French with New Spain, 30; 32; officially assigned by viceroy to accompany Ramón expedition into Texas, 38; suffered a severe fall from his horse, 48.

Jordán, Captain Juan, occupied Pensacola, anticipating the Spanish expedition of Arriola and the French expedition of Le Moyne d'Iberville (q. v.), 5.

Jumanos, petitioned for missionaries; request heeded, 312.

La Navidad de las Cruces, place visited by the Mendoza expedition; here Fathers Nicolás López, Juan de Zavaleta, and Antonio de Acevedo joined main body of the expedition, 317.

Le Moyne de Bienville, Jean Baptiste, repulsed English intruders on the Mississippi, 9; placed in command of third fort built by French, 9; explored the Red River country with St. Denis, 20; urged St. Denis to persuade the Indians against aiding Spaniards, 113; received word from France regarding war with Spain; ordered to attack Pensacola, 114-115.

Le Moyne d'Iberville, Pierre, led expedition to Gulf of Mexico, 3-4; arrived at Pensacola, 6-7; went on to Mobile Bay, reached the Mississippi, established Fort Maurepas, 6-7; built other forts along the river, 12; presented memorial proposing an alliance between France and Spain to safeguard Spanish dominions, 12; occupied Mobile Bay, 15.

López, Father Nicolás, *Custodio* of New Mexico, was requested to send

Mobile Bay, visited by scouting party of Martínez but no settlements were found there, 9; again investigated by Arriola in search of English colonies; discovered fort and fleet nearby flying English flag, 10; French settlements were found there, 10-11; occupied by Iberville who received orders to that effect from French King, 15; Martínez reported new encroachment by French on Spanish domain, 15; designs of St. Denis to seek control of all the Indian nations between Mobile and Espíritu Santo Bays, 39; visited by Roldán by order of Varona, 114.

Montero, Juan, Intendant of the Canary Islands, received orders of the King to locate at Espíritu Santo Bay, instructions for settlement, 270; published proclamation to Islanders and its results, 271-272; suggested transportation at expense of *Cabildo* but his proposal was not approved, 272; 273.

Nuestra Señora de Atoche, visited by Mendoza expedition, 316-317.

Nuestra Señora de Belén, visited by Mendoza expedition, 315.

Nuestra Señora de Guadalupe, third mission established in 1716 at Nacogdoches; formal possession given to Father Margil for the Zacatecan friars, 59-60; inspected by Alarcón, 105; reëstablished by Aguayo, 142; rebuilt by Father Margil by order of Aguayo; Solemn High Mass celebrated by Father Margil and sermon delivered by Father Espinosa at its reëstablishment, 155-157.

Nuestra Señora de Guadalupe de Albuquerque, pueblo organized near Mission Nuestra Señora de Guadalupe, 105.

Nuestra Señora de Guadalupe, place visited by Mendoza expedition (near the Río Grande), 317.

Nuestra Señora de la Límpida Concepción, place visited by Mendoza expedition near present day McNary, 314.

Nuestra Señora de la Purísima Concepción, second mission established in 1716 in East Texas; official possession given to Father Espinosa for the Querétaran friars; Father Vergara appointed minister; made mission headquarters, 59; inspected by Alarcón, 103-105; visited by St. Denis for an interview with Aguayo, 139-140; prepared for restoration by Fathers Vergara and Sánchez; visited and reëstablished by Aguayo; possession given to Father Espinosa for the Querétaran friars, 151-154; Cadodachos present at ceremony, 153; moved to the Colorado River and later to San Antonio, 238-243.

Nuestra Señora de la Soledad, place visited by Mendoza expedition due west of Fort Hancock and McNary, 314.

Nuestra Señora de Loreto, presidio at La Bahía del Espíritu Santo in extreme need due to inefficiency of Diego Ramón as Captain, 176; conditions at the post; revolt of the mission Indians, 179-188; its removal to a new site on the Guadalupe River, 185-188; investigation into the death of José Domingo Ramón by Almazán, 181-183; attacked by coastal Indian tribes, 181-183; Diego Ramón removed; Don Juan de Bustillo y Ceballos appointed, 183-185; inspected by Rivera; garrison in splendid condition; salaries of soldiers reduced, 222-223; Don Gabriel Costales appointed Captain and given instructions, 257-261.

Nuestra Señora del Espíritu Santo de Zúñiga, mission founded by Aguayo in 1722, 147; Father Agustín Patrón as resident missionary, his work, 167-169.

Nuestra Señora del Pilár, presidio near Mission San Miguel de Linares de los Adaes; its new site selected by Aguayo, stockade built and garrison supplied with soldiers under Captain Don Joseph Benito de Arroyo, 144-145; 158-159; its condition under

lished in East Texas; further financial aid for operation requested, 65-66; viceroy informed by *Fiscal* of the desire of the French to penetrate into the country of the Tejas, 70; Father Olivares entered into conferences with the viceroy regarding missions and settlements on the San Antonio River; viceroy requested a written report which was transmitted to the *Fiscales* for consideration, 72-73; favorable recommendations by *Fiscales* Espinosa and Velasco; report of Velasco given in detail, 73-75; the *Real Acuerdo* approved recommendations of the *Fiscales,* 77-78; the *Junta General* convoked by the viceroy decided in favor of the expedition to San Antonio, 78; appointment of Alarcón as Captain General and Governor, 78-79; Alarcón received instructions to be observed by him to be carried out according to the will of the officials and especially of the viceroy, 88-91; relief expedition obstructed by floods; abandoned at Lake Santa Anna; *Junta de Hacienda* advised the viceroy to send new supplies to East Texas, 98-100; failed to realize the full importance of Father Sáenz de San Antonio's mission, 111; their policy regarding the frontier system of New Spain, 171-172. (See also Presidial administration.)

Sumesta, Father Fray Juan de, visited the Indian nations in the region of Junta de los Rios, 327.

Tejas Indians: Alliance suggested with them by the Council of the Indies to prevent the encroachments of foreigners in the Spanish dominions, 14-15; visited by St. Denis several times, 20; contact with these Indians was the purpose of the Espinosa-Olivares-Aguirre expedition into Texas in 1709; no contact was made, 22-23; coöperated with St. Denis, 28-29; Bernardino, Chief of the Tejas, accompanied St. Denis to the Río Grande, 30-31; relationship of Ber-

nardino, 29-30; attacked at the Colorado River by coast Indians, 30; St. Denis attempted to locate Father Hidalgo among these Indians but was unsuccessful, 33; physical features and natural resources of the region described by St. Denis in his report demanded by the viceroy, 33-35; *Junta* approved sending missionaries to the Tejas to prevent incursions of foreigners and their illicit trade on Spanish dominions, 34-35; Ramón expedition, with the guidance of St. Denis, approved by the viceroy and provided with an escort of soldiers for the settlers and missionaries, 35-36; Ramón expedition had for its purpose the settlement of East Texas and the Christianizing and civilizing of the Tejas Indians, 35-38; 40-41; informed in advance regarding the approach of the Spaniards into their region, 54-55; exchanged welcomes, courtesies and services, 55-58; assisted in erecting temporary quarters at the presidio for Ramón and his party; also gave similar aid to the missionaries to afford them shelter, 57; missions established and built with the services of the natives, 59-60; the desire of the French was to penetrate into the country of the Tejas and to dispose of their goods in the frontier provinces, 70; these Indians and their region described in the report of Father Olivares to the viceroy, 70-72; Velasco, the *Fiscal,* makes a similar report, 73-75; temporary location of the Presidio de los Tejas moved from the west side of the Neches to a place a quarter of a league from Mission of Nuestro Padre San Francisco de los Tejas, 96; conditions at the presidio and mission, 96-98; relief expedition necessary, 99-100; twenty-three nations in revolt, 100; welcomed Alarcón to the Mission of Nuestro Padre San Francisco de los Tejas; pueblo reorganized and called San Francisco

Valero, 102-103; greeted Alarcón with great ceremony at La Purísima Concepción Mission; reorganized pueblo and named it Concepción de Agreda, 103-105; at Mission San José de los Nazonis, Alarcón made his inspection and reorganized the Indian pueblo; called it San José de Ayamonte, 105; at Mission of Nuestra Señora de Guadalupe the Indians fired a salute and the governor after a scrutiny of the establishments reorganized and named the pueblo Nuestra Señora de Guadalupe de Albuquerque; at Mission Nuestra Señora de los Dolores he followed the same routine and called the pueblo Nuestra Señora de los Dolores de Benevente; at Mission of San Miguel de Linares, Alarcón examined the records and the buildings and gave the name of San Miguel de Cuellar to the pueblo, 105-106; attended the closing ceremonies of the Alarcón visit to East Texas, 107; paid their respects to Aguayo, 139-140.

Tobar, Baltaser de, *Fiscal,* concluded correctly that English vessels in the Gulf were in reality French, 10; his recommendations for expulsion of French were heeded, 10.

Urioste, Domingo de, friar, Franciscan lay brother, accompanied the Fathers of the College of Santa Cruz of Querétaro and the Ramón expedition of 1716 to Texas, 45; 46.

Urrutia, Captain Joseph, lived among the Tejas Indians for ten years, 30; desired as one of the leaders in the Ramón expedition of 1716, 62; his fitness and experience urged as reasons for his selection by Father Margil; appointed protector of the Indians in Nueva León and could not

be relieved of his duties at that post, 63.

Varona, Don Gregorio Salinas, Governor of Santa María de Galve, notified the viceroy of New Spain of French trading expedition to Río Grande, 21; his earlier career, 21; warned the viceroy regarding French designs for occupation of Pensacola, 113-114; invited to general council of war, 113; sent to explore Espíritu Santo Bay, 113-114.

Velasco, Doctor, *Fiscal,* discussed trading activities and movements of the French and especially of St. Denis since their occupation of the Gulf coast, 24-26; makes a report recommending the establishment of a mission on the San Antonio River and its occupation by settlers, 73-75.

Vergara, Father Gabriel, Franciscan missionary of the College of Santa Cruz of Querétaro, sent with Ramón expedition of 1716 to Texas, 45; 46; among the missionaries who spent Holy Week at Mission of La Punta, 44; mentioned on the list checked by Ramón when party entered Texas, 45; 46; appointed by Father Espinosa as minister of La Purísima Concepción Mission, 59; awaited the arrival of Aguayo in San Antonio, 136; sent by Aguayo in advance to Mission Concepción, 151-152.

Villasur, Captain Pedro de, ordered by the Governor of New Mexico to lead an expedition to the Panana nation; suffered a severe defeat, 332; account of the expedition, 333-335.

Zavaleta, Father Juan de, missionary, joined main body of the Mendoza expedition at La Navidad de las Cruces, 317-318; greeted by Jediondo Indians carrying Cross and the French flag, 321.

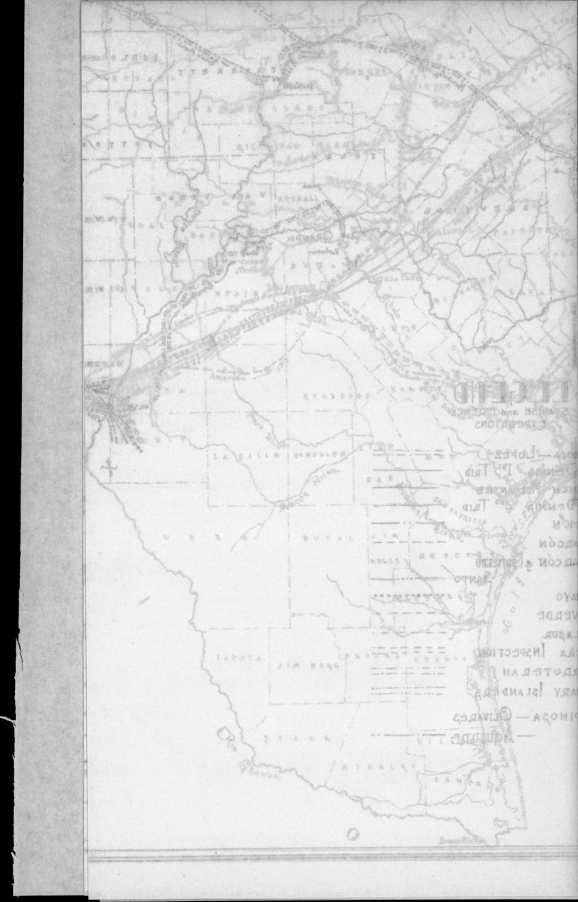

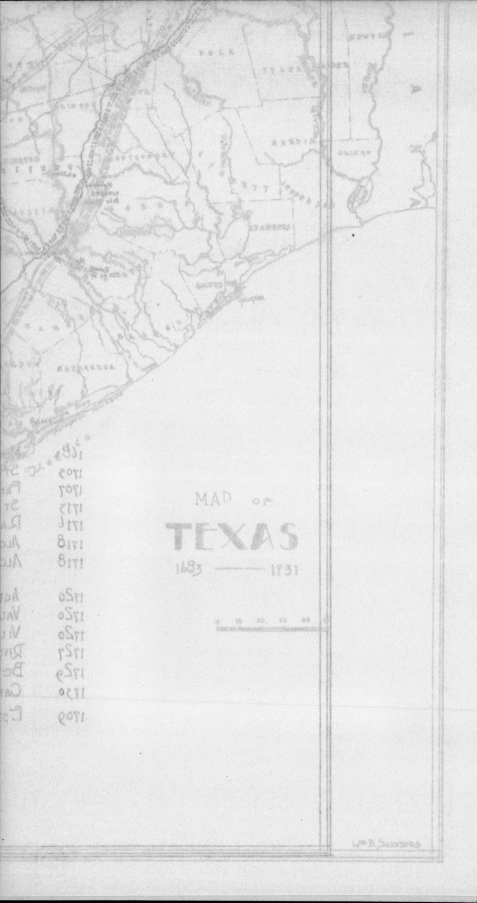

MAP OF

TEXAS

1683 ———— 1731